THE REAL THING

Cultural Studies of

the United States

Alan Trachtenberg, editor

MILES ORVELL

The Real Thing

IMITATION AND

AUTHENTICITY IN

AMERICAN CULTURE,

1880 – 1940

The University of North Carolina Press

Chapel Hill & London

Library of Congress Cataloging-in-Publication Data

Orvell, Miles.
The real thing: imitation and authenticity in American culture,
1880–1940 / by Miles Orvell.
p. cm.
Bibliography: p.
Includes index.
ISBN 0-8078-1837-2. ISBN 0-8078-4246-X (pbk.)
1. United States—Civilization—1865–1918. 2. United States—
Civilization—1918–1945. 3. United States—Intellectual
life—1865–1918. 4. United States—Intellectual life—20th century.
5. Material culture—United States. 6. American literature—History
and criticism. 7. Photography—United States—History.
8. Imitation. 9. Authenticity (Philosophy) I. Title.
E169.1.O783   1989   88-20886
973—dc19   CIP

The author is grateful for permission to reproduce the following:

From *Collected Early Poems* by William Carlos Williams. Copyright 1938
by New Directions Publishing Corporation. Reprinted by permission of
New Directions Publishing Corporation.

From *Paterson* by William Carlos Williams. Copyright 1946, 1948, 1949, 1951,
1958. Copyright 1963 by Florence H. Williams. Reprinted by permission of
New Directions Publishing Corporation.

From *Imaginations* by William Carlos Williams. Copyright 1970 by Florence H.
Williams. Reprinted by permission of New Directions Publishing Corporation.

A substantial portion of Chapter 1 first appeared as "Reproducing Walt Whitman:
The Camera, the Omnibus and *Leaves of Grass*," in *Prospects* 12 (1987) and is
reprinted by permission of Cambridge University Press.

An earlier version of Chapter 3 was awarded a Reva and David Logan Grant in
Support of New Writing on Photography and appeared as "Almost Nature:
The Typology of Late Nineteenth Century American Photography" in
Views: Supplement (Fall 1986). It is reprinted in revised form by permission
of the Photographic Resource Center in Boston and the Logan Grants.

93 92 91 90 89 5 4 3 2 1

To Gabriella

CONTENTS

Foreword by Alan Trachtenberg / ix
Acknowledgments / xiii
Introduction / xv

PART ONE
The Condition of Future Development

Chapter 1: Whitman's Transformed Eye / 3

PART TWO
A Culture of Imitation

Introduction / 33
Chapter 2: A Hieroglyphic World: The Furnishing of
Identity in Victorian Culture / 40
Chapter 3: Photography and the Artifice of Realism / 73
Chapter 4: The Romance of the Real / 103

PART THREE
Inventing Authenticity

Introduction / 141
Chapter 5: The Real Thing and the Machine-made World / 157
Chapter 6: The Camera and the Verification of Fact / 198
Chapter 7: Not "Realism" but Reality Itself / 240

Epilogue: The Dump Is Full of Images / 287

Notes / 301
Bibliography / 341
Index / 375

*M*iles Orvell describes his subject in *The Real Thing* as a "history of cultural forms," a notion that evokes a kind of historical writing more familiar in Europe than in the United States. *Kulturgeschichte*—the tradition of Vico, of Hegel, of Herder and Burkhardt and Huizinga—has never flourished here. Why this should be the case raises a cultural question in its own right. Of course, the term *United States* by itself seems to confine culture to Eurocentric categories. In the 1870s the American Lewis Henry Morgan produced a great cultural study of the languages, politics, architecture, and clan systems of the New World cultures known as Indian, but for white Americans Europe provided the measure of culture. And in the light of Europe the United States seemed too recent to have developed genuine forms of its own. The notion of newness provided a happily convenient explanation of the "thinness," as Henry James put it, the deficiencies of depth and dimension the United States presented in the eyes of "old world" cultivation.

For most of its history an outpost of Europe, can it be said that, before its leap into modernity ahead of Europe, the United States developed significant cultural forms of its own? Just that question has been raised persistently by writers like Emerson, Whitman, James himself, John Dewey, Van Wyck Brooks, and Lewis Mumford. If not a tradition of cultural *history*, there is a distinctly American tradition of cultural *criticism*. The keynote has been an exhortatory plea for recognition and nurture of the native, the home-grown. "I ask not for the great, the remote, the romantic; what is doing in Italy or Arabia; what is Greek art, or Provençal minstrelsy; I embrace the common, I explore and sit at the feet of the familiar, the low. Give me insight into today, and you may have the antique and future worlds. What would we really know the meaning of? The meal in the firkin; the milk in the pan; the ballad in the street; the news of the boat." Thus wrote Emerson in 1837, and immediate responses appeared in the aggressively "American," experimental works of Thoreau and Whitman. It would take more than three generations before a group of young intellectuals turned to the writing of history as a means of reclaiming a native culture, an "authentic" tradition, in Orvell's term. The "usable past" of Van Wyck Brooks, Lewis Mumford, and Constance Rourke arose precisely from a rejection of "imitation," of the mechanically produced "mass culture" of small distractions and repetitive pleasures in the mass media of the early twentieth century. Out of that "usable past" enterprise sprung the conception of an "American studies," of culture as a historical subject too broad and complex and many-sided to fit easily into the standard academic divisions of "departments" and "disciplines." American cultural history—a hybrid field—found its home in the interstices between departments and disciplines.

There are signs of change now, as the culture concept has been adopted freely in many areas of humanistic study. Orvell's book, inaugurating a series focused on the study of culture past and present in the United States, offers a very favorable augury. In its treatment of "imitation" and "authenticity" not as ideas but as categories of cultural experience, *The Real Thing* reveals its kinship with a line of scholarship concerned with identifying unities and tensions within broad regions of American life. The line reaches from Mumford and Rourke in the 1920s and 1930s to the scholarship of John Kouwenhoven, Henry Nash Smith, Leo Marx, and Warren Susman more recently. "Interdisciplinary" makes the common method seem too mechanical and programmatic, but this bruised term nevertheless captures a feature of the book's procedure: its bringing into simultaneous focus whole regions of experience separated by the conventional disciplines of academic labor—the literary and the domestic; the verbal and the visual; the material and the intellectual; the "useful" and the "fine," the "high" and the "low." In this effort it resembles the European genre of *Kulturwissenschaft*, which described systematic relations among the arts, languages, technology, religion, moral codes, and law and customs, seeking common origins for these phenomena, and "morphologies," or nexii of interrelatedness. Less concerned with totalities of relations, more pointed in his analytical probings, Orvell still shares the motive of viewing a whole through the particular forms of connectedness among its parts.

The argument advanced by *The Real Thing* contributes a new set of terms for an old set of problems: how to gauge the role and influence of technology, of "the machine" in American cultural life, particularly in the expressive media of literature, photography, and the arts of design. Orvell has something fresh and original to say about these matters. By proposing "imitation" and "authenticity" as the large categories within which Americans have experienced, conceived, and adapted themselves to the swirling changes of modernity, he offers a new gauge or measure of cultural form, a way of identifying and describing forms in their material and experiential manifestations. His shrewd choice to restrict his investigation to literature, photography, and design—the word, the image, the thing—allows him to range among diverse cultural spheres and phenomena, to apply the analytical concepts of "elite," "popular," and "mass" across the variety of expressive modes, of styles and artistic movements. Moreover, the book places its crosshatched examination within the framework of a historical argument that accounts for the dialectic between imitation and authenticity against a background of social differentiation: the growing split between a "mass" culture born of nineteenth-century technologies of reproduction and a twentieth-century culture centered in a modernist or machine aesthetic that viewed the same technologies as opportunities for "authentic" creation and experience—for a new experience of "reality." While nineteenth-century mass culture cherished imitations of familiar experiences as "the real thing," twentieth-century modernist culture abhorred tradition and used the tools of replication to devise new "real things."

But the schema describes only the framework, the outer form of the argument. Page by page the book offers analyses rather than abstract arguments. A wonderfully detailed account of a pervasive obsession with what is "real," the book tactfully allows the evidence to speak for itself. Readings of the familiar and unfamiliar—daguerreotype galleries, Whitman's poems, the interior furnishings of a Victorian sitting room, theatrical spectacles, the Sears catalogue, Stieglitz's photographs, Frank Lloyd Wright's houses, and Gustav Stickley's chairs and tables—are woven together into an elegant texture of insight and surprise. At every turn specific detail is allowed to brush against the grain of the argument, toughening its fibers. Rather than the categories themselves, the subject is better understood as the tensions between them. And in this light, as an account of alternating conceptions and practices of the arts to define and achieve "reality," the book looks beyond its period to our own, to the aesthetic fashions of "post-

modernism," in which imitation recurs as a sophisticated displacement and critique of modernist "authenticity." Orvell provides a valuable historical perspective on the latest turn in the dialectic. Thus the
book joins its forebears among the cultural critics of the 1910s and
1920s, who launched their quest for cultural history out of a need to
clarify the confusions and controversies of their own time.

Alan Trachtenberg

ACKNOWLEDGMENTS

*L*ooking back to the beginnings of this study, about ten years ago, I realize that the earliest of the ideas eventually worked out here were sparked by my reading of some of Lionel Trilling's essays on reality in America and by John Kouwenhoven's classic, *The Arts in Modern American Civilization.* Lewis Mumford's writings, with their gigantic intelligence and humane center, remained an enduring influence, as did the example of Alan Trachtenberg, who so often seemed, as I turned to new areas of investigation, to be already luminously there. Add to these intellectual compass points the dozens of other scholars in whose debt I feel. Their names are in the notes to these chapters, and their prior efforts enabled a work of this kind—which is an effort at synthesis—to come into existence.

I am indebted to the College of Arts and Sciences at Temple University for granting me the two study leaves that were essential for the composition of the book; and I am grateful to the Faculty Senate Committee on Research and Study Leaves for additional support in the form of research grants. I thank also the staff of Paley Library, especially the Inter-library Loan Department, for their cooperation in securing far-flung materials. And Iris Tilman Hill, Editor-in-Chief at the University of North Carolina Press, has provided the kind of intelligent support and thoughtfulness for which any writer must be very grateful.

One writes a book like this in a solitude surrounded by other books and, in my own case, interrupted only by visits from the cats (my thanks here to Eden and Kadie for long service); but the time away from the desk is just as important. Conversations with colleagues at Temple have contributed directly and indirectly to my own ideas, and I want to thank especially Richard Chalfen, Allen Davis, Joseph Margolis, Jay Ruby, and Morris Vogel. My thanks also to friends and colleagues in English—especially Robert Buttel, Richard Kennedy, Monica Letzring, Morton Levitt, Philip Stevick, Alan Wilde, Roy Wolper—for their encouragement and support over many years.

Robert Greenberg, also of Temple, and Jane Tompkins read an

early version of the Whitman chapter, and their acute suggestions were influential on the later development of the study. Jean Caslin and Susie Cohen contributed many helpful suggestions to the chapter dealing with nineteenth-century photography during the course of editing an earlier version of it for publication by the Photographic Resource Center in Boston. Thomas Riggio and Sharon O'Brien read an earlier draft of the entire manuscript, and their responses in matters small and large were most valuable; for their warm friendship and for the hours of talk *not* about this book I also thank them.

To other special friends I want to say special thanks for providing the background against which long years of work may happily take place: to Herb Simons, gamesman and rhetorician, for sharing with me his profound and riotous meditations; to Paul Wachtel, affluent in acuity, sagacity, and levity, for his prodigal friendship.

Most of all, thanks to Gabriella Ibieta, for her consistently keen advice on the manuscript and for always being equal to the fortunes of the day; she was courageous enough to marry a man finishing a book and has been a steadfast anchor for more than my craft.

INTRODUCTION

$\mathcal{T}$his study argues that the tension between imitation and authenticity is a primary category in American civilization, pervading layers of our culture that are usually thought to be separate, from commercial design and advertising to literature. More specifically, I argue in this book that a major shift occurred within the arts and material culture from the late nineteenth century to the twentieth century, a shift from a culture in which the arts of imitation and illusion were valorized to a culture in which the notion of authenticity became of primary value. One might describe this change, in rough terms, as a change in the meaning of a phrase that remains central to both nineteenth-and twentieth-century culture, "the real thing." Put simply, the nineteenth-century culture of imitation was fascinated by reproductions of all sorts—replicas of furniture, architecture, art works, replicas of the real thing in any shape or form imaginable. It was a culture inspired by faith in the power of the machine to manufacture a credible simulacrum; yet it had not fully absorbed the methods of the machine, and in the end it was a culture of types, of stylizations, of rounded generalities. The culture of authenticity that developed at the end of the century and that gradually established the aesthetic vocabulary that we have called "modernist" was a reaction against the earlier aesthetic, an effort to get beyond mere imitation, beyond the manufacturing of illusions, to the creation of more "authentic" works that were themselves real things.

I am not asserting that a culture of authenticity entirely *replaced* the earlier culture of imitation; nothing so neat took place. In fact, as I shall reiterate later, the nineteenth-century culture of imitation remained (and still remains) a strong part of the mainstream of twentieth-century industrial popular culture. But what developed around the turn of the century was a counterthrust to the mainstream culture, an effort on the part of a number of intellectuals and artists to revitalize a culture thought to have grown moribund, an effort that centered on values of authenticity. Shifts in taste may seem like swings of the pendulum, but they are signs of deeper currents as well: in this case, as I shall argue, the move from imitation to authenticity has deep roots in a new self-consciousness about American culture that was being engendered by a number of intellectuals (most notably Van Wyck Brooks), and it has roots too in a freshly creative response to the machine as an agent for revolutionizing American society along lines previously not imagined in the nineteenth century.

This effort to move America from a culture of imitation to one of authenticity is, then, partly a response to a set of outworn aesthetic conventions and partly a response to a change in the technological environment, centering on the meaning of the machine. Whereas the earlier period saw the machine as an agent for democratizing luxury and diffusing high culture through imitations of elite forms, the twentieth-century culture of authenticity was based, conversely, on a functionalist ethos that sought to elevate the vernacular into the realm of high culture. Inspired by the machine's capacities to record and analyze reality and to build new artifacts, a number of artists evolved forms that similarly emphasized underlying structures, fragmented shapes, and detailed textures. The tension between imitation and authenticity, I argue, has been a key constituent in American culture since the Industrial Revolution and assumes crucial importance in the shift from the nineteenth to the twentieth centuries that we have called—in all its encompassing multiplicity—modernism.[1]

Let me pause a moment at the outset over the phrase that will recur throughout this study—"the real thing"—a phrase that unites both Henry James (who wrote a story with that title) and Coca Cola; a phrase that is at once concrete (thing), abstract (real), and etymologically redundant (res = thing); a phrase that points, in all its ambiguity, to what has been a recurring metaphysical preoccupation for Americans. The philosopher Philip Wheelwright puts it most grandly when he writes, "The problem of reality is man's ultimate problem; his judgment, 'Such-or-such is more real, or more deeply real, than something else,' is a major expression of his intellectual faith."[2] In more mundane terms, when we call an experience or a thing "the real thing," we are identifying a quality of intensity that is otherwise lacking in the featureless background that constitutes the main hum of experience. But what is background and what foreground may shift like the figure and ground of a Gestalt test. "Heaven knows what we mean by reality," D. H. Lawrence wrote in *Studies in Classic American Literature* (1922). "Telephone, tinned meat, Charlie Chaplin, Water-taps, and World-Salvation, presumably. Some insisting on the plumbing, and some on saving the world: these being the two great American specialities."[3] And one could still make a case, nearly seventy years after Lawrence, that the practical and the spiritual remain primary antithetical categories in American experience.

Wheelwright's "intellectual faith" in what is real is not only a function of abstract philosophical reasoning but also of historical circumstance, with all its conditioning of perception and understanding. As Walter Benjamin writes, "During long periods of history, the mode of human sense perception changes with humanity's entire mode of existence. The manner in which human sense perception is organized, the medium in which it is accomplished, is determined not only by nature but by historical circumstances as well."[4] Though the European Marxist's perspective sits uneasily with the complexities of American culture, I follow Benjamin at least to the extent of seeking a nexus between the technological and the cultural, and more particularly in emphasizing as a key element the advent of the mechanical reproduction of images.

One might imagine that the concept of authenticity begins in any society when the possibility of fraud arises, and that fraud is at least possible whenever transactions—whether social, political, commercial, or aesthetic—routinely occur, especially when the society becomes so large that one usually deals with strangers, not neighbors. This would be even more likely in a society like that of nineteenth-century America, one that lacks the fixed social hierarchies of a rigid class system and in which there is at least the theoretical possibility of social mobility. And when the material fabric of the society is, over a short period of time, revolutionized by the rapid mechanization of production, where the factory manufacture of goods replaces the work of the artisan and the workshop, then the problem of what "the real thing" really is might become even more acute. All of these factors of course characterize American society from the mid-nineteenth century forward, and it is in this period especially, as I see it, that the problem of authenticity, of naming "the real thing," begins to take on truly significant proportions.

The transition from the late nineteenth-century world to that of the twentieth century has been described in many ways, but let me here emphasize a tension one might discern between the social world and the intellectual world, a tension between—to borrow Wallace Stevens's words—a violent order and a violent disorder. For on the one hand there was the gradual imposition of order as the force of technology grew stronger in the social world: underpinning the consumer society was a rapid growth in organization systems—integrated research teams and hierarchies of management, business conglomerations, and government bureaucracies, a move toward the "incorporation" of America, as it has been called, that took place at many levels in our culture.[5] And, correspondingly, there was the gradual movement from a plural society of diverse immigrant groups toward a more homogenized social order, a more "Americanized" population—a move accomplished not without the sometimes forceful suppression of differences.

Against the tendency toward the formation of larger and larger systems of order, the early twentieth century witnessed a breaking up of many long-held notions of order and stability that governed the intellectual and scientific world. The world no longer presented, on closer inspection, an aspect of order and coherence, of solid forms and surfaces; what might previously have gone unnoticed or been written off as anomalous would seem, given new instruments of observation and new theories of the physical universe, to be rudimentary evidence for entirely new hypotheses about the world. What had been invisible was made visible in the form of X-rays; infinitesimal temporal moments were revealed through high-speed photography; the atomic world of the infinitely small, and the astral world of the infinitely large, opened up unimaginably on either side of humanity's normal vision; forces one could not see directly—electricity, magnetic fields —yet had newly visible effects. The mind had to accommodate itself to these changed conceptions of physical reality and to technologies that afforded instantaneous communication across great distances and seemingly unlimited energy sources.[6] Along with these changes in scientific apprehension, the psychological and philosophical foundations of perception were changing accordingly, as the physical seemed to border on the metaphysical. A gap was opening wide between what was commonly assumed in everyday life—the conventional—and what was scientifically understood. Underneath "the surface forms of ordinary consciousness," as one recent critic has written, there was a more significant reality, understood variously as a sensory flux, a "chaos of sensations," a "real duration," a "stream of consciousness," or as "immediate experience."[7]

Thus even as the technological sphere grew more and more successful in imposing order on a burgeoning consumer society, a growing realization of instability and uncertainty flowed increasingly from the scientific world. Henry Adams, whose experience of the changes from the nineteenth to the twentieth centuries was as deep as anyone's, summed up the new scientific outlook in a neatly compact, unendingly problematic sentence: "In plain words, Chaos was the law of nature; Order was the dream of man."[8] The artist, like the intellectual, was caught between the recognition of chaos and the dream of order; and it is out of these two impulses that the modernist culture of authenticity was born, with its consuming effort to restore contact with real things, yet do so in a way that recognized the new scientific reality that was part of the changed air one breathed in.

So many issues might be relevant to the concern at the heart of this essay—the shift from a culture of imitation to a culture of authenticity—that I feel the need at the outset to define the scope of this volume, and to announce certain assumptions I will be making. First, some disclaimers: I am not writing an essay in the history of ideas or in social history or in popular culture studies. Moreover, the philosophical or religious problem of reality, the epistemological problem of how we know the world, the semiological problem of the correspondence of sign and thing, are all outside the range of what I have undertaken in this study. Rather, I am writing an essay in the history of cultural forms, and what I am interested in is how the notion of authenticity has affected the arts in America.

Any culture establishes the limits within which all people—including artists—have experiences, limits created by the material environment and the technological base, by the conventional meanings attached to objects and actions, and by the vocabulary of concepts and words that serves as the interpretative context for experience. Singular events and the peculiarities of personal psychology certainly influence artists, but so do the gradual and nearly invisible social forces that are tied to our modes of production and our material culture. Yet while the artist is thus a product of the complex set of forces shaping all individuals in a given culture, we nevertheless rightly attribute to him or her the power to fashion the materials of the given world—in the work of art itself—and to thereby effect an alteration in the consciousness of the age through the organization of the art work. Herbert Marcuse puts it too strongly, however, when he states in a late work that "the truth of art lies in its power to break the monopoly of established reality (that is, of those who established it) to *define* what is *real*."[9] Artists may define what is real, but whether they can break the monopoly of established reality is another question. Against Marcuse we must place Clifford Geertz, for whom the artist is rooted in a complex system of cultural signs and things, and for whom any interpretation of the work of art must derive from this "common world in which men look, name, listen, and make."[10]

My own approach falls somewhere in the middle zone that allows the art work its power to define reality by altering our consciousness, but sets it in the context of a cultural dynamic that is the critic's business, in turn, to elucidate. From this point of view, my attempt at crossing levels of culture (high to low) and genres (literary, visual, material) has as its goal the *systemic* understanding of American culture. The kind of integrative history I am aiming at would help explain, as Neil Harris put it in another context, "not only the origins of stylistic transformation but also their relationship to contemporary thought and opinion," an approach that combines aspects of commercial and technological history with "the history of taste, opinion, and artistic style."[11] Building on the many recent vertical studies of particular movements and figures, I hope in this study to provide a horizontal overview, a way of connecting problems and issues that have been seen in isolation, but that are, I think, parts of a larger whole.

The nature of my overall argument has dictated the structure of this book, and I want to describe it briefly. The two main parts encompass the shift from what I call a "culture of imitation" (Part 2) to a "culture of authenticity" (Part 3); in the former, as I have suggested, the arts revolve around various kinds of replications of nature within the vocabulary of conventions and types governing current notions of "realism," while in the latter the arts attempt to get beyond imitation, beyond the manufacturing of illusions, to the creation of works that are themselves real things.[12] But stating the shift in these terms may be a little misleading, because the reaction *against* the genteel typologies of the older realism in fact begins in the 1890s and is the subject, in part, of chapter 4, "The Romance of the Real." Moreover, it is important to affirm that the nineteenth-century culture of imitation continues into the twentieth century (through the present, in fact) as a main current in popular culture—movies, television, popular fiction, amusement parks, popular graphics, and so forth.

The modernists I examine in Part 3 often saw themselves as reviving a Whitmanesque notion of the artist who speaks for and creates his culture holistically, and this intention is crucial to an understanding of their work; but the artists I deal with had an ambivalent relationship with the mainstream of American culture they were trying to influence. When they were not aspiring to a democratic popularity, they were likely to scorn the inertia of a middle-class culture they could not shape into the form of a receptive response. Hence when I speak of the development of a "culture of authenticity" I am speaking of a movement within the broader stream of American culture, a movement that had its roots in an intellectual elite (who were looking back to the democratic Whitman) and that spread its influence in varying degrees beyond that core.

The opening chapter, on Walt Whitman, is a kind of prologue to the whole, and there I have offered Whitman as the writer who, perhaps more than any other, was attempting consciously to model his work on the changed conditions of modern life, which encompassed the conditions of commercial life, the technology of manufactures, and the invention of the daguerreotype. Beginning with Whitman allows me to examine the mid-nineteenth-century background to Victorian culture in America when mechanization—with its related cultural ramifications—first had a significant impact on our society. And the discussion of Whitman also provides the base for several later chapters, for the impact of the poet's life and works was felt throughout the modern period. Moreover, the Whitman chapter establishes the parameters for the integrated approach I shall pursue, somewhat differently, in Parts 2 and 3—through a more detailed consideration, in separate chapters, of the three broad areas of my concern: material culture, photography, and literature.

Why these three areas? My inclusion of literature needs the least explanation, because writers have characteristically articulated the concerns of society with sensitivity and due complexity, thus providing central evidence for the student of cultural change. I include photography because it is an art that is in many ways allied to literature (in its descriptive capacity) and, as the literal medium par excellence, has served as a model—through several permutations—for literary realism. (Photography is not peripheral to our culture, as is still sometimes thought, but on the contrary quite central.)[13] Also, photography stands mid-way, so to speak, between the descriptive and image-making art of literature and the concreteness of the material world that is inevitably its subject matter. Material culture—by which I mean architecture and design and household furnishings—likewise is essential for an examination of authenticity and imitation in American culture, because the material environment surrounds us inescapably, conditioning our experiences and providing a tangible measure of changing notions of "the real thing."

The three areas I focus on are thus complementary, forming what I intend to be an integrated whole within each of the main parts. Moreover, I am counting on something like a cumulative or synergistic effect, as the reader proceeds, with one chapter acting upon another, both forward and backward in the sequence. There is of course some danger in taking such a broad sweep of things, but I have tried to counteract the potential dispersion by offering some fairly detailed, specific readings of individual figures and texts, seeking to generalize on the basis of selected major figures who are at the same time representative of larger currents.

One further advantage to the synchronic examination of material culture, photography, and literature is that it offers three increasingly smaller circles of investigation, from the point of view of audience, or communities of consumption. Allowing for exceptions, there is by and large a decreasing progression in the size of the audience as we move, within each major part of the book, from material culture, to photography, and then to literature. Thus the circle is largest at the outset of Parts 2 and 3, for one can assume that the greatest number of people interact with the objects of their environment and are affected by the appearance and significance of material designs, just as houses and furnishings provide a nearly universal means of personal expression. And one can assume that a slightly smaller set of people (but still large) will have contact with the visual environment that has been created by photography and the various forms of photographic reproductions. And, pursuing the logic, literature will tend to have the smallest audience, which may be considered elite—by education and background if not always by income. Consequently, if one is seeking a view of culture that is integrative, these overlapping zones provide a ready framework within which to test generalizations.

Although I concentrate on the period from about 1880 to 1940, this book derives from, and inevitably relates to, contemporary experience. For anyone sensitive to the ambiguities of representation, everyday life in America offers endless riches and an abundance of metaphysical conundrums to contemplate. If the later nineteenth century can be described as a culture of imitation, and the first part of the twentieth century as a culture of authenticity, then our own time might be called a culture of the factitious. We have a hunger for something like authenticity, but we are easily satisfied by an ersatz facsimile. And the facsimiles are all around us: we can, for example, eat a hamburger in a Philadelphia fast-food place surrounded by cowboy artifacts and other souvenirs of the Wild West, receiving with our tray the friendly greeting "Happy Trails" from the cashier; following her advice, we find ourselves at Grand Canyon National Park, where an official sign near the parking lot leads the tourist in search of the awesome to a specially designated spot, guaranteed to yield excellent snapshots; still out West, we can tour a deactivated intercontinental nuclear missile silo, making sure to wear hard hats ("this is the real thing," the museum founder says); visiting Disney World, we can enjoy the automated Indians eternally pounding corn along the banks of a man-made river; we can stand outside a store window in SoHo and watch a live mannequin display clothing ("the extreme we aspire to," a teacher of the robot-skill says, "is having someone stare at you through the window, trying to figure out whether you're real or not"); we can hear a confident voice on television promoting the docudrama *Roots* by saying, mystifyingly, "there you have it . . . some of it fact, and some of it fiction, but all of it true, in the true meaning of the word."

During the last twenty-five years Americans have not merely tolerated the facsimile representation with grudging good humor. They have loved it. One has to remind oneself of this fact or one will utterly fail to understand something as innocent as the recent report in a news magazine that the most fashionable designers are making polyester clothes for the richest people in America. As one designer in this mode put it, "I love it when they don't try to look real." This apparent reversal of ontological priorities may be simply a new expression of the perennial quest in clothing and decorative styles for the fashionably artificial. More likely, it is a late blossoming of an attitude that has pervaded the contemporary artistic sensibility for at least two decades—visible in the popular writings of Susan Sontag in the 1960s as a willingness to take style seriously (or, I should say, playfully) without worrying about deeper significance; visible in the deadpan delight in the textures of contemporary popular culture to be found in the writings of Donald Barthelme and Max Apple; in the monumental versions of our least monumental artifacts—lipstick, an icepack, an electric fan—created by Claes Oldenburg; and in the sculptured cartoon caricatures of streets and subways by Red Grooms. This new sensibility—which we have called postmodernist, and which I shall say more about in the Epilogue to this study— has clearly gone beyond *worrying* about imitation and authenticity, though it is everywhere concerned with it. Thus in this context one can understand a critic's recent remark that "for modern man everything that exists does so only in and through representation."[14]

Obviously, we are a long way from Wright Morris's assertion—published in 1979, but speaking out of an earlier, modernist sensibility— that we Americans have a hunger for what is "real," and that the word itself "vibrates in our consciousness more persistently than the word 'truth.'"[15] Morris is speaking of our appetite for photographic veracity, a legacy of the 1930s but there may still be a large measure of validity in what he says—witness the contemporary taste for the "primitive," the "folk," the "natural," and the "organic" in many other categories. The fact is that the contemporary rage for the factitious exists alongside of the contrary appetite for the authentic; we are dealing, in the contemporary period, with two ends of the same pole. (And it is a pole that Americans have been straddling since the nineteenth century.)

We have had several excellent guides to the ontological ambiguities of American popular culture over the last twenty-five years, and they inevitably form the backdrop against which the present essay should be read. Daniel Boorstin's pioneering study, *The Image: A Guide to Pseudo-Events in America* (1961), for example, explored, from the point of view of social history, the pseudo-worlds of journalism and advertising, tourism, public relations, and Hollywood movies, positing a hypothetical "real" world that eludes popular experience as the individual constantly mistakes the pseudo for the real event.[16] For Dean MacCannell, too, reality and authenticity lie always, for modern people, elsewhere; in his more specialized study, *The Tourist: A New Theory of the Leisure Class* (1976), MacCannell combines a social scientist's observation of everyday life with a semiotician's analytic framework, to describe the "front" and "back" spaces in the tourist's experience of staged attractions and his quest for the ever more au-

thentic encounter.[17] More subtly attuned to the nuances of the factitious American landscape (though less systematic) is the Italian
semiologist Umberto Eco, whose *Travels in Hyperreality* (1986) ex-
plores the confusions between copy and original on many levels of
popular culture—from wax museums to amusement parks and ghost
towns. Eco is a connoisseur of representations and confesses his own
fascination with the imitation, which he regards as having reached a
climax of perfection—if that is the word—on the West Coast of the
United States. (The West Coast is farther than the East Coast from the
source of "original" culture—which ultimately is Europe in Eco's European view—and hence is in greater need of simulations.)[18] For the
French sociologist Jean Baudrillard, however, America is merely a
more intense embodiment of the universal condition of Western culture; applying a phenomenological approach to the problem of authenticity, Baudrillard has argued that the simulation has become the
ineluctable experience for the modern person, as "signs of the real"
are universally substituted for "the real itself."[19]

These works have elucidated the nuances of contemporary experience, but they have generally not explored the origins of our consuming metaphysics, nor have they related the arts systematically to the
society from which they spring. While this study originated, then, in a
need to understand aspects of contemporary experience, I attempted
to get at the root of the issue in nineteenth-century America and
discovered that the movement from the late nineteenth century to
around 1940 seemed to complete a cycle from one extreme to another. I have chosen to stop short of carrying my discussion into the
post–World War II period—except for a brief epilogue.

This study is limited to an exploration of American experience
(which includes at times a consideration of the meaning of Europe)
primarily because of my own interests and limitations, but one may
legitimately ask whether the movement described here may also be
found in European culture, given the currents of influence running
across the Atlantic, and given the common industrialization process.
Without opening up a subject that lies outside the scope of this work,
let me suggest only that one major difference lies in what each place
has meant to the other. That is, America had Europe to look to as the
"home" culture, the originator of style, the source of artistic models—
not until well into the twentieth century does the import-export traffic begin to run from the New World to the Old—so that the challenge

for the American artist was to define himself against the European. Europe, however, had no "Europe." Its cultural evolution could take place for most of the period under discussion here in what Americans, at least, often took as a freer climate of experimentation. Another difference worth noting is that, given the relative shortage of workers in the nineteenth century and the abundance of resources, the machine had a more enthusiastic reception in America than in Europe; and the habit of ingenious adaptation and invention has remained strong into the twentieth century. Thus for the artist wanting to connect with American society, especially with its machine-made forms and its will to consumption, Whitman's imperative—"to enter into the essences of the real things"—has remained strong.

From another perspective, this entire study might be framed within the larger and older question of how American culture has distinguished itself from European culture—a problem that has concerned American scholars for generations, with its particular formulations in terms of the frontier and the East, the country and the city, redskins and paleskins, vernacular and cultivated traditions. My own effort is to situate this tension within our more recent sense of the distinctive consumer society that evolved in America, and to broaden the perspective by incorporating the significance of technology to all aspects of American life and arts—a significance that is often underestimated. In examining the interconnections between imitation and authenticity, I am looking at something that is, if not exclusively American, at least characteristically so; and I am looking at its peculiarly American twist, for in no other culture is the notion of "the real thing" so open a window into understanding.

Part One

THE CONDITION

OF FUTURE

DEVELOPMENT

Whitman's

Transformed

Eye

*I*n trying to understand the relationship between the American artist and the new technological civilization of the nineteenth century, we can do no better than begin with the poet who attempted to reinvent poetry in America and who would thereby provide a model for so many artists coming after him, who were likewise seeking to establish an art appropriate to the conditions of the country. More than any other artist of his time, Whitman had tried to reproduce in his work the entirety of American civilization—its industrial and urban character as well as its spiritual, aesthetic, and demotic wealth. The lifelong creation of *Leaves of Grass* was to be a kind of counterpart to the United States, an epic embodiment of the national character and landscape, a poetic equivalent of the new reality of America, and also, of course, the picture of an ideal self—"Walt Whitman, a kosmos"—that the poet created out of his historical identity to serve as a model for his readers.

Whitman is our first modern poet because he was first to invent a new form appropriate to the modern age, a form that would reflect the new relationship between part and whole that a mass civilization would establish, a form that could contain within the bounds of the artwork the rich particularity and clashing contradictions of American life. That form is, of course, the free-verse catalogue—a series of unrhymed lines of varying length, sometimes numbering over a hundred at a stretch, each of which names some single, concrete, complete image of a person or thing or place; it is a form that stands classical epic poetry on its head, making what used to be an extended pause in the action into the main substance and structure of the poem.

There can be no single explanation for Whitman's great invention, but we can, to begin with, offer certain literary precedents for Whitman's verse.[1] Milton, and much later Carlyle, for example, had argued that rhyme was not essential to poetry; and the popular Englishman Martin Farquhar Tupper gave supporting evidence of a sort in his thousands of lines of sententious wisdom, composed in a verse that was indeed unrhymed, but otherwise wholly congenial to the sentiments and imagery of the parlor. Moreover, Emerson's advice in "The Poet" about meter-making arguments undoubtedly gave Whitman strength in his experiment, along with Emerson's notion that "bare lists of words are found suggestive to an imaginative and excited mind."[2] A reviewer for the *London Examiner* tried to give a lineage to the anomalous Whitman and came up with the following description, which Whitman had the good humor to include among the reviews at the back of the 1856 *Leaves of Grass*:

> Suppose that Mr. Tupper had been brought up to the business of an auctioneer, then banished to the backwoods, compelled to live for a long time as a backwoodsman, and thus contracting a passion for the reading of Emerson and Carlyle? Suppose him maddened by this course of reading, and fancying himself not only an Emerson but a Carlyle and an American Shakespeare to boot when the fits come on, and putting for his notion of that combination in his own self-satisfied way, and in his own wonderful cadences? In that state he would write a book exactly like Walt Whitman's "Leaves of Grass."[3]

The reviewer was probably not far from the mark; what he left out, however, was at least as important—namely, those "influences" that came not from the printed page but from the contemporary urban world that Whitman experienced so deeply and fully. Whitman was certainly right when he said that "my 'Leaves' could not possibly have emerged or been fashion'd or completed, from any other era than the latter half of the Nineteenth Century, nor any other land than democratic America."[4] An enormous cultural sponge, Whitman had spent the fifteen years before the first edition of *Leaves* in and out of journalism and had absorbed as much as anyone the transformations in American life in the mid-century—the growth of cities and manufactures and technology, the new scientific theories and discoveries, the currents of Orientalism and German philosophy, and not least the flourishing popular culture of his time—newspapers, opera, phrenology, photography, and exhibition halls.[5] The poet must "flood himself with the immediate age as with vast oceanic tides," Whitman wrote in the 1855 Preface, and that is exactly what Whitman had done, until he contained enough to "let it out," as he put it in *Song of Myself*.[6]

Modern criticism of Whitman has indeed taken notice of the influence of popular culture on the development of the poet (Paul Zweig's recent biography most effectively), but in a somewhat piecemeal fashion. The popular urban culture of the mid-nineteenth century was crucial to the poet, providing Whitman with an angle of vision and a coherent matrix for his vision. In particular, I shall argue that the camera provided the foundation for Whitman's way of looking at the world, and that the exhibition hall, in all of its various forms, provided a model for the structure of the long poem Whitman never stopped writing.

Whitman's project was nothing less than a "readjustment of the whole theory and nature of Poetry," as he put it in "A Backward Glance," "for democratic America's sake."[7] And what that came down to, first of all, was looking at the world with new eyes. Remy G. Saisselin has recently argued that the city in the nineteenth century transformed the eye of the observer, as novel kinds of urban spaces and entertainments, like the arcade, the panorama, and the department store, were created to satisfy a growing population of consumers. Saisselin affirms, moreover, that an unprecedented variety of aesthetic observer evolved along with these changes in urban experience: no longer was the observer a person "of taste in contemplation before a picture or a landscape ... [but a] flaneur in the modern city."[8] (On the very first page of the 1855 Preface, Whitman had exalted the country's "details magnificently moving in vast masses" and the "tremendous audacity of its crowds and groupings.")[9] Saisselin is speaking here primarily of the European city, of Paris especially, but his observations are valuable in considering the sources of Whitman's art, for they point to a relationship between poetry and the urban milieu that has been generally overlooked.

Saisselin associates this new urban observer with the photographer, whose gaze was also ubiquitous, surveying urban types and spaces. In fact, during Whitman's formative years—the 1840s—the camera was just being introduced to America and was an immediate popular sensation, taking on myriad functions from the portrait to the landscape, from the art photograph to the scientific study; and it became, I would argue, a crucial metaphor and model for the poet's own creative processes, standing for the peculiarly modern apprehension of reality.[10] For Whitman approached the world not on terms of an extended meditation, as did Bryant, Longfellow, and Emerson, but with the relatively brief perception of discrete particulars made possible by the camera. Susan Sontag has remarked on how twentieth-century photography has fulfilled Whitman's own large aesthetic embrace of the world—indeed parodied it in recent years—by embracing low subjects, the ugly, along with the beautiful; what she failed to note was the degree to which Whitman's own eye was transformed by photography.[11]

"Poet! beware lest your poems are made in the spirit that comes from the study of pictures of things," Whitman warned, "—and not from the spirit that comes from the contact with real things themselves."[12] But what exactly does it mean to model your poem on "real things themselves"? The particular kind of "contact" Whitman wanted is based not upon the traditional imagery of painting, with its inevitable distance from reality, and its idealization of actuality; rather, it is based upon the new mechanical process of representing the reality immediately before the camera lens that had become, by the 1850s, a common feature of urban life, one that was changing the way the world was perceived and structured. In fact, Whitman may be the first poet to throw out the traditional Horatian analogy of poetry to painting (*ut pictura poesis*) and put in its place what would become, for many writers, the new prevailing analogy: *ut camera poesis.*[13] Emerson had offered Whitman an image that would be close to the latter's own habits when he had pictured the rich poets as mirrors, "carried through the street, ready to render an image of every created thing."[14] But Emerson's mirror was not quite what Whitman needed; it suggested a removal from reality that was at odds with the poet's need for "contact," for a poetry in which "nothing is poetized, no divergence, not a step, not an inch, nothing for beauty's sake, no euphemism, no rhyme." For his approach to the world Whitman preferred instead the contemporary, the scientific metaphor—not the mirror but the camera: "In these Leaves everything is literally photographed."[15]

Edward Everett Hale was alert to just this quality in Whitman—his concrete picturing of reality—when he noted in a review that some parts of *Leaves of Grass* "strike us as real,—so real that we wonder how they came on paper."[16] Hale's phrasing interestingly recalls the universal amazement that greeted the first permanent transfers of visual images of the real world onto a flat surface—the daguerreotype process, which was at its peak of popularity in the late 1840s and early 1850s.[17] Whether or not the allusion was intended by Hale, it is one the poet himself used on several occasions and it is a telling metaphor for Whitman's creative process, at times explicitly named, at other times only hinted at obliquely.

The notion of the poet as camera plate, for example, seems hovering in the background of the famous lyric about the making of the poet in the 1855 edition:

> There was a child went forth every day,
> And the first object he look'd upon, that object he became
> And that object became part of him for the day or a part of
>   the day,
> Or for many years or stretching cycles of years.[18]

Whitman here pictures himself as taking the imprint of the objects of the world, the city, the country, crowds, streets, goods, absorbing the world into the receptive plate of his consciousness until the later "development" of his poetry. Five years later, another poem about his formative years (taken to refer to the New Orleans sojourn) would make the metaphor even more explicit:

> Once I pass'd through a populous city imprinting my brain
>   for future use with its shows, architecture, customs,
>   traditions (p. 109)

More inventive, if less explicit, is the metaphor Whitman uses in "Crossing Brooklyn Ferry" (1856), which likewise speaks of the poet's genesis and seems to offer allusions to chemical processes (cosmic as well as photographic) and to the new technologies of mass production, as if Whitman's "representative" quality derived from his being "reproduced" by contemporary industrial processes (with a touch of alchemical ones too, perhaps):[19]

> I too had been struck from the float forever held in
>   solution,
> I too had receiv'd identity by my body (p. 162)

In retrospect, it seems inevitable that Whitman would introduce himself to the world with a frontispiece daguerreotype portrait of himself (reproduced as an engraving) that sets the style and tone of the whole of *Leaves of Grass* to follow and establishes implicitly its relationship to several major strands in the popular scientific culture of the age. (The soul "makes itself visible only through matter," Whitman had written in an early notebook.)[20] Whitman calls attention to the photographic image in one of his audacious self-reviews, this one written for the *Brooklyn Eagle*, when he notes that "its author is Walt Whitman and his book is a reproduction of the author. His name is not on the frontispiece, but his portrait, half-length, is. The contents of the book form a daguerreotype of his inner being, and the title page bears a representation of its physical tabernacle."[21] It is a striking conception, a linked circle of equivalents: portrait equals author equals book equals inner being equals body equals portrait equals book. . . . Taking the mechanical process of the daguerreotype as his starting point, Whitman moves to an interlocking vision of his volume—"a reproduction of the author"—that fulfills in practice the theories of organic form that Emerson, Greenough, and others were contemporaneously developing in their essays.[22] It is not just that the portrait shows us the author of the poem that follows; the represented image is also the subject of the poem.

Moreover the photographic image embodies exactly the kind of representation of self Whitman was aiming at in the whole of *Leaves of Grass*: it was simultaneously a literal image and a representative one, both a "real thing" in itself and a larger, more suggestive, exemplary type of itself. ("Convey what I want to convey by models or illustrations of the results I demand," Whitman had written to himself in a notebook of the mid-1850s.)[23] Mathew Brady had capitalized on this aspect of photography early on, simultaneously exploiting and bestowing a national celebrity status upon politicians, soldiers, writers, and other prominent figures. And interestingly Whitman claimed, in conversation with Horace Traubel in later years, that he himself gave Brady the idea of a gallery of great historical figures, thinking how much better it would be, "rather than having a lot of contradictory records by witnesses or historians—say of Caesar, Socrates, Epictetus, others—if we could have three or four or half a dozen portraits—very accurate—of the men: that would be history—the best history—a history from which there could be no appeal."[24] Incidentally, Whitman's recollection is probably flawed—Edward Anthony's National Daguerreotype Miniature Gallery was founded a year or two before Brady opened his similar collection in 1845—but it is significant that Whitman should so readily identify himself with Brady's purposes as to make the claim.[25] In any case, daguerreotypes of famous persons—from the arts, politics, religion, the military—reached the public not only through the many galleries in the major American cities, but also through the publication of books based on the gallery as metaphor—Plumbe's *National Plumbeotype Gallery* (1847), with its mass-produced lithographs, and Brady's dozen lithographs, published as *The Gallery of Illustrious Americans* (1850). In taking himself as a national prototype, then, Whitman had the precedent of the portrait galleries, just as in taking himself as a representative spiritual type he had the sanction of Emerson's *Representative Men* (1850).

The fact that Whitman used a daguerreotype portrait as a surrogate for his name (the title page, set in type by Whitman himself, otherwise lacks any authorial identification) is itself symptomatic of the visual orientation of *Leaves of Grass*, and in subsequent editions photographs would continue to play an integral role in the poet's theatrical presentation of himself, with the image changing as the poet's self-conception changed.[26] But just as important, in this first edition, is the particular image offered, which was clearly as carefully constructed as the lines that follow it. For Whitman strode into American poetry in 1855 in a manner deliberately and self-consciously calculated to overturn his reader's assumptions about the place and provenance of poetry in modern society.

What does a poet look like? Glance at the frontispiece portraits of Whitman's contemporaries and you see *gentlemen*: black coat, shirt closed at collar, black tie, hat off in deference to indoor protocol. Usually you see a bust of the author, rarely a view below the waist. (Even ten years later, Marcus A. Root, in one of the major discussions of photography of the time, would affirm that the poet or historian or editor should be photographed in a seated position, since to do otherwise would embarrass him by the novelty of the attitude; "statesmen, lawyers, clergy men, and public speakers generally," on the other hand, should be taken in a *"standing posture."*)[27] Practically the first thing Whitman rushed to tell his reader, as witness the frontispiece, was that he was not sedentary, and not a gentleman. The engraving facing the title page, based on a daguerreotype taken in the summer

Frontispiece, Leaves of Grass, *1855 edition, engraving based on*
daguerreotype of Whitman made by Gabriel Harrison
(Courtesy of Pierpont Morgan Library, New York City)

*Full-plate daguerreotype of Henry Wadsworth Longfellow, ca. 1850
(Courtesy of Longfellow National Historic Site, Cambridge, Mass.)*

of 1854 by Gabriel Harrison (a well known "artistic" practitioner), is a conscious assault on the Longfellow conventions and an effort to establish in their place a new type of poet who challenges the restrictive authority of gentility: floating in space on the large quarto page is the figure of a man, seen from the knees up. He is standing with one arm akimbo, hand on hip, the other hand in his pocket; his face is bearded, he is wearing a broad-brimmed hat tilted at an angle, and a blouse (no formal jacket) open at the throat, exposing his undershirt; his trousers seem made of durable, sturdy cloth. It is an image of informality, of casualness, of man outdoors; we are looking at a kind of worker, perhaps; certainly not a gentleman in a study.

Sometime around 1855 Whitman wrote a note to himself for an undelivered lecture on *Leaves of Grass* (why should not the poet assume that he would become instantly famous, that he would lecture?) in which he distinguishes himself from the traditional literateur: "Literature to these gentlemen is a parlor in which no person is to be welcomed unless he come attired in dress coat and observing the approved decorums with the fashionable."[28] The lack of dress coat came across clearly to his contemporaries, who thought it worth remarking in several of the first reviews of *Leaves of Grass*. One, for example, noted the absence of superfluous appendage of coat or waistcoat, the "air of mild defiance, and an expression of pensive insolence in his face."[29] An English reviewer alert to violations of social class caught Whitman's stance even more directly, and with some offense: "This portrait expresses all the features of the hard democrat, and none of the flexile delicacy of the civilized poet. The damaged hat, the rough beard, the naked throat, the shirt exposed to the waist, are each and all presented to show that the man to whom these articles belongs scorns the delicate arts of civilization."[30] But the image is more of a puzzle, more of an incongruity, than at first appears, for others have properly seen through the rough pretense to an essentially civilized poet underneath. Thus a British reviewer in 1856 notes the portrait of a "bearded gentleman in his shirt-sleeves and a Spanish hat."[31] And more recently Gay Wilson Allen has added the nice observation that despite the nonchalance and unconventionality of the image, the poet "does not appear to be rough, disorderly, sensual, or even fleshy if the word means overweight. His Van Dyke beard is neatly trimmed, his hat looks like an expensive beaver, and his genial countenance has a certain air of refinement."[32]

These inconsistencies reflect perhaps the instability and ambiguity of costume semantics, but they are worth calling attention to because they more importantly argue certain tensions within Whitman, pointing to the willed fusion of contraries within his own person that was an essential part of the cultural program he was announcing. Whitman in 1855 was an iconic oxymoron, embodying a central contradiction that would remain throughout his lifetime, the contradiction between his working-class sympathies and his elite literary ties, his identification with the common people and his sense of apartness. "The genius of the United States [is] always most in the common people," he could say in the 1855 Preface: "Their manners speech dress friendships—the freshness and candor of their physiognomy —the picturesque looseness of their carriage."³³ But elsewhere in *Leaves of Grass* he would depict himself starkly separated from the "common people"—"apart from the pulling and hauling stands what I am." That doubleness—"Both in and out of the game and watching and wondering at it"—was shared of course by Thoreau and Emerson, by Hawthorne and by Melville; yet Whitman, unlike the others, turned his inconsistencies and ambivalences into an act of social affirmation, achieving wholeness, or at least the appearance of wholeness, in his persona and poem, if not exactly in his life. What Erik Erikson would say of national identity in general—that it is based on opposing characteristics, and derives its "unique style" from the ways in which these "opposite potentialities" are counterpointed rather than allowed to "disintegrate into mere contradiction"—is no less true of Whitman, whose contradictions were much more a source of his complex identity than the bland assurance of "Song of Myself" ("Do I contradict myself? / Very well then I contradict myself") would lead us to think.³⁴

The daguerreotype frontispiece can take us even further into an understanding of Whitman's connections with popular notions of representation, for it insists that we notice the sheer physicality of the image, a frank acceptance of the body that is of course carried explicitly into the poem and that marks the influence of phrenology on Whitman.³⁵ Surely Walt's personal pride in his own phrenological reading—he had it printed on several occasions as proof of his ample capacities—led him in the first place to offer his body as frontispiece signature. But clearly it is not for Whitman a question of the body *or* the soul; rather, it is a fusion of the body *and* the soul, a union of opposites, that Whitman repeatedly affirms in his poem, and this union is the ground on which the other unifications of opposites in *Leaves of Grass* are also built. For the vision Whitman carried into the making of his poem affirmed not only the oneness of body and soul, but the parallel oneness of the form of the poem and its purpose.

Paul Zweig has most recently made clear just how deeply Whitman was influenced by the currents of phrenology that were flowing through New York society in the 1840s and 1850s.[36] I myself want to emphasize the sense in which the whole foundation of phrenology provides a parallel premise for Whitman's invention of a poetic form. For implicit in the phrenologist's practice of reading the bumps on the cranium is the assumption that the outward form of the skull was an index to the individual's mental faculties, social proclivities, and personality: to the phrenologist, in other words, outer equals inner. And despite the inner conflicts and dodges represented in *Song of Myself*, despite the terrible doubt of appearances that Whitman exposed in moments of acute self-confrontation, the aesthetic principle of *Leaves of Grass* affirms a similar identity of appearance and reality. In making this identity his foundation principle Whitman of course runs deeply counter to such contemporaries as Hawthorne and Melville, for whom ambiguity of appearance and concealment of purpose were central concerns.

In addition to phrenology, another important influence was the "science" of physiognomy, a way of understanding character that evolved in the late eighteenth and early nineteenth centuries based on a reading of the face. Physiognomy was largely based on John Caspar Lavater's widely popular *Essays on Physiognomy*, in which an equation is posited between facial type and the moral and personal qualities of the individual. For Lavater, "physiognomy [is] the Science of discovering the relation between the exterior and the interior— between the visible surface and the invisible spirit which it covers— between the animated, perceptible matter, and the imperceptible principle which impresses this character of life upon it—between the apparent effect, and the concealed cause which produces it."[37] Whitman's "Faces," a poem first published in the 1855 edition, is based on just this notion of congruence, with many of the lines consisting of a distinct metaphor sealing the character of each subject within a brief but vivid description, ranging from bilious satire—

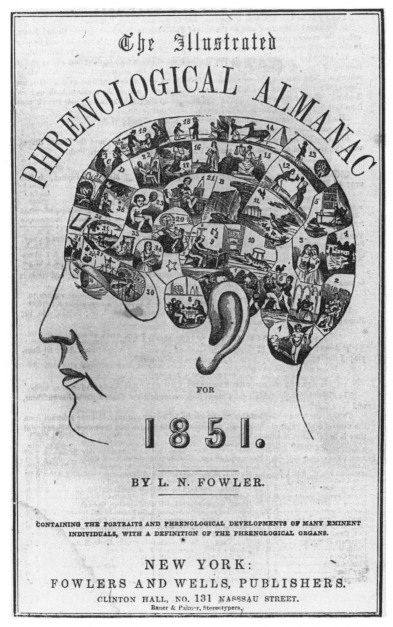

Cover of The Illustrated Phrenological Almanac for 1851, *by L. N. Fowler,*
published by Fowler and Wells
(Courtesy of New-York Historical Society, New York)

This face is a dog's snout sniffing for garbage,
Snakes nest in that mouth, I hear the sibilant threat.
This face is a haze more chill than the arctic sea,
Its sleepy and wabbling icebergs crunch as they go (p. 464)

to a more benign portraiture—

Behold a woman!
She looks out from her quaker cap, her face is clearer
and more beautiful than the sky. (p. 467)

Though Lavater admitted the fallibility of the physiognomist, he held firm to the science itself, using a huge variety of graphic representations of the face as the material for his studies; but the practice of reading faces extended to everyday situations as well in nineteenth-century America, as *Godey's Lady's Book* shows in discussing the variety of ways women's feelings are registered: "There is the timid glance of modesty, the bold stare of insolence, the warm glow of passion, the glassy look of indifference," etc.[38] That this catalogue of appearances (including "the open frankness of candor") might induce the reader to compose her face as well, leading to the theatricalization of manners, was perhaps inevitable; but the goal was a character of simplicity and courtesy, evidencing a harmony of inner quality and appearance.[39]

Whitman's own school for learning the face was the street and crowds that he loved so much, but it was also, and perhaps more importantly, the daguerreotype gallery. There Whitman learned not merely the art of observation, but the art of organization as well. It was in the daguerreotype gallery that one was allowed to do what would otherwise have been difficult in polite society: stare. (The exactness of the reproduction, together with the common frontal pose, would make the experience far more vivid than looking at a painting.)[40] We know, in fact, that the act of staring, of reading a face, of imagining a character in the image before him, particularly excited Whitman, who frequented the many daguerreotype galleries in Manhattan and wrote about them on several occasions during the 1840s: "You will see more *life* there—more variety, more human nature," than anywhere else, he wrote in the *Brooklyn Eagle* on July 2, 1846. Broadway, of course, had its full share of the more than one hundred galleries in Manhattan and Brooklyn at the time, including Mathew Brady's and John Plumbe's, where the visitor typically would enter a large room furnished comfortably with carpets, seats, lamps, and above all with the samples of the daguerreotypist's art hung on the surrounding walls. (The picture itself would be taken in a smaller "operating room" off the main gallery.) "What a spectacle!" Whitman wrote after his visit to Plumbe's: "In whatever direction you turn your peering gaze, you see naught but human faces! There they stretch, from floor to ceiling—hundreds of them. Ah! what tales might those pictures tell if their mute lips had the power of speech! How romance then, would be infinitely outdone by *fact*." And he goes on to imagine several dramatic biographies—e.g., "Is the husband yet tender to his bride?"—in the faces on view. He is especially fascinated by the eyes of the portraits, which sometimes go beyond "what comes from the real orbs themselves." Clearly what added to Whitman's pleasure was the dialectical fancy that the daguerreeotype, inviting the romance of speculation, was at the same time a "fact." The gallery was an "immense Phantom concourse," he wrote, "speechless and motionless, but yet realities."[41]

But it was not simply as a place where he might exercise his imagination or learn the subtleties of physiognomy that the daguerreotype gallery served Whitman. It was also, by its very structural properties, an organizational model for *Leaves of Grass*, providing a microcosm of the diversity of American society, a way of gathering into one whole the plurality of peoples and types that composed America.

The daguerreotype gallery was only one of a whole category of new urban structures that were providing fresh experiences in the mid-nineteenth century. John H. I. Browere, as early as 1828, opened a "Gallery of Busts," consisting of life masks that he had made in his travels around the country, and that he hoped would be the basis of a national museum.[42] And busts of a more "scientific" nature were on display in the numerous phrenological galleries throughout the 1840s and 1850s, serving as models of types of character and personality. (The phrenological bust itself, with its separate faculties spatially mapped, was yet another amalgam of discrete elements.) Another instance is P. T. Barnum's Gallery of American Female Beauty, instituted in the year *Leaves of Grass* was first published, as part of a scheme for an international beauty contest based on submissions from all over the country, which were to be judged by the New York

*Interior of Mathew Brady's National Portrait Gallery at Broadway and
Tenth Street, opened in 1860, from an engraved advertisement*

public's "votes" for their favorites.[43] (Incidentally, Barnum's rather
different attempt to define the illustrious—his living gallery of freaks
and oddities—did not meet with Whitman's approval.)

All of these various galleries served a variety of purposes: they codified regional types and informed Americans of the great variety of
their countrymen; they might also, on closer look, affirm the value of
the individual personality, *against* the type, in a period becoming
more and more subject to the homogenizing experiences of such
cultural forms as—precisely—the gallery. But they also, most simply
and most importantly, served as amalgamating wholes capable of
containing the accumulation of discrete particulars that was an ongoing feature of a civilization that was growing by leaps and bounds.
The gallery—like the panorama and exhibition halls, which I shall
consider later, and like the urban grid and the department store—
provided a model of flexible yet coherent organization.

This way of organizing parts within a whole we might call the omnibus form—a structure of variable size and shape, containing an
expandable number of particulars, not unlike the actual omnibuses
the poet liked to ride along Broadway. The omnibus form was so

important to Whitman because what he was seeking, as a self-consciously *modern* poet, was precisely a way of organizing experience—the "broad show of artificial things"[44]—that would be commensurate with the multiplicities of the new age, a form that would be equal to his culture's habits and experiences. What David Grimsted has said of late nineteenth-century melodrama applies equally well, I think, to these omnibus forms of Whitman's age—that "if there are certain common assumptions that bind together a particular society in a given age—what Alfred North Whitehead calls 'first principles almost too obvious to need expression, and almost too general to be capable of expression'—perhaps nothing is more revealing of them than the most popular of cultural forms."[45] For Whitman, the first principles were the spectacles that had come to dominate urban culture—from the great displays of daguerreotypes in the Broadway galleries to the exhibition halls he loved to frequent.

In seeking the proper shape of containment, Whitman evidently arrived at a formal equation between poet, poem, and gallery early on. How conscious he was of the gallery as a model is evident from a poem written before the 1855 edition and not published in Whitman's lifetime, "Pictures," which makes explicit the connection between the poet's mental storehouse of images and the public storehouse of images. It begins,

> In a little house pictures I keep, many pictures
>   hanging suspended—It is not a fixed house,
> It is round—it is but a few inches from one side of it to
>   the other side,
> But behold! it has room enough—in it, hundreds and
>   thousands,—all the varieties;
> . . . .
> And there, on the walls hanging, portraits of women and men,
>   carefully kept (p. 642)

Ranging from scenes of contemporary America to scenes of world history, Whitman's "Pictures" evokes, at the beginning of his career, the sense of wonder the poet felt at the power of the word to create a world by speaking it. Although Whitman did not publish the entirety of this long poem in his lifetime, he did like the opening well enough to print it many years later (1880) as a short poem, "My Picture-Gallery."[46]

In taking over the trope of the gallery and adapting it to his own poetic purposes, Whitman does not simply name things, places, objects, persons; rather, he provides a descriptive epithet that concretizes the thing observed, animating it in a quick, sure sketch, as in this section from "Song of Myself" (which, handily, begins with an image of a gallery):

> The connoisseur peers along the exhibition-gallery with
>   half-shut eyes bent sideways,
> As the deck-hands make fast the steamboat the plank is
>   thrown for the shore-going passengers,
> The young sister holds out the skein while the elder sister
>   winds it off in a ball, and stops now and then for the
>   knots,
> . . . .
> The pedler sweats with his pack on his back, (the purchaser
>   higgling about the odd cent;)
> The bride unrumples her white dress, the minute-hand of the
>   clock moves slowly,
> The opium-eater reclines with rigid head and just-open'd
>   lips (pp. 42–43)

It is no wonder that Eakins loved Whitman's work, given the painter's similar conception of the dramatic moment as the artistic subject; both were seeking to preserve the spectacle of concentrated action, the point of thoughtful engagement. (Eakins's own photographs were often used to model his paintings, and Eakins was particularly interested in Eadweard Muybridge's motion studies.) In Whitman's catalogue form, the poet had invented the literary equivalent of the quick sketch—the capturing of significant movement in an economical line that sums up a character. And this is the same direction in which the new art of photography was moving, especially after picking up shutter speed by 1855. Whitman's verse played with speed as a variable, with images we would want to linger over, as we linger over pictures in a museum or animals in a zoo, yet all within a context of great volume, urging us to move on to the next line as soon as one has registered.

That sense of movement we have when reading Whitman suggests another implicit model for the structure and content of *Leaves of*

Grass: the panorama. Like the gallery, the panorama is an omnibus form, encompassing within its boundaries a multiplicity of images, scenes, facts; but while the gallery is an architectural space through which the viewer wanders at will, the panorama is a large painted surface, which was displayed in two different ways—either mounted on the walls of a cylindrical viewing room, encompassing the viewer at the center; or unrolled from a drum before a stationary audience, the scenes passing in view as the canvas was unfurled. In the former case, the viewer's eye moves across the detailed scene, reading the parts at his or her own pace; in the latter instance, the pace and view are determined by the unrolling canvas; but in either case the viewer must assimilate the shifts of perspective and integrate the experience into a whole. Painted panoramas were hugely popular in New York, especially during the 1840s and 1850s (though continuing for decades more), with several exhibits running simultaneously, some displaying the American landscape (the West was a favorite), and others such exotic subject matter as "Egypt and the Holy Land," "The Antediluvian World," and "Voyage to the Moon." Where the gallery, especially the daguerreotype gallery, featured images of illustrious persons, the panorama offered the unified image of an illustrious landscape, either as an object of admiration in itself or peopled with historic figures and incidents.[47]

There were also during these years exhibitions of panoramic landscape views in more direct representational media—the daguerreotype and the scale-model—which claimed a unique mimetic authority. Robert H. Vance, for example, exhibited his images of gold-rush California in 1851, boasting of his three hundred views that they were "no exaggerated and high-colored sketches, got up to produce effect, but are as every daguerreotype must be, the stereotyped impression of the real thing itself."[48] Yet another daguerreotypist, H. E. Insley, of New York, conceived the idea of producing a series of daguerreotypes featuring American cities and communities, and he called for images from across the country. And in New York City in 1846, E. Porter Belden put on display a much-acclaimed, carved wooden miniature model of the city. "It is a perfect *fac-simile* of New York," one of the promotional flyers announced, "representing every street, lane, building, shed, park, fence, tree, and every other object in the city."[49]

Behind the enthusiasm for panoramas and models lay a combination of appeals. Contemporary commentators evince, at the most basic level, a sheer delight in the accuracy of representation: here was an art that was literal and informative, giving "exact" likenesses and a general knowledge of places beyond the experience of most city dwellers, especially on the East Coast. (Scenes closer to home but distant in time could also fascinate the public; Whitman delighted, for example, in F. Guy's "A Snow Scene in Brooklyn," "a literal portrait of the scene as it appeared from his window," created by the painter's constructing a large frame in his window enclosing the desired view, thus containing the reality of the street within the perimeter of the painting.)[50] The panoramas deliberately appealed to all classes (you did not need to read to enjoy them), and often were presented in theaters where the artist, or some other person, would narrate the scenes as they unfolded before the audience. Though painted somewhat crudely, judged by the academic standards of the day, the panoramas made up in scale and size what they may have lacked in subtlety, evoking the wildness of the American continent, and the drama of world-historical scenes, on an almost mythic scale.[51] Yet to the contemporary viewer, the illusion of reality was apparently very strong, as an 1849 letter about a Mississippi panorama makes clear: "the artist had succeeded in imposing on the sense of the beholder and inducing him to believe that he is gazing, not on canvas, but on scenes of actual and sensible nature."[52]

The panorama appealed as well to the nationalistic sense of the average American, confirming his need for a physical setting commensurate with his dreams about America, and rivalling—or surpassing—the more established imagery of Europe. Here was a vicarious experience of travel, of sights and scenes, without the necessity of undergoing hardship; and the viewer's delight in its encyclopedic "completeness" must have matched his delight in its accuracy. The American landscape, with its vast expanse of variegated scenery, seemed especially designed for display in the panorama.

Whitman was surely voicing this popular response to the American geography when he declared in his 1855 Preface, "The United States themselves are essentially the greatest poem." (If poems could be "real things," why could real things not be "poems"?) And he went on, characteristically, to define the poet's role as tallying the Me and the Not Me, the soul and reality. The American bard must respond to "his country's spirit ... he incarnates its geography and natural life and rivers and lakes. Mississippi with annual freshets and changing chutes, Missouri and Columbia and Ohio and Saint Lawrence with the falls and beautiful masculine Hudson, do not embouchure where they spend themselves more than they embouchure into him."[53] If Whitman was indeed the poet of panoramas, encompassing in his imagery a sense of space and scale that rivalled the synoptic effects of the visual panoramas, he produced his effects by doing what no actual panorama could do—i.e., by making leaps of space and scene beyond the means of any merely physical traveler, as in the astonishing Section 33 of "Song of Myself," which begins, "I skirt sierras, my palms cover continents, / I am afoot with my vision":

> Scaling mountains, pulling myself cautiously up, holding
>   on by low scragged limbs,
> Walking the path worn in the grass and beat through the
>   leaves of the brush,
> . . . .
> Where sun-down shadows lengthen over the limitless and
>   lonesome prairie,
> Where herds of buffalo make a crawling spread of the
>   square miles far and near,
> Where the humming-bird shimmers, where the neck of the
>   long-lived swan is curving and winding,
> . . . .
> Looking in at the shop-windows of Broadway the whole
>   forenoon, flatting the flesh of my nose on the
>   thick plate glass,
> Wandering the same afternoon with my face turn'd up to the
>   clouds, or down a lane or along the beach (pp. 62, 63, 64)

By moving the reader's eye from scene to scene, Whitman imitates the unrolling of the painted panorama before the viewer's sight, thus giving shape in his geographical catalogues to the new sense of American space that had already found popular expression in the galleries and exhibition halls of the country.

Whitman's invention of an ever-expandable verse form mirrored the new nation's sense of its natural resources and population; but it was also a perfect vehicle for celebrating the new material wealth of the country, a wealth more and more based on commerce, technology, and manufactures. During the period of Whitman's maturity,

America went from the beginnings of industrialization to an economy more and more dominated by mechanization: in the workplace, in the home, in transportation technologies. By the start of the Civil War, America was still predominantly an agricultural nation, but between 1840 and 1860, the years of Whitman's poetic maturation, net income from manufacturing grew threefold, from $162 to $495 million. Moreover, manufacturing began to account for a proportionally larger share of the national commodity output during the mid-century, rising from 17 percent in 1839 to 47 percent in 1879. The combination of rich resources and technological mastery was making America the fastest growing society in the world.[54]

Among the materials the poet must assimilate, Whitman had declared in his 1855 Preface, were "the factories and mercantile life and laborsaving machinery." And to Emerson (in an 1856 letter) he had added that among the things the poet must establish contact with were "real articles, the different trades, mechanics ... money, electric-telegraphs, free-trade, iron and the iron mines."[55] While Whitman thus celebrated the new technological civilization, Emerson himself had come to fear that the machine would get between man and his natural eyes: "Machinery is good," he wrote in his journal, "but mother-wit is better. Telegraph, steam, and balloon and newspaper are like spectacles on the nose of age, but we will give them all gladly to have back again our young eyes."[56] And though Whitman would himself later feel that materialism was undermining the life of the spirit, his initial confidence in his own transformed eye was sufficient to encompass happily the growing industrial density of the civilization.

From the first edition of *Leaves of Grass* in 1855 Whitman had enunciated a whole new department of American poetry by virtue of his affirmation of the common, everyday things of the material environment, and by his direct treatment of things. The new poets, he had written in the preface to *Leaves of Grass*, "shall find their inspiration in real objects today, symptoms of the past and future"; into the poet shall "enter the essences of the real things."[57] And it is this aspect of Whitman that a reviewer of the 1855 edition particularly emphasized when he wrote, in the *United States Review*, that the author of *Leaves of Grass* is a "lover of things," and of men and women; he is surrounded by common objects, the sweeping movement of "commerce, manufactures, arsenals, steamships, railroads, telegraphs, cities with paved streets, and aqueducts, and police, and gas— ... all the features and processes of the nineteenth century."[58] That Whitman himself had written the review—yet another of the many he had composed in his effort to celebrate himself and encourage his readership to do the same—makes all the more evident how important the point was as a foundation principle.

The chief vehicle for the display of manufactured goods—before the advent of the department store later in the century—was the trade fair or exposition. There one could see gathered at one time and in one place the otherwise dispersed evidence of the manifold changes in the U.S. economy. Like the public gallery, the exposition was a nineteenth-century invention that combined education and entertainment, framing within its halls an encyclopedia of objects, a dictionary of technological miracles that subsumed the individual thing under the aggregate spectacle. The first such display of arts and manufactures was held in London in 1851 in a glass and iron structure that came to be known as the Crystal Palace. New York followed almost immediately (1853) with its own world's fair, also housed in a "Crystal Palace," but distinct from the London exposition in that New York's proclaimed an ostensibly democratic purpose—to raise the level of taste in America, to diffuse art among "the mechanic and tradesman as well as the opulent and noble," as the illustrated catalogue put it; "if the beautiful were daily placed before us, surely our social life could not fail to be ameliorated and exalted by its silent eloquence."[59] What was in fact placed before the visitor was an enormous range of the fine and practical arts, with many European examples, and many American goods that seem from the present perspective virtually indistinguishable from the European articles; if there was a democratic, an American aesthetic, it was more visible in the rhetoric of the catalogue than in the objects on display.

Still, Whitman was enthralled by the Crystal Palace, as much by the building as by its contents. "Iron and glass are going to enter more largely into the composition of buildings," he wrote prophetically in 1857. The Crystal Palace was "an original, esthetic, perfectly proportioned American edifice—one of the few that put modern times not beneath old times, but on an equality with the best of them."[60] It was, we might say in retrospect, an architectural parallel to *Leaves of Grass*, a functional, organic structure, compendious in its myriad containments, inviting multitudes, modern and scientific; both were

Bird's-eye view of New York Crystal Palace, 1853, by John Bachman
(Courtesy of New-York Historical Society, New York)

commensurate with the requirements of a democratic art. (In his notebooks he had inscribed, "Rules for Composition—A perfectly transparent, plate-glassy style, artless, with no ornaments.")[61]

Whitman probably visited the Crystal Palace as much as any other American of his time, enthralled by the "phantasmagoria" (to use Walter Benjamin's word) that all such exhibitions offered to the nineteenth-century urban observer.[62] "I went a long time (nearly a year)," Whitman wrote, "days and nights—especially the latter—as it was finely lighted"; he was especially interested in the display of European art, and in the "fabrics and products and handiwork from the workers of all nations."[63] These were of course the years when Whitman was composing the first *Leaves of Grass*, and the exuberant materialism of the world exposition seems to have entered into the spirit of Whitman's own affirmation of the real things of America, as the large container of the hall itself would have reinforced the evolving design of the poem.

*Interior view of New York Crystal Palace for Exhibition of
the Industry of all Nations, 1853
(Courtesy of New-York Historical Society, New York)*

Thus in reinventing poetry for the modern age, Whitman had found models in urban popular culture far more significant than we have previously realized. In photography, Whitman had found a central metaphor for his own creative processes, a way of looking at the world that was attentive to fact, literal in its reporting, yet suggestive of typicality. Moreover, like the new photographic techniques of imprinting living shapes upon a chemically sensitized plate, Whitman's verse was both art and science, comfortable with its literalism, yet striving for a lifelike representation of self and nation that was anything but mechanical. Given the equation between poet and poem, the deliberately stylized daguerreotype portrait that appears as the frontispiece in the 1855 edition could not have been a fitter emblem of the poet who would reproduce himself so self-consciously in the pages that follow.

And in eschewing the tight organization of conventional poetry in favor of a loose, free-flowing, disorganized encyclopedia, Whitman had found the literary equivalent for one of the key patterns in nineteenth-century popular culture, the organizational principle underlying the gallery, the panorama, and the exhibition hall—the containment of an infinitely expandable number of parts in an encompassing whole. The one book, *Leaves of Grass*, could grow from edition to edition simply by expanding or rearranging at any point: he had found a form perfectly suited to a society of discrete individuals, loosely associated as members of a non-hierarchical collection (at least in theory), a society in which number and volume were becoming ruling principles. By echoing the omnibus structure of the gallery in his poetry, Whitman was taking from the popular culture of his time one of the determining forms of experience, transforming a visual model into a literary one, and in the process implicitly evoking the power of popular forms to educate the common reader. Moreover, in discovering the formal equivalent, in poetry, for the new urban, industrial culture, Whitman managed to have it both ways: he was modern, alert to the latest scientific discoveries, he was at one with Broadway and the Crystal Palace and the Galleries; but he had also invented a form that was flexible, organic, and breathing, a "handmade" form that took its exact shape from the length of the variable line and from the thought, that could go on for a few lines, or a few thousand lines.

Thus the exemplary wholeness of *Leaves of Grass*, its power as an act of social ethics, lay in its providing an ideal remedy of sorts for the inadequate definition of "being human" that was evolving out of the nineteenth century's response to technology and industrialization; for if one strong characteristic of urban industrial life was its separation of man from nature and from his work, and the loss of Emersonian wholeness, then Whitman was providing in his poetry and person a way of embracing that same civilization on an ideal plane where the self was not constrained by the new technologies, but rather was enlarged. Locating Whitman within the matrix of mid-nineteenth-century popular culture may likewise enlarge our own reading of *Leaves of Grass*. Whitman's achievement was not to have escaped his time and entered the literary pantheon of transcendental values; it was to have immersed himself in his time and in the most character-istic features of its urban culture; it was to have devised a structure that, like the steamboat or the locomotive, was a new invention, an expression of the energies and needs of his culture in a substantially new shape. For the artist intent on finding forms that could reflect a contact with the real things of American life, with the authentic, with the forces of contemporary science and technology, with the totality of American civilization, Whitman would provide, as we shall see, a durable touchstone and inspiration, especially to those coming of age in the twentieth century, when his example would gain a relevance it never had in the nineteenth.

Part Two

A CULTURE

OF IMITATION

*I*n deliberately taking his stand at the center of his age and entering into the "essences of the real things," Whitman had knowingly embraced the whole of America's growing industrial civilization; and images of a thriving urban economy, of mechanics and laborers, flicker throughout the early editions of *Leaves of Grass*. At times—especially in the journalism of the 1850s and 1860s—Whitman could sound like the cheeriest of boosters, waxing prosaic over the "immense variety of manufactures, works, foundries, and other branches of useful art and trade carried on in the limits of our expansive and thriving city." Doorknobs, cups and saucers, dishes, pitchers, doorplates, piano keys, clock faces—nothing was too humble for Whitman to celebrate.[1] This was the Whitman who read "Song of the Exposition" at the fortieth annual Exhibition of the American Institute in 1871, celebrating the arrival of the new muse on American shores with a humor his readers often overlook: "Smiling and pleas'd with palpable intent to stay, / She's here, installed amid the kitchen ware!"[2]

For Whitman, as for many in the late nineteenth century, the new force of mechanization was identified optimistically with the spirit of national progress. Senator Orville H. Platt, for example, speaking at the 1892 Patent Centennial Celebration in Washington challenged his audience to a thought experiment: "Try to imagine what our social, financial, educational, and commercial condition would be with an absolute ignorance of how steam and electricity can be used in the daily production of things for our sustenance and comfort; with an absolute ignorance of the steamboat, the railroad, the telegraph, the telephone, the modern printing press, and the machinery in common daily use."[3] Thus was the machine incorporated into an already existing religious tradition that gave people dominion over nature: the exploitation of "crude matter" to achieve greater comfort was part of a providential plan that furthered the individual's power.[4]

This celebration of America's growing wealth and of a newly arising technological civilization was part of a middle-class culture that thrived on a traffic in representations and replications of every possi-

ble sort. The popular culture in America was rapidly becoming, after
the Civil War, at once a culture of consumption and a culture of
spectatorship. Richard Altick in *The Shows of London* (1978) details
the extraordinary variety of spectacles that caught the fascinated eye
of the British public, and many of these had a second life across the
Atlantic, or were imitated and adapted for American consumption.
During the 1870s and 1880s spectator entertainment grew from its
rudimentary pre–Civil War forms into more and more elaborate spectacles: circuses, minstrel shows, vaudeville, light musicals, sports,
road shows. Barnum was of course the great innovator in such eclectic entertainments, and he featured during the mid-century the usual
jugglers and gypsies, giants and dwarfs, but also ventriloquists and
automatons, and other forms that evinced the growing taste for representations—"dioramas, panoramas, models of Niagara, Dublin,
Paris and Jerusalem," as the promotional literature put it.[5]

The popular theater, too, in the last decades of the century catered
increasingly to a taste for lifelike imitations that floated easily over
the border between life and art. It was an excess of such theatrical representations—which might include everything from real food
eaten on stage to real horses used to enact battle scenes—that
prompted the critic William Thayer to argue in 1894 that the sensationalism of the theater had dulled the viewer's imagination, a symptom of the same disease—"epidermism"—Thayer saw manifest in the
taste for realism in literature.[6]

But the disease was already far advanced in American culture, and
growing ever stronger, as the practice of imitation supplied the matrix for cultural forms in virtually every sphere. The climax of this
aesthetic of replication—though by no means the end of it—was, one
might say, the whole of the Chicago Exposition of 1893. The fair was
divided into two apparently different geographical areas: on the one
hand, a Midway Plaisance, with shows and rides, pleasures and ex-
citements; and on the other, the hugely impressive great Court of
Honor, an environmental stage worthy of a deMille extravaganza on
the Roman Empire. (Of the latter, Louis Sullivan wrote, "Thus ever
works the pallid academic mind, denying the real, exalting the fictitious and false.")[7] John Cawelti has justly seen in the Court a monument to elite taste and in the Midway the messy vitality of popular
culture, with the distance between the two an anticipation of the split
that would characterize modern society.[8] Yet both the popular Mid-

way and the elite Court shared at bottom a similar aesthetic of replication: in the official exposition there were not only the imitation palaces made out of ephemeral staff, but also replicas of home-grown structures: a reproduction of St. Augustine's Fort Marion offered by the state of Florida, for example, and a replica of the clock tower on Independence Hall—together with the actual Liberty Bell—displayed by Pennsylvania. Meanwhile, moored at the Lake Front were replicas of the *Niña*, the *Pinta*, and the *Santa María*, built in Spanish naval yards. As for the Midway, it featured replicas of German and Turkish villages, a street in Cairo (with dancers), a Moorish palace, a Viennese cafe, villages from Algeria, Tunisia, Austria, and Dahomey, a Japanese bazaar, etc., with people from these places as "actors."[9]

And where the Columbia Exposition's Midway left off, amusement parks and the cinema were soon ready to take over. Coney Island, for example, which endured long into the twentieth century, originated in the same late nineteenth-century industrial aesthetic of replication, offering not only mechanized rides and thrills, but also a series of simulated disasters—the Fall of Pompeii, the eruption of Mount Pelée, the Johnstown and Galveston Floods, not to mention a burning four-story building that was repeatedly set ablaze and extinguished.[10] The cinema, itself a product of the late Victorian imagination, would soon make those actual repetitions unnecessary. But one of the initial "improvements" on the cinema—Hale's Tours—suggests that movies were not enough, or at least that the appetite for replication knew no limits. Hale combined moving pictures with a moving audience in a bizarre hybrid that simulated movement through a landscape via a pseudo-railway: rocking platforms, circulating air, clicking track sounds, and front and rear scenic projections convinced Hale (as he tried to convince his audience) that "it is impossible not to imagine that you are actually on the train."[11] But we surely miss the point of Hale's Tours if we see them as simply substitutes for an audience that could not afford train travel; even for the experienced traveler there was the primary marvel of the *recreated* experience.

One dominant mode in the popular culture in the late nineteenth century was thus the tendency to enclose reality in manageable forms, to contain it within a theatrical space, an enclosed exposition or recreational space, or within the space of the picture frame. If the world outside the frame was beyond control, the world inside of it could at least offer the illusion of mastery and comprehension. And on a more elementary aesthetic level, the replica, with its pleasure of matching real thing and facsimile, simply fascinated the age. Nothing better illustrates this characteristic pleasure in replication than the Victorian parlor, with its artifical flowers and marble fruit; and—to anticipate a later chapter—nothing was more at home in the Victorian parlor than the stereograph collection, inevitably including an abundance of still-life images.[12]

The pervasive growth of the spectatorial habit in America is adroitly suggested by William Dean Howells in *A Hazard of New Fortunes*, when he shows us the voyeuristic excitement of riding on the New York elevated, in which the rider gains a "fleeting intimacy" with the urban dweller in the apartments seen from the traveling car. "March said it was better than the theater, of which it reminded him. . . . What suggestion! what drama! what infinite interest!"[13] Where Whitman, nearly half a century earlier, had sought connection with his fellow New Yorker—whether on omnibus or ferry or pavement— Howells's March delights in the more distanced quality of representation; it is like the theater, only better.

The theatricalizing of experience that Howells epitomizes in his character harmonized fully with a consumer culture that in other respects was offering imitations of every kind in place of the real thing. For this was the triumph of the machine—that in its capacity to produce imitations it could supply everything from entertainment to necessities in virtually unlimited quantities. But to the more thoughtful observers of change, it was precisely the machine's capacity to imitate that raised the knottiest issues. And the question first posed by industrial technology in the nineteenth century would become the question we are still trying to answer: how has the machine, with its power to produce replicas and reproductions, altered our culture? Has it, for example, degraded the quality of civilization by flooding our world with sham things? Or has it enlarged and democratized the base of culture? That question was debated during the years following the Civil War in terms, especially, of the ubiquitous chromolithograph, which became a symbol of the new culture. The whole problem of the cheap art reproduction sums up a good deal of the class conflict surrounding the advent of a culture of imitation and is worth a closer look.

Improving aesthetically with a rapidly advancing technology, the chromos, as they were called, entered the home as premiums offered by salesmen, or through direct purchase, or through the agencies of galleries, museums, religious, and fraternal organizations. They offered images drawn from a huge range of subject matter—allegories of childhood, manhood, and old age, of marriage and bachelorhood, historic battles and heroes, steamboats and railroads, urban buildings and street scenes, sublime landscapes, fruit, vegetables, meat, flowers and babies, horses and deer and fish, Beethoven, Washington, and Yankee Doodle.[14]

The problem with the chromos was not just that they were cheap and therefore widely available; it was that the reproductions could be of quite good quality, and the better they were, the more they challenged the elite classes. The socially aspiring middle-class reader had an ally in the Beecher sisters, who in *The American Woman's Home* advised him or her of the charms of reproductions "of the best class"—not only chromos, but plaster statuettes as well, "providing always that they are selected with discrimination and taste."[15] And publishers often guaranteed the accuracy of a reproduction, happily oblivious to the paradoxes they were courting, as when a chromo, available in two sizes ($5 and $20) was promised to be "certified . . . a *fac-simile* of the original."[16] So good was the quality that one observer at the mechanics' exhibition stood amazed before a display of chromo wonders "which challenged the observer to tell how they differed from the original paintings at their side."[17] But to others, that was just the problem: to the degree that the chromos (and other kinds of reproductions) erased the difference between the original and the reproduction, they called into question some of the fundamental values of cultural entitlement.

To champions of an egalitarian culture, the chromos epitomized the goal of a heritage accessible to all. As James Parton argued in *The Atlantic*, they harmonized well with "the special work of America at the present time, which is not to create, but to diffuse; not to produce literature, but to distribute the spelling book."[18] But just because of their democratizing tendency, the chromos also represented, to more conservative critics, the chiefest evil, the erosion of barriers between the classes. The most consistent voice here was that of E. L. Godkin, editor of *The Nation*, who argued that the copy of a painting destroyed the unique qualities of the original and led to a distorted appreciation of art.[19] The society that the British-born Godkin saw shaping up around him was a "pseudo-culture," lacking in moral and mental discipline, a society brought about by the rapid acquisition of wealth. To Godkin the chromo was part of a series of debasements of culture—along with lyceum lectures, magazines, and newspapers—all of which "diffused through the community a kind of smattering of all sorts of knowledge, a taste for 'art'—that is a desire to see and own pictures—which, taken together, pass with a large body of slenderly-equipped persons as 'culture.'" Godkin campaigned against the chromo for years, but what confirmed his view of the age and brought about this definitive attack was the scandalous Beecher affair (the charismatic minister was tried for adultery but later acquitted) which, Beecher being a champion of egalitarian culture, Godkin took as an epitome of what he christened the "chromo-civilization."[20]

The division within the culture over the value of the chromo was, typically, evident in the singular person of Mark Twain, who in this, as in so much else, mirrored the popular taste. In *Connecticut Yankee*, for example, Hank Morgan surveys his sparsely furnished sixth-century apartment and feels acutely the lack of decoration: "It made me homesick to look around over this proud and gaudy but heartless barrenness and remember that in our house in East Hartford, all unpretending as it was, you couldn't go into a room but you would find an insurance chromo, or at least a three-color God-Bless-Our-Home over the door; and in the parlor we had nine."[21] Twain's irony, confusingly, seems to cut both ways: against the backward barrenness of the British, but also against the excesses and banality of Hank's own nineteenth-century Hartford. A letter to Andrew Lang from the same year (1889) indicates that he was puzzling much over the larger implications of the whole chromo question: for he defends himself there against Matthew Arnold's recent attack on the vulgarity of American culture by identifying his own art with the egalitarian ethos of the chromo; but he then argues that the ultimate purpose of the reproduction is to advance the masses, finally, toward the real thing.[22] Are the old masters to be scorned? or approached at last?

Perhaps the middle ground in the debate had already been struck by Edward Bruce who, surveying the Centennial exhibition in Philadelphia, saw no inherent contradiction between the democratizing tendencies of the age and true cultural achievement—at least if one looked far enough ahead. For Bruce saw in the magnificence of America's industrial progress and in the "vastly increased" number of "cultivated minds," in the swelling museums and galleries and libraries, in the universal distribution of literature and the universal copying of artworks, a promise of achievement yet to come. As for just now, "The age, recognizing perforce the inherent capabilities of the race as a constant quantity, contents itself so far with endeavoring to adapt and reproduce, or at most imitate, such manifestations of the artistic sense as it finds excellent in the past. The day for originality may come ere long."[23] Yet even the sanguine Bruce cannot withhold his disgust, at the Centennial, from the "depressing atmosphere of fraud" that is all about him in the mechanisms that replace human labor by machines and real things by shams. Standing before an "immense iron wheel devoted to the drying of paper collars," which he grandly styles a "monument to sham," Bruce prophecies a bionic future that would await its fulfillment in the twentieth century: "Soon we shall have sham paper collars, then enameled skins, and then the costume of Vortigern's Pict, and the fever called buttoning and unbuttoning shall be, as Poe craved, ended at last." (Poe, who had imagined the "Man Who Was Used Up," is surely an appropriate allusion here.) In all this, in the fashions of consumption beginning to sweep the country, Bruce saw the machine and its products bringing "the American people within its yoke and manacle."[24] There were others with fears similar to Bruce's, of course, but their cautious response to the machine forms part of a reaction to technology that I want to explore in a later part of this study.

The pervasiveness of the culture of imitation in the late nineteenth century can best be grasped through a more detailed examination of three interrelated areas of cultural expression, which will occupy the following three chapters. The first deals with the middle- and upper-class world of material goods that was more and more creating identity in America and supplying the vocabulary of self-expression. What things meant to the middle class in this new world of reproductions and replicas will be the subject of "A Hieroglyphic World." A major part of that world was the photographic image; photography was arguably the most widely experienced and therefore most influential of replicated forms, and it will be examined in the second chapter of this section. The third major area of consideration will be literary realism; although the mimetic goals of realism were, broadly speaking, in harmony with the nineteenth century's culture of replication, during the 1890s a breakdown in conventional realism occurred in the writing of a younger generation that paved the way for the modernist revolution that followed in the twentieth century.

A Hieroglyphic
World

The Furnishing of Identity

in Victorian Culture

*W*riting with the privileged hind-
sight of 1920, Edith Wharton provided the key to an understanding of
late nineteenth-century manners when she remarked in *The Age of
Innocence* on the "elaborate system of mystification" that formed the
social ritual of bourgeois society. "In reality they all lived in a kind of
hieroglyphic world, where the real thing was never said or done or
even thought, but only represented by a set of arbitrary signs."[1] And
one could take Wharton's observation one step farther: the hieroglyphic world of the American middle and upper classes during the
decades following the Civil War encompassed the whole fabric of
social communication, including the material objects that furnished
the individual with his or her visible identity. So dense is the system
of decorative signs in the period that one might easily think that the
most characteristic expression of the Victorian mind was *matter* in all
its shapes and sizes, textures, surfaces, and substances. In this chapter I want to look first at the structural and aesthetic properties of this
hieroglyphic world, which is the material foundation of the late nineteenth-century culture of imitation; and I want then to explore its
moral and spiritual significance, using evidence from popular culture
and also from works of fiction that more self-consciously and complexly treat the moral and spiritual ramifications of the artificial
world of the consumer. For however disparate the evidence—from
the Sears catalogue to Henry James—the culture as a whole reveals
an interconnectedness, at the heart of which is the central importance of *things* as signs.

The American passion for consumer goods was part of a larger
pattern of growing consumption in Western industrial cultures gener-

ally, beginning in the eighteenth century and becoming more and more institutionalized by the middle of the nineteenth century. At the center of the web of consumption—especially for the growing urban population—were the department stores, their majestic interiors, modeled on palaces and temples and cathedrals, giving to the act of buying a grand and sacred character. Like the more sporadic and more spectacular world trade expositions, they were conceived as expressions of high national purpose, sharing with the official fairs a similar ethical, practical, and aesthetic orientation. Thus, when Siegel-Cooper installed in its New York store a copy of the Daniel Chester French statue, *Republic*, from the 1893 Chicago Exposition, and when John Wanamaker installed in his Philadelphia store the great eagle from the 1903 St. Louis World's Fair, these were merely crowning manifestations of a longstanding continuity between our officially certified national purpose and merchandising.[2] Looking back in 1900 on the 1876 Centennial, Wanamaker spoke of it as opening "a new vision to the people of the United States. It was the cornerstone upon which manufacturers everywhere rebuilt their businesses to new fabrics, new fashions and more courageous undertakings. . . . The continuing outgrowth of that exhibition has revolutionized the methods of almost every class of mercantile business in the United States."[3]

But the expositions and stores existed not merely to be venerated, but most emphatically to be patronized. In order for the economy to function properly, old inhibitions to spending—a reverence for the virtues of frugality and restraint—had to be cleared away: desire had to be created and legitimized.[4] This goal the stores accomplished through a variety of techniques—accommodating services, lowered prices, comfortable surroundings; above all they accomplished the virtual reconditioning of the American consumer through the appeal of newly attractive store windows and advertisements, which encouraged him or her to reason not the need, but simply to buy. (There is a nice congruity in the fact that L. Frank Baum, the author of the quintessential tale of desire and self-transformation, *The Wizard of Oz* [1900], was also the founder and editor of an early trade journal for window decorators, *The Shop Window*.)[5] The success of this effort is registered in the growth of the economy itself, but also, more vividly, in the various depictions—graphic and literary—that dramatize the state of desire.

Perhaps none excelled Theodore Dreiser in dramatizing the nuances of this emotion so central to the consumer's emotional economy. Early stories—echoing journalistic illustrations—describe the longing of the individual outside, on the street, looking at the department store windows and the homes of the comfortable;[6] but it is Sister Carrie who occupies the central place in this gallery of unfulfilled desire, and Dreiser's depiction of her initiation into the mystery of the department store bears the mark of an archetype in American experience: "[she] passed along the busy aisles, much affected by the remarkable displays of trinkets, dress goods, stationery, and jewelry. Each separate counter was a show place of dazzling interest and attractions. She could not help feeling the claim of each trinket and valuable upon her personally, and yet she did not stop. There was nothing there which she could not have used—nothing which she did not long to own."[7] The psychology of the passage is acute, especially in the last sentence, where use and desire, reason and need, interfuse. By the end of the novel, Sister Carrie has gained success and its material rewards, but Dreiser's insight into the conditioning of desire is to show us a Carrie who is, at the end, still restless and haunted, even in her comfort.

Essential to the legitimizing of desire on a mass scale was the inculcation of a belief that, first of all, there was *enough* for everyone, that in fact there was *more than* enough, that indeed there was *so much* that it must be very natural, very easy, and almost a God-given right, to own things. Supporting this belief was an aesthetic of abundance that is visible virtually everywhere one looks in the material culture of Victorian America, the result of an industrial capacity that could indeed supply a seemingly limitless supply of things. From 1873 to 1898, as Ray Ginger has observed, the capacities of production were in excess of the market's capacity to absorb goods, and overproduction was widespread—an excess capacity to "mill flour, to make watches, to manufacture stoves."[8] This excess capacity shows up in the marketplace in several different ways, as more and more goods come before the consumer. For one, there is a shift from the relatively random assortment of things in the general store to the vast expansion in the variety of goods available in the department store. Moreover, one-of-a-kind items in the general store are found in multiples in the larger department stores. And, in the department store, goods are carefully subdivided according to kind and variety, as things are seen, inevitably, as members of larger categories.

In fact, the abundance of products in the marketplace created the necessity, embraced enthusiastically, of imposing system and order on a scale previously unknown. (One sees this tendency not only in the realm of practical aesthetics and business, but in the sciences and social sciences too, encompassing everything from Mendeleyev's periodic table of the chemical elements, to Melville Dewey's decimal system, which itself was probably modeled on the classification scheme used at the Philadelphia Centennial.)[9] Every product had its place in the visible scheme of display, and also in an invisible structure of inventory, bookkeeping, and warehousing. The ordering of things in the department store was of course a practical matter, a way of facilitating sales, but there was also the more playful display featured on occasion at fairs and exhibitions, in which goods were massed to form huger versions of themselves that mightily signified the strength of their numbers. Polyisomorphs, we might call such structures—a fifty-foot high obelisk of olive oil bottles in the shape of an olive bottle, a monster cheese weighing 22,000 pounds, a giant tower of beer bottles.

The Victorian expression of abundance, along with its concomitant rage for order, are nowhere more evident than in the busy pages of the mail-order catalogue, which came of age in the 1880s and 1890s. For those displaced from the metropolis, unable to enjoy the street theater of the store windows, the sales catalogue—from Sears or Montgomery Ward, especially—served as a surrogate for the three-dimensional display, offering the advantage, besides, of being amenable to solitary contemplation and unencumbered dreaming.[10] Virtually anything was available through the catalogues—anything one might want to put in a house, on a house, or around it, including the house itself.[11] While the department store display case was crowded with the actual objects on sale, massed together to show their virtue, the pages of the catalogue were filled to capacity with images of discrete things, classified by kinds, each image standing for a potentially infinite storehouse of actual goods. The catalogue was crowded as well with page after page of densely set type, a text that flowed in and around the objects like a wash of reassuring sales talk, the whole looking like the patterned wallpaper of the period, bound in book form. The catalogues were known as "wish-books"—inviting as they

Food counter in R. H. Macy's Department Store, Herald Square, 1902,
photograph by Joseph Byron
(Courtesy of Museum of the City of New York)

were—and the wish was finally tempered only by the price of the article itself: according to its price was the thing known and assigned its ontological space in the universe of the catalogue. Thus of a dozen varieties of chairs or lamps or harnesses or bonnets or suspenders or rings, each item was marked at finely graduated prices. By thus codifying the world of things, the merchant was implying two principles: that material things had their qualities and classes, just as did people; and that the goods they were selling were fairly priced. (That is, you got what you paid for.)

The excess capacity that distinguished the marketplace was visible as well in the home, which was the linchpin in the late nineteenth-century consumer culture. A main focus of Victorian aesthetic effort, the home expressed the abundance of energy that was basic to

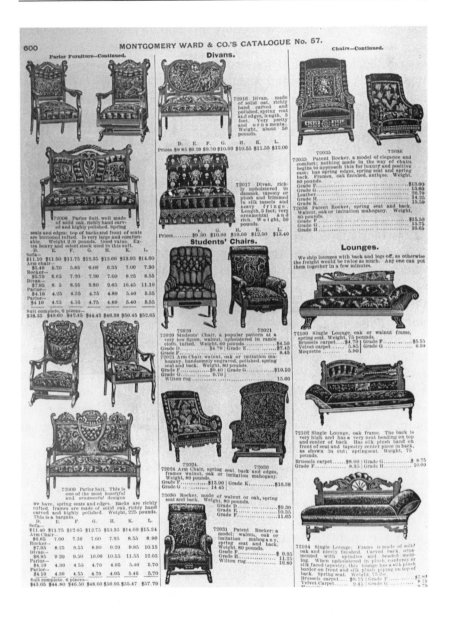

Parlor Furniture, page from Montgomery Ward and Co.'s Catalogue no. 57, 1895

the Victorian conception of healthy functioning and that was visible in countless other ways: interminable novels, gargantuan, multi-course meals, lavishly styled dresses, luxuriating drapes, high ceilings, bursting families, and shelves stuffed with bibelots. In the home, it has often been observed, was refuge from the commercial whirlwind, and there the family could preserve its sense of autonomy. There a man was still his own master, even if his stature in the workplace was shrinking; and there woman had a key role in managing the domestic economy, a role that was becoming increasingly honored and spiritualized.[12] It was as if, in the words of Donald Lowe, "the private space of the family could compensate for the estrangement in the public world."[13] (Even Whitman, who more characteristically exhorted the American to take to the open road, wrote that "it is in some sense true that a man is not a whole and complete man unless he *owns* a house and the ground it stands on.")[14] Despite the efforts of reformers throughout the nineteenth century to encourage more practical communal living arrangements, the privacy of the home remained sacrosanct.[15]

The home was the center of the moral and spiritual universe, "an unfailing barrier against vice, immorality, and bad habits," as Andrew Jackson Downing wrote in 1850.[16] And the vision of progress, of an egalitarian culture of homeowners, came together in a middle-class ethic that elevated the worker to the status of independent homeowner as well, as Henry Ward Beecher enunciated with clear conviction in his July 4 oration in 1876:

> [T]he average American household is wiser, there is more material for thought, for comfort, for home love, to-day, in the ordinary workman's house, than there was a hundred years ago in one of a hundred rich men's mansions and buildings.... The laborer ought to be ashamed of himself—or to find fault with Providence that stinted him when he was endowed—who in 20 years does not own the ground on which his house stands, and that, too, an unmortgaged house; who has not in that house provided carpets for the rooms, who has not his China plates, who has not his chromos, who has not some picture or portrait hanging upon the walls, who has not some books nestling on the shelf, who has not there a household he can call his home, the sweetest place upon the earth. This is not the picture of some future

*Interior of Mrs. Leoni's residence, 1894, photograph by Joseph Byron
(Courtesy of Museum of the City of New York)*

time, but the picture of to-day, a picture of the homes of the workingmen of America.[17]

Beecher, one of the most popular orators of his time, was sketching a picture that was already reinforced by the popular Currier and Ives chromos that featured happy homesteads and warm interiors. The only obstacle to the realization of these dreams of domestic bliss was the simple lack of money.[18] But even that obstacle eventually became less of a problem with the advent of the five-and-dime stores, which Dreiser praised, in 1911, as "a truly beautiful, artistic, humanitarian thing," bringing the "stock of overproduction" within the "range of the poor," and thereby democratizing the fulfillment of desire.[19]

The aesthetic character of the home offered in many ways a sharp contrast to the nineteenth-century workplace, a contrast between a "flat prosaic atmosphere," as Mario Praz has written, and the sur-

roundings of comfort and leisure, "which must propitiate [the worker's] dreams and illusions."[20] Yet swings of fashion—from the ornate
but relatively restrained furnishings of the mid-century to the clut-
tered eclecticism of the 1880s and then to a somewhat more simplified, chastened expression in the 1890s—make generalization about
Victorian domestic style somewhat hazardous.[21] Let me nevertheless
take as a norm of middle-class style what Kenneth Ames has called
the "commercial aesthetic," a picturesque eclecticism that mixes
"Renaissance, Baroque, Classical, and wholly invented." Turned out
by the large manufacturers of Grand Rapids, these eclectic designs
pervaded the households of America, giving substance to Beecher's
July 4th vision of a prosperous republic.[22] Ironically, however, it was
anything but a republican style; rather, it was essentially imitative
of vaguely aristocratic modes—highly decorated surfaces, dramatic
curves, allusions to traditional European high styles. Looking for status, middle-class Americans tried to reproduce in their homes the
trappings of a generic aristocracy, objects rich in narrative signs suggesting allegorical fantasy and far-off places—leaves, claw feet, em-
bellished figures.[23]

But I am not so much interested in the pieces themselves as in the
way they were ordered and given meaning within the Victorian environment. And one characteristic that remains more or less constant
thoughout the period (as compared with the notably different style of
the early twentieth century, at least), is the quality of abundance we
have noted as a key feature of the marketplace. From the advent of
machine production in the 1840s to the end of the century, the middle-class aesthetic featured a densely decorative style, an interior
stuffed with things, whether it was the display of bric-a-brac on the
shelf, or the pillows on the divan, or the jumble of photographs pop-
ping out of the album, or the pages of the homemade scrapbook.

These interiors are visible in the many photographic records of the
time, and they are reflected as well in the literature of the period,
as in this concentrated and detailed description from William Dean
Howells's *A Hazard of New Fortunes*, a *locus classicus* for the type.
Howells's main characters, the Marches, have been looking for a furnished apartment, and they come upon this specimen, done up by
Mrs. Grosvenor Green.

> [W]herever you might have turned round she had put a gimcrack
> so that you would knock it over if you did turn. . . . At every door

hung a portière from large rings on a brass rod; every shelf and dressing-case and mantel was littered with gimcracks, and the corners of the tiny rooms were curtained off, and behind these portières swarmed more gimcracks. The front of the upright piano had what March called a short-skirted portière on it, and the top was covered with vases, with dragon candlesticks and with Jap fans, which also expanded themselves bat-wise on the walls between the etchings and the watercolors. The floors were covered with filling, and then rugs and then skins; the easy-chairs all had tidies, Armenian and Turkish and Persian; the lounges and sofas had embroidered cushions hidden under tidies ... There was a superabundance of clocks.[24]

And so on. Mrs. Green has the appropriate mix of objets d'art and mass-produced objects, the whole adding up to a case study of material fetishism no less interesting for being a furnished apartment designed for renting; for Howells has evidently strived to express a kind of typical ideal of the period's taste for excess.[25] And the point of Mrs. Green's effort is that more is more; it is not the individual thing that matters, but the volume of things. Howells's satire captures what is most characteristic in the material culture of the Victorian period—its love of abundance, of numberless bibelots, of illusions of receding space and hidden corners—along with its love of artifice, of replication. And that latter point suggests the second major principle of the Victorian material aesthetic that I want to explore: the aesthetic of imitation.

At every level of society individuals sought an elevation of status through the purchase and display of goods whose appearance counted for more than their substance. The result was a factitious world in which the sham thing was proudly promoted by the manufacturer, and easily accepted by the consumer, as a valid substitute for authenticity. At the bottom of this aesthetic was the machine. Though scholars of the decorative arts may have overestimated the degree to which the machine was used in the production of household goods, in general it lowered the cost of labor and made possible the production of less expensive objects designed in the approximate style of higher-priced, hand-made goods, but with relatively less ornamentation and simpler lines.[26] For the consumer this meant not only an abundance of objects available, but a variety of styles and ornamentation that gave to the middle class a new vocabulary of expression based on the language of the upper classes.[27] Thus *the imitation* became the foundation of middle-class culture, exemplifying, as Jean Baudrillard would say, the inevitable tendency of technology to substitute the fabricated world for the natural one.[28]

Of course imitation materials were in use in America long before the industrial revolution. During the Colonial period, for example, canvas floor coverings were painted in black and white alternating squares to resemble marble tiles, while wooden stairs were often painted in swirling marble patterns; in fact, cheaper wood furniture was not infrequently painted in grain-like patterns—at all levels of society—as much for the sheer pleasure in decoration as to elevate the status of the object. Still what was in occasional evidence before the nineteenth century becomes the core of consumer society after the mid-1800s, pervading both houses and furniture. Trade catalogues from the late nineteenth and early twentieth centuries unabashedly proclaimed the excellence of their ersatz fabrications: linoleum (invented in 1863) patterned to look like marble, wood parquet, carpet, and mosaic; hollow concrete blocks cast in metal molds and made to resemble stone (1912); asbestos shingles that "harmonize with the natural surroundings" and are "as durable as stone," to name just a few.[29]

For the consumer seeking the proper signs in this hieroglyphic world, guides were essential, and two of the most trusted were the Beecher sisters—Catharine and Harriet, sisters of Henry Ward Beecher—who offered counsel on a wide range of topics relating to household economy.[30] In their books, as well as in the many others on the market, the essential paradox of consumerism flourished: encouraged to believe he or she lived in a world of unfettered personal expression, the consumer in reality was a member of a strictly rule-governed society. Page after page promulgated the canons of good taste, advising the reader on the best combinations of rugs, furniture, and accessories, all the while affirming the individualism of the homemaker. As one writer put it, in a volume published to coincide with the 1893 Chicago fair, "The Japanese-Eastlake-Morris-Cook influence has made women think for themselves, and moved the more cultivated and self-reliant among them to act upon the principle that their home is as individual a possession as their wardrobe, and may as honestly express their personal taste and convictions."[31] Some in-

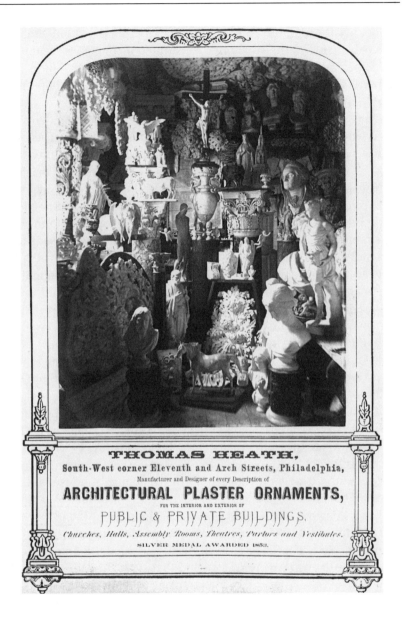

Architectural plaster ornaments, manufactured by Thomas Heath,
Philadelphia, trade advertisement
(Courtesy of Library Company of Philadelphia)

dividuality there surely was in household expression, but the language available to the consumer constituted a collective vocabulary
of ready-made forms and conventions. In this sense, as Mario Praz
has written, "furniture reveals the spirit of an age" perhaps even
more than the other arts.[32]

What was the spirit of the age thus revealed? A terrific drive upward, with the *appearance* of elevated status serving just as well,
almost, as the real thing. The clamor for such signs grew so great that
by 1885 one furniture company felt free to admit that its products
were copies, but that they were otherwise equivalent to originals:
"The renewal of old fashions has not only brought the genuine pieces
out of their obscurity, but the demand being much greater than could
be supplied by the real thing, has led to the making of copies . . .
Mssrs. Sypher & Co. produce copies of these old pieces which are
in every way as handsome and as well made as the originals."[33]
And many of the domestic economy manuals during the post–Civil
War period advised using cheap materials in place of more expensive ones; with unblushing egalitarianism, they would proclaim that
"cheap luxury is easily obtained" through "elegant imitations" of the
high French style in various materials.[34] (All of this was made even
easier after the invention of installment buying in the late nineteenth
century.)

Of course there were critics of such practices, the most influential
of whom was the landscape architect A. J. Downing, who, as early as
1850, had made the authenticity of the house a point of virtue, insisting on "truth" in all aspects of home design—use of materials, suiting
of design to setting, and above all in the matching of house-type and
scale to the buyer's social class. Thus there are farmhouses, cottages,
and—at the upper end—villas, and it is a "foolish ambition," Downing
warned, to "build cottages and wish to make them appear like villas."
Standing on a belief in the fixity of social class that the American was
eager to overturn, Downing asserted that it is "false in taste as for
a person of simple and frank character to lay aside his simplicity
and frankness to assume the cultivation and polish of a man of the
world."[35]

The consumer's risk in such efforts of advancement was that the
engine of instant elevation could mightily backfire. Abraham Cahan
records in *The Rise of David Levinsky* (1917) how his main character,
Levinsky, has been wandering through the Ghetto of the Lower East

Side of the 1890s and comes across a mother and two children who have been evicted for non-payment of rent and who are on the sidewalk watching their pile of furniture: "What puzzled me," David remembers, "was the nature of the furniture. For in my birthplace chairs and a couch like those I now saw on the sidewalk would be a sign of prosperity."[36] And Dreiser, who had earlier taken the aspirations of a Sister Carrie so seriously, in his later years wrote a little satire called *The Fine Furniture*, about a woman, Opal, who is married to a logger and who insists on squandering their money to purchase a set of furniture wholly inappropriate to their geographical and social milieu; in order to keep the newly arrived pieces clean the whole logging camp society must be excluded from their house, and even the woman's husband must eat in a shed. When the couple is finally ostracized by the community for their "superiority," they put the fine furniture in storage and move away.[37]

As these fictions suggest, the consumer lived in a world where dream and desire were continually cultivated, often at his or her peril. For it was also a world where *caveat emptor* served as the rock-hard reality principle. A variety of evidence attests to the fact that the ancient tradition of slightly deceptive trading had reached something close to an art in the American nineteenth century, not least of which is the widespread appearance in fiction and popular humor of the archetypal figure of the confidence man, who elicits a typically mixed response in literature as in life—horror at the immorality of his chicanery and admiration for the skill with which he carries off the trick. How closely these figures were intertwined with common experience is suggested in David Crockett's description of Job Snelling, a Massachusetts peddler, who "bragged of having made some useful discoveries, the most profitable of which was the art of converting mahogany sawdust into cayenne pepper, which he said was a profitable and safe business; for the people have been so long accustomed to having dust thrown in their eyes, that there wasn't much danger of being found out."[38] And Mark Twain recalled, in *Life on the Mississippi*, overhearing a conversation between two salesmen (or "scoundrels," as Twain calls them) who try to top one another in boasting of their respective facsimile products, oleomargarine and cottonseed "olive" oil: "Maybe you'll butter everybody's bread pretty soon, but we'll cottonseed his salad for him from the Gulf to Canada, and that's a dead certain thing."[39]

That the earlier nineteenth-century practices continued throughout the century is evident from an advertisement that Macy's felt
impelled to place in the *New York Herald* in 1875: "Every article sold
in this establishment is guaranteed to be what is represented. Any
article sold from this establishment not suiting, or not being what it
is guaranteed, will be exchanged or the money refunded."[40] Despite
the possible ambiguity in phrasing ("guaranteed to be what is represented"?), Macy's was reassuring its customers of its good faith. And it
was not uncommon for advertisers to warn that others' products were
"base imitations," with some going so far as to offer rewards for the
arrest of persons selling such frauds.[41]

The masterpiece in this genre of resourceful advertising was the
Sears catalogue, whose genius it was to carry honest representation
almost to the point of fraud, while still maintaining the good will and
trust of the consumer. Stories of hoaxes played on the customer
would naturally be circulated by local rural merchants who wanted to
discourage their own customers from dealing with mail-order firms;
but Sears actually did engage in some shady if imaginative practices
in its early days, such as advertising a complete set of furniture for
$1—leaving to the consumer the discernment of the word "minia-
ture" in minuscule type. And these practices of limited deception continued into the twentieth century, with catalogue pages advertising
"Our Genuine Pisani Stradivarius Model Violin" (for $45), or cameras
that looked exactly like Kodaks and were manufactured in a factory
pictured on the page and blazoned "Rochester." Only the the very
attentive customer might see that the camera was made in Rochester,
Minnesota, and not in George Eastman's New York town.[42] (It seems
not inconceivable that Sears established his camera factory in the
homonymous Minnesota town in order to profit from the confusion in
the first place.)

The consumer might even himself be recruited into the game of
misrepresentation, as in the ad for a "Trainmen's Special" watch,
which says exactly what it is, but isn't exactly what it seems: "This is a
cheap trading watch, made to look like the most expensive 23 jeweled, adjusted railway watch made ... it is stamped '23 jewels, adjusted' ... It is essentially a trading watch. We have sold thousands
of these movements to auctioneers, horse traders and other traders,
peddlers, jewelers, publishers and scheme houses for premiums, etc.
for while we sell it for just what it is, in interior construction a plain 7

jeweled American movement, it has all the appearance of a movement that you would pay $25.00 or more for." Such an ad functions almost like a play within a play, legitimating the principal fiction ("trust us") by allowing the consumer a glimpse at a world outside the catalogue, where the buyer must beware. If the consumer wanted to enter more actively into the game of trust, hoax, and pratfall, he might purchase, for 19 cents, "the smallest Kinematograph in the world." Look through the eyepiece at the dancing girl, invite your friends to do so, and "as soon as a small knob is turned a small spray of water is released and shot into the operator's eye."[43] As Melville had demonstrated so brilliantly in *The Confidence Man*, where trust was shadowed by doubt, where no rugs were glued to the floor, all things were possible; but if a buyer got stuck with a $5 watch instead of a $25 one, or a shot of water in the eye, he could of course pass on the experience to the next trusting stranger. Being on the winning end of such transactions was yet another way of elevating one's status in a democracy, where all were equally vulnerable.

Stepping back from these examples of trading practice to look more generally at the Victorian interior, one might almost say that Burton Benedict's observation about world's fairs during this period is true as well of the whole panoply of consumer culture, from the home to the department store—that in such places "man is totally in control and synthetic nature is preferred to the real thing."[44] But we should be wary of condescending to this culture of replications, for it is hard to know where nature ends and technics begin in man's making of things.[45] And indeed it was often precisely the purpose of the Victorians to confuse the realms of artifice and nature as part of an overall aesthetic in which the imitation became a central category, not merely endured, but exulted in.

Thus the middle-class environment typically indulged in fanciful representations and theatrical juxtapositions: of paper flowers with real flowers, of wax or marble fruit with real fruit. In the display of such household artifacts—the small objects made affordable to a prospering society—one sees repeatedly a reveling in the artifice of materials and a love of playing true against false, natural against artificial. Such clashes were part of a shared popular aesthetic that worked by confusing and delighting the senses and incidentally paying homage to the transformations of the artisan. One can see the

reasoning behind the love of such juxtapositions in the advice offered
by the Beechers to the homemaker interested in ornamenting a room
with pictures: try German ivy. "Slips of this will start without roots in
bottles of water. Slide the bottle behind the picture, and the ivy will
seem to come from fairyland, and hang its verdure in all manner of
pretty curves around the picture. It may then be trained to travel
toward other ivy, and thus aid in forming a green cornice along the
ceiling. We have seen some rooms that had an ivy cornice around the
whole, giving the air of a leafy bower."[46]

The Victorian habit of mixing nature and art also had its antecedents in the eighteenth-century taste for complexly patterned collages
comprising a variety of things real and artificial—hair, wax, mica
flakes, shells, stamps, dried flowers, paper twisted into rolls. But
the nineteenth-century taste was more fantastic, more exuberant, at
times an exhibition of technological prowess, at other times a sheer
delight in the metaphysics of substance and the ventriloquism of objects that could be made to speak with unexpected voices. Thus, iron
furniture might be shaped into twigs and branches, horns and antlers
mounted in a mirror frame; wardrobes might turn into bedsteads,
and bedsteads into tables and chairs.[47] To the American followers of
Eastlake, "purpose is always to be declared—there is to be no disposing of a bed by day in the wardrobe or the lounge-box: the bed is a
bed, and the wardrobe a wardrobe unmistakably."[48] But popular taste
ran against such admonitions.

There is a classic summation of that popular taste—its love of decorative artifice—in Mark Twain's *Life on the Mississippi*, where he offers the definitive catalogue of the mid-century "House Beautiful,"
with its fake Corinthian columns outside and its plaster fruit, wax
flowers, and artificial Napoleons inside. But consider the similar description of the Grangerford parlor in *Huckleberry Finn* (Chapter 17)
which, because it connects revealingly with Twain's more general
view of American society in the book, is worth a longer look. Huck
describes the scene:

> There was a clock on the middle of the mantelpiece, with a pic-
> ture of a town painted on the bottom half of the glass front, and a
> round place in the middle of it for the sun, and you could see the
> pendulum swinging behind it.... Well, there was a big outland-
> ish parrot on each side of the clock, made out of something like
> chalk and painted up gaudy. By one of the parrots was a cat made

of crockery, and a crockery dog by the other; and when you pressed down on them they squeaked but didn't open their mouths nor look different nor interested. They squeaked through underneath. There was a couple of big wild-turkey-wing fans spread out behind those things. On the table in the middle of the room was a kind of lovely crockery basket that had apples and oranges and peaches and grapes piled up in it, which was much redder and yellower and prettier than real ones is, but they warn't real because you could see where pieces had got chipped off and showed the white chalk, or whatever it was, underneath.

Huck's deadpan description seems to leave nothing out, turning the whole parlor into a ticking, chiming, squeaking still-life menagerie, an environment that represents well the Victorian taste for illusion and mimesis.

The scene functions as well as a kind of emblem of the larger themes in the book as a whole. For the Grangerford parlor, with its disguises and ambiguities, is a microcosm of the entire world of charades and hoaxes and masquerades and schemes through which Huck must navigate. In fact, one might say that Twain's work, generally, with its frequent preoccupation with doubles, with false identities and look-alikes, is in many ways the fictional counterpart of the aesthetic of replication that governs the Victorian household, and a clue to Twain's immense popularity may lie in his resonance with such basic habits of perception. For Twain's is a world in which outer signs mean more than inner quality, in which one could gain immense wealth and status overnight by selling the signs of wealth and status to an anxiously aspiring middle class. In such a world the domestic aesthetic of artifice and replication mirrors the larger social sphere where newcomers must constantly be evaluated.

Twain's critique of the household—and of the larger world of which it is a microcosm—has enough good humor in it to pass cunningly into the popular currency. A more conservative and satiric treatment of similar issues can be found in Frank Norris's early novel, *Vandover and the Brute* (1895), which extends matters of decoration into a more serious social and moral critique of a society that is symptomatically deranged. For Norris sets up, within two adjoining chapters, a contrast between the family homes of two young women, Ida Wade and Turner Ravis. Ida's father is a self-made merchant whose business is carpet cleaning; her mother, of an artistic turn, gives lessons in "painting on china and velvet." In contrast, Turner's family is "one of the best" in the city: they are "old-fashioned," they have family traditions and customs, they go to the right schools and belong to the right clubs.

The two houses tell the same stories, as Norris implicitly decodes each detail in building his description: the Wades's house is decorated with "meaningless" millwork, sports two Corinthian pillars with iron capitals "painted to imitate the wood of the house, which in its turn was painted to imitate stone." Inside, the parlor features a cheap piano, a carpet and sofa, an Alaskan "grass basket" filled with photographs, an inverted sewer-pipe filled with cattails tied with a ribbon; a "huge easel of imitation brass" holds a large crayon enlargement of a baby photograph, draped (as is everything else in the room) with yellow cloth; an unwound clock stands in an artist's palette, above which is a photogravure of a lion looking at the spectator. "In front of the picture were real iron bars, with real straw tucked in behind them." Opposed to Ida Wade's house of illusions, of artifice playing against nature, is Turner Ravis's house, about which Norris tells us just enough to make plain the difference: the pictures on the Ravis walls were "oil paintings of steel engravings and genuine old-fashioned chromos, beyond price to-day. Their furniture and ornaments were of the preceding generation, solid, conservative. They were not chosen with reference to any one style, nor all bought at the same time. Each separate piece had an individuality of its own. The Ravises kept their old things," etc.[49] And of course the two young women reflect their homes: Turner Ravis is a model of order and self-discipline, decorous and reliable; Ida Wade is fun-loving, adventuresome, and unfortunately all too susceptible to Vandover's brutish advances. (She ends a suicide.) Norris's pointed tale reveals the degree to which decorative style could be used as a code for character, and the degree to which it could presumably shape character in a society based on such hieroglyphic signs.

Learning to tell the true from the false, the lie from the truth, learning trust and mistrust, was part of an acculturation process that shows up again and again in nineteenth-century culture, from the "operational aesthetics" of P. T. Barnum, with its hoaxes and hybrids (and we recall that Twain's favorite book was Barnum's autobiography), to the serious literature of Poe, Melville, and James.[50] In the hieroglyphic universe of nineteenth-century America, confidence men, lifelike portraits, purloined letters that are invisible because too obvious—all abound; and the characteristic stories of the period are filled with plots of mistaken identity, disguise, detection, and discovery.

Underlying middle-class Victorian taste lay an imitation of American upper-class taste; and underlying American upper-class taste lay an imitation of European traditions—the hierarchical designs of the royal courts, with their heavily ornate surfaces, their swirling forms, their aristocratic connotations.[51] Indeed one cannot talk adequately about reproductions and replicas, about the meaning of things in general for Americans, without talking about the aesthetic and social and moral meaning of Europe. Despite our growing mastery in things industrial and technological, the dominant assumption was that we were still vassals to Europe in the arts.

Thus the Centennial, for example, was seen as an occasion to "soften manners and counteract the now unmitigated exercise and influence of mere industrialism," by supplying examples of the decorative arts from abroad that would replace the "common, pretentious and ugly objects of our everyday life."[52] Twenty-five years earlier, at the London Crystal Palace, an American observer remarked proudly on the simplicity of American goods; lacking the costly excesses of the aristocratic European nations, Americans produced "articles of utility and comfort, and for the advantage of the middling classes, who are the great producers of the world, as distinguished from the nobility and gentry"; with the improvement of manufacturing processes, the mimicking of elite European designs soon became widespread.[53] And by the 1893 Chicago Exposition, whole rooms were featured in the various European pavilions, providing tangible and coherent models for American taste.

The architecture of the Chicago Exposition itself was the most emphatic statement of where elite values lay at the end of the century: with its huge palatial structures festooned with statues and decorative embellishments, the whole looked like a fantasy of Imperial Rome, if not a three-dimensional stage set out of Thomas Cole's *The Course of Empire*. The White City (so called because of the color of the chief building material, staff, which was selected for its speed of construction and ease of destruction) became a national symbol of America's coming of age on the world scene, a dreamed self-image of might and power interpreted to the populace by an illustrious team of Eastern architects. It might also be read as a sign of America's continued rivalry with, and consequent submission to, European standards; this in effect was the view of Louis Sullivan, who contributed one of the few consciously "American" designs and would later say that the Columbian Exposition had set back American architecture for generations. Meanwhile, Europeans who came to Chicago looking for something distinctly American were disappointed to find a facsimile of Europe and turned instead to downtown Chicago, with its modern office buildings, as a more authentic expression of the American spirit.

The exposition at Chicago was symptomatic of a shift that had taken place since the Centennial in America's orientation toward Europe and the past. Until approximately the 1890s, for example, the emulation of European architectural models consisted of relatively free adaptations, eclectic designs, such as the Queen Anne, which at best modulated into a distinctively American shingle style.[54] During the last decades of the century, however, the excesses of Victorian eclecticism became purified in two different ways, as Richard Guy Wilson has pointed out. On the one hand there was the effort toward simplification, derived from Ruskin and Morris, and which would develop into the functionalism of the Arts and Crafts movement. (This will be examined in more detail in a later chapter.) On the other hand was the "scientific eclecticism" of McKim, Mead, and White, and of Van Brunt, with their scorn of unscientific heterogeneity and their striving for a kind of archeological purity and accuracy of design.[55] It was out of the latter impulse that the Columbian Exposition itself was built.

Symptomatic of the orientation to Europe, and of the new emphasis on simplification, was the influential volume, *The Decoration of Houses* (1897), written by Edith Wharton in collaboration with the architect Ogden Codman, and in which the virtues of the Italian Renaissance were celebrated. Wharton and Codman argue for a harmony of architecture and decoration based on simplicity and proportion, a reaction against the excesses of Victorian taste.[56] The success of Grand Rapids in providing eclectically styled furniture for the middle-class market was, of course, what was wrong with America, from the elitist viewpoint of Wharton and Codman. Addressing their counsel to an upper-class (or would-be upper-class) audience, the two

Basin and Court of Honor, looking East from the Grand Plaza,
Chicago World's Fair of 1893
(Courtesy of Avery Architectural and Fine Arts Library,
Columbia University)

wove the language of social distinctions into their judgments and warnings: they decried, for example, the "vulgarity of the pinchbeck article flooding our shops and overflowing upon our sidewalks." (They might almost be talking about the immigrants of the Lower East Side themselves.) And elsewhere: "vulgarity is always noisier than good breeding," and one should therefore not mix good pieces with bad. If all of this encouraged the middle-class reader to believe that he or she could actually learn to "pass" as a social aristocrat, one had to remember that the game was risky; fine discrimination and money were essential, for mere imitation of one's social betters, by the use of cheaply manufactured parlor furniture in "pseudo-Georgian or pseudo-Empire," was offensive to good taste.[57]

Lacking the necessary resources, however, the middle class would

have to settle for the European derivatives that were the staple of the
marketplace; only the very rich could be free of Grand Rapids and
could go back to the presumed source of Culture—the Continent. As
Baudrillard says, for the self-made man, the "authentic" European
object supplies the signature of his paternity; "l'authenticité vient
toujours du Père: c'est lui la source de la valeur."[58] The first preference of the traveler, on his rapacious tour of Europe, would be to
bring back an original chunk of Culture—vase, painting, table, statue,
rare book; failing that, one could patronize American artists who
would supply one with hand-made artifacts, exact reproductions of
the real European thing.[59] This is the sort scorned by Robert Herrick,
in his novel *The Common Lot* (1904), in the person of a widow who
collects furnishings for her new house, "Forest Manor": she is "the
modern barbarian type that admires hungrily and ravishes greedily
from the treasure house of the Old World what it can get."[60]

Perhaps the archetype in this category was the wealthy Bostonian,
Isabella Stewart Gardner, and her grip on the imagination must still
have been strong in 1926 when Lewis Mumford excoriated her in his
The Golden Day. Gardner, like so many other millionaires at the end
of the nineteenth century, was trying to answer the question of the
moment, which was, as historian Hugh Dalziel Duncan put it, "no
longer one of how to let people know that one was rich, but of indicat-
ing to one's peers that one knew how to be rich 'in style.' "[61] The
official doctrine of genteel culture, fostered by Harvard's Charles Eliot Norton, among others, held that art was a civilizing, spiritual
force, that it would counteract the materialism of America's business
culture, that it would take one from "the world of matter to that of
spirit," as Helen Horowitz has put it.[62] And the locus of style, civilization, and culture became the Italian Renaissance, which, through the
writings of Pater, Symonds, and Burckhardt, was the subject of new
interest.[63]

But of course it took immense wealth to counteract the abuses of
vulgar materialism. And though an E. L. Godkin might argue in
Scribner's that the wealthy in America should construct public monuments and buildings instead of grand private houses, those at the
apex of the social pyramid tended to demonstrate their love of beauty
and their spiritual greatness by a correspondingly great display of
wealth along European lines, with the Italian palaces of the Medici
serving as their favorite models.[64] Thus their mansions were filled

with period rooms, evidence of a desire to create, in the midst of a commercial society where fortunes were based on coal, railroads, and iron, a fantasy of aristocratic status.[65] To make that fantasy credible was the challenge. First, an object had to *look* costly, and *be* costly. (A spoon designed to look like silver but actually made of baser metal, as Veblen observed, falls markedly in our estimation of its worth when we discover its "false" nature.) Second, it had to evince the good taste of the owner. (Wharton and Codman: "To the art-lover, as distinguished from the collector, uniqueness *per-se* can give no value to an *in*artistic object.")[66]

The novelist Frank Norris corroborates this point exactly in his novel, *The Pit*, when he shows us the self-made millionaire Jadwin, at the height of his fortune, vaunting his art gallery to his friend Gretry. After parting some heavy curtains, the two enter Jadwin's theatrical two-story high gallery. "It was shaped like a rotunda, and topped with a vast airy dome of coloured glass. Here and there about the room were glass cabinets full of bibelots, ivory statuettes, old snuff boxes, fans of the sixteenth and seventeenth centuries. The walls themselves were covered with a multitude of pictures, oils, water-colors, with one or two pastels." After examining the room the mightily impressed Gretry murmurs, "This certainly is the real thing, J. I suppose, now, it all represents a pretty big pot of money."[67] Precisely! (As Tocqueville had observed early in the nineteenth century, "in the confusion of all ranks everyone hopes to appear what he is not.")[68] Jadwin's demonstration is climaxed by his setting in place a perforated roll of music and thus "playing" the overture from *Carmen* on his mechanical organ.

One of the most acute dissections of this tendency of the aspiring American to worship at the shrines of European material culture comes in a short story by D. H. Lawrence called simply, "Things," in which the lines between idealism and materialism, between the aesthetic and the industrial components of American civilization, and between America and Europe, are all sharply and satirically drawn. Earlier, in *Studies in Classic American Literature* (1923), Lawrence had lambasted American tourists in Europe, who exclaim over the cupolas at Saint Mark's, " 'Don't you think [they] are like the loveliest *turnips* upside down; you know'—as if the beautiful things of Europe were just having their guts pulled out by these American admirers."[69] In "Things" he gives these tourists a name and a history: the Melvilles, who start from New England and wind up, at last, in Cleveland. And although the story takes place in the first decades of the twentieth century it caps a tradition of American infatuation with Europe that flourished in the late nineteenth century.

Lawrence's Melvilles are "idealists" (aptly named) who, before the War, seek the beautiful life in Europe, nourishing their inner souls with the beautiful "things" they collect on their travels, all the while scorning Europeans as themselves "materialistic." "Of course they [the Melvilles] did not buy the things for the things' sakes, but for the sake of 'beauty,'" Lawrence writes. But the glow fades from their things after a year or two, and they shuttle back and forth between Europe and America until Erasmus Melville finally is forced (on account of pinched funds) to accept a job at a midwestern university. With resignation at first, but afterwards with great joy, the Melvilles, surrounded by their things—"Bologna cupboard, Venice bookshelves, Ravenna bishop's chair, Louis-Quinze side-tables"—become cultural celebrities, showing off in their "best European manner." Living with the contrived superiority of European aristocrats, surrounded by their fine things, the Melvilles proclaim, "we prefer America." Amidst the furnaces of Cleveland, "with red and white-hot cascades of gushing metal, and tiny gnomes of men, and terrific noises, gigantic," Erasmus says to his wife, "Say what you like, Valerie, this is the biggest thing the modern world has to show."[70]

Lawrence's compact satire makes its point craftily: in the twentieth century, all that is left of the epic quest of American idealism— suggested by his naming the couple after the great New England searcher after ultimate truths, ultimately disillusioned—is the quest of materialism and the drive toward social superiority. In Cleveland the contradictions of American society flourish, and the American wants it both ways: the industrial might, the vulgar strength of his factories; and the refinement of European "culture." But he cannot have it both ways without giving up some essential vitality. It was a point Lawrence had made more explicitly in *The New Republic* in 1920. "It is an insult to life itself to be *too* abject, too prostrate before Milan Cathedral or a Ghirlandajo," he wrote in "America, Listen to Your Own." "Let Americans turn to America, and to that very America which has been rejected and almost annihilated. Do they want to draw sustenance for the future? They will never draw it from the lovely monuments of our European past. These have an almost fatal narcotic, dream-luxurious effect upon the soul. America must turn again to catch the spirit of her own dark, aboriginal continent."[71] It was a point Whitman had made before, and that some others were making in the early twentieth century. But it was not what most Americans wanted to hear, or could understand. For genteel America, the fascination with Europe was at the heart of the struggle for identity. And the greatest anatomist of that struggle, writing in the last decades of the nineteenth century and into the twentieth, was Henry James, who defined the nuances of the theme from every angle.

We do not normally think of James in the context of the growing consumer economy of the late nineteenth century, but the question of ownership is a key one in his work throughout his career, and his fiction offers a powerful critique of the upper end of the consumer world.[72] Two of James's fullest treatments of the relationships between people and things are *Portrait of a Lady* and *The Spoils of Poynton*, and I want to consider them in some detail here, for they offer a psychological investigation of ownership that brings us inside the mentality of consumption and thus warrants a closer look.

The primary characters in *Portrait*—Isabel, Osmond, and Ralph—are all Americans, transplanted to the arena of self-discovery and culture, Europe, where the question turned over again and again is, as Madame Merle (another American) puts it in a conversation with Isabel, "What shall we call our 'self'?" James is taking the great preoccupation of Whitman and transforming it into the vocabulary of a consumer culture in which ownership—of things, of people—is a major part of the definition. Madame Merle has the famous passage:

> When you've lived as long as I you'll see that every human being has his shell and that you must take the shell into account. By the shell I mean the whole envelope of circumstances. There's no such thing as an isolated man or woman; we're each of us made up of some cluster of appurtenances. What shall we call our "self"? Where does it begin? where does it end? It overflows into everything that belongs to us—and then it flows back again. I know a large part of myself is in the clothes I choose to wear. I've a great respect for *things*! One's self—for other people—is one's expression of one's self; and one's house, one's furniture, one's garments, the books one reads, the company one keeps—these things are all expressive!

James wants us to be somewhat skeptical of Madame Merle's "bold analysis of the human personality," as he archly calls it, partly as a way of setting us up for Isabel's quite contrary opinion, which will set in motion the drama of the story: "I don't agree with you. I think just the other way. I don't know whether I succeed in expressing myself, but I know that nothing else expresses me. Nothing that belongs to me is any measure of me; every thing's on the contrary a limit, a barrier, and a perfectly arbitrary one."[73] Isabel here announces a freedom of the self that is idealistic in the extreme, a self that would have no material hindrances, a self that would claim a freedom to expand and fulfill itself without restraint; and it is precisely James's contrivance to lure such a self into a relationship that seems at first to fulfill that idealism but that ends in a blank confrontation with the firm barriers set up by the magnetic Osmond.

For Osmond is the person for whom things are the whole of self-definition, and Isabel herself becomes a crucial possession. Isabel's marriage is based, for her part, on a fatal misreading of Osmond's character: "His pictures, his medallions and tapestries were interesting; but after a while Isabel felt the owner much more so, and independently of them, thickly as they seemed to overhang him." It is a misreading because in the case of Osmond the showy accumulation of minor treasures is, Isabel eventually realizes, the whole of his substance. For his part, Osmond sees Isabel as "a silver plate, not an earthen one," silver because he could then "tap her imagination with his knuckle and make it ring." For Osmond the language of love is imbued with the imagery of replication: Isabel is to be a "reproduction" of himself, but of a special kind; he does not want, in his wife, to "see his thought reproduced literally—that made it look stale and stupid; he preferred it to be freshened in the reproduction even as 'words' by music."[74]

Isabel may not be completely suffocated by Osmond's sterility, but her sense of oppressive limits, of barriers to the expression of the self, could not be greater than at the end of the *Portrait*, when she decides to stay with her husband. She has inevitably become a part of Osmond's "cluster of appurtenances," a part of *his* expressive shell, to use Madame Merle's phrase, as Osmond is a part of Isabel's. The drama of *Portrait of a Lady* thus flows out of the meaning of ownership and mistaken appearances, and in ways that are not at first apparent, perhaps, James's novel connects with a society in which buying and selling, collecting and displaying objects, have become a central preoccupation and a governing metaphor.

In *The Spoils of Poynton* (1897), written more than a decade after *Portrait*, *things* are even more explicitly a part of James's subject, or rather, not the things themselves, but the passions they excite. For *Spoils* is about avidity, "that most modern of our current passions," as James calls it in his preface, "the fierce appetite for the upholsterer's and joiner's and brazier's work, the chairs and tables, the cabinets and presses, the material odds and ends, of the more laboring ages."[75]

The novel actually depicts two different worlds of things, and at first glance they are poles apart: on one side is Mrs. Gereth's collection at Poynton (the "spoils" of the title), an assemblage of objects whose perfection, we must assume, makes them worth fighting for. These are the things—paintings, furniture, bibelots—that in an age of mass production are the relics of the romantically imagined artisan. On the other side is the world of the Brigstocks, which, according to Mrs. Gereth at least, is of "an ugliness fundamental and systematic, the result of the abnormal nature of the Brigstocks, from whose composition the principle of taste had been extravagantly omitted ... they had smothered [their house] with trumpery ornament and scrapbook art, with strange excrescences and bunchy draperies, with gimcracks that might have been keepsakes for maid-servants and nondescript conveniences that might have been prizes for the blind." In the bedrooms are souvenirs "from some centennial or other Exhibition."[76] The contrast with Poynton could not be clearer; and yet, both Mrs. Gereth's world of taste and the Brigstocks's house of vulgarity evince a similar set of values: in both worlds, things have been richly treasured and avidly saved. And the drama really centers less on the conflict between taste and vulgarity than on the passion for things more generally.

Three women constitute the epicenters of the book: Mrs. Gereth, whose present business is to find a suitable candidate for her son Owen's hand and hence the trusted management of Poynton; Fleda Vetch, whom Mrs. Gereth has settled on as her choice; and Mona Brigstock, who wants Owen and all his appurtenances, and whom, because of her vulgarity, Mrs. Gereth abhors. Fleda's own background is petit bourgeois, but she can move from that world to the world of the Gereths because of her fine intelligence and sensibility, and because she is an artist. (How good an artist remains undemonstrated; she has spent a year in France studying with impressionist painters.) Moreover, her intermediary status, between Gereths and Brigstocks, seems indicated by her father's character: like everyone else in the novel, he is a collector, with a taste that seems less than Gereth and more than Brigstock. He likes old things, flea market treasures—"brandy-flasks and matchboxes, old calendars and handbooks"—and he prides himself, James tells us with deadpan irony, on "having a taste for fine things which his children had unfortunately not inherited."[77]

James is not, in *The Spoils*, interested in the old things themselves, but in things as a religion, and that is the very phrase Mrs. Gereth uses in telling Fleda about the history of her accumulations: "Yes . . . there are things in the house that we almost starved for!" For the Gereths evidently lacked means at first, and their treasures were gained through self-sacrifice: "They were our religion, they were our life, they were us! and they're only *me*—except that they're also *you*, thank God, a little, you dear!"[78] Mrs. Gereth's eagerness to give up her treasures, provided they are to the right person, sharply qualifies her own avidity, and moves our understanding to a new level: it is not the mere possession of things that fuels Mrs. Gereth's resistance to Mona Brigstock, but her sense that under Mona's hands the things would be desecrated because not appreciated, and that her own life, so bound up with the accumulated things, would consequently be destroyed. "It was the need to be faithful to a trust and loyal to an idea."[79] Mona, for her part, cares nothing for the things themselves; she has no appreciation of their worth and insists on owning them only because she wants everything coming to her with Owen.

And Mona does gain the objects legally and materially at the end, but only briefly: for the book ends with a fire that destroys everything at Poynton. But the spoils had already been "dematerialized" before the fire: the action of the novel is, in a sense, the process whereby their true value comes more and more, for Fleda and Mrs. Gereth, at least, to reside in their personal and symbolic meaning, and not their physical embodiment. And James's final ironic disposal of the property, out of everyone's hands, comes like a burning judgment on Mona's cupidity. Yet whatever the material value of the spoils had been, James has supplied midway through the book a judgment upon the *things* that comes back to us in retrospect: Fleda had found it impossible to work at Poynton. "No active art could flourish there but a Buddhistic contemplation."[80] The spoils are death to the imagination.

There are no Americans in *The Spoils of Poynton*, and it may be for that reason that James can stand back from the battles and give to his tale a distance and irony that make all of the characters part of a unified comedy of jealousies and disasters. And by excluding the international theme, James was able to focus more purely on the moral dimensions of his story. But his exploration of the ways that matter can grip the spirit, and his demonstration of a transcending of that state, make it clearly relevant to American culture, and like many of James's novels, it was initially serialized in *The Atlantic Monthly*. At a time when the possession of European art treasures and bric-a-brac was considered the mark of social and spiritual distinction to the American, James's short novel has the force of a complex Vanitas, a memento mori.

Again and again, around the turn of the century, as the saturation of *things* reached the limit of containing space, the social and spiritual grace afforded by material objects was put to the question. And Nietzsche's observation on the European bourgeoisie would apply to America as well: "Men of the seventies and eighties . . . were filled with a devouring hunger for reality, but they had the misfortune to confuse this with matter—which is but the hollow and deceptive wrapping of it. Thus they lived perpetually in a wretched, padded, puffed-out world of cotton-wool, cardboard, and tissue-paper."[81] The actual stripping of that stuffed world to its functional bare bones would await the modernist movements of the twentieth century; but the same "hunger for reality" noted by Nietzsche can be seen in America as a note of dissidence within the general chorus of contentment, a feeling that something, amid the spendors of Victorian materialism, had been left out.

Disenchantment took many forms, but the one most relevant in the present context is the curious ambivalence toward the grand idea of progress itself, with all its material trappings. Here and there, within the novels and popular culture of the period one sees, against the main current of material advancement and the growth of cities and factories, a significant reverse current of nostalgia, carrying the individual backward to a simpler time.

A detailed and explicit challenge to the dominant ethos can be found, for example, at the center of Henry Blake Fuller's novel, *With the Procession* (1895), which poses the question, What is the ultimate value of change, of upward mobility, of material things? Fuller's critique of progress comes through most clearly in a scene featuring Mrs. Bates, an arriviste Chicago aristocrat whose motto, "Keep up with the procession," supplies the book's title; Mrs. Bates lives surrounded by royal splendor, Baroque magnificence, but her connection with her possessions is at best tenuous. She has in fact no real use for them except as part of a stage setting to impress her visitors. The secret behind the show is revealed to one guest—the book's heroine—who summarizes her discoveries, following Mrs. Bates's tour of the ostentatious house: "she doesn't get any music out of her piano, she doesn't get any reading out of her books; she doesn't even get any sleep out of her bed."[82] (It is used to lay hats and coats on.) Mrs. Bates's genuine emotional center is a private room reached through a secret passage, a place redolent of her past, with its comfortable and homely middle-class furnishings—an old, cracked mahogany bureau, a shabby writing desk, a threadbare carpet, an old piano, well-worn books, and so forth.[83] Fuller gives us, in this depiction of Mrs. Bates's inner sanctum, an embodiment of her nostalgia, the "backstage" glimpse behind the facades of conspicuous consumption.

The backward pull that the novelist was depicting was also being reflected in the popular culture, where stories of rural manners and characters, literary marmalade, were consumed avidly by the urban reader along with popular Currier and Ives chromos of country customs and domestic rural scenes. (The urban population between 1880 and 1900 was doubling.) And, as Lewis Mumford observed, with the dying away of traditional folk forms during the late nineteenth century, a scholarly and elite audience began its acts of archival repossession, savoring the "authenticity" of ballads and stories that were rooted in the preindustrial past.[84] The same taste for the past showed up in the new interest in antique furniture which began around the same time, fostered by leaders of the household art movement.[85] And, most revealing of all, the rise to success and national prominence began to carry with it a ritualistic public tribute to one's humble origins: the interviews with the famous, for example, which were drawn from *Success* magazine and collected in a 1903 volume called *Little Visits with Great Americans,* are filled with memories of rural boyhood, of poverty and raw beginnings.[86]

It was as if the middle-class American were trying to hold onto his "real" self amidst the rapid changes of society. The pervasiveness of nostalgia, whether in genre paintings of blacksmiths, still-life images of old and worn things, or recollections of life on an earlier Mississippi, was a way of habituating men to the present, of retaining a sense of proportion and scale, of human stature, during a period when the individual's capacity to assimilate change was being pushed to the limit. The culture of consumption was making it possible for the American to jump several rungs in the social ladder in a single generation, in a process that would only accelerate into the twentieth century; but it was also generating a sense of the "real" self as a remnant one left behind, and that too would remain a consistent feature of American experience, a part of the national mythos, extending into the twentieth century.

That sense of movement forward against a current of nostalgia finds its classic expression twenty-five years after the generation of Fuller in Fitzgerald's *The Great Gatsby*. Gatsby personifies the immense longing that is a part of the dream and that finds its partial fulfillment (as with Dreiser's Carrie) in the showy appearance of things. As an epitome of the consumer culture, Fitzgerald offers us the scene with Nick and Daisy, on a tour of Gatsby's mansion, when the self-made man stops to show them his shirts. One by one he throws them onto the table, "shirts of sheer linen and thick silk and fine flannel, which lost their folds as they fell and covered the table in many-colored disarray." Of course we sense the incongruity between thing and feeling in these shirts: they are symbols of achievement, sacred objects removed from an ark, and they make evident the sublimity of Gatsby's power of self-elevation (he had started with only his rules of self-discipline) and the pathos of his need to manifest that power.

Yet Gatsby surprises us by his indifference to the actual things themselves. His real desire is to recapture a dream of desire that is based on repossession of Daisy. His longing is nostalgic, seeking to regain the distance that is the premise of the romantic glow. Again, Carrie comes to mind, with her rocking daydreams; but Carrie, though an earlier creation, is in some ways a figure more contemporaneous with our own time; her desires are vaguer and less satiable than Gatsby's; she is a precursor of a rootless, pathological mass consumption society.[87] Gatsby, the grander, more romantic figure, is connected by Fitzgerald to the aboriginal American urge to settle the wilderness of a new continent: moving forward, he is simultaneously "borne back ceaselessly into the past."

When Gatsby's father comes for his son's funeral, he brings with

him, in addition to a childhood copy of *Hopalong Cassidy*, a photograph Gatsby had sent him of his mansion on West Egg, which he
shows admiringly to Nick. "He had shown it so often that I think it was
more real to him now than the house itself."[88] Fitzgerald's sentence
reverberates. The house is, of course, an apt symbol of Gatsby's
dream; and so is the photograph itself, for it represents a moment
fixed in time past and lifted into the realm of permanence. That it
might seem "more real" to the father than the house itself seems also
uncannily right, and captures the son's similar sense of a more intense reality attending an object seen at a distance.

What has made *The Great Gatsby* so central a text for American
culture is its powerful and tragic embodiment of the dilemma at the
core of the hieroglyphic world: to possess one's fortune in a society in
love with representations may be, in the end, to possess merely the
signs and images of aspiration. To furnish one's identity in such a
world may be, at last, to furnish pictures for an album of photographs.

Photography and

the Artifice of

Realism

*W*hile the typical middle-class home in the late nineteenth century was becoming the center of material consumption, furnished with outward displays of the soul's spiritual and commercial status, it was also becoming the center of another, related form of consumption: what could not be owned outright, given limitations of space, time, and money, could be encompassed by a surrogate ownership in which photographic images brought a vast cyclopedia of world culture and symbols into the eye of the parlor, making the American a connoisseur of replicated experience.[1] The camera was arguably influencing the character of American culture as much as any other single technology, and thus the way photography was practiced and the way people thought about the medium are necessarily significant aspects of the whole culture. The photograph took many forms in the home, from the stereograph card, which had established itself in America as a popular entertainment by 1860, to the print hung on the wall as decoration, and, in the last decade of the century, the printed portfolio album. Into the parlor thus came an extraordinary gallery of sights: the great art works from European museums and the homespun sculptures of the Rogers groups; architectural views of the city, industrial scenes, railroad trains, and bridges, along with the old mill stream and other rural vistas; there were mountains and deserts, pyramids and local court houses, miniatures and staged tableaux.

By 1900 vicarious experience had become a major commodity in the American marketplace and the habit of surrogates had grown strong and indelible in American life, preparing the ground for the mass market visual narratives that were to come in the twentieth century in the form of movies and television. Within twenty years of the invention of photography in 1839 it became a commonplace to

Residence of Thomas Donaldson, Philadelphia, late 19th century
(Courtesy of Library Company of Philadelphia)

speak of the practical advantages and pleasures of "touring" without having to leave home: "With a pile of pictures by their side, which cost almost nothing," even the humblest Americans "can make the European tour of celebrated places, and not leave the warm precincts of their own firesides," *Scientific American* wrote on June 2, 1860. In the next decade, photographs of scenery and archeological remains, especially, were being promoted as worthy household decoration, and the delights of vicarious experience were frankly acknowledged. ("It is pleasant to lean back in one's chair and be transported to distant countries at a glance.")[2] And with the advancement of printing technology later in the century, a "portfolio of national photography," *Camera Mosaics*, could be introduced to the reader as an "extension of picture galleries" surpassing "all the treasures of art in Rome and Florence and Paris and Dresden, and the feast is spread by the sitting-room window or under the fireside lamp."[3]

But few claims for the mimetic capacity of photography could sur-
pass the one made in 1894 by James William Buel, in advertising his
record of the Chicago Exposition. When Buel announced his plan to
publish *The Magic City: Portfolio of the Chicago World's Fair*, a series
of consecutive weekly numbers consisting of sixteen to twenty photographs, he billed it as a "permanent re-opening of the Grand Columbian Exposition." "In some respects," he claimed, "this splendid portfolio is better and more to be desired than an actual visit to the
Exposition, for through the magic agency of photography the scenes
are transferred in marvelous beauty and permanent form to the
printed pages, while the accompanying historical descriptions make
plain and clear myriads of intricate and wonderful things, many of
which were not comprehended by those who saw them."[4] Putting
aside the slight exaggeration typical of such notices, there is still
something daring and prophetic in Buel's pitch, almost a metaphysical challenge to our common sense: the photograph is "better" than
the real thing.

The photograph was part and parcel of a middle-class culture that
accepted replications of every sort—from furnishings and architecture to fine art prints—as the natural advantage of living in an advanced, technological world. In reducing the world to proportions
that could be taken in at a glance, in holding it still long enough to let
us look closely, photography opened up a whole new world to consciousness. This new imagination is most evident in the writings of
Oliver Wendell Holmes, who himself had a strong influence on the
reception of the camera, not only through his published essays in *The
Atlantic* during the 1860s but through his design for a cheaply produced stereoscope, the rights to which he gave away freely so as to
encourage the popular enjoyment of photography. In Holmes—the
Boston Brahmin who was both physician and novelist—we see the
literary and scientific intelligence of the Victorian era at full play with
photography, fascinated by both the optical and the aesthetic possibilities of image-making. He inspects the self-portraits of friends and
correspondents, entranced by the revelations of character to be read
in the furnishings of their homes; he revels in the scientific uses to
which the stopped motion of the image lends itself—a new way to
understand walking, for example; he holds up, to the view of one eye,
one half a stereo card, while with the other eye he looks at the scene
originally stereographed, and discovers a perfect match between re-

ality and image; he takes his readers on a tour of American and European scenes (beginning of course with Niagara Falls); he notes the accidents recorded by the image, the traces of authenticity—clotheslines, marks on a drumhead, fragments of London street signs—that will sensitize generations of artists to the power of the detail in literary and visual description.

Yet while one side of Holmes's mind is thus entranced by the literal, descriptive power of the camera, its ability to make us appreciate the concrete thingness of reality, to "duplicate" the world before us, another side of his imagination responds to a rather different quality of the stereograph, its capacity to transport us, away from the literal, into a kind of "dream-like exaltation of the faculties," one that leaves the body behind.[5] And it is not only the viewer who is thus disembodied, it is the image itself, which is separated, in the stereographic process, from its concrete, original substance. In a famous passage in "The Stereoscope and the Stereograph" Holmes writes with speculative abandon on the possible future of photography: "*Form is henceforth divorced from matter.* In fact, matter as a visible object is of no great use any longer, except as the mould on which form is shaped. Give us a few negatives of a thing worth seeing, taken from different points of view, and that is all we want of it. Pull it down or burn it up, if you please. We must, perhaps, sacrifice some luxury in the loss of color; but form and light and shade are the great things, and even color can be added, and perhaps by and by may be got direct from Nature."[6] The passage has at times been taken more seriously than it was intended—Holmes's wit is often on the edge of whimsy—yet it does sound a prophetic note. For in speaking thus of photography as "this greatest of human triumphs over earthly conditions, the divorce of form and substance,"[7] Holmes is not only (as has been noted) assimilating photography to the nineteenth century's characteristic view of technology as an aggressive conquest of natural constraints, a triumph of man's will over earth's resistance; he is also talking about technology as a process whereby what is produced and sold is, increasingly, an image, an appearance, a look, a constellation of imagined attributes, rather than the strictly utilitarian object. Holmes's whimsical look forward to a Borgesian "enormous collection of forms" such that "they will have to be classified and arranged in vast libraries, as books are now" has of course materialized, along with our contemporary truism that, as William Ivins put it in concluding his

Prints and Visual Communication, "at any given moment the accepted report of an event is of greater importance than the event, for what we think about and act upon is the symbolic report and not the concrete event itself."[8]

Holmes thus offers a first paradoxical experience of the camera: an appreciation of its ability to direct our close attention to "the real thing" and of its simultaneous capacity to estrange us from ourselves and from reality, to compel our entrance into the aesthetic world of the image. Our contemporary conception of photography is in many ways narrower than Holmes's, shaped as it has been by our predilection for "straight photography," which we think of as an "honest" use of the medium. Thus, looking at the nineteenth century, we have tended to find antecedents and exemplars for our own time—the great descriptive photographers of the Western landscape and of the geological expeditions, the documentary photographers of the city, the makers of unvarnished portraits, the journalistic artists of the Civil War, the scientific students of motion.[9] Our conservative taste can hardly prepare us for the discovery that the Victorians, in their own fascination with the new medium, luxuriated in the many diverse forms it might take, one moment celebrating its capacity for a seemingly literal imitation of reality and the next its use as a vehicle for fantasy and illusion. An early work on the stereoscope, for example, affirms that through the camera "truth itself will be embalmed and history cease to be fabulous"; yet a later chapter, on photographic amusements, speaks without any sense of contradiction of creating "spirit" photographs and of recreating historical scenes in costume. And these conjunctions remain in the literature of the period.[10] We have put off to one side the practitioners of illusion, of staged tableaux, of table-top photography, relegating them to a minor facet of the popular interest in photography, peripheral to the medium's destiny as a realistic form, a medium of truth and revelation.

Yet the nineteenth century's practice of photography was founded on an understanding of the medium as an illusion, and the realism of Victorian photography is properly understood as an "artificial realism," in which the image offers the viewer a representation of reality, a typification, a conscious simulacrum—though a simulacrum that elicited a willing suspension of disbelief. The view of nineteenth-century photography that I am presenting here builds on A. D. Coleman's formulation of the "directorial mode" to describe works in which the photographer manipulates the subject in front of the camera, as opposed to works of straight photography, in which the implicit claim is that the image is a record of untouched reality.[11] Coleman posits as well an intermediate category, wherein the photographer stands ready to seize a moment from the flux of time, thus blending his subjective sensibility with the "facts" of nature, but this mode depends on a technology of instant photography that was largely beyond the nineteenth-century photographer. All three strategies do overlap, as Coleman explains, but where his concern is with tracing the distinctions among the practices, as background to an understanding of the self-conscious directorial mode of the twentieth century, my own effort is to stress the core assumptions *shared* by virtually all practitioners of late nineteenth-century genres, whether artistic, documentary, or portrait.

The history of photography, it might be said, is the history of the countless efforts to overcome the *limitations* of the medium, to expand upon what a representation of reality might be. And to examine the nature of photography during this period is, in large measure, to expose the varieties of artifice designed to enhance the power of the representation. The photographic print is by nature inherently limited as a representation of reality by virtue of its reduced size, its flatness, and its limited angle of vision—the window the lens affords on the world. In fact, there were efforts to overcome each of these limitations. I have already mentioned the stereograph, with its fraternally twinned images that could immerse the viewer in the full three-dimensional depth of the scene, eliminating the flatness of two-dimensional representation; stereographs also enlarged the field of vision so that, as Holmes observed, the object appeared not as a miniature, but as life-size. But the stereograph of course required a special viewing mechanism; for the more traditional flat picture format, viewed with the unaided eye, other means were employed to overcome the reduction of image size. Thus the commercial galleries commonly featured life-size enlargements of portraits, which might be hand colored to enhance the illusion of the image, and could thereby compete with the painted portrait. With the painted landscape the photographer was less able to compete; at great pains, mammoth plates—some over 17″ by 20″—were carried into mountainous landscapes in order to render a sharper, more detailed image than was possible with an enlargement of an ordinary negative plate. But the results, while impressive, could not compare with the more dramatic effects and much grander sizes of the landscape painter.

Meanwhile, the limitation of viewing angle was overcome through the development of panoramic photography. The technique here was to combine several plates into a single larger whole to produce a sweeping vista—of city or wilderness—that was supposed to evoke the experience of actually being in a landscape; one of the most ambitious of such hybrids of realism and artifice was an 1888 publication called *Panorama of the Hudson, Showing Both Sides of the River from New York to Albany*, "the first photo-panorama of any river ever published ... one hundred and fifty miles of continuous scenery accurately represented from eight hundred consecutive photographs." Though the river width varies from a half mile to four miles, the pictured river remains uniform. With each photo showing both sides (printed so as to blend in the water), the reader is required repeatedly to turn the book upside down to get the opposing bank right side up; the technique produces some awkward perspectives when bridges must be photographed, but there is no problem showing boats—they have been drawn in—and virtually every page shows at least one such vessel floating on the water.[12] Such panoramas obviously required a considerable suspension of disbelief: the viewer accepted the book-apparatus as a kind of model, an artificial construction made out of "real" pictures.[13]

But the problem with all such efforts to stretch the physical limitations of the two-dimensional photographic print was that they inevitably intruded upon the viewer's ability to become immersed in the world of the image. The form overwhelmed the content, calling attention to the very artificiality of the medium that the format was designed to overcome. More successful in creating the illusion of reality were photographs that accepted the framed window and focused instead on the dramatization of the image within the frame. The photograph here allied itself with a theatrical event, or with pictorial representation, as if the photographic rectangle were a proscenium arch or a framed canvas. An extreme example of such work is that of the popular theatrical photographer Napoleon Sarony, whose reputation was based on his representations of actors and actresses in their most famous roles, complete with props. In a photograph that makes the pictorial analogy explicit, Sarony recreated the popular painting by

William Notman, "Exhausted," from Cariboo Hunting Series, *ca. 1866
(Courtesy of Notman Photographic Archives, McCord Museum,
McGill University, Montreal)*

Adolph William Bouguereau, *The Captive* (1891), which was itself, as Ben L. Bassham points out, based on a model of photographic realism.[14] In Sarony's look-alike photograph, *The Butterfly*, a young girl with angel's wings sits naked on a stone balcony, holding a butterfly aloft in one hand. Sarony's literal representation of an imaginary conception is clearly intended as a tour de force, but what detracts from the illusion is the palpably artificial look of the "stone" balcony—an obvious studio prop.

Still, Sarony's extreme example points to a major tendency within Victorian art photography: the synthesis of the extremes of artifice and mimesis, a synthesis based on a typological realism in which the approximation of the image to reality was viewed as a triumph of technology and art over the inherent limitations of the medium. In the 1860s, for example, the famous Montreal photographer, William Notman, published a series of photographs depicting a caribou hunt, including shots taken in a snowy, nighttime landscape. These were technically "impossible" outdoor shots, each separate scene depicting a distinct phase of the hunt—going out in the snow, becoming exhausted in a snow storm, arriving at camp, shooting the animals, sitting around the campfire, among others. Notman's caribou sequence was enthusiastically reviewed by the *Philadelphia Photographer* in May of 1866, and the terms of the discussion move us closer to an understanding of how the photographic community conceived of the relationship between camera image and reality. The writer— probably the editor, Edward Wilson—was ecstatic about the effects achieved, admitting, for example, that he could only guess how the storm was created, "but that the artist has given us a remarkable photograph of a snowstorm without snow, we cannot deny." And he concludes his detailed discussion, "No pains or expense have been spared to secure these results, and we have never seen anything more successful and true to nature, without being wholly nature itself. Oh! what a future is there for photography!"[15] "True to nature, without being wholly nature itself." Here we are near the heart of the Victorian photographic aesthetic; by examining the theory and practice of the Englishman Henry Peach Robinson, we can come yet closer to an understanding of the nature of photographic representation during this period.

Robinson is now known primarily for a few combination prints that appear regularly in standard histories of photography, where he is

treated typically as an important though aberrant figure who prosely-
tized on behalf of the sensational (in its day) but now vaguely dis-
reputable aesthetic of pictorial photography. Yet Robinson is, I would
argue, not peripheral to an understanding of nineteenth-century photography, but quite central to it. With the publication of his textbook
Pictorial Effect in Photography (1869), which went through four editions in America by 1897, Robinson became among the most influential of writers on photography in the latter part of the century.[16]

Robinson generally treats photographic compositional principles as
similar to those in painting, but with certain differences to be observed—a respect for probability, for example—because photography
is a more literal medium. Yet what is most interesting about his principles is how he draws the line between a merely "factual" representation and a more "artistic" one. On the one hand, Robinson advises
against the purely fantastic—cherubs or mermaids—claiming that
"photographs of what it is evident to our senses cannot visibly exist
should never be attempted." Yet, on the other hand, the bare presentation of facts alone constitutes an excess of literalism, a "tyranny of
the lens."[17] The photographer should be free to construct an image
using studio accessories such as artificial logs covered with ivy, tufts
of grass, painted backdrops, etc.; he might also pose his models to
represent some particular dramatic moment, and he might add together different elements from two or more negatives to create what
was called a combination print.[18]

Thus at the core of Robinson's practice was the careful balancing of
mimesis and artifice to achieve a kind of general truth that evoked an
aesthetic frisson as the observer caught on to the process. The peculiar refinement of Robinson's aesthetic has not been observed sufficiently; yet it is consistent from the early *Pictorial Effect* to the later
Elements of a Pictorial Photograph. As he says in the earlier book, "A
great deal can be done and beautiful pictures made, by the mixture
of the real and artificial in a picture. It is not the fact of reality that
is required, but the truth of imitation that constitutes a veracious
picture. Cultivated minds do not require to believe that they are
deceived, and that they look on actual nature, when they behold a
pictorial representation of it."[19] And Robinson reminds us, using
Ruskinian principles, that we prefer a marble figure to a waxwork:
the former does not try to look like what it is not. Similarly, Robinson
says in his later work, "We must know that it is a deception before we

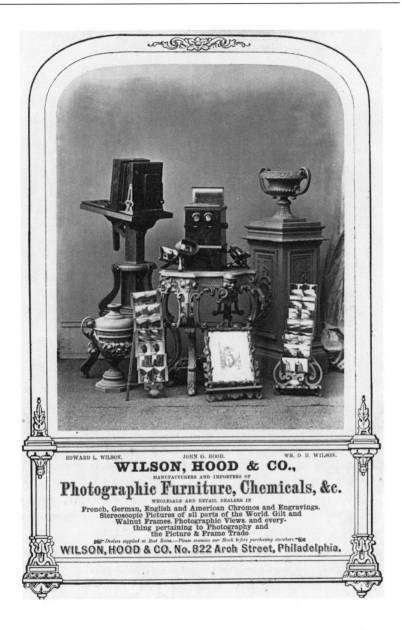

Photographic furniture, chemicals, etc., Wilson, Hood and Co.,
Philadelphia, trade advertisement
(Courtesy of Library Company of Philadelphia)

Henry Peach Robinson, study for a composition picture, 1860
(Courtesy of Gernsheim Collection, Harry Ransom Humanities Research
Center, University of Texas at Austin)

can enjoy it; it must be a gentle surprise, and not a delusion."[20] We
have been condescending to pictorialist photography for so long that
we have forgotten that sophisticated viewers, at least, were well
aware of the staging and in fact savored precisely the ontological
ambiguity of the resulting image.

Robinson may have pushed pictorial effect to the brink of aestheticism. As generally understood and practiced, however, Robinson's notion of pictorial photography defines a kind of "artificial realism" that
was shared by a wide variety of photographic strategists. The Phila-
delphian Marcus A. Root, for example, whose book, *The Camera and
the Pencil* (1864), preceded Robinson's volume by several years, had
earlier enunciated principles that would anticipate Robinson's balancing of mimesis and artifice: "Although strictly obliged to imitate
reality, the photographer may, nevertheless, sometimes unite the ele-

ments of the scene he would represent. He may, in fact, *compose* the scene he wishes to reproduce, by choosing the personages; giving them costumes, . . ."[21] (Root would give temporal license to the photographer as well, calling for the reproduction of the pageant of history "with the vividness of living reality.")[22] Even the great daguerreotypist Albert Southworth (who is regarded as a master of literalism) stated while in a retrospective mood, "the artist, even in photography, must go beyond discovery and the knowledge of facts; he must create and invent truths and produce new developments of facts. . . . Nature is not all to be represented as it is, but as it ought to be, and possibly have been."[23] And we find this flexibility again at the end of the century in articles appearing in the principal American photography journals. John Bartlett, for example, writing in the *American Journal of Photography*, argues that the photograph must be intensely realistic; yet despite this seeming expansion of the pictorialist sphere to encompass a grittier realism, Bartlett's own strategy remains embedded in a studio vocabulary and an avoidance of the "commonplace" (that is, literal record): his subjects are carefully positioned amidst artificial backgrounds in a manner recalling Robinson.[24]

The practice of photography during the late nineteenth century was raising questions about the nature of truth that would only gradually become fully articulated. If, at the center of the problem was the degree to which the camera—a mechanical instrument—could deliver a picture of reality that was truthful, the real issue was of course buried in the question itself: what was a "truthful" picture of reality? Was truth to be found in literal exactitude or in artistic generalization? The pictorialist compromise was to place the answer somewhere in between the extremes, and to develop a practice that understood the photographic representation to be a *type* of reality. The practice of using human models, for instance, itself transformed the question of what was "truthful" to the question of what was "convincing." The photograph based on a model is not a proposition in the form "This is an X"; rather it becomes a statement in the form, "This is a *representation* of an X." And once an image is accepted as a representation, then the question is no longer, "Is the representation more or less truthful?", but rather, "Is the representation more or less convincing?"

The strongest argument that it was the effectiveness of the picture that mattered—the degree to which it was *convincing* rather than *true*—was made by Robinson at the end of *The Elements of a Pictorial Photograph*. There he challenged his reader to examine seven of his rural genre photographs, and to guess in each case whether he had used a model or a "real" person as the subject. In fact, it is difficult to tell; but more important is the implication in Robinson's challenge— namely, the assumption that verisimilitude is as good as verity. The *effect* is all, the *means* nothing, Robinson claims: "The poet says, in default of the real thing, 'Tis from a hand maid we must paint our Helen.'" Of course Robinson is careful to warn his reader against dressing up just anyone; if he wanted a peasant represented, for example, he would be careful to use old clothes on an intelligent, malleable model. Aesthetic considerations are at issue, not questions of verifiability. Moreover, he scorns the detective camera's candid snapshots as producing unsatisfactory groupings.[25] Robinson is working within the genre of "art" photographs, and that, of course, is the key point: for the kind of "truth" that is relevant to art, in Robinson's understanding, is a general truth, through which, in effect, the literal capacities of the camera are subverted.

The pictorial aesthetic that Robinson represented offered a good deal of freedom, but it was nevertheless circumscribed by codes of probability and convention that would become apparent only when they were transgressed. And the transgressions served to define more clearly the core of the aesthetic, as in the case, later in the century, of F. Holland Day. Day was a master craftsman, a superb printer, a medievalist, and an aesthete, on familiar terms with the literary and art circles of his day; but he was also clearly an elitist, who, as Estelle Jussim puts it, "objected to the very accuracy of photography as catering to the demands of the masses for representationalism."[26] Day's studies of young women and men feature exotic costuming, sensitive posing, and dramatic lighting; they are representations of imagined inward states, often using a vocabulary drawn from mythology and religion.

Perhaps the culminating effort in this line was the *Crucifix* series he undertook in 1898; after starving himself satisfactorily and growing a beard, Day featured himself in an elaborate, pre-Hollywood version of the Crucifixion, complete with imported cloth and cross from Syria. Though Day was not without his defenders (notably the

F. Holland Day, Crucifix with Roman Soldiers, *1898*
(Courtesy of Library of Congress)

English photographer Frederick Evans), by and large people were outraged. At issue was not simply the blasphemous nature of the project (his critics thought it might have been better had he cast someone other than himself in the leading role), but what was seen as the failure of Day's art. Instead of transporting us to an aesthetically intact, dramatized Crucifixion, we are made aware, through the clarity of Day's lens and the fully revealing distance from the figures, of the tricks and artifice. As a critic of the day wrote, "we are looking at the image of a man made up to be photographed as the Christian Redeemer, and not at an artist's reverent and mental conception of a suffering Christ."[27] Just before the *Crucifix*, Day had made a series, *The Seven Last Words of Christ* (1898), which depicted the agony of Jesus (again F. Holland Day), exclusively in close-ups of the face, at dramatic angles, using soft focus. These images were felt to be more "convincing" than the Crucifix, chiefly because we are not aware of the physical actuality of the model. In short, the response to Day's work suggests that the issue in question was how convincing a representation the photograph provided, not the initial premise, which viewed the photographic subject as a general representation of reality, *a type*.

By type, however, we must understand not the scientist's general summation of a class; rather, the typology of nineteenth-century photography is—to borrow a word from poetic terminology—metonymic, whereby the pictured subject, with all its concrete particularity, *stands for* a more general class of like subjects. The individuality of the subject is thus presented on its own terms while it simultaneously serves the larger purpose of representing a general category.[28] Understanding the typological synthesis of specific thing and general meaning allows us to comprehend what may otherwise appear to be, as a recent study has it, "the bewildering notion that the camera somehow extracts what amounts to a Platonic ideal form behind the shifting variability of Nature."[29] But that is precisely the point: with varying degrees of sophistication, the photographic community did accept a typological concept of the photo-representation, whereby the image was viewed as both a mimetic and an artificial construction, both specific and general.

By far the greatest number of photographs taken during the nineteenth century were portraits of individuals, and we must test this notion of the typological representation by examining the center of popular practice—the commercial portrait. At first glance the portrait would appear to be an exception to the rule I have been proposing. The goal of the photographer—if he prided himself on the "artistic" quality of his work—was to capture the living quality of his subject, "the *soul* of the original,—that *individuality* or *self*-hood, which differentiates *him* from all beings, past, present, or future," as put by Marcus Root.[30] The concept of truth expressed here thus seems quite different from the general truth of pictorial photography; rather it appears to be a truth that resides in the particular subject, and the effort of the photographer is to find that truth and reveal it. The greatest portrait photographers—Southworth and Hawes, Brady, Gardner —were thought to do just that, and the photographic journals were filled with practical advice on how to capture the sitter's unique personality—despite the encumbrances necessitated by a long exposure time.[31]

Yet in the process of discovering the sitter's "individuality," a kind of generalization was nevertheless aimed at. The advent of instantaneous photography in the 1870s and 1880s would eliminate the need for stiffly held poses.[32] But commercial studios were slow to adopt the new technology, and for reasons that go to the heart of how the portrait was conceptualized: for if the portrait was to capture the unique truth of the sitter, it was to capture it in the manner of a painting, to find the pose that might sum up—in effect, generalize—the sitter's personality, a posture of dignity and repose; the instantaneous moment was more likely to result in a distorted expression, rather than the more *typical* truth of individuality aimed at.

In fact, the portrait became even more of a generalized statement in the years following the Civil War, as the sharp-focused eccentric individuality of the early daguerreotype style gave way to a softer, more artificial ideal of self-representation. The whole practice of retouching a negative was of course one very widespread method of normalizing a particular sitter by, one might say, removing the rough edges; if there were defects of complexion or other oddities that could be removed, it was the common practice of studio photographers, beginning around 1868, to remove them, with the added fashion of a slightly diffuse effect (replacing the previously universal ideal of the sharp focus) coming in around 1870. The great German photographer Hermann Vogel (with whom Stieglitz later studied) was one in-

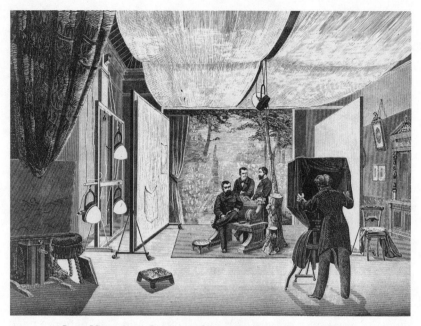

Late Victorian photographic portrait studio, engraving

fluential advocate of retouching, arguing that while photographs will
furnish representations "more correct than any other art," they may
not be absolutely correct; corrections of lens distortion and of other
defects by retouching were necessary because "it constitutes the art
of photography to present the reality true and beautiful."[33]

Although some protested the loss of "personal identity" in the
newer styles, the age demanded an image of its own grace. Along
with the Victorian hall-stand—which allowed everyone coming in or
leaving the house to check his appearance—the studio portrait afforded an occasion for defining the self in conformity with prevailing
norms of appearance and taste.[34] Where the first daguerreotype portraits, like earlier painted portraits, had often featured some visible
sign of the sitter's character or achievement (tools of the trade, etc.),
the studios supplied a readymade background and social status for
the patron in search of an image: the nearly universal accoutrements
for the American portrait studio were the balustrade, column, and
curtain in the 1860s, followed later by more bucolic and exotic set-

tings—rustic bridges, hammocks and swings, palm trees and parrots—for an increasingly urban audience.[35]

The representation—or sometimes misrepresentation—of self and class that might result was not without its critics: one observed in the *Philadelphia Photographer* (1871) that a typical studio photographer entertains all social classes, "the aristocratic and educated" as well as the "uncouth and unlettered." And while the former might look at home amidst the marble hall background, with columns and pretty furniture (the writer is evidently not troubled by the contrivance of the setting), the lower-class customer is clearly out of place: "If you desire to place him in a position suitable to his style and condition in life, you had better fill up and make surroundings of rudeness, and a pig, horse, and bullock." He recommends finally a "plain, spotless, even background" as suitable for all social classes.[36] A few years later, another writer argued less invidiously that the aristocratic pretensions of the photo-backgrounds were simply inappropriate for a country claiming to be a democracy: "Old style backgrounds, painted sharply and representing palaces and marble columns, etc., are inadmissible, and absurd to use in America, where such things do not exist, and doubt if they would appear in good taste in any place except with royalty for the subjects."[37] But these arguments for restraint and an appropriately egalitarian background in portrait photography were clearly running against the current.

Regardless of the background used, any studio portrait was singular and could represent only so much of the complex human personality. As Oliver Wendell Holmes had written, different portraits of our friends will show us wholly different sides of their characters, for our friend is "not one, but many, in outward appearance, as in the mental and emotional shapes by which his inner nature made itself known to us."[38] Holmes's own imagination here interestingly marks the limit of nineteenth-century photographic practice; for the photographer did not, at this time, have the theoretical capacity to incorporate different views of human personality within the same photographic construct. The closest we come is the occasional instance in the nineteenth century of the multiple portrait, as practiced, for example, by the Boston firm of Southworth and Hawes, who constructed a circle of poses looking like a lunar cycle of faces.[39] With the subject's head turned at different angles and arranged symmetrically around a single large image at the center, it is the mounting as a whole that is so striking. But the Southworth and Hawes example makes little attempt to bring out *different* sides of the subject's personality, showing us instead merely different sides of the face; it is an aesthetic study of variations on a single theme, not unlike the different poses assumed by a subject during a given sitting. Holmes's sense of the multiplicity of the human personality would await the twentieth century for true photographic expression, as, for example, in Alfred Stieglitz's extensive series on Georgia O'Keeffe.

The characteristic nineteenth-century interest in the *typical*, and the photographer's pursuit of the general truth of portraiture finds its most extreme expression in the theory of the composite portrait developed by the English scientist Francis Galton, who had a considerable following in America. Galton's composites are made by combining individual portraits into a single homogenized facial image and are thus not to be confused with the composites of the artistic pictorial photographers, who made combination prints using individualized images to compose a synthetic whole containing all of its parts. By photographing an individual as many as twenty times and printing a single composite print at the end, Galton argued that he would avoid the hazard of the single image and would arrive at an averaged expression that was the sitter's true self. "A composite portrait represents the picture that would rise before the mind's eye of a man who had the gift of pictorial imagination in an exalted degree," Galton wrote.[40] (Note Galton's association of his method with the artistic temperament.) Put together twenty different photographs of twenty different individuals, Galton believed, and it was possible to reveal the purity of type: Italian, Pole, Jew.

The composite may be based on the credible scientific notion that a comparison of items within a given class should yield knowledge of their shared, general characteristics. And it may also remind us, plausibly, of Charles Sanders Peirce's more or less contemporary notion of "the real" as a kind of infinite consensus—what is "ultimately agreed by all who investigate," independent of "what you or I or any finite number of men may think about it."[41] But the photographic composite, in Galton's hands, became a tool for devising stereotypes in the interest of defining racial lines.

Galton, a cousin of Charles Darwin and the founder of eugenics, had begun his composites at a time when immigrants were viewed by many in England and America with grave suspicion as a threat to the

Twelve Boston physicians and their composite portrait, ca. 1894,
from McClure's Magazine, *September 1894*

established social order. Knowing what they looked like (for it was assumed that all members of a given ethnic group looked alike) would help society defend itself against their potential criminality and radicalism. A camera enthusiast, George Iles, wrote, "Just as truth has been substituted for tradition in the case of animal movement, so we shall here replace vague impressions of foreigners and of special classes at home by exact and easily compared pictures."[42] Yet Galton's approach was really diametrically opposed to the studies of animal movement by Eadweard Muybridge to which Iles refers. Where Muybridge separated what was perceived as continuous movement into its constituent parts, Galton corralled individuals into a forced whole.

Nevertheless, Galton's notion of an ideal composite, anticipating the logic of racial purity of the twentieth century, had its vogue in the late nineteenth century. For example, in the Anthropological Building of the World's Columbian Exposition there stood the twin statues of the ideal American male and the ideal American female.[43] Whitman had sung longingly of his own "divine Average," his ideal mothers and robust men, but his vision had been at bottom an inclusive one, a vision of plurality, not of the monolithic purification of gender. In the name of science, Galton had carried photography far from its typological character, creating in his composites parodies of the concept of the type: not the individual raised to the power of the general, but the individual blurred and blended into a social identity that imprisoned him or her.[44]

Given its various efforts to overcome the limitations of the medium, photography in the nineteenth century could not be said to operate within what one might call a purely photographic aesthetic. (That would await the twentieth century.) Instead, the medium borrowed from existing approaches in other forms and genres: from the tourist sketch, the painted portrait, the staged tableau, even—as in the composite—from the scientific illustration. But what about the use of photography as a *historical record*? Was not the inherent literalism of the medium the great strength of the camera when used as a recording device, and was not that literalism at odds with the typological representation outlined above? One would think so; and certainly in the early years of the medium, as we have seen, a belief in the truth of the image was widespread. Because the photograph was made by sunbeams, it was understood, as Joel Snyder has put it, "to provide information of an unbiassed kind"; it assured "the audience of the absence of a 'narrator,' or of an agent who is directing the attention of the audience."[45] Yet, interestingly, as photography was gaining popularity through the stereograph market (from the 1850s to approximately 1910), some viewers apparently did need assurance from a credible source, serving indeed as a kind of surrogate narrator, that the image was "truthful," as in this inscription to be found on the back of some early stereograph cards: "I have looked these views carefully over and find them very correct. I was present when they were taken. The pictures and statuary are in their original places."[46] The views are "very correct"? Does the need for such a statement indicate that the photograph was believed implicitly, or that it was not?

The issue is a complicated one, for what one finds is that photographs presented as historical records—whether of events, landscapes, or people—were offered as literally true, but were in fact the product of an often doctored presentation. What one finds, in short, is that even while the image was presented as a "document," the photographer was constructing a *general* representation, a simulacrum of the real thing. Once again, verisimilitude was the goal, though verity was the claim.

What are we otherwise to make, for example, of Alexander Gardner's representations of the Civil War? Gardner presented his scenes of battlefields and encampments to the public in the *Photographic Sketch Book of the War* (1866) by claiming their utter veracity: "Verbal representations of such places, or scenes, may or may not have the merit of accuracy; but photographic presentments of them will be accepted by posterity with an undoubting faith."[47] He was right, of course: posterity did accept the images with undoubting faith—until, that is, the meticulous studies of the photographs and the localities made by William Frassanito demonstrated that that faith had been misplaced. Thus, for example, Gardner had identified Union soldiers as, at times, Confederate soldiers; he had labeled one of his pictures "Field where General Reynolds Fell," even though the photographer had been nowhere near the field where Reynolds actually fell; he had dragged the same corpse from one location, where he had photographed it a first time, to another location (a sharpshooter's nest) for a second photograph and presented them both as records of different victims in different locales.[48] From a purely pragmatic point of view,

Gardner's reasons for misrepresenting his images are not difficult to construe: given constraints of time and events, he could expose only a limited number of negatives on the battlefield; but he had many more stories to tell, and so he paired a plausible image with a convincingly written narrative, and the viewer could never tell the difference. In Gardner's *Sketchbook* the narrative in fact dictates the viewer's reading of the image. And what this suggests most notably for our purposes is that Gardner was playing upon his audience's beliefs in the veracity of the medium while taking for himself a much more flexible view of photographic practice, whereby the manipulations of the photographer were permissible in the interest of achieving a rhetorically convincing effect.

The example of Jacob Riis similarly straddles the categories of fiction and documentary, artifice and mimesis. It is symptomatic of our confusion over late nineteenth-century photography that recent commentators cannot agree on a definition of Riis's virtues. While one critic might applaud his style for being appropriately crude, direct, and honest, another might laud it for being deceptively artful, shrewdly calculating.[49] And the nineteenth-century response reflected a similarly divided sense of what Riis was after: witness the reviews of *How the Other Half Lives*, which celebrated the volume for the "accuracy" of its scenic descriptions, and also for its fictive vigor—"enormously more interesting than any novel that ever was written or that ever will be."[50] These inconsistencies in the response to Riis point to a photographic practice that was acceptable in its own time but appears inconsistent to us now.

For Riis, the documentary mode was much less exacting in its purity than we would like to think; it allowed for a flexibility of practice in the streets (similar to Gardner's on the battlefield) that places it within the same broad field of pictorialist practice, with its franker manipulations of staged subjects. True, Riis did not employ models to pose as the urban underclass; he did not, at least, clothe his subjects, or drag them into a studio in order to better control the content of the image, as did Sigmund Krausz, for example, in his *Street Types of Chicago: Character Studies* (1891).[51] Yet we miss something important if we fail to see the degree to which Riis manipulated his representation of poverty to reflect a preconceived image of the poor, turning his subjects into types before the eye of the camera.

This technique is most evident when Riis gains the cooperation of his subjects to *play themselves* for the camera. Riis was fond of staging "candid" shots in which he would position various street boys in a corner staircase, or in the crevice of a building, or in some other typically "forgotten" place, and ask them to feign sleep (one can see the smiles playing on their lips). The vulnerability of childhood, coupled with the vulnerability of sleep, was a doubly pathetic combination. Other times we see children working in a sweatshop or saluting the flag in a classroom, their eyes sneaking a look at the camera they were presumably to "ignore." We do not know how often Riis paid his subjects, but he does tell us that he offered a tramp ten cents to sit for a picture, and that the tramp demanded a quarter if Riis wanted the pipe in his mouth as well. Riis paid for the pipe.[52] And Riis reports that in several shots of a gang of youths, they enacted for his camera the mugging of a victim, and indeed they were excited at the prospect of photo-notoriety and themselves mugged for the camera's eye. Another gang insisted on bringing a sheep into the picture. These images are interesting just because they reveal so much about the interaction between photographer and subject, reveal what Riis could not have intended—the degree to which he was creating an artificial image of the urban poor. Or, to use the terms invoked earlier to frame this discussion, Riis gives us, with the often willing and knowing collaboration of his subjects, a metonymic typology of urban slums, representing for us "the poor," "the miserable," "the other half." He is after the general truth of a general category, and the finer truths of individuals necessarily escape him.

A similarly illustrative use of photographs is evident in the anthropological photography of the late nineteenth century, brought to a climax in Edward Curtis, whose sensibility was formed by nineteenth-century practices, though his work spans the years from the turn of the century to 1930, when the final volume of his monumental *The North American Indian* was published. Curtis aimed "to picture all features of the Indian life and environment" with a kind of objectivity that he is careful to state at the outset: "Being directly from Nature, the accompanying pictures show what actually exists or has recently existed (for many of the subjects have already passed forever), not what the artist in his studio may presume the Indian and his surroundings to be."[53] Yet as Christopher M. Lyman has shown, Curtis's representations were contrived in a variety of ways. They may not have been taken in a studio, but they otherwise reflect the

Jacob Riis, Showing Their Trick, Hell's Kitchen Boys, *ca. 1889
(Courtesy of Jacob A. Riis Collection, Museum of the City of New York)*

photographer's active mediation, his interposing of an idealized image of Indian life upon his subjects: by dressing them in the appropriate picturesque modes (supplying props—for example, headdresses —where necessary); by eliminating from their immediate surroundings artifacts that may have been adopted from white culture (for example, alarm clocks, brand names on canvas tenting); by changing day to night (in his darkroom) and adding other kinds of dramatic lighting in order to enhance the romantic aura of the Indian.[54]

Likewise we have evidence now that even among expeditionary photographers like Timothy O'Sullivan, the camera was treated as an expressive, rather than as a strictly literal medium. This can be seen, for example, in O'Sullivan's practice of tilting the frame for emphasis and effect, or in his series of six photographs of the Green River in Colorado from the exact same vantage point at different times of the day.[55] (O'Sullivan's posing of human subjects in his pictures also seems to be expressive and not simply for purposes of measuring space.) And Martha Sandweiss has noted that William Henry Jackson on occasion would piece together separate negatives to compose an enhanced, more artistically attractive combination print of a given scene.[56] These practices point to a use of the medium that is consonant with the generally pictorialist sensibility of the nineteenth century I have been sketching. As such, they seem to qualify Rosalind Krauss's otherwise cogent argument that O'Sullivan and other landscape photographers were merely producing "views" (to use the nineteenth-century terminology) of singular sights that together compose a catalogue of information for some institutional sponsor, whether governmental survey, stereo company, or railway line. The expeditionary photographers may not have thought of themselves as artists, as Krauss argues, but even when seemingly most literal, the nineteenth-century professional was striving for a rhetorical effect.[57]

The movement from the end of the nineteenth century to the beginning of the twentieth saw a subtle but definite change in the way photography was viewed outside the circle of professionals: from a passive medium to an active medium. Though photography was from its beginnings a product of artistic manipulation and technological experimentation, it presented itself to the popular imagination as an art of the machine in which the passive character of the mechanical process was its dominant characteristic, as opposed, say, to the active processes of the scientific imagination. Here, for example, is geologist Clarence King, who led Timothy O'Sullivan through the Southwest around 1870, and who offers a typical contrast between the passivity of the camera and the activity of the scientist as he recounts a pause in his own geological investigations: "I was delighted to ride thus alone, and expose myself, as one uncovers a sensitized photographic plate, to be influenced; for this is a respite from scientific work, when through months you hold yourself accountable for seeing everything, for analyzing, for instituting perpetual comparison, and as it were sharing in the administering of the physical world."[58] King's implied metaphor of the mind as passive camera plate turns up as well in a more sophisticated form at the end of the century in the analogy between the mind and the camera: "Has the Brain a Photographic Function?" asks the *American Journal of Photography* in 1897, suggesting that visual images are "impressed" upon the brain, and later reactivated, in the same manner as the photographic process.[59]

But if there was any basis for thinking of photography as passive during the time when the camera was fixed on a tripod while the subject waited for the release of a shutter, that began to change with the development of new technologies of photography; and with these changes the whole set of assumptions held by photographers and—especially—viewers began to change.[60] With the faster shutter speed of the modern camera, the stream of time could be interrupted and motion could be broken down into its constituent parts; King's notion of photography as a passive recording of nature persists through the century, but during the last decade a new way of thinking about the camera begins to be formulated, one that in effect takes the terms King has opposed to photography—the probing, analyzing, and active observing of scientific work—and transfers them to photography itself. Eadweard Muybridge's studies in animal movement, which received wide publicity, were the significant catalyst.

Experimenting with the design and placement of his cameras, Muybridge succeeded in representing the stopped motion of, first horses, then virtually every kind of creature that could move across a field of vision. The arrangement of that motion against a grid background, with the individual frames themselves presented on the page in a grid-like structure, gave an aura of scientific discovery to the visible increments of movement, and had a startling effect upon people's confidence in their unaided vision. No one had ever *seen* what Muybridge revealed; our notions had been approximate, and often incorrect; the artists had been wrong. (Though it is important to note that Muybridge himself did not recommend that the artist slavishly follow his stop-motion images, recognizing a difference between an artistic rendering and a literal recording.)[61]

A world of observation had opened up with high-speed sequential photography, and Stieglitz's aesthetic of instantaneous photography would flow from the same technical possibility, eventually making the contrived arrangements of the pictorialist photographer seem outmoded. Moreover, as the hand-held "detective" camera became popular among enthusiasts, what had been a passive historian, a witness to events after they had happened, became now an active intruder upon private and public life; legal minds worried about the loss of our right to privacy, while psychologists spoke of our need to incorporate our previously hidden selves into our concept of being.[62]

The camera was becoming, at the turn of the century, the symbol of a kind of intrusive presence in society: a culture that had been fascinated with spectacles and replications of reality, and that had brought myriad photographic microcosms into the parlor, was itself becoming the spectacle. (Even Walt Whitman, after commencing his career with a deliberately photographic representation of self, would complain, late in life, "I've been photographed, photographed, and photographed, until the cameras themselves are tired of me.")[63] And the subject who had composed a self with the help of the knowing professional and in the safe confines of the photographic studio, was being turned out into the streets. With the camera becoming lighter and falling into the hands of the amateur, the metonymic typology of photography would yield to the autobiographical particularity of the family album; the pictorialist synthesis would gradually fall apart before the instantaneous aesthetic of Stieglitz, and the documentary photographer would have to defend his practice in a community of viewers less likely to believe what they saw. Yet the full absorption of these various changes in the technology and practice of photography lay ahead, in the twentieth century. To look back on the practice of photography in the late nineteenth century from our own perspective is to see a world of artificial realism in harmony with a culture of replications, where what was offered as almost nature was sufficient.

Along with photography, literature was a part of this culture of replications, and the aesthetic of *types* was as characteristic of the conventional popular literary work as of the photographic work. Yet toward the end of the nineteenth century, in the movement of literary realism—as in the contemporaneous new movements in photography mentioned above—there occurred the momentous breakdown of the culture of replications, with its typological aesthetic. In the debates surrounding the advent of realism, with their self-conscious polemics and cultural battle cries, the problems of representation, and of fact and fiction, were argued keenly and with a full realization of the social and aesthetic ramifications of the issues. And, significantly, photography would itself play a key role in establishing a model for a kind of factuality and intensity in representation, and would serve as an important catalyst in the whole shift from a culture of replication to a culture of authenticity.

The Romance of
the Real

*T*he debate surrounding literary realism in the last decades of the century was simultaneously a debate about *what* the legitimate subject matter of fiction ought to be and about *how* to see and represent it. The word itself—realism—meant different things to different people, and was variously high or low, uplifting or vulgar, idealistic or literal, depending on who was speaking about what. The earlier realism—with which I will by and large not be concerned in this chapter—is in harmony with the culture of imitation that I have outlined in earlier chapters: one would find it regularly in such magazines as *Atlantic Monthly*, *Harper's*, and *Scribner's Monthly*, which would grace the parlor table, along with the photo album. It is a fiction of genteel heroes and heroines and recognizable local types, a fiction of uplifting sentiment in harmony with a Christian ethos, a fiction of small-scale subjects and interiors.[1] My focus here will be instead on the shift that occurs in the meaning and conception of "realism" late in the nineteenth century: from a realism that was in harmony with the culture of imitation and that reaches its complex and grand culmination in the illusionistic fiction of Henry James; to a realism that encompasses the new movements of "veritism" and "naturalism" and that takes its inspiration from the younger generation of writers who identified with the West and Middle West. Put more simply, it is a movement that attempts to bring literature and life closer together. In that newer realism one can see, in effect, the beginning of the breakdown of the culture of replication, a process that will result in the modernist art that develops more decisively after the turn of the century.

I will be dealing primarily with the period of the 1890s, for it is in that decade especially that the literature of local color, a staple of middle-class consumption along with sentimental romances and historical fiction, was giving way to a literature attempting to introduce new subject matter that had long been denied expression. During the 1890s the fundamental premises of literary representation were being questioned profoundly by writers like Frank Norris and Stephen Crane, who—influenced in part by photography—were pushing the conventions and techniques of mimesis to the breaking point. The new movement in literature is in many respects allied to similar fresh currents in American painting: the anti-sentimental, Howellsian treatment of portrait subjects in Thomas Eakins, for example, whose celebration in other works of the oarsman and the surgeon located a new kind of heroism in American painting; the fierce, almost Darwinian natural world of Winslow Homer; or the group of new realists around Robert Henri—John Sloan, William Glackens, and others—who were finding, like Norris and Dreiser, inspiration in the drama of city streets, harbors, and quotidian scenes. The movement in literature, however, was in the vanguard, perhaps because of the stimulating contact between fiction and journalism that was developing after the Civil War and also because of the generally less academic, less institutionalized environment of literature. And the changes that did occur in fiction are visible with an often explicit self-consciousness that makes clear the tensions and issues involved.

To write about something, to acknowledge seeing it, is to confer existence upon it, and to the defenders of genteel culture, there were some things one did not allow to exist. What was at stake in the politics of literary realism was both the definition of culture and the defense of a social class. The class of comfort, which expressed itself in the parlor magazines of the period and in the founding of museums and orchestras, and which found its spiritual base in New England, strived to maintain its dominance over an America becoming increasingly plural in its peoples and its arts. For the changes in American society in the late nineteenth century were many—increasing immigration, the growth of cities, the agitations of labor—and these were unsettling the traditional authority of middle- and upper-class values and were forcing consideration of the fate of "culture" in America.

The fears of the establishment were clearly visible as early as 1872 in an address to college students delivered by Charles Dudley Warner and reprinted in *Scribner's Monthly*. Warner is in many respects the quintessential man of letters of the period—newspaper editor, essayist, biographer, travel writer, successor to William Dean Howells as occupant of the "Editor's Study" at *Harper's*, and editor of two major codifications of the literary culture of the time, the *American Men of Letters Series* and the *Library of the World's Best Literature.* (Yet it is his association with Mark Twain—the two friends collaborated in the writing of *The Gilded Age*—that has made him best remembered in the twentieth century.) In his address to the graduates of Hamilton College, his own alma mater, Warner raised the question, "What Is Your Culture to Me?" That question, which provides the title for his essay, is one of the few moments when Warner enters into the imagination of the lower classes. For the most part, the distinguished alumnus is "answering" the question from the point of the view of the "cultured" class, attempting to persuade them of their responsibility to pass on to the masses the fruits of their own heritage.

In Warner's Arnoldian model, culture is equivalent to the "best" works of the elite classes, works that are housed in the university and in the library; such works of culture develop the "higher part of man's nature." Warner emphatically adjures the educated classes of America to extend their spiritual wealth to the benighted lower classes and thus to help overcome the growing materialism of the country. In the background, most importantly, is a sense of impending class warfare, should the elite class fail to respond to the growing restlessness of the laboring class. "Unless the culture of the age finds means to diffuse itself, working downward and reconciling antagonisms by a commonness of thought and feeling and aim in life, society must more and more separate itself into jarring classes, with mutual misunderstanding and hatred and war." The specific threat Warner foresees—and he was prescient in this regard—is from the "great movement of labor," which is "real, and gigantic."[2]

Warner represents here the viewpoint of the genteel literary critics of the period who were unwilling or unable to acknowledge the validity and vitality of a popular culture that was gaining strength in the last decades of the century. In practical terms, this meant a ban on certain subjects that might be considered "commonplace" (that is, lower-class). Warner, in an essay ten years later, in 1883, phrased the matter delicately: "Do not misunderstand me to mean that common and low life are not fit subjects for fiction, or that vice is not to be lashed by the satirist [note the implied connection], or that the evils of a social state are never to be exposed in the novel ... But when the mirror shows nothing but vice and social disorder . . . the mirror is not held up to nature, but more likely reflects a morbid mind."[3] The function of art, according to the genteel position, was not to expose reality, but to uplift the spirit. The novelist and editor Maurice Thompson, who often published in southern journals, put the matter baldly when he argued that art, in the face of increasing social unrest, must keep the social boundaries intact. "The great masters of art," he said, "lift us above the mire of degrading things." But to his horror, he found that in the fiction of the new realism, "we are hobnobbing with persons with whom we could not in real life bear a moment's interview."[4] Here is the crux of the matter: to admit such characters into the pages of the genteel magazines and novels was tantamount to admitting the vice and disorder of the lower classes, the whole plurality of urban life, into the front parlor.

To the younger generation of realists, coming of age in the 1890s, admitting such persons into the realm of fiction was precisely the point of their efforts. And Hamlin Garland, with the blunt manners of the West, satirized the cloistered habits of the elite writer in exactly the same terms with which Thompson had defended himself. Devising a dialogue between the "aristocrat" and the "Western radical," Garland has the former declare, "I don't like the common American in life, and I don't like him in books." To which the radical replies (and Garland is with him, unequivocally): "You have no sympathy with the American people of middle condition. . . . From your library, or from the car-window, you look upon our life; that is the extent of your knowledge of our conditions, at best."[5] The realists of the 1890s were conducting, then, not simply a literary program, but a social and political one as well: admitting the common people into fiction was giving them a status denied in polite society.[6]

Realism and reform seemed, for a moment in the early 1890s, to be as friendly as a cat and his cream. Clarence Darrow, a year before he resigned his lucrative job as a Chicago railroad counsel to defend Eugene Debs in the aftermath of the Pullman Strike, signaled his growing sympathies for the underclasses when he rushed to the defense of realism. Associating its truth-telling mission with the progress of social justice, Darrow wrote, in the *Arena*, "The world has grown tired of preachers and sermons; to-day it asks for facts. It has grown tired of fairies and angels, and asks for flesh and blood. It looks on life as it exists to-day—both its beauty and its horror, its joy and its sorrow. It wishes to see all; not only the prince and the millionaire, but the laborer and the beggar, the master and the slave."[7] Realism was thus equivalent to democracy, and the crux of the issue was the power of "the fact"; for the new realist was to be as impartial in his respect for fact as the scientist. As Darrow put it, the artist of the day was "telling facts and painting scenes that cause humanity to stop, and think, and ask why one should be a master and another be a serf."[8] (This was precisely the point Twain had made in *Connecticut Yankee* in 1889, using the same equivalence of fact, science, and democracy.)

That one word, "fact," became the point of fusion between social and literary motivations, gathering almost a mystical quality, as in Jacob Riis's invocation in the preface to *Children of the Poor*. "Ours is an age of facts," he wrote. "It wants facts, not theories, and facts I have endeavored to set down in these pages. The reader may differ with me as to the application of them. He may be right and I wrong. But we shall not quarrel as to the facts themselves, I think."[9] Riis's assumption that there is anything quite as simple as "the facts themselves," and his faith in them, may seem to us somewhat naive, but it was part of a growing middle-class culture that valued objectivity increasingly.[10]

Resistance to the power of "fact" came from the genteel establishment, which associated *facts* with *science* and viewed both as threats to the established order of conventions and assumptions. The writer of a lengthy letter to *The Dial*, for example, after dissecting with a good deal of energy the varieties of realism—imitative, literal, and selective, all of them "stimulated by the passion for the actual"— lamented the limitations of an age in which "all departments of human culture are fast being swallowed up by science which assimilates what it can and rejects the rest."[11] As this writer makes plain, facts were associated with the masses (once again, the "lower" order was threatening the "higher"): "Facts please the many simply by reason of their sheer force and reality; the crowd seek not truth but sensation in either reality or its transcript. . . . There are those, however, who aim at a higher Realism, who seek for the truth of things and the inner reality of facts."[12]

This notion of a "higher Realism" gave a lofty ring to the defense, and it was along these lines that the critic and editor Hamilton Wright Mabie (author of such volumes as *My Study Fire* and *The Life of the Spirit*) put the case for literary idealism as a more *complete* realism:

"All that the Idealist asks is that life shall be seen not only with his eyes but with his imagination. His descriptions are accurate, but they are also vital; they give us the thing not only as it looked standing by itself, but as it appeared in the complete life of which it was a part; he makes us see the physical side of the fact with great distinctness, but he makes us see its spiritual side as well."[13] Deriving from John Ruskin, this synthesis of the ideal and the real, the former lying within the shell of the latter, was the essence of the genteel aesthetic and was widely disseminated in a variety of forms.[14]

In fact, the same formula of a "higher Realism" was used by William Dean Howells, who during the 1880s and 1890s attempted to make realism acceptable to genteel culture. In articulating his theory of literary representation in the mid-1880s, Howells, in this as in so much else, tried to strike the middle road, balancing the requirements of realism against the obligations of genteel culture, exhibiting thereby the the adroitness of a tightrope walker holding a china tea cup. This exemplary performance was an effort to associate himself with the power of "fact," but not with the coldness of science (or, if he could help it, the vehemence of social protest), as in this statement from the "Editor's Study" in 1886: "When realism becomes false to itself, when it heaps up facts merely, and maps life instead of picturing it, realism will perish too."[15] Occupying the interesting middle terrain of a growing middle-class culture, embodying in his criticism and fiction the tensions that were charging the debate over the new realism, Howells was arguably the most influential critic and editor of his day.

Characteristically, Howells was friend to both Henry James and Twain and stood somewhere in between the two in his tastes, deeply appreciative of James's power and subtlety, but hospitable to the fresher voices and subjects coming from outside of New England. The possibilities for the novelist that James had failed to see in America, Howells saw in abundance, and in his 1889 review of James's study of Hawthorne, he objected to the latter's famous list of What Was Missing in America, claiming that there was in the United States "the whole of human life remaining and a social structure presenting the only fresh and novel opportunities left to fiction."[16] From his various editorial positions, the influential Howells was the champion of the younger realists—up to a limit—against the restraints of the elite establishment.

What had made Howells such an excellent editor and literary mentor for the middle classes was his respect for the limits of parlor taste (where sex was forbidden) coupled with his healthy occasional challenge to accepted practices and subjects. Howells had thrived for years in a culture in which, as he had put it, "the fate of a book is in the hands of the women." Yet his position as man of letters in a world of business embodied a degree of ambiguity that by the early 1890s was clearly causing him discomfort. He was only too aware of the grotesqueness of an artist *selling* his work in a market and of the disproportion of reward to labor. He thought of himself as "allied to the great mass of wage-workers," yet the masses, he knew, did not recognize his kinship.[17] Nor did the wealthy classes have any use for the writer, although he served them by amusing them. The writer's peculiar fate, as Howells saw it, was thus to occupy an uncertain middle position between the upper and lower classes, unable to bridge the gap between them, yet otherwise exploiting the virtues of the middle class and its representative quandaries.

Howells's innately moderate and modest temperament has been, as Lionel Trilling observed, his undoing for the twentieth century, with its twin appetites for evil and for abstraction.[18] We have tended to condescend to Howells and his Biedermeier world, viewing him as an essentially compromised figure; we forget that he was the only writer of his standing in the elite community who opposed the state's actions in the Haymarket Affair; and we forget that Howells, in the 1890s, before he settled into a more comfortable mood of reminiscence, was articulating a utopian socialism—see, for example, *A Traveler from Altruria*—that was deeply critical of the American social and political structure, albeit in a genial form.[19] Howells's unfortunate utterance that the proper business of the American novelist is with the more "smiling aspects of American life," since they were the more typical, has stayed with us, despite his acknowledged importance to a generation of realists who themselves handled some quite unsmiling aspects of American life, as indeed Howells did himself, at least on occasion.

The closest Howells came to dramatizing the conflict of cultures that was implied in the challenge of realism was in his 1890 novel, *A Hazard of New Fortunes*. There the riches of the commonplace would find their expression in the new materials of the city that Howells had recently come to know. For like the Marches in the novel, Howells in 1888 had left one literary job in Boston (with the *Atlantic*) to take

another in New York (with *Harper's*), and the contrast between the
two places—the former with its deathlike pallor and conservatism,
the latter with its panorama of immigrants and revolutionaries, laborers and aristocrats, aspiring artists and boorish millionaires—interested Howells greatly.

In *A Hazard* Howells examines the whole process of learning to see
that was at the ethical and aesthetic core of the new realism. The
early chapters of the novel, especially, are filled with detailed descriptions of the life of the city. And everywhere we are viewing New York
through the eyes of the Marches, for Howells is at least as much
interested in depicting *how* they see New York as *what* they actually
see. Basil March, as a magazine editor, is an appointed guardian of
the genteel Bostonian culture, and in his encounter with the pluralistic society of New York City, Howells has represented the conflict
between the establishment culture and the lower classes that had
preoccupied Warner two decades earlier. Time and again Howells
comments on the Marches' perceptions, often critical of their remote-
ness from the reality of what they see. "They liked to play with the
romantic, from the safe vantage-ground of their real practicality, and
to divine the poetry of the commonplace," he tells us early on.[20]
Strolling around Washington Square amidst a parade of Italian and
French and Spanish faces, Howells tells us that "They met the familiar picturesque raggedness of Southern Europe with the old kindly
illusion that somehow it existed for their appreciation, and that it
found adequate compensation for poverty in this."[21] Seeing a hungry
man stooping to eat a cracker from the street, Basil goes after the
man and asks him (he can hardly believe what he saw), "Are you in
want—hungry?" The man, who is French, accepts a coin from March
and then lapses back, as Howells puts it, into the "mystery of misery."
Basil is shocked, but he consoles his wife, and himself, with the probable rarity of the event, and also with its universality: "And what part
of Christendom will you live in? Such things are possible everywhere
in our conditions."[22] Through such incidents Howells shows us the
resistance to comprehending new "facts" that the Marches exemplify.
They assimilate the shocking poverty of the city to their comfortable
perceptions, which remain, for the most part, unchallenged.

After several such experiences, Howells is prepared to offer us a
more radical perspective on the contrasts of luxury and poverty in
New York. Out walking with his son Tom one Sunday morning, March

is made unhappy by the site of "frozen refuse melting in heaps, and particularly the loathsome edges of the rotting ice near the gutters, with the strata of waste-paper and straw litter, and egg-shells and orange-peel, potato-skins and cigar-stumps." (Who said Howells saw only the smiling aspects?) March says to himself, whimsically, that the poor must be fond of such surroundings, since "You always find them living in the worst streets," to which his son Tom seriously replies, "Every sort of fraud and swindle hurts them the worst. The city wastes the money it's paid to clean the streets with, and the poor have to suffer, for they can't afford to pay twice, like the rich." Basil is shocked by Tom's radicalism and relieved to find out that its source is old Mr. Lindau, a former teacher of Basil's, now living in New York, and a committed socialist. Basil approves his son's common sense in recognizing that the system is not perfect, but that "it's about the best there is."[23] The reasonable person accepts the failures, frauds, and hard times that are inevitable. Howells has by this point already provided sufficient ironic distance from the Marches for us to see the complacency behind such commonly held common sense. But how far in the direction of radical criticism does Howells himself allow his story to go?

Lindau is the chief proponent of the critical view in *A Hazard of New Fortunes*, and he embodies the radical potential of the novel. "Dere *iss* no Ameriga any more! . . . No man that vorks vith his handts among you has the liperty to bursue his habbiness. He iss the slafe of some richer man, some gompany, some gorporation, dat crindt him down to the least he can lif on, and that rops him of the marchin of his earnings that he might pe habby on."[24] But Lindau's sharp attacks are carefully flattened by Howells in several ways. Though Howells validates Lindau by making him a Civil War veteran (one who, moreover, has refused his pension—for a lost arm—from the government he does not respect), he is, equally significantly, a foreigner—and thus one whose un-American views can all too easily be explained as an aberration. More importantly, how can we—assuming we are genteel—take seriously the views of anyone who speaks with such an outrageous accent? Howells himself mocks it, in his own authorial voice, when he reflects, on one occasion, on how Lindau could no longer denounce Fulkerson (the wealthy backer of the magazine for which Lindau does translations) "as the slafe of gabidal," "though Fulkerson's servile relations to capital had been in nowise changed by

his nople gonduct."[25] And when Lindau dies at the end, the victim of a
policeman's club received during a strike, he is judged to have "died
in the cause of disorder." Thus Howells manages, in *A Hazard of New
Fortunes*, to affirm his radicalism, and also to deny it, containing it
safely within the margins of bourgeois tolerance, both having and
eating his cake.[26]

Middle-class realism as Howells practiced it thus deliberately observed certain limits. It was a form that spoke to a cautious but curious audience, and during the course of *A Hazard of New Fortunes*
Howells pauses several times to tell us by implication what the realist
novel is and what it is not, and to place it within the larger framework
of American culture. At one point, for example, March asks directions
of a "shabby-genteel ballad-seller," whose wares—doleful treatments
of "the wrongs of the workingman," or gay songs of the "high seas," or
"the poetry of plantation life"—are strung on a cord against a wall.
March buys "a pocketful of this literature, popular in a sense which
the most successful book can never be." In a sentence notable for its
syntactical complexity, Howells distances his own middle-class art
from the artless speech of the street ballad: "Where they [the ballad-
makers] trusted themselves, with syntax that yielded promptly to any
exigency of rhythmic art, to the ordinary American speech, it was to
strike directly for the affections. . . ."[27] But if the novel was more fastidious than the ballad, and perforce a less popular form, it was to
be distinguished from the other extreme of American culture—the
showy expression of the "prosperous commercial class, with unlimited money"—on still other grounds. The New Yorkers on promen-
ade, for all their wealthy display, look "dull": "fashion and comfort
were all that they desired to compass, and the culture that furnishes
showily, that decorates and that tells; the culture, say, of plays and
operas, rather than books."[28] The novel of realism was, by implication, part of a culture that esteemed seriousness of purpose and complexity of form; it encompassed a range of social observation and
political and philosophical issues that were beyond the reach of the
more showy, elite culture.

Against the two extremes of popular and elite culture, then, Howells defines the novel as a middle-class form. But he is also interested
in distinguishing the serious novel of realism from its possible com-
petitor for the attention of the parlor reader—the sentimental novel.
At several points during the course of *A Hazard*, Howells inserts pas-

sages that ironically open a door on the alternative perspective of sentimentalism, and then close it gently. When it appears, for example, that Alma Leighton has decided to refuse Beaton's marriage offer, March defends her refusal against his wife's wish for a "happy ending" to their relationship. Against the sentimental convention, he opposes the harder facts of common sense. "I believe that this popular demand for the matrimony of others comes from our novel-reading. We get to thinking that there is no other happiness or good-fortune in life except marriage; and it's offered in fiction as the highest premium for virtue, courage, beauty, learning, and saving human life. We all know it isn't."[29]

In short, Howells knew well what kind of novel he wanted to write in *A Hazard* and was at pains to make clear to the reader the fidelity of his picture to "real life," as opposed to the more sensational and sentimental worlds of fiction that were passing for popular at the time. In moderation was Howells's genius. Yet ironically, Howells admitted, twenty years after the novel's appearance, that it had failed to catch the public's attention in serial form and that its great success as a completed volume was due to the violent strike scenes that climax the book, "the material of tragedy and pathos."[30] The public had evidently been ready for at least the fictional representation of social unrest, but Howells followed his moderate instincts in holding back from the more extreme implications of his novel, conveniently eliminating his most radical characters in one way or another. For it was his conviction that at bottom America was not Russia, that a social revolution was more than unlikely and that the middling character of the civilization finally balanced the extremes of social class—in the same way that realism balanced the extremes of the popular and elite genres.

Yet Howells may have ultimately paid a price for his shrewd sense of what the reading public would tolerate and what the middle-class novel ought to represent. As the decade of the 1890s progressed to its end, the rapid changes in taste and the rise of the younger generation of realists left Howells in a rear-guard position. Against the charge that the "present bounds of American fiction are not wide enough, or rather they are too strictly patrolled by the spirit of the young girl," Howells rose in defense. He would allow happily that "American novels are full of clever details, witty conversations, and delicate touches," but he would not at all allow that "the wolfish problems of existence are never grasped and handled firmly in them."[31] Howells's notion of the "wolfish" problems, the "real problems of existence" was, however, somewhat restricted: it would include economic problems (financial reverses, downward mobility) and domestic ones (manners and marriage), along with "civic and moral and religious problems." All such considerations could be safely read by Howells's still-imagined ideal reader, the young lady and her family.[32] What Howells specifically was ruling out of course (and he was too polite even to mention it) was the problem of sexuality. Wanting to preserve the novel as a family genre, he pushed himself to declare that books that deal with such matters "do not present a true picture of life, as a whole or in any large part."[33] But in thus accepting the limitations imposed by "good taste," Howells left himself open to the charge of defending a golden mean of mediocrity.

In "Problems of Existence in Fiction," Howells had listed a number of writers who, he felt, did actually deal with the real problems of existence, among them Henry Blake Fuller, Harold Frederic, Stephen Crane, and Henry James. Howells does not mention the midwesterner Hamlin Garland here, but he was of course aware that the parlor world of Victorian fiction was experiencing fresh gusts from the West. In 1894 Garland had brought out *Crumbling Idols*, which called excitedly for a literature that could regenerate American culture. And behind Garland one can hear the rhythm and vocabulary of Walt Whitman—kept alive for years as a cult object by his worshiping followers—now beginning to surface and enter the more central currents of American culture. Confirming the strength of the "common" folk, Garland takes up Whitman's themes (though without the latter's imagination): America's "great railways, bridges, tunnels, transportation facilities, were perfected by minds which rose out of the common ranks of American life. The genuine American literature, in the same way, must come from the soil and the open air, and be likewise freed from tradition."[34]

Another westerner, of even greater importance than Garland, is missing from Howells's account—Frank Norris—for he had only recently, in 1898, had a first adventure novel published. Yet what is remarkable, and speaks volumes for Howells's catholicity, is the fact that just two weeks after his defense of the "young lady" as the guardian of taste, Howells was hailing Norris's second novel, *McTeague*

(1899), in terms that practically reverse his defense of American fiction in the earlier essay. Writing in the same journal, *Literature*, Howells reopens the whole question of whether American fiction shall include "the passions and the motives of the savage world which underlies as well as environs civilisation," and leaves it now to the reader to decide.[35] Accurately citing the strong influence of Zola on Norris, Howells prophecies that the future importance of American literature on the world scene will come from the new force of western literature embodied in *McTeague*. On the crucial question of the writer's donnée, his choice of subject, Howells meets Norris more than halfway, willing now to stand against the genteel critic's horror of such characters as McTeague: "Polite readers of the sort who do not like to meet in fiction people of the sort they never meet in society will not have a good time in *McTeague*, for there is really not a society person in the book."[36]

Like Garland, Norris was picking up where Whitman had left off, greeting the new muse of American fiction, in 1901, in terms that explicitly recall Whitman's robust woman of the "Song of the Exposition." Fiction, Norris urged, was not an affair of velvet jackets and "studio hocus-pocus," but of the outdoors, the marketplace; and the new muse was no delicate mademoiselle "but a robust, red-armed *bonne femme*, who rough-shoulders her way among men and among affairs, who finds a healthy pleasure in the jostlings of the mob and a hearty delight in the honest, rough-and-tumble, Anglo-Saxon give-and-take knockabout that for us means life.... [She is] unashamed to know the clown and unashamed to face the king."[37] We do not know what the readers of the *Boston Evening Transcript* (where it appeared) thought of all this, but just two years earlier the journal's reviewer had recoiled from what he considered Norris's gloating over morbid details of vulgar low life in a review of *McTeague*.[38]

Norris himself was explicit about the requirements of an authentically realistic art (which he called, ardently, "Romance"): writing in the *Wave* in 1897 of all the as yet unwritten stories of San Francisco, he urged excitedly that younger writers "get hold of them." "It's the life that we want, the vigorous, real thing, not the curious weaving of words and the polish of literary finish."[39] But what did it mean to get "the real thing" on paper? In *McTeague*, inspired perhaps by Zola and by a need to look closely at the brutalities of contemporary life, Norris had pushed his romantic characterizations to the limit of credibility while maintaining a sense of the texture of his characters' lives. *McTeague* had begun with the details of McTeague's digestion ("thick gray soup," etc.) and ended with the primitive dentist handcuffed to his enemy (whom he has just murdered) in the middle of a desert; in between Norris exulted in a frank depiction of sexual appetites and the passion for money.

But these are lower-class characters: the fastidious might not like reading about them, but their lives are consistent with genteel expectations about such creatures, and at least Norris (and his reader) could hold the seamy material at a distance; at least the story was about a class of characters whom we, gentle readers, could expect to be different. In *Vandover and the Brute*, written around the same time as *McTeague*, we are in an entirely different world from the latter novel, the world of genteel San Francisco society, of college men and social dances, of artists and businessmen, in short, the world of "culture" that Howells and James, *mutatis mutandis*, wrote about. And it is specifically Norris's intention to introduce into this world the shattering force of "the brute," not in the form of an alien intruder dressed in a befouled costume, but as an active component within the personality of the genteel hero himself. If anything would satisfy Howells's adversary in his demand for a "wolfish" fiction, it was Norris's *Vandover*, for in it the hero literally goes down on all fours, naked, and barks "wolf." Although neither Howells nor anyone else had the chance to read *Vandover* in the 1890s (Norris failed to find a publisher and it appeared posthumously in 1914), *Vandover* extends the concerns of realism importantly beyond the limits Howells and the marketplace had drawn. As such, *Vandover* adds a new dimension to our understanding of the conflict of classes and cultures that Warner had anticipated years earlier in his graduation speech, "What Is Your Culture to Me?"

Vandover and the Brute raises in dramatically unexpected form the question of how real realism could be. Or perhaps, How *unreal* realism could be? For *Vandover* does test the limits of credibility, particularly where the title character is concerned; yet its triumph is to bring into fiction a fresh dimension of moral realism along with a profound critique of genteel culture.[40] The story centers on the son of a comfortably monied San Francisco business man, Vandover, who is in the process of developing his artistic talent when he yields to temptation and seduces a young woman, Ida Wade, who is a notch or two below him socially. Ida commits suicide, and Vandover's guilt is immense. The young artist's weak character gives way gradually to gambling, whoring, and the squandering of his family fortune following the death of his father; sliding further into lassitude and vice, Vandover's degeneration is all too visibly symbolized as a mutation into animality, and at several points in the novel he gets down on all fours and howls. (Norris labored under certain theories of lycanthropy.) *Vandover* ends, stunningly, with the once-promising artist and debonair young man cleaning workers' cottages on property he used to own: "Prone in the filth under the sink, in the sour water, the grease, the refuse, he groped about with his hand searching for the something gray that the burnisher's wife had seen. He found it and drew it out. It was an old hambone covered with a greenish fuzz."[41] Norris is unflinchingly, grittily "European," dealing with materials that Americans held traditionally at more than arm's length.

Vandover and the Brute is a bitter indictment of Victorian society, from top to bottom.[42] Recalling Melville's *Israel Potter* and anticipating West's *A Cool Million*, it is at least partially a parody of the Horatio Alger story of the hard-working youth who slowly but surely gains success. Norris ends the novel with the utterly debased hero on the floor, finishing up his cleaning work and looking up into the eyes of Oscar, a young boy of the working class who is clearly, by the sign of his energies, destined to rise in society: "For an instant the two remained there motionless, looking into each other's eyes, Vandover on the floor, one hand twisted into the bale rope about his bundle, the little boy standing before him eating the last mouthful of his bread and butter."[43] Norris's final freeze-frame suggests much about social mobility in America, upward and downward.

It would be possible to read the novel as a bizarre and pessimistic tale of lycanthropy, of evolutionary degeneration and determinism, or as a novel about sexual guilt.[44] But there is good reason to see *Vandover* as a parable about culture conflict that internalizes within the hero the warring "higher" and "lower" elements that were so agitating to social theorists of the time. (The same that had concerned Charles Dudley Warner much earlier.) Norris has imagined "the brute" as a collection of all the horrors that the Victorian order held in check (the same ones that were on Warner's mind earlier) amalgamated in an indistinct but powerful impulse toward disorder: the power of the laboring classes, the power of unrestrained sexuality, the power of indulgence and dissipation. Thus as Vandover "loses" the struggle between indulgence and discipline, between sexuality and control, he devolves from a well-to-do young gentleman to a speechless member of the proletariat. Seeing that potential inherent in Vandover, Norris was implicitly raising all sorts of questions about the natural hegemony of the ruling class.

Vandover and the Brute is also a story about the power—or power-lessness—of art. It is the artistic side of Vandover's temperament, Norris tells us, that holds the potential for his salvation. Yet as the story unfolds, the course of Vandover's development and career reveals the defects of the genteel art culture. Vandover gains gradual mastery of drawing technique by copying out of "A Home Book of Art," with its sentimental pictures of idylls, gypsy girls, lonely women, and allegories of "Spring," "Youth," "Innocence." And he progresses from copying lithographed reproductions of minor studies to successful life studies. Yet Vandover's imagination, despite his abilities, is fundamentally warped by the sentimentalities of genteel culture. His conception of art is rooted finally in the banalities of the "Home Book of Art," and from them he cannot escape.

In the later stages of Vandover's disintegration, his artistic skill and powers of observation desert him, the connection between mind and hand is severed, and he can produce only "grotesque and meaningless shapes, the mocking caricatures of those he saw in his fancy," while a "numb feeling" comes into his head.[45] Finally, his money and his talent gone, he is reduced to "furnishing" his room with lettered signs that can now only stand for the missing representations and other furnishings of his cozy bourgeois life. "Naked, exhausted, Vandover slept profoundly, stretched at full length at the foot of the bare, white wall of the room beneath two of the little placards, scrawled with ink, that read, 'Stove here'; 'Mona Lisa here.'"[46] Norris's humor is brilliantly mordant and relentless. Signs have now replaced objects, which were themselves signs of culture. In the next chapter he has Vandover doing the only artwork left to him—painting "those little pictures on the lacquered surfaces of iron safes"—until even this becomes impossible.[47] In the early days, Vandover's father had always given his son some money as a reward for his talented productions. That initial equation of money and art Norris now drives to its grimly ironic conclusion.

The failure of Vandover's art is symptomatic, Norris implies, of the failure of genteel culture generally. For in his aesthetic universe there is no correspondence, no connection, between art and reality. Caught in a shipwreck (he had left San Francisco for a time in order to restore his spirits following Ida's suicide), Vandover discovers himself at last in a "rolling lifeboat" plunging in a "tumbling ocean." "There was nothing picturesque about it all, nothing heroic. It was unlike any pictures he had seen of lifeboat rescues, unlike anything he had ever imagined. It was all sordid, miserable, and the sight of the half-clad women, dirty, sodden, unkempt, stirred him rather to disgust than to pity."[48] The discrepancy between conventional representation and reality is absolute; art has in no way prepared him for experience. Unable to escape the early influences of the sentimental and melodramatic modes so popular during the period, Vandover's imaginative failure is total.

Yet *Vandover* stands as final evidence of Norris's own power to transcend the limits of Victorian platitudes and sentimentalities and to give, in the fact of its own representation, the lie to the conventional models of art that Vandover himself carried to his doom. For Norris's fable points to one more moral: that "art" has no power at all to save—either the individual or the culture—unless we mean by it something more than false heroics and trite sentimentalities. Only to the degree that it gave the reader "the vigorous, real thing," as Norris had put it earlier, could the novel lay claim to being an art of serious powers and purposes.

But how close to "reality" should one go in depicting that "real thing"? Where did art stop and science begin, for example? These were theoretical questions that were at the center of literary debate and that we need to explore further.

Realism offered a challenge not only to the traditionally defined materials of fiction, but also to the whole manner of literary representation that governed the production of literary effects. Writing in "The Editor's Study," his monthly forum at *Harper's Magazine*, Howells summed up succinctly the major issues at stake in the literary theory of the late nineteenth century in a speech he imagines being made by a pedant to a scientist.

I see that you are looking at a grasshopper there which you have
found in the grass, and I suppose you intend to describe it. Now
don't waste your time and sin against culture in *that* way. I've got
a grasshopper here, which has been evolved at considerable
pains and expense out of the grasshopper in general; in fact, it's a
type. It's made up of wire and cardboard, very prettily painted in
a conventional tint, and it's perfectly indestructible. It isn't very
much like a real grasshopper, but it's a great deal nicer, and it's
served to represent the notion of a grasshopper ever since man
emerged from barbarism. You may say that it's artificial. Well, it *is*
artificial; but then it's ideal too; and what you want to do is to
cultivate the ideal. You'll find the books full of my kind of grasshopper, and scarcely a trace of yours in any of them. The thing
that you are proposing to do is commonplace; but if you say that it
isn't commonplace, for the very reason that it hasn't been done
before, you'll have to admit that it's photographic.[49]

Howells thus offers us, in the "wretched pedantry" of the speaker,
several points for analysis which open up into the largest questions of
the time involving the nature of literary representation.

The first thing to observe is that this is an argument about literature, and yet Howells has cast the young writer in the role of a scientist. The deliberate analogy being proposed between the scientific act
of description and the literary one raises a host of secondary questions: is an accurate description the same as an artistically "true"
one? And how is such a true description best achieved? Through the
use of established models and conventions or through direct observation? In pursuit of the real, should the writer-cum-scientist avoid the
"commonplace"? Should he avoid the "photographic"? Or should he
emulate the objectivity of the camera? In short, how close to "the real
thing" should "realism" come? Since what is at stake is the picturing
of reality, it should not be surprising that these questions were dealt
with often in stories about artists, where the pictorial arts are of interest in their own right and also as analogues to the process of literary representation.

In fact, the whole problem of representation was itself a major
theme in late nineteenth-century pictorial art, and before turning to
fictional treatments, I want to at least allude to the issue as it surfaces
in painting. For during the 1880s and 1890s many artists were explor-

ing the nature of replication in the trompe l'oeil mode of painting, reviving a genre that had high popularity in seventeenth-century Dutch art. Though the common criticism was that trompe l'oeil was strictly literal, or merely photographic, that there was no imagination involved in the production of such works, in fact trompe l'oeil painting often fooled more than the eye, achieving a sophisticated complexity of composition and a metaphysical density that are not at first apparent. William Harnett's paintings, for example, carried extreme disorder to the point of complex order, featuring tabletop arrangements of pipes, books, jugs, musical instruments, etc., that are on the verge of violent discombobulation such that their physical balance could only be the result of the utmost care in placement. And John Haberle, the Laurence Sterne of illusion, painted doors and drawers stuccoed with coins and money and newspaper clippings, in arrangements that defy the logic of space: in *A Bachelor's Drawer*, for example, objects that seem to be lying flat inside a drawer appear on closer examination to be stuck onto the outside of the drawer that is shut in some hypothetical bureau. If all art is a kind of lying, trompe l'oeil art, by being so frankly duplicitous, was also frankly truthful, making transparent the artifice of representation.[50] In Howells's terms, the trompe l'oeil artists were representing grasshoppers that looked real *and* artificial at the same time.

Such an interruption of the *illusion* of art was the very thing to be avoided by the more traditional of the realists—Henry James, for example—who would conceal as much as possible the technique by which belief was obtained. To invite inspection of their artifice, or to exploit the literal was to court sensationalism.[51] That point is made transparently clear in a satiric tale by Henry Blake Fuller, "Dr. Gowdy and the Squash," that deals explicitly with trompe l'oeil painting. Fuller, whose Jamesian sensibility and refinement were at odds with his Howellsian preference for American materials, was at his best in satirizing Chicago affairs and the arts. "Dr. Gowdy" is really a parable of culture conflict in the Midwest, with equal scorn for the literary and artistic crudities of "veritism," for the middle-class inspirational view of art, and for the commercializers who exploit popular taste. At the center is the painter Jared Stiles, a rustic who gains fame in Chicago for his paintings of squashes with real seeds pasted onto the canvas. Dr. Gowdy, whose uplifting sermons on art had originally inspired Jared, is shocked by the "discordant mingling of the simulated and the real" in his would-be disciple. "I've never seen anything worse," he exclaims to a tour group who are viewing Stiles's latest work, "unless it's that." "He pointed to another painting past which they were moving—a den of lions behind real bars. 'That's the final depth,' he said."[52] But Jared goes on to paint bigger and better squashes—with real squashes attached to the fence-post frames; he leaves the Midwest and travels East to peddle his wares before delighted audiences who cry, "Which is which?"[53]

Though Fuller targets the vaudeville aspects of trompe l'oeil painting, "Dr. Gowdy" has a broader point that relates it to the movement of realism in late nineteenth-century arts generally. For the "cardinal tenet" of Fuller's new western artists, most from rural backgrounds, was that "a report on an aspect of nature was a work of art," a tenet that, to Fuller's thinking, threatened the whole definition and status of art.[54] If art is merely an exhibit of facts, the real thing itself, then where was the artist? where was the imagination?

Those were also questions that Henry James had dealt with more penetratingly in his appropriately named tale, "The Real Thing," which appeared in 1893, as the debate over realism was reaching a crisis. Here the definition of truth—literal vs. artistic—is treated in terms similar to those raised by Howells's grasshopper earlier, that is, in terms of "models." One day a couple of aristocrats, Major and Mrs. Monarch, walk into a London artist's studio. (It is the artist who narrates the tale.) The Monarchs have fallen on hard times and are now seeking work as models, expecting that the illustrator, who has been commissioned to do drawings for a series of novels dealing with upper-class English life, will be able to use them. The artist is compassionate and takes them on, but discovers eventually that he is better off employing his usual lower-class models, who have the ability to pose convincingly as aristocrats, rather than the aristocrats themselves. For although the latter advertise themselves as "the real thing" and hence would seem to be better than any possible model, the artist finds their very authenticity limits his own powers of plastic expression. He is too bound by their fixity as individuals to use them with the flexibility that art requires. Instead, he finds that his drawings of them seem like copies of photographs: Mrs. Monarch is "insurmountably stiff." "I could see she had been photographed often, but somehow the very habit that made her good for that purpose unfitted her for mine."[55] She can serve, in other words, as a literal icon of her class, credibly embodying the details of correct appearance, but she is incapable of any variety or motion.[56]

The lesson the artist draws is central to James's own whole aesthetic as an artist. Time and again in the notebooks and prefaces we hear him exclaim against the "fatal futility of Fact," as he called it in the preface to *The Spoils of Poynton*; he wants only the germ of the story overheard at dinner, not the whole thing, with its merely literal, vulgar details. In fact, a respect for mere accuracy may work against the artist. As the illustrator in "The Real Thing" puts it, "In the deceptive atmosphere of art even the highest respectability may fail of being plastic."[57] For James, who had begun in the 1890s seriously to write plays and to court the audience in front of the proscenium, the artist was a kind of magician, and the "deceptive atmosphere of art" is a phrase that goes a long way to explain the peculiar Jamesian artistry: the control of angle in depicting a scene visually, the control of what the reader knows at any given moment, all to achieve a calculated effect.[58]

James's willingness to acknowledge "the deceptive atmosphere of art" was not an admission that the work of art itself should give away its secrets. Rather, the illusion of life must remain strong and unbroken. By implication, what was not to be tolerated was the mixing of the real and the artificial. In the fullest flowering of the older realism that was congruent with the culture of imitation, the distance between art and life had to be kept clear.

James would doubtless agree with Howells's pedant in shunning the "photographic" as too "commonplace" for art. (By the time he came around to using Alvin Langdon Coburn's photographs for the frontispieces to the New York Edition, James had grown in his appreciation of photography; but even so, Coburn's images, soft enough to harmonize with James's nuanced prose, were specifically not to compete with the text, but were rather to set the stage for the novel's action.)[59] But photography in the 1890s was already beginning to have a significant effect on the way many younger writers thought about literary representation. For the distinction between truth and accuracy that was at the core of the realist's self-definition was inevitably sharpened by comparisons with photography, which in the 1890s was becoming more and more a part of the common consciousness, as the periodical press increasingly reproduced photographs to satisfy the popular taste. Despite the photographers' often licentious practice (see the preceding chapter), the camera still maintained, with the general public and with most writers, its reputation as a completely truthful medium of representation. But precisely its widespread acceptance as a metaphor for truth would give it an ambiguous status as a model for literature.

At one end of the spectrum were those who would concede photography's literal truthfulness and *for that very reason* would deny that it was an art. The necessity for art to idealize nature was a premise of the genteel critics gathered around the *Atlantic*, especially, and this assumption carried well into the twentieth century. As Charles Dudley Warner put it in 1883 (and he stands for many others), "A photograph of a natural object is not art; nor is the plaster cast of a man's face, nor is the bare setting on the stage of an actual occurrence."[60] John Burroughs, who learned much from Emerson's essays and from his friend Walt Whitman, said virtually the same thing twenty years later: "The real itself, however faithfully set forth, has no charm. A photograph is barren; the rudest sketch of the same, seen by a true artist, has far more power to touch and move the soul."[61] (It was in the context of this idealistic conception of art that photographers themselves sought to overcome the presumed barrenness of the medium by emulating painting through a variety of techniques—carefully posing the subject, manipulating the photographic plate in the darkroom, using soft-focus lenses, etc. The result was the romantically impressionistic photography of the Photo-Secessionists.)

At the other end of the spectrum were those who felt that this same factual quality of the photograph was exactly what gave it persuasive exemplary value for fiction: the objectivity of the camera was a kind of middle excluding the extremes of sentimentality and tasteless excess (that is, sexuality), as in Joseph Kirkland's somewhat grandiloquent plea in 1893 for an art that tells only the truth, but "not all the truth," a fiction written under a "starry firmament of illimitable light which the mind of man has discerned and the spectroscope and camera of prose fiction have made available to each of us."[62] Howells, who had all along occupied this middle ground, also invoked the camera as an ideal of neutral observation: Norris's *McTeague*, which he reviewed in 1899, Howells found too brutal in its depiction of life; but by and by, Howells predicted, Norris will put in the "noble and tender and pure and lovely" too, achieving thereby "something of the impartial fidelity of the photograph."[63] This was exactly what he himself was shortly to strive for in his travel book on England, which he called, invoking the new taste, *London Films*, and which he opened with an elaborate analogy between the amateur photographer and the writer who carries his "mental kodak" with him, subsequently serving up to the reader his "photographs" of various scenes.[64]

Though opinion remained divided on whether or not it was a good thing for a work of fiction to be "photographic," by 1900 one meaning of the term had become clear: it meant objective, factual, a faithful delineation of life. And usually urban life was meant. When *Sister Carrie* was published in 1900, it elicited a chorus of agreement on the quality of its realism: it was "written out of real life"; it was "logical and photographic"; with its actual names of streets and businesses, it was "a photograph of life in a large city"; its chief merit lay in its "photographic description"; and so on.[65] The Jamesian illusion of life was giving way to a quality of authenticity that was expressed in terms of the metaphor of the mechanically reproduced image. And the terms were well chosen in one respect at least, for Dreiser had an announced interest in the visual arts, especially photography.

Yet the "objectivity" of *Carrie* was itself of course an illusion. Dreiser's particular slant toward urban description had its visual roots in the Ash Can painters (Everett Shinn was a friend) and in the photography of Alfred Stieglitz, the acknowledged master of the New York Camera Club in the 1890s—about whom Dreiser wrote three magazine articles around the turn of the century.[66] And the peculiar magic of Dreiser's style, as of Stieglitz's, was a synthesis of objective *and* subjective elements. Indeed the basis of Dreiser's admiration for photography was essentially Stieglitz's own principle: the transmutation of a mechanical image into a *personal* impression. (Stieglitz's first book of photographs was titled *Picturesque Bits of New York* [1887].) The photographer, Dreiser wrote, "must catch his own impression, then so manipulate and soften the cold facts of the negative that the concrete manifestation will satisfy" others.[67]

If Dreiser's own depiction of the city in *Sister Carrie* was "photographic," it was so by virtue of just such a dramatic and personal impression of the city, as for example in this description of Broadway, as seen by the excluded Hurstwood at the end of *Carrie*: "This was the hour when the theatres were just beginning to receive their patrons. Fire signs announcing the night's amusements blazed on every hand.

Cabs and carriages, their lamps gleaming like yellow eyes, pattered by. Couples and parties of three and four freely mingled in the common crowd, which poured by in a thick stream, laughing and jesting."[68] There is no attempt to be exhaustively descriptive; rather, details are picked out with a certain haphazard but concretely representative quality—the Fifth Avenue loungers, the great hotels lit up, the night "pulsating with the thoughts of pleasure and exhilaration."[69] It is "objective" description, but colored by an attitude—Hurstwood's isolation—that makes it work as fiction.

A similar subjectivity colors Stephen Crane's prose style, which was also seen as "photographic," and in a sense that offers a final perspective on the period's understanding of photography and on the varieties of illusion encompassed by the notion of realism. What was "photographic" in Crane was not the objectivity or impartiality of his presentation, but on the contrary its power to startle the reader by its vividness. Crane's fidelity to experience seemed revelatory; he was sensationalistic in a way that was itself a sensation, and his treatment of New York life in *Maggie: A Girl of the Streets* held the reader's attention, not only because of the relative novelty of the subject matter but because of the quality of the prose. This was the case for Norris, for example, who did not particularly like *Maggie*, but was much impressed by Crane's genius for description and epigram: "The picture he makes [in *Maggie*] is not a single carefully composed painting, serious, finished, scrupulously studied, but rather scores and scores of tiny flashlight photographs, instantaneous, caught, as it were, on the run."[70] Norris's use of the term "flashlight photograph" alludes to the new magnesium flash-powder, which was used in experiments in the late 1880s by Jacob Riis. (The newspaper report of Riis's first results, published with drawings based on photographs, was called "Flashes from the Slums.") Norris offers a description of Jimmy's truck driving, from *Maggie*, to illustrate his point, but a better passage might be the following: "Eventually they entered a dark region where, from a careening building, a dozen gruesome doorways gave up loads of babies to the street and the gutter . . . Withered persons, in curious postures of submission to something, sat sucking pipes in obscure corners. A thousand odors of cooking food came forth to the street. The building quivered and creaked from the weight of humanity stamping about in its bowels."[71] Whatever is "photographic" about such a passage comes from the widely known photographs of Riis, which were exposing scenes of the other half to the middle class for the first time; but Crane's style clearly goes beyond neutral description to a kind of expressionistic intensity. (And so does Riis's own prose at times in *How the Other Half Lives*.)

Riis would naturally come to mind because of the subject matter in *Maggie*; but the startling vividness of Crane's prose style evoked, for others, a quite different photographer—Eadweard Muybridge, whose experiments in high-speed motion photography were widely known by the 1890s. To Harold Frederic, for example, reviewing *The Red Badge of Courage*, Crane had gone beyond the conventions of literary description in the same way that Muybridge had gone beyond the traditional painter in the depiction of the motion of horses: "At last, along comes a Muybridge, with his instantaneous camera, and shows that the real motion is entirely different."[72] To Frederic, Crane's vivid battlefield descriptions surpassed even first-hand accounts, where the writer was likely to be overwhelmed by his experience. Crane had, of course, no battle experience, and was born several years after the Civil War had ended. He had, however, obviously made the most of his sources, and among them, undoubtedly, was Alexander Gardner's *Photographic Sketch Book of the Civil War*; Timothy O'Sullivan's famous *Harvest of Death*, for example, published in Gardner's *Sketch Book*, surely had made its impression (along with Gardner's prose captions) on the young writer who wrote: "The men saw a ground vacant of fighters. It would have been an empty stage if it were not for a few corpses that lay thrown and twisted into fantastic shapes upon the sward."[73]

Part of the marvel of *The Red Badge of Courage* was that Crane himself had not yet seen battle first-hand at the time he wrote it. His sources were literary and pictorial. Perhaps for this very reason—that Crane's own imagination was tutored by the representations of reality that were everywhere a part of the culture of imitation—Crane more than any other writer of his time raised the question again and again in his writings: How do we learn to see? And that question leads to others: How does culture precondition experience? What makes a true report? How close can a narrator come to his subject? Where does life end and the art begin in constructing the illusion called "realism"? What gives Crane a certain contemporaneity, and at the same time allowed him to break the limits of Jamesian realism, is his implicit preoccupation, throughout his career, with questions like these about the whole process of representation, questions that constitute the problem of realism. In the phases of Crane's career we can see the effort to approach ever closer, in art, to the real thing.

It is clear from Crane's early newspaper sketches, which report on the amusements of the Jersey shore, that the young writer was captivated by the new forms of popular entertainment, including the steam-powered mechanical rides, the tintype galleries, and the camera obscura.[74] In fact, he defined his own work as a series of "sharply outlined pictures, which pass before the reader like a panorama, leaving each its definite impression."[75] But while his own writing may draw some structural inspiration from the visual displays that caught the popular imagination, in other respects Crane stood at some distance from the whirligigs and rocking horses of the amusement parks: "let the people sit and dreamfully rock themselves into temporary forgetfulness," he wrote in an 1894 article on "Coney Island's Failing Days," positioning himself with respect to mass culture in a way that would anticipate many twentieth-century writers.[76] In his own fiction, he was less likely to let the people dream; his effort was directed, rather, toward an exposure of the dangers of the dream, the potential for self-deception, if not self-destruction, in the illusions that coerce mass society. And it is as parables of disillusionment that I want to discuss Crane's fiction.

A closer look at *Maggie* and *The Red Badge of Courage*, together with "The Blue Hotel," reveals Crane's increasingly complex treatment of the problem of preconditioned seeing.[77] *Maggie*, Crane's earliest long fiction, is in some ways his most interesting in this regard because it is least consistent: it is a criticism of melodrama that is itself melodramatic. Hamlin Garland praised it as "the voice of the slums ... written by one who has lived the life," yet Crane had not lived in the city when he first drafted the book, and what we hear most clearly, I think, is the sharply observant voice of the writer, not the voice of the slum.[78]

For Crane makes it quite clear that Maggie is to be seen as a victim of her illusions. Thus in the dastardly bartender Pete, for example, she sees "the ideal man. Her dim thoughts were often searching for far-away lands where the little hills sing together in the morning."[79] And her dream of escaping from the slum life around her is fed further by the plays to which Pete takes her, melodramas in which the heroine is rescued from her "treacherous guardian by the hero with the beautiful sentiments."[80] The appeals of Victorian melodrama, as David Grimsted has shown, were various: the depiction of the reality of evil and the triumph of good; the confirmation of order in the universe; the simultaneous hatred of class distinctions and vicarious identification with the upper class.[81] Maggie is a textbook case, for she responds to all of these appeals, especially to the depiction of the virtuous poor who triumph over the wicked wealthy.

But Maggie also wonders—and here Crane captures beautifully the contradictory appeals of popular culture—if she herself can acquire the "culture and refinement she had seen imitated" on the stage. The process of disillusionment that Maggie undergoes—Pete proves a hollow knight, her dreams of escape come to nothing—is an education in perception that presumably leaves her with no alternative but suicide. Crane judges ironically the appeals of popular drama and the naiveté of an audience for whom the presentation on stage is "transcendental realism"; but if the stage is not "realism" then by implication the novel *Maggie*, which tells these truths, *is* realism.[82]

But what kind of "realism" is this? If melodrama is the realism of the masses, the realism of *Maggie*, one is tempted to say, is the melodrama of an elite audience. For although Crane presumably stated his purpose clearly in inscribing a copy of *Maggie* for his friend Hamlin Garland—to show "that environment is a tremendous thing in the world and frequently shapes lives regardless"—still he solicits our interest in Maggie mainly on the grounds of her uniqueness, not her typicality. Environment is important, yes, and "frequently" shapes lives, yes, but the whole process is particularly noteworthy, Crane implies, when the person being crushed is someone of Maggie's exceptional virtue. For Crane is careful to make Maggie singularly appealing: "She grew to be a most rare and wonderful production of a tenement district, a pretty girl."[83] And Crane was not alone in developing the romantic side of realism. Norris, for example, seeking to enlarge the domestic range of Howellsian realism, urged the writer to find Romance in the realism of urban life. "Look for Romance—the lady of the silken robes and golden crown, our beautiful, chaste maiden of soft voice and gentle eyes—look for her among the vicious ruffians, male and female, of Allen street and Mulberry Bend."[84] (Maggie's robes were not quite silken enough for Howells, who thought *Maggie* "wonderful," but not fit for the parlor table.)[85]

Yet Crane too had his doubts about the suitability of Maggie and her friends to appear at the table of fiction, doubts that are visible in the acrobatic style he employs to keep himself at a distance from them. Whether or not pretty girls are so rare in tenement districts, Crane has a special affection for his heroine and a corresponding contempt for the characters surrounding her.[86] He is at pains to distance himself, by his narrative rhetoric, from the speech of his characters, as in this passage, depicting Pete and Maggie in a saloon:

> He was extremely gracious and attentive. He displayed the consideration of a cultured gentleman who knew what was due. "Say, what's eatin yeh? Bring d'lady a big glass! What use is dat pony?"
>
> "Don't be fresh, now," said the waiter, with some warmth, as he departed.
>
> "Ah, git off d'eart!" said Pete, after the other's retreating form.
>
> Maggie perceived that Pete brought forth all his elegance and all his knowledge of high-class customs for her benefit.[87]

What can one say, except that Crane—for all his attempt to render his subject intimately—superciliously keeps himself (and therefore his reader) at a distance. Whitman of course never read *Maggie*, but in 1889 in conversation with Horace Traubel he spoke against a quality he found in the French and in our own humorists (Bret Harte and Twain), "a tendency I always dislike, never will accept—a superciliousness which seems to hold them from mixing with the event, the fact, they describe . . . as though with the insinuation, 'see how far we are removed from all that—we good gentlemen with our dress suits and parlor accomplishments!' "[88] Certainly the criticism would be apt with respect to *Maggie*, which evinces Crane's anxiety to remove himself from the picture he draws so vividly. Yet in later works Crane moved closer to his subject, and it is to these we turn next.

That shift is evident in the work that suddenly brought Crane major public recognition, *The Red Badge of Courage*, in which the author seems to identify effortlessly with the point of view of his main character, a youth enamored of the adventure of war. But one basic aim of *The Red Badge* is similar to that of *Maggie*: to demonstrate the distance between popular culture and actuality, in this case the grave separation between the heroic storybook ethos of war and the actual experience of it.

The hero, Henry Fleming, enlists in the war fully primed with the expectation of drama and glory: "He had burned several times to enlist. Tales of great movements shook the land. They might not be distinctly Homeric, but there seemed to be much glory in them. He had read of marches, sieges, conflicts, and he had longed to see it all. His busy mind had drawn for him large pictures extravagant in color, lurid with breathless deeds."[89] The war is thus seen by young Fleming as a chance to have a share in a glorious enterprise of the sort he had thought impossible in the humdrum round of modern life, which held the passions in check by the force of education and "firm finance."[90]

What Fleming in fact experiences is the confusion and degradation, the suffering and tedium, the death and disfigurement, of actual combat. *The Red Badge* is the story of a species of psychological trauma that had been largely ignored by previous writers. Even Whitman, whose *Specimen Days* had detailed the suffering of war from the vantage point of the soldier's hospital bedside, had celebrated the heroism of the infantryman on and off the battlefield: "We hear of some poor fighting, episodes, skedaddling on our part. I think not of it. I think of the fierce bravery, the general rule." And again, "courage and scorn of death the rule, exceptions almost none."[91] For Crane, trepidation is the rule, skedaddling his theme. Not surprisingly, *The Red Badge* met with less than enthusiastic response from some former Civil War officers, who considered Fleming a satire on the American soldier.[92] But the reception was otherwise extremely favorable, and the "reality" of the battle descriptions convinced many a veteran that he had served with Crane himself, who was born in 1871.

The Red Badge succeeds as psychological realism where *Maggie* does not, because of Crane's identification with Fleming's point of view. Yet Crane's empathy has its limits, and critics have argued for decades about exactly what those limits are: is Crane sympathetic to Fleming, illustrating the moral growth and greater self-understanding that seem to result from his adventures ("He felt a quiet manhood, nonassertive but of sturdy and strong blood")?[93] Or is Crane detached and ironic at the end of the novel, showing us Fleming's false sense of his own importance, even at the end ("He beheld that he was tiny but not inconsequent to the sun")?[94] And the final line of the book does little to clear up the ambiguity: "Over the river a golden ray of sun came through the hosts of leaden rain clouds." With its dual emphasis on sun and clouds, and its intimation of a divine providence that remains enigmatic, the sentence leaves matters unresolved.[95]

Our capacity for self-deception continued to fascinate Crane; and if he seems problematically comfortable with irony and ambiguity in *The Red Badge*, Crane seems at least to have the ironies under firmer control in the short story, "The Blue Hotel." Like the earlier novels, "The Blue Hotel" contrasts the expectations bred by popular romance —this time stories about the wild West that were feeding the urban imagination—with the actualities of experience: trying to understand the Swede's apparent fear on arriving in Nebraska, one character conjectures, "It seems to me this man has been reading dime novels, and he thinks he's right out in the middle of it—the shootin' and stabbin' and all."[96] Like Maggie and Henry Fleming, the Swede's literary illusions are undercut by experience: the dangerous West of gamblers and killers turns out to be a friendly hotel on the prairie. But the pattern in "The Blue Hotel" differs from the other works in that the Swede does not undergo disillusionment when he ought to. Instead, he pushes the environment to respond to him as he had expected it would, coercing from the docile cardplayers in the hotel a violent response: he accuses young Johnnie of cheating, he beats him in a fistfight and then goes on to celebrate his victory in another hotel, where he provokes an otherwise perfectly civil gambler into stabbing him mortally.

"The Blue Hotel" seems, then, to be about the discrepancy between preconception and experience and about the grave consequences of fulfilling the expectations of one's imagination, of acting in real life as if it were literature. But Crane complicates that simple moral by the ending of the tale, in which the Easterner and the cowboy—witnesses to the original incident in which the Swede accuses Johnnie of cheating—ruminate over the actual events. The Easterner now claims that Johnnie *was* cheating, and that his own refusal to support the Swede makes him—as well as the cowboy and the others—accomplices in his murder. In that case, the Swede's fears of the immoral and lawless West are somewhat justified: he is after all the victim of something more than his imagination. And yet, Crane does not let us settle on this as the final meaning of the story. The cowboy is made, in the last line, to cry out "blindly into this fog of mysterious theory: 'Well, I didn't do anythin', did I?'"[97] The phrase "fog of mysterious theory" restores our uncertainty about guilt and innocence in this instance and recalls to us that whatever the silent complicity of the others, the Swede was still the prime architect of his own demise.

Again and again Crane built his fiction at the epistemological intersection of experience and preconception, testing the adequacy of our various collective representations of reality to the thing itself. This is nowhere done more deliberately and methodically than in "An Experiment in Misery" (1894), which was written around the same time Crane was writing *The Red Badge* and represents a turning point in Crane's effort to achieve authenticity by deliberately closing the distance between author and subject. For the "subject" of the experiment is the narrator himself, the reporter, who at the outset wonders aloud to a friend, as they stand regarding a tramp, how the tramp feels. The homeless of the big cities, the refuse of an industrial system grown callous, had long received journalistic attention of the sort that presumed to report knowingly, from above, on the conditions of the poor; but, as the reporter's friend points out, "You can tell nothing of it unless you are in that condition yourself. It is idle to speculate about it from this distance." Closing the distance becomes the aim of the "experiment," shifting one's safe, middle-class perspective to that of the underclass. And the method the reporter arrives at is to dress up in tattered clothing and set out to live the life of a tramp with only a couple of dimes in his pocket, ready to "discover his point of view or something near it," as the reporter says.[98] Thus the conventions of popular understanding shall be tested by the reality of experience.[99]

But experience of what, exactly? Can the reporter fail to escape the inherent vicariousness of the experience? the inauthenticity of his costume drama? "Shortly after the beginning of this journey the young man felt his liver turn white, for from the dark and secret places of the building there suddenly came to his nostrils strange and unspeakable odours, that assailed him like malignant diseases with wings. They seemed to be from human bodies closely packed in dens; the exhalations from a hundred pairs of reeking lips; the fumes from a thousand bygone debauches; the expression of a thousand present miseries."[100] What we have here—as throughout the story—is the youth's experience of the tramp's life, not the tramp's life itself, as how could it fail to be? And the story is most honest and most convincing when it makes us aware of the observer's viewpoint, as when reporting on the sounds of the sleepers: "But to the youth these were not merely the shrieks of a vision-pierced man: they were an utterance of the meaning of the room and its occupants."[101]

There are really two versions of "An Experiment" to consider. In the original version, which appeared in *The New York Press* on April 22,

1894, Crane supplies the frame I have alluded to earlier—the conversation between the reporter and his friend that provides the occasion
for the experiment in the first place; and he supplies a conclusion as
well, which I shall get to in a moment. But when he published the
piece in *The Open Boat and Other Stories* (1898) he omitted the frame,
leaving us instead with a "story" about a young man who is "going
forth to eat as the wanderer may eat, and sleep as the homeless
sleep."[102] Except for the ambiguously tentative phrasing, there is no
indication in the later version that the young man is not himself one
of the homeless and hungry. And when the story ends, it is with the
youth confessing himself an outcast from society: his eyes look out
guiltily from beneath his lowered hat, as he wears "the criminal expression that comes with certain convictions."[103]

Without the frame we are offered a tale from *within* the urban
maelstrom, a fiction with a strongly expressed sense of the alienation
of the bottom dog. With the frame, we have an experiment in shifting
perspective, an epistemological inquiry that unfolds a schema for the
realist enterprise, an ironic presentation of the place of the imagination in modern society. And with the frame, the youth's convictions
seem more honestly tentative at the end: he is less willing to claim a
general truth as the result of his masquerade. His friend (from the
start of the frame) asks him whether he has discovered the tramp's
point of view, and the youth replies: "I don't know that I did, . . . but
at any rate I think mine own has undergone a considerable alteration."[104] There is inevitably a touch of the absurd to Crane's framing
premise: the youth who would be a tramp goes to the "studio of an
artist friend, who, from his store, rigged him out in an aged suit and a
brown derby hat that had been made long years before."[105] Nevertheless this costume fantasy represents a significant shift in the nature of
realism: Crane's youth might have borrowed his clothes from the artist in Henry James's "The Real Thing," but the artist himself in the
James story would never have worn them. And here is a difference
between the realism of James (and his generation) and the realism of
Crane (and his): both stories were written within a year or two of
each other, but they conceive of the problem of representation in
completely opposed ways: for James and his artist, the studio is a
place to learn to see, and art is a matter of creating an illusion. Crane
moves outside the studio and into the street, and thus demonstrates
the new conditions for seeing that a new realism required.

But pushing realism out of the studio and into the street was not without risks for the realist. Putting himself consistently on the line as a reporter, fusing his life and his art, Crane nearly lost both while covering a story about running guns to Cuba, when the steamer *Commodore* was wrecked off the coast of Florida in 1897. Following his rescue, Crane wrote a "factual" news account of the event which leaves off where "The Open Boat" takes up. One of Crane's most famous pieces, "The Open Boat" is subtitled, "*A Tale Intended to be after the Fact: Being the Experience of Four Men from the Sunk Steamer* Commodore"; and the words "tale" and "fact" should alert us to the mixed company in "The Open Boat." Whatever its genre, Crane's narrative voice here is as free from irony as it ever will be: "It would be difficult to describe the subtle brotherhood of men that was here established on the seas. No one said that it was so. No one mentioned it. . . . And after this devotion to the commander of the boat, there was this comradeship, that the correspondent, for instance, who had been taught to be cynical of men, knew even at the time was the best experience of his life."[106] As an early instance of what we would now call "non-fiction journalism" "The Open Boat" takes Crane's experimental approach to its ultimate conclusion: the early investigations of the discrepancy between melodrama and reality end in a real-life melodrama that is no costume-drama (as "An Experiment in Misery" might be called), but a mathematical limit of realism. The problem of Howells's grasshopper—whether to represent it with a tried and tested cardboard model or to depict it more literally, or even photograph it—has been solved: the artist has become the grasshopper.

One last tale by Crane might be mentioned here as a kind of coda to this discussion, for it is a satire on the fashion of extreme realism in the theatre that is also a reflection on the danger of crossing the thin line between artifice and reality, a warning to the realist imagination to observe the prudent limits of illusion. The macabre "Manacled" was published in 1900 and is about an actor who, in pursuit of ever greater realism, has himself manacled on stage with real manacles when the role calls for it. One day a fire breaks out in the theater, and as (real) flames engulf the building, everyone successfully flees—the whole cast and audience—all except the actor himself, who must hobble, still wearing his locked manacles toward the exit. Alas, he dies in the effort; yet to the actor's mind, habituated to the creation of illusion, the fire is not quite really real: "What a fool I was not to foresee this!" he exclaims near the end. "I shall have Rogers furnish manacles of papier-mâché to-morrow."[107] Stories of naifs rushing up to rescue the stage heroine or otherwise mistaking the actions of the drama for the realities of life have long been a part of the Western mimetic tradition.[108] Crane turns the proposition around and shows us an audience making no mistake about the reality of the fire, but rather an actor—an artist—who has fatally confused art and life, who has substituted reality for illusion, real thing for artifice. (It is as if, following the close call of the *Commodore* shipwreck, Crane himself was drawing a new lesson about the possibly dire consequences of too close an engagement with the subject of one's fiction.)

In an interview with William Dean Howells in 1894, the young Crane abruptly concluded by asking the master impatiently what the future of realism would be: would realism "capture things," as had seemed possible just recently, or—as seemed to Crane—was there an imminent counter wave of genteel repression, of sentimentality. In Crane's report, Howells has the last word—a word of assent to the fears of the young writer thus interviewing him: "What you say is true. I have seen it coming. . . . I suppose we shall have to wait."[109] Realism eventually regained its momentum, and would indeed come to dominate the popular midstream of American fiction in the twentieth century. But, ironically, to a generation of modernists and iconoclasts in the teens and 1920s, Howells, the champion of realism, would come to symbolize the genteel restraints from which the writer must free himself.

Meanwhile, Crane himself, after his death in 1900 at the age of 29, passed rapidly from public view. But a series of acts of critical recognition beginning in the 1920s made him, along with Twain, among the most influential of the realists, especially for the generation of Hemingway and Anderson. What saved Crane was the intensity of his vision, which was based on a penetrating recognition of how culture can shape our seeing, and on how the writer can break through to a representation of the real thing, thus closing the distance between art and life. A new generation of writers in the twentieth century would in effect follow Crane's experiments in looking at the heterogeneity of American society and would begin to ask of the previously unrecognized elements of the population the question that never really had occurred to the genteel culture: "What is *your* culture to me?" They would also follow Crane in attempting to change the work of art from an artful illusion of reality to a more intense encounter with the real thing itself; in the process they would take Howells's grasshopper and examine it keenly under the modernist microscope.

Part Three

INVENTING AUTHENTICITY

INTRODUCTION

*I*n turning now to the twentieth century, my interest lies in the counter-response on the part of many artists and intellectuals to the culture of imitation previously explored. But I want to reiterate unmistakably that the culture of imitation that was at the core of nineteenth-century culture remained (and remains, even now) a significant component of twentieth-century culture, alive and well in the various popular arts that assumed an aesthetic of realism and replication. Thus popular literature still adhered, for many decades, to the aesthetic canons and world-view of sentimental realism, as did the narrative plots of Hollywood movies and, after World War II, television soap operas; European "aristocratic" models still prevailed in the material environment, with their elaborate, molded decorative embellishments signifying the consumer's putative social status; and types and genres remained in vogue in photography, especially in advertising, where stereotypes of the nuclear family, of courtship, of social class distinctions, prevailed in the print media and, subsequently, in television. In short, the culture of imitation has been well entrenched in twentieth-century America. At the same time, however, a new culture was developing in the early decades of the century—one that aimed at the creation of a kind of authenticity deemed otherwise lacking in the culture of imitation that maintained its old grip during this period. That new culture was continuous with the impulse of the younger generation of realists in the 1890s, but the new culture of authenticity derived its form more specifically as a response to the vast consumer culture that was implacably taking shape in the early decades of the twentieth century.

To describe that consumer culture, one must begin with the pervasiveness of the machine and all its ramifications. The expansion and refinement of energy sources like oil, coal, and hydroelectric power, coupled with the advent of new building technologies, together with the widespread application of mass production methods, resulted in a society whose economic base and visible appearance were being radically transformed. Industrial photographs from the end of the nineteenth century and the beginning of the twentieth often unwit-

141

tingly reveal the growing incongruity between the human form and the scale of the new machine-made world: the engineer, the mechanic, the logger, the miner, the construction laborer, stands on his bridge, or locomotive, or elevated rail line, or building, dwarfed by the stark immensity of the constructed thing. And the abstract force of the machine was embodied, in more enigmatic terms, in the many photographs of massive generators, dynamos, giant presses, huge drills, and other machines for the manufacturing of things, that came increasingly to public exposure after the turn of the century, advertising the might of modern industry. The power of the machine was creative, but it seemed evident especially after World War I that it was also destructive, for its brute power had figured so importantly in the winning of the war and in the enormous casualties and suffering inflicted. In both negative and positive terms, the machine became, in the early twentieth century, of overwhelming economic and symbolic significance, and the artist and intellectual, one way or another, had to come to terms with it.[1]

In the nineteenth century, the machine was used predominantly to create consumer objects that enthusiastically mimicked handcrafted things (furniture, household objects, clothing, and accessories); in the twentieth century it was used increasingly to manufacture objects that were themselves machines—telephones, phonographs, coffee makers, toasters, vacuum cleaners, and, for children, electric trains and talking dolls. To take just one example, over the period from 1900 to 1920, the number of telephones increased from about 1 million to 7.5 million, and by 1930 it had risen to over 20 million. But at the center of the United States economy, it became increasingly evident, was a machine that was not originally an American invention, but that was soon modified and adapted to American conditions—the automobile. Ford's Model T, brought out in 1908, totaled approximately a half million sales by 1916, but by 1927, when production ceased—to be replaced by the Model A—15 million cars had rolled off the assembly line. And not just cars were being sold during these years. A whole way of life went along with them—roads, roadside services, travel industries, vacation industries, petroleum industries, new habits of commuting, new residential patterns, new social habits, new sexual habits. An industrial technology adept at the mechanical reproduction of things and visual media became even more expert in the early decades of the century, creating the base of a vast economy with a

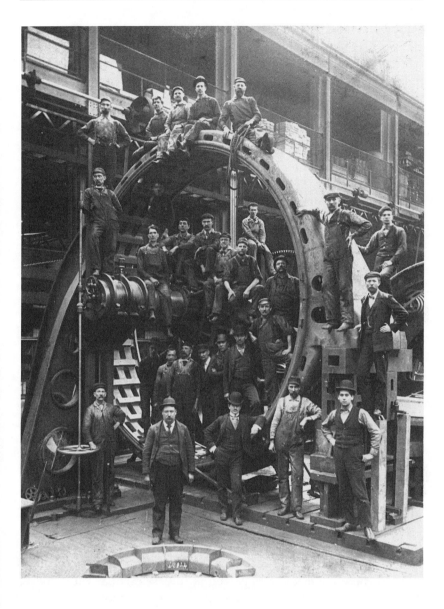

Employees of Westinghouse Electric, ca. 1900
(Courtesy of Library Company of Philadelphia)

common denominator of popular taste that grew as fast as the power of advertisement could create it.

Pictures had been used in advertising since the 1880s, but beginning in the 1890s photographs—with the evident appeal of their "realism" and "sincerity"—were used more and more.[2] As Edward Steichen, himself a leading commercial photographer during the 1920s and 1930s put it, "the frank objectivity of the photograph found favor with the businessman and with his client, the public."[3] In many such photographs, the product itself was singularly featured, bathed in dramatic studio lighting and viewed from an angle that emphasized its abstract design. Whereas, in the late nineteenth century, an attractive window display was marked by the sheer quantity of goods on view (as the pages of the sales catalogue were abundantly furnished with print and drawings), advertisers after 1910 began to move away from the mixed display toward the more particularized line of goods. "High class goods," as one trade writer argued in 1911, "cannot be crowded in a window."[4] For it is evident that the way objects were treated mirrored social relations: only in the pawn shops were goods crowded in uncomfortable disorder, jostling one another as in an urban tenement. Meanwhile, print advertising featured less copy and more white space, as the consumer's individual connection with the object was emphasized.

The world of the ads was a paradise in which things were more real than in our everyday world, yet that "reality" had to be guaranteed over and over again. Coca Cola's famous ad campaign of the late 1960s and 1970s—"It's the Real Thing"—had an earlier wide visibility in a campaign in the early 1940s; but the concept itself goes back at least to 1908, when the ad copy urged the consumer, "Get the genuine."[5] Scanning the ads of the early decades of the century, one repeatedly encounters products that offer themselves as some more intense experience of themselves, a more emphatic, more "real" version of their virtues: cigars imported from Cuba "are real cigars"; "The Durham-Duplex is a real razor"; Faultless Pajamas will give you "real sleep"; the Wellington Pipe offers "a good smoke with a real pipe"; Kaffee Hag coffee is "Not a substitute—but *Real Coffee* that lets you sleep"; Clicquot Club is "A really dry Ginger Ale"; Fleischmann's Gin is "The Real American Mixer"; Hires has "real Root Juices"; Vermont Maid is "Syrup with that real Maple Sugar Flavor." And indeed the "reality" of American products increases through the 1940s to the

Coca Cola advertisement, 1942
(Courtesy of Coca Cola Company, Atlanta, Georgia)

point where consumers have to be reassured that virtually everything they are buying is real: real tobacco, real noodle soup, real lemon meringue pie, real orangeade, real medicine, real flavor, real cake, real cold tablet.[6]

It was as if there were some defect in everyday reality that had to be remedied by the more authentic reality of the object to be consumed. The arts would attempt to remedy the defect of "reality" in complex ways that shall be described, placing them in a subtle dialectic with the consumer culture. On the level of popular culture and advertising, the need was addressed in terms of a restless consumption of material goods, forever falling short of ultimate satisfaction. In the words of one writer in the early 1920s, there was a gap between "our own poor weary world of reality" and the blissfully perfect reality of the ads—"a world of well regulated bowels, cornless feet, and unblemished complexions, a world of perfectly fitting clothes, completely equipped kitchens, and always upright and smiling husbands."[7] But the gap could be bridged by the act of consumption, and the function of the world of advertising and the media was to make the passage from here to there an intensely desired one.

The consumer lived nervously on the edge of this world, which was constantly liable to reverse itself into a false image of itself; as if shams and frauds were flooding the marketplace, threatening the authenticity of the consumer's paradise. Only in English, as Leo Spitzer has written in a classic essay on advertising, "are there so many prefixes which tend to unmask false values: pseudo-, sham-, make-believe, makeshift-, mock-, would-be-, fake-, phony-, semi-, near-, baloney-, synthetic-, etc."[8] And with good reason: the ersatz object was a staple of the consumer paradise.

Upton Sinclair gave a vivid, if somewhat paranoid, vision of such a world in *The Jungle* (1905), a world where "The storekeepers plastered up their windows with all sorts of lies to entice you; the very fences by the wayside, the lampposts and telegraph poles, were pasted over with lies." It is a world where the unwary—especially those newly arrived in the country—were at the mercy of the unscrupulous: "How could they find out that their tea and coffee, their sugar and flour, had been doctored; that their canned peas had been colored with copper salts, and their fruit jams with aniline dyes?"[9] Sinclair's turn of the century critique, a characteristic rhetorical admixture of anger and precise information, anticipates the more elaborate description of commercial legerdemain offered by Edmund Wilson in the fuller flush of the advertising culture, when he epitomized the new American couple, Mr. and Mrs. X, and the world of advertising they had come to inhabit: "It is a formidable undertaking," Wilson wrote, "to persuade people to invest . . . in health-builders made of cheese, fat-reducers containing cascara, coffee made of dried peas, gelatine made of glue, olive oil made of cottonseed, straw hats composed of wood shavings, sterling silver that is lead cement, woolen blankets, silk stockings and linen sheets all actually woven of cotton, sealskin coats that are really muskrat"—and the list goes on. "Mr. and Mrs. X," Wilson concluded, "will grow more and more to resemble the men and women depicted in the advertisements, insipid, fatuously cheerful, two-dimensional, spic and span."[10]

But no reaction to the consumer paradise was more extreme, perhaps, than Henry Miller's, when he looked back, in *Tropic of Capricorn* (1939), on the years before he went to Paris in 1930 and described the peculiar misery of American prosperity: "All department stores are symbols of sickness and emptiness, but Bloomingdale's is my special sickness, my incurable malady. . . . In Bloomingdale's I fall apart completely: I dribble onto the floor, a helpless mess of guts and bones and cartilage. There is the smell, not of decomposition, but of misalliance. Man, the miserable alchemist, has welded together, in a million forms and shapes, substances and essences which have nothing in common."[11] Whatever lightness of tone Wilson could muster has turned sour and grotesque by dint of nearly a decade of the Depression.

Behind the creation of the putative consumer paradise was the reality of the factory, and there, the heroic image of the body that Whitman had constructed as a model for his countrymen—the body electrically charged with sensuality, graceful in its movements, creative in its labors—was of little relevance. Not Whitman, but Frederick Winslow Taylor and the system of scientific management guided the factory manager. As the body accommodated itself to the new demands of the industrial world, the border between human motion and automatic motion became increasingly blurred. We have a glimpse into the new strangeness of this manufacturing world, in a description, around the turn of the century, of a factory in which wax records are being produced for speaking dolls. A visitor observes that each of the girls in the factory has a stall where she speaks into a recording device the words to be repeated by the doll, "and the jangle produced by a number of girls simultaneously repeating 'Mary had a little lamb,' 'Jack and Jill,' 'Little Bo-peep,' and other interesting stories, is beyond description. These sounds united with the sounds of the phonographs themselves when reproducing the stories make a veritable pandemonium."[12]

How close the order of the factory was to a kind of chaos was made even more clear in Chaplin's *Modern Times*, where Charlie, the worker on the assembly line who has been fashioned into a mindless moving component of the production process, would become a symbol of twentieth-century experience. The stylized imagery of the film might make us forget the more serious point, that only in his madness, which follows his descent into the inner gears of the machine, does Charlie regain the spontaneous, dancelike freedom of the body. William Dean Howells had had a premonition of these possibilities when, at the Philadelphia Centennial, he had stood and stared at the huge and powerful Corliss engine, and at the idle engineer at its side, oiling the thing: "This prodigious Afreet is his slave who could crush him past all semblance of humanity with his lightest touch. It is, alas! what the Afreet has done to humanity too often, where his strength has superseded men's industry."[13]

If factory workers were seeming less and less distinguishable from the objects they were producing, the consumer was also making an awkward adjustment between the body and material things, an adjustment, or maladjustment, that gradually found expression in a new kind of comedy of objects in the twentieth century. Buster Keaton was the popular embodiment of this maladjustment, raising ineptitude to the level of comic ballet; his short of 1922, for example, *The Electric House*, demonstrated how many things could go wrong at once in the new, artificial environment, and how close to chaos was the new order of things. Meanwhile Rube Goldberg, beginning in the early years of the century, offered cartoon readers a similar new kind of comedy, exploring the borderline between order and chaos in his extravagant devices that combined animal instinct, machine design, and the operations of chance to effect some dubiously practical end. Keaton and Goldberg were anticipating in their zaniness the lighter side of what would become a staple of sociological theory: industrial civilization, said Marcuse, "transforms the object world into an extension of man's mind and body."[14]

Yet the perceived result of this increasingly mechanized environment is visible in an image that recurs in the writing of the teens and 1920s, the image of a connection broken, a distance opening up between men and nature, between men and the world: T. S. Eliot's "Gerontion" complains, sitting amidst the detritus of world civilizations, "I have lost my sight, smell, hearing, taste, and touch." And William Carlos Williams proposes a similar diagnosis for American culture, writing in *In the American Grain* (1925) that behind the miraculous "energy that goes into inventions here," was a "fear that robs the emotions; a mechanism to increase the gap between touch and thing, not to have a contact."[15] As the abstract lessons of the new sciences of uncertainty and relativity were infiltrating popular consciousness, a feeling emerged of a growing distance between the senses and the "real world" whose physical structure seemed to defy our sensorium. By the time these sentiments passed to Nathanael West, at the beginning of the Depression, they had evolved into a kind of self-parody, as in the mad schoolboy's diary that Balso Snell discov-

Trade photograph, advertising permanent-wave machine, ca. 1920
(Courtesy of Library Company of Philadelphia)

ers in West's satire, *The Dream Life of Balso Snell* (1931), which puts the case most clearly (and with morbid excess): "Reality! Reality! If I could only discover the Real. A Real that I could know with my senses. A Real that would wait for me to inspect it as a dog inspects a dead rabbit."[16]

The lack of "reality" was felt especially keenly by those writers who focused on the city, or on the pervasive environment of advertising. Lewis Mumford, for example, surveying urban culture at the start of the 1920s, declared pessimistically that "the highest achievements of our material civilization—and at their best our hotels, our department stores, and our Woolworth towers are achievements—count as so many symptoms of its spiritual failure." And his vision of the urban commercial thoroughfare, with its sad flaneurs, constitutes an epitome of the twentieth-century malaise: "Up and down these second-hand Broadways, from one in the afternoon until past ten at night, drifts a more or less aimless mass of human beings, bent upon extracting such joy as is possible from the sights in the windows, the contacts with other human beings, the occasional or systematic flirtations, and the risks and adventures of purchase."[17] In what seems a conscious allusion to Whitman's great flow of Broadway traffic, with its promise of a prosperous democratic civilization, Mumford depicts a commercial landscape become a Waste Land. What Mumford had given general expression to, Dos Passos embodied in the individual voice of his autobiographical narrator in "The Camera Eye" of *U.S.A.*, who once again invokes Whitman. We see the "Eye" narrator walking the streets, "inquiring of Coca-Cola signs Lucky Strike ads pricetags in storewindows scraps of overheard conversations stray tatters of newsprint yesterday's headlines sticking out of ashcans," looking for a formula in action and speech that will eliminate the civilization of the dollar and restore the "storybook democracy" of Whitman.[18]

The felt distance between people and the world was a product not only of the fabricated material environment, but of the information environment as well—movies, photography, newspapers—with its increasingly important function as mediator of experience. In one of the earliest serious studies of the cinema, *The Art of the Moving Picture* (1915), Vachel Lindsay wrote that "moving picture nausea is already taking hold of numberless people, even when they are in the purely pagan mood." They were victims, Lindsay said, of "photoplay delirium tremens" and the solution was escape to the outdoors.[19] Yet the outdoors, according to the Congregationalist minister and popular healer Gerald Stanley Lee, was no solution either: "I find that the machines about me everywhere have made most people very strange and pathetic in the woods," he wrote in his synoptic, impressionistic *Crowds* (1913); "They cannot sit by brooks, many of them; and when they come out to the sky, it looks to them like some mere, big, blue lead roof up over their lives."[20] If the real world had thus turned into its simulacrum, the movies had helped foster the condition. As the silent era was giving way to a whole new set of talking conventions, Elmer Rice constructed a thoroughgoing spoof of Hollywood silent conventions in which the distance between reality and convention was the repeated source of satiric barbs: "When the dawn came (with its customary panoramic effects and its routine enlargement of birds and the young of domestic animals), I crept softly out of the cottage, and repaired to the barn."[21]

The psychology dominating the twentieth-century consumer culture was most acutely analyzed during the 1920s by Walter Lippmann, who, in *Public Opinion* (1922), argued that belief was founded in modern society on opinions created by the technological media. Relying upon a constructivist psychology drawn in part from John Dewey and William James, Lippmann's premise was that "most facts in consciousness seem to be partly made. A report is the joint product of the knower and known, in which the role of the observer is always selective and usually creative." We do not, in other words, see things "directly"; we see them and remember them according to our conditioning, and what we see consequently are conventional, pre-formed images that we impose on the real world. Thus in the mind of the public, "Real space, real time, real numbers, real connections, real weights are lost. The perspective and the background and the dimensions of action are clipped and frozen in the stereotype." And the prime agents in creating our stereotypes, Lippmann argued, are the mass media, especially the visual reproductions of the camera and the motion picture that had come to dominate the public fictions of entertainment and information. "Photographs have the kind of authority over imagination to-day," Lippmann wrote, "which the printed word had yesterday, and the spoken word before that. They seem utterly real. They come, we imagine, directly to us without human meddling, and they are the most effortless food for the mind conceivable. . . . The shadowy idea becomes vivid; your hazy notion, let us say, of the Ku Klux Klan, thanks to Mr. Griffiths, takes vivid shape when you see the Birth of a Nation."[22] It would not be long before Studs Lonigan and his friend Pat would would sit in the darkened movie house in the final volume of Farrell's *Studs Lonigan* trilogy, watching newsreels with disbelief and indifference until at last the gangster movie comes on the screen: "Now we'll get the real stuff," Pat says.[23] The fiction of the newsreels has yielded its place to the more intense, more involving, more credible fiction of the crime movie. The "reality" of the screen fiction has replaced the reality of experience.

What was at stake in defining thus what was "real" and what was "unreal" was the value structure (as much as the ontological one) of American culture. The supposed arbiters of taste and value in the culture—the genteel editors and the university academics who had already made a stand against realism—had grown remote from the new centers of power, industry, and the media. They could only observe mordantly, or grotesquely, or—as in the case of philosopher George Santayana—wanly, the crisis at hand: "The truth is that one-half of the American mind, that not occupied intensely in practical affairs, has remained, I will not say high-and-dry, but slightly becalmed," Santayana wrote in his famous essay, "The Genteel Tradition in American Philosophy" (1911).

> It has floated gently in the backwater, while, alongside, in invention and industry and social organization the other half of the mind was leaping down a sort of Niagara Rapids. This division may be found symbolized in American architecture: a neat reproduction of the colonial mansion—with some modern comforts introduced surreptitiously—stands beside the skyscraper. The American Will inhabits the skyscraper; the American Intellect inhabits the colonial mansion. The one is the sphere of the American man; the other, at least predominantly, of the American woman. The one is all aggressive enterprise; the other is all genteel tradition.[24]

In the chemistry of the genteel tradition, Emerson's vitality had grown ossified, and was even being credited with having generated the split in American culture that so many intellectuals were worrying about. (Waldo Frank: "Emerson supplied the dualism which our material obsession needed to survive.")[25] The remaining nineteenth-century sources of renewal—Whitman, William James—would be left for a new generation of artists and intellectuals to repossess and make over into a living culture.

If indeed they could. For Santayana's critique—anticipated by Henry James's distinction between an uptown culture of the arts and a downtown culture of business—reflected a society in which the artist and intellectual felt increasingly estranged, his power to define "reality" usurped by the forces of capital and commerce. Yet as the sense of a culture divided between the practical life of commerce and the spiritual pursuit of beauty pervaded the intellectual climate in the first decades of the new century, a number of artists and intellectuals resolved to make whole the split.

Perhaps the most influential formulation of the problem—and of its solution—lay in Van Wyck Brooks's 1915 volume, *America's Coming-of-Age*. Using terms from the vernacular, Brooks distinguished between two opposing extremes in American life, extremes that, in his argument, had existed from early on—the "highbrow" and the "lowbrow." The contrast offered a powerful descriptive tool for analyzing what was wrong with America:

> What side of American life is not touched by this antithesis? What explanation of American life is more central or more illuminating? In everything one finds this frank acceptance of twin values which are not expected to have anything in common: on the one hand, a quite unclouded, quite unhypocritical assumption of transcendent theory ("high ideals"), on the other a simultaneous acceptance of catchpenny realities. Between university ethics and business ethics, between American culture and American humour, between Good Government and Tammany, between academic pedantry and pavement slang, there is no community, no genial middle ground.

Brooks's formulation would determine the agenda of his own criticism of American letters in the years that followed, and it would significantly shape Lewis Mumford and others as they too sought to analyze what was usable in the American past.[26]

For Brooks—as later for Mumford—what was needed was a unity of cultural expression. The split between "highbrow" and "lowbrow" must be resolved by our finding, both as individuals and as a society, a middle ground that united these two extremes of American culture. "Where is all that is real, where is personality and all its works, if it is not essentially somewhere, somehow, in some not very vague way, between?"[27] For Brooks did not want to suppress the "lowbrow" element, or improve and elevate it into the province of "true" culture, as had Charles Dudley Warner. Brooks was picking up on a receptivity toward the street that had already been evident in the realists of the 1890s, but now, for Gilbert Seldes, E. E. Cummings, and others, was becoming an even more important component of American civilization. For the new commercial culture had an indisputable vitality, and in retrospect it is impossible to imagine the Modernist arts without it; the popular culture of twentieth-century industrialism—movies, cartoons, jazz, skyscrapers, advertising—provided a transfusion of energy and a handbook of rhythms and forms for the artists who were breaking with the outworn traditions of the genteel culture.[28]

And indeed there was a seeming paradox in the artist's position vis-à-vis modern industrial culture. On the one hand the machine was the source of the anomie, the distancing from "reality" that was so pervasively sensed; yet on the other hand, the industrial vernacular civilization that was evolving in the twentieth century offered an aesthetic excitement and a variety of popular forms that energized the vocabulary of the arts. The machine could even be envisioned as the foundation for a more egalitarian society, as in the work of the designers and architects who sought its rational adaptation to the needs of a mass society. Distinguishing between these two aspects of the machine civilization—its deleterious social effects vs. its exciting aesthetic and utopian possibilities—was precisely the problem for many artists and intellectuals in the early decades of the twentieth century.

For this reason, Brooks's formulation of the problem was especially persuasive, for it seemed to sum up the dilemma, and the challenge, of the time. The dilemma was that the artist and intellectual had indeed, as Santayana suggested, come to seem irrelevant, recessive, floating gently in the backwater, as he put it. And the challenge for the American artist who would come to terms with his time and not simply rely on nineteenth-century formulas, was to confirm, in the arts, a kind of authenticity that was contemporary, connected with the energy of twentieth-century civilization (which was a technological energy) and yet an authenticity that was separate from the social and personal distortions of business and commercial values.

Yet, significantly, for all the striking out for some new thing that would be fully commensurate with the twentieth century's newness, the artist felt the need to connect with a tradition of creation that derived from American conditions, American materials, and an idealized American political ethos. Especially during the Depression, when the dislocations of the present seemed overwhelming, a part of the contemporary impulse, a part of the maturity the American artist wanted to claim, involved establishing a lineage, connecting with a past that seemed a source of stability and value. So that when Harold Rugg, for example, praised Alfred Stieglitz in the celebratory volume of 1934, *America and Alfred Stieglitz,* he did so in terms that consciously set the photographer in the tradition of the arts generally in America, looking back to Emerson, Whitman, and Sullivan: "These men also strove to create the tradition of the American thing. They tried to visualize the unique indigenous American person."[29]

It is this effort in the arts to come to terms with the technological and commercial reality of American civilization, while defining an aesthetic of authenticity that was often deliberately subversive of the culture's practical values, that I turn to in the following chapters. There were heroic models of authenticity standing all around the artist in the city—the skyscrapers, the bridges, the dynamos—but insofar as they were products of a commercial civilization that eroded the individual's power, they were ambiguous symbols, at once heroic and menacing. The culture of authenticity that was aimed at by the artists who were addressing the problem consciously was integrally based on the machine, but in a cautious, almost circumspect way. At the risk of oversimplifying and amalgamating tendencies that were not ever codified as such, one might define the culture of authenticity in the early twentieth century as one that would restore, through the work of art, a lost sense of "the real thing." In more specific terms, it sought to reconnect the worker and the thing made, and yet celebrate the positive virtues of the machine; it would affirm social values that allowed the individual his or her development while affirming also a community of individuals; it would be based on a functional articulation of parts to whole and simplicity of design, yet it would be complex and subtle; it would eschew unnecessary ornamentation, yet it would value the work of the hand; it was progressive in its orientation to the future, yet founded on a past that was defined in "American" terms. In short, it was a kind of balancing act, an effort at cultural synthesis, and fraught accordingly with certain irreconcilable tensions. Many of the artists and intellectuals I consider in the following three chapters offered themselves as guiding lights of our culture— picking up where Whitman had left off—but for the most part they were standing outside the mainstream of American popular culture as it flowed through the marketplace, and their relationship to the great public was to some degree a vigorous and imaginative, but disappointed, courtship.

I want to begin, in the following chapters, by examining the effort to confront the challenge of the machine in the areas of architecture and design, where the possibility of shaping the material environment was most tantalizing; then I want to explore the twentieth-century vocabulary of photography and its pursuit of the real thing, which was located between the spheres of art, commerce, and propaganda; and finally I want to examine the effort by three literary artists—each of them influenced in varying degrees by photography or by the whole aura of technological civilization—to create a modern literature of authenticity and restore the Whitmanesque patrimony to our prodigal culture.

FIVE

The Real Thing
and the
Machine-made World

$\mathcal{D}$uring the first decades of the twentieth century, the city changed in ways that were beyond the imagination of the nineteenth century: new neighborhoods expanded rapidly to encompass more and more space, as trolley and elevated train lines connected outlying regions to the inner cities; simultaneously, buildings—equipped with elevators—soared to a height that left the nineteenth-century walk-up structures far below; meanwhile, underneath the city, layers of tunnels crisscrossed one another, providing routes for trains, subways, and the myriad other wires, cables, and conduits that compose the infrastructure of the modern city. Underlying many of these changes were new technologies of manufacture, new forms of factory organization, and new kinds of energy, including a rapidly increasing system of electrification, manifest not only in the streetcars and streetlights of the city, but within the household as well—in the form of vacuum cleaners, irons, lighting fixtures, telephones, and, beginning around 1920, radios and refrigerators. Meanwhile, outside the home, and outside the city, roads were being constructed to carry a volume of automobiles that increased exponentially. Mechanization was pervading every sphere of American life, producing an expanding world of greater speed and greater comfort, a world of exhilarating change.

Yet the exhilaration of the new machine age brought with it, inevitably, a note of anxiety that is heard occasionally amid the general chorus of enthusiasm. Consider, for example, a passage like the following from the volume, *Crowds: A Moving-picture of Democracy*, written for a popular audience in 1913 by the minister and health advocate Gerald Stanley Lee: "What is the thing, the real thing in the Hand-made World, that fills me with pride and joy, and that I cannot and will not give up? . . . And what is it in the new Machine-made

World which, in spite of the splendid joy, a rough new, wild religion there is in it, keeps daily filling me as I go past machines with this contradictory obstinate dread of them?"[1] Lee's question acutely sums up the misgivings that lay behind many other meditations on the machine. And the more the world was filled with machine-made things, the more questions were generated regarding the impact of the new technologies on daily life and work: would the machine, for example, support traditional values, or utterly destroy them? Would it liberate the artist and designer, or make them obsolete in the face of engineering and science? Would its powers of fabrication be used to transform raw materials into simulacra of foreign cultures, or would a form of expression develop that would be representative of indigenous American culture—assuming there was such a thing? The machine's power to shape the material environment was ineluctable, and its example was both inspiring and daunting.

Looking at the interconnected areas of architecture and design, where the effects of the machine are most visible, I want to explore the pursuit of an ideal of design based on a supposed "right" use of the machine, an ideal that would correct the earlier culture of imitation, with its misuse of the machine to mimic the work of the craftsman, and establish instead a more authentic, more real use of materials in conformity with honest principles of construction. These values come out of the late nineteenth-century Arts and Crafts movement, which reaches its fullest public expression in the early decades of the twentieth century in the work and career of Gustav Stickley, and it is with Stickley that I begin. Though Stickley's own influence had waned by the mid-teens, his ideas took on an even more complex elaboration in the work of Lewis Mumford, who was influential in establishing the importance, for the modern period, of Louis Sullivan and Frank Lloyd Wright. But the tension between the machine as a democratic force—the foundation of a culture of authenticity—and the machine as an instrument to realize the goals of industrial capitalism remains constant, especially in the work of the great industrial designers of the 1930s, which culminates in the 1939 World's Fair. By the start of World War II, the goal of a popular, machine-based consumer culture that retains its ties to the craft tradition is only partially realized, most notably in the work of Russel Wright. That the goal of such a synthesis remains a persistent thread in American material culture of the early twentieth century is itself significant evidence of how cultural values condition and modify technological implementation, and of how intertwined the effects of ideas and of material conditions are upon one another.

Gustav Stickley's importance to the cultural historian lies not only in the fact that his furniture surpasses in quality any other made in the Arts and Crafts style in America; it lies at least as much in his role as a publicist for a philosophy of design and living that was widely influential during the first decades of the century.[2] Through a variety of forms, Stickley succeeded in putting before the public a total philosophy of design, social ethics, and education that offered a critique of mass culture at the same time that it attempted to become a part of and to change mass culture. Reacting against the excesses of the Victorian household and looking forward to the greater austerities of the modern period, Stickley is a major transitional figure whose importance we have only recently begun to estimate; and he is especially interesting in the present context, for while he articulated an ideal of simplification and craftsmanship, he yet affirmed the place of the machine in modern production.

To Stickley, household furnishings were part of a larger program to express and meet the needs of American culture, and his influence was exercised through the printed word as much as through the wooden chair: from 1901 until 1916, Stickley published a magazine called *The Craftsman* that served as a vehicle for articulating an integrated philosophy of arts, society, housing, urban design, and education, with articles on everything from Ruskin and Morris to folk music and the American Indian.[3] Behind the diversity of topics in *The Craftsman* was a broadly didactic, if not indeed utopian purpose. For household furnishings were only the beginning; at the most general level, Stickley would defend *The Craftsman*'s breadth (against a correspondent who questioned an article on the photographer and reformer Jacob Riis) by saying that "the whole Craftsman movement is really a movement for the bettering of men," and that Riis "is a true Craftsman, making of himself an ideal, noble, free, American citizen."[4] Stickley thought of himself as addressing not the leisure class, but the professional and laboring middle classes—"they are the real Americans"—and, picking up where Whitman had left off, he saw the twentieth century as the "Age of the people."[5]

Stickley's self-consciously American ethos paradoxically evolved out of a combination of foreign influences—Carlyle, Ruskin, and Morris; Japanese prints and architectural forms; European design magazines—all rounded off by a trip to England in the 1890s.[6] As a youth, Stickley had learned furniture construction from an uncle, and the first designs to come from his own workshops were based on Colonial and Shaker models; Stickley expanded his reproductions at his Syracuse workshops during the 1890s to include Louis XV, Italian Renaissance, Chippendale, etc.—all forms he would later condemn on the grounds that they were imitations of the past, and as such unrepresentative of contemporary American life. During the high period of Stickley's production (from around 1900 to 1916), the typical Craftsman design, in contrast to the earlier lines produced by the Grand Rapids manufacturers, was marked by simplicity of line, absence of ornamentation, and a dark-stained solid oak construction. Heavily solid and rectilinear, Stickley's chairs, settees, desks, and other pieces were widely imitated and found a responsive chord in a middle-class market seeking a simplification of the elaborately ornamented pieces popular during the Victorian period.[7] Americans were no longer interested in following the advice offered earlier by such Victorian guides to abundance as Harriet Spofford, who counseled her presumably agile readers, "Provided there is space to move about, without knocking over the furniture, there is hardly likely to be too much in the room."[8]

At the heart of Stickley's aesthetic was an argument that rooted our sensory experience of the object in our *knowledge* of the thing. In this view, an appreciation of a piece of furniture came from an understanding of how it was made. Accordingly, Stickley argued that we like things that are plain and unornamented, rather than objects "made by machinery with intricate processes which we cannot understand."[9] Following Ruskin and Morris, he held machine-carved ornament to be absurd and false, "counterfeiting a slow, patient, intelligent operation."[10] But Stickley was not therefore arguing nostalgically that "craft" meant hand production only; rather, the worker should master the machine as a useful tool, taking advantage of labor-saving machinery that would leave him—at least theoretically—free to express his own individuality in the finishing of a piece.[11]

Underlying Stickley's "religion," as he called it, lay a critique of American culture that was rooted in the notion of authenticity as the fundamental value lacking in our society. "The time is ripe for the

Living room designed by Gustav Stickley, from The Craftsman, *April 1902*

birth in this country of a national art—an art that shall express the strongly individual characteristics of the American people, but, like all art, it must spring in the first place from the common needs of the common people." Thus the commercialized object, created to satisfy artificially induced needs, was anathema. Believing that his own pieces constituted "a true expression of the collective thought of the age," Stickley inveighed against the forces of mass advertising that increasingly were governing the marketplace.[12] The sale of goods is gained "through the hypnotic influence of words," he complained. "People are told what to think about this trash that is sold," just as they are told what to believe in books, magazines, and theater. In a market ruled by fashion, he said, "we have made impermanency a basis of commercial valuation" as opposed to the traditional styles (and permanent values) of the handmade folk object.[13] As the nation grows older, he wrote, we "begin to stand on our own feet and to cherish our own standards of life and of work and therefore of art, we show an unmistakable tendency to get away from shams and to demand the real thing."[14]

But demanding the real thing meant breaking free from the pervasive influence of an impoverished urban culture and a faulty educational system. He told the story of a class on the Lower East Side that had been asked if it had ever seen a cow. Only one child had—and that cow was in the window of a dairy. "It was a picture," Stickley wrote, "or a terra cotta cow the lad had seen, and he had taken it for a true representation." All of which was an argument for an education that was less dependent on "merely theoretical knowledge" and more on nature: "the education that comes from contact with real things is real and vital, and cannot be developed in the closet or the schoolroom." Children need "closer contact with real things, with real work, with real life."[15] It was precisely this belief that impelled Stickley, in 1908, to acquire 600 acres in New Jersey and build there, by 1911, Craftsman Farms, which was intended to be a model school, farm, and crafts community for children.

Although Craftsman Farms failed to materialize as an ideal educational community (instead, Stickley's own family moved into the impressive main house on the property), behind it lay a constellation of good intentions that amplifies the meaning of the Arts and Crafts movement in America: the intent to unify hand and brain, spirit and body, laborer and tool, labor and management, and, not least, to unify the social classes.[16] Labor was seen as a restorative, fostering a connection—between people and tools and between people and real things—that had been lost. In thinking about constructing an ideal community, Stickley was moving in a direction that had been widely promoted in America by the Englishman C. R. Ashbee; and the latter's ideal of uniting the worker and his work, with the individual becoming master of the tool, chimed well with Stickley's ideas.[17] And here the Arts and Crafts movement dovetailed as well with the manual training movement, which, with advocates like Calvin Woodward, Felix Adler, William James, and John Dewey, saw the public school as a place where the hand and head could be educated together.[18]

The particular balance of hand and machine that Stickley was seeking was doubtless formulated under the influence of Oscar L. Triggs as well, who had written frequently for *The Craftsman* and was the author of *Chapters in the History of the Arts and Crafts Movement* (1902). Even more than Stickley, Triggs had sought to incorporate the machine into the ideal labor community, defining for it a function apart from hand processes: "Order, exactitude, persistence, conformity to unbending law, these are the lessons which must emanate from the machine," Triggs wrote, quoting Prof. J. A. Hobson. "Machinery can exactly reproduce; it can, therefore, teach the lesson of exact reproduction, an education for quantitative measurements."[19] Right use of the machine, accordingly, would be to let it take care of basic functions and primitive needs, leaving to the individual the exercise of his craft. Triggs thus looked forward to the emancipation of labor and the development of industrial socialism, a vision he set forth in his *Chapters in the History of the Arts and Crafts Movement*: "The machine in doing the drudgery of the world is undoubtedly an instrument for the furthering of industrial liberty. Voluntary co-operative individualism is the goal toward which the whole industrial world is now tending."[20] Drawing on Tolstoy and Whitman, along with Ruskin and Morris, Triggs found a place for the machine in society, while still maintaining the primacy of the workshop community based on individually meaningful hand work.

Yet in wishing to secure meaningful work for the laborer, both Stickley and Triggs were running against the current of industrial practice, as Thorstein Veblen made clear in a review of Triggs's volume in 1902. However much he might applaud the abstract goal of humanizing and beautifying industry, of bringing art "into the everyday work of the industrial classes," Veblen charged the Industrial Art League with running "on sentimental grounds rather than on grounds of reasoned practicality." Striking the Arts and Crafts movement in its soft utopian underbelly, Veblen declared, matter-of-factly, that "Modern industry, in so far as it is characteristically modern, means the machine process," for "a democratic culture requires low cost and a large, throughly standardized output of goods." He went on, "Since the machine process is indispensable to modern culture, both on business grounds and for reasons of economy, this limits the immediate scope of the arts-and-crafts salvation to those higher levels of consumption where exigencies of business and economy are not decisive." To the degree that Triggs was incorporating the machine into the industrial process, he was acting in accord with economic and technological demands; but just to that degree, he was inevitably defeating his own higher purposes, for the machine process, to Veblen, will "root out of the workmen's scheme of thought whatever elements are alien to its own technological requirements and discipline."[21]

Stickley resisted the logic of the machine (as Veblen described it) for years, but finally the marketplace won the argument. His manufacturing procedures—use of hand labor, exacting standards of quality, careful treatment of finishes—raised the prices of his goods to the point where he was inevitably catering to a somewhat limited, comfortably middle-class audience. Nearly identical furniture could be had more cheaply from Stickley's competitors in the Arts and Crafts line, including his own brothers' company—L. & J. G. Stickley. (The Sears catalogue also listed Craftsman-style furniture, oblivious to ideology and indifferent to its placement on the same page as their Roman Empire designs.) So that while Stickley was proselytizing for Craftsman designs and freely offering his own detailed plans to do-it-yourselfers, he was simultaneously warning the consumer against the crude work of competitors—"Mission," "Handcraft," "Crafts-Style," "Roycroft," and "Quaint." Meanwhile, Stickley's brothers, lacking any allegiance to an overall philosophy of craft and untroubled by thoughts of William Morris, could advertise their own designs in a spirit woundingly antagonistic to Gustav's: "The Work of L. & J. G. Stickley, built in a scientific manner, does not attempt to follow the traditions of a bygone day. All the resources of modern invention are used as helps in constructing this thoroughly modern product." They even went so far as to compare the construction of their seat cushions to the methods used in the making of automobile seats.[22] By 1911, Stickley himself, who had written of the laborer that "the greatest thing in work is your own development in the process," was inveighing against the wasteful practices of labor unions and praising Frederick Winslow Taylor's system of "scientific management."[23] The carefully framed synthesis of craft tradition and machine technology was falling apart. Where the craft ideal did remain, in ceramics or woodworking, it had devolved into hobbies for the leisure class, or as relief for the middle class from their harried, workaday worlds.

Stickley's last ambitious effort—to institutionalize the Craftsman culture in a Manhattan skyscraper—embodied the paradoxical quality of the moment. Following his move to New Jersey in 1911, Stickley gave up on the utopian Craftsman Farms and instead invested his energy and money in a building off Fifth Avenue that housed commercial floors, architectural services, library and lecture hall, and the offices of *The Craftsman*. But the stresses and tensions between simplicity and luxury were beginning to crack the Craftsman cosmos:

While articles in *The Craftsman* celebrated nature and the Whitmanesque virtues of the common folk (for example, Ernest Crosby's "I do not wish to be above people. / I wish to be with people"), other articles discussed practical solutions to "the Servant Problem."[24] Striving to maintain his solvency, Stickley was shifting his emphasis from a Whitmanesque conception of "the people" to an audience comprising "people of culture and taste" who were looking "to make life better and truer by its perfect sincerity," as a Stickley ad put it; but what that came down to in practice was often bumpy vases and high sentiments.[25]

Toward the end, Stickley's own line of goods reflected concretely and depressingly the compromises forced upon him. The market demanded cheaper goods, including the once anathematized period reproductions, and Stickley had to comply. Writing in the last year of *The Craftsman*, Stickley tried to be faithful to his original principles, yet at the same time trim his sails to the winds of the trade. Where previously the unornamented, severe style of the Craftsman line was declared to be the only honest design, now honesty was defined by a different standard, and reproductions were said to be still "honest" because such copies "truly represent a period or the desire of the owner of the house." Defending himself against his conscience, Stickley made a fine distinction: "There is something that borders on immorality in imitation period furniture. It is dishonest, for it assumes to be something that it is not and should be as scorned as counterfeit gold. Faithful copies are an entirely different matter and are not to be ranked with the loose, untruthful shams, so commonly offered for sale. If furniture is sold under period names it should be the best possible representative piece. A chair that is sold as Gothic or Jacobean or Chippendale should be a truthful reproduction of a characteristic example of the work of those times."[26] Stickley was backpedaling fast, producing Colonial pieces to suit the tastes and trends of the period, a nostalgic looking backward to slower, more secure times, the times before the machine had changed everything.

Trying to join his own radical enterprise with the forces of commerce, industry, and modernism, Stickley failed in the most visible and American of ways—the Craftsman Building closed in 1916 and Stickley went bankrupt. Still one must say that although the synthesis of machine and organic form, of hand and brain, structure and decoration, matter and spirit, form and purpose, did not hold in the particular democratic form Stickley had aimed at, the goal of synthesis retained a powerful hold on the imagination and would be picked up by others, *mutatis mutandi*, in subsequent years.

While Stickley was fighting his rear-guard battle to keep alive a humanistic synthesis and yet stay financially solvent, the machine was playing a larger and larger role in daily life, fostering a growing enthusiasm for technology and for the engineer, evident at all levels of the culture. The civil and mechanical engineer had been featured, and celebrated, for decades in the middle-class magazines (*Scribner's*, *Century*, *Harper's*) as a kind of culture hero, along with the great inventors like Bell and Edison.[27] The little magazines, too, caught the fever, hailing the machine as a source of new energy, an inspiration for new forms that would replace the stuffy conventionality of genteel culture. "I have already turned from an Art Exhibition," George W. Vos wrote to the editor of the little magazine, *The Soil*, around the time of Stickley's bankruptcy (1916), "to marvel at the coordination and the real art of a steam shovel, ripping out great handfuls of boulders and earth." (Alfred Stieglitz, ever interested in the changing city, had earlier made a photograph of just such a machine.) Although Vos evidently wanted to preserve some contact with the humanistic values of the Arts and Crafts movement—he invoked William Morris as a precursor of the "simplification" that marks machine design—he imagined the artist of the future to be the engineer, and the new aesthetic was based on the structure and movement of machine processes: "There are splendid curves in steam lines, in belts, and in all moving machinery."[28] The adulation of the engineer held on through the 1920s, with continued enthusiasm among the avant-garde, who were looking for some contact with the forces that were changing the visible face of the modern city. One particular enthusiast was Jane Heap, editor of *The Little Review*, who in 1927 introduced a special supplement to a number dealing with the "Machine-Age Exposition," affirming that "there is a great new race of men in America: the Engineer. He has created a new mechanical world, he is segregated from men in other activities." Heap wanted not only to celebrate the engineer, but to foster a "union with the architect and artist," which would bring about "a new creative force," important for "the life of tomorrow."[29]

Yet Heap's promulgation was issued in the same year, 1927, that

"Just Like Original Colonial Furniture," advertisement from
Country Life, *1916*

Rockefeller agreed to finance the restoration of Colonial Williamsburg. And it was symptomatic of the period's ambivalence in the face
of radical change that the backward-looking impulse could coexist
with an equal and opposite enthusiasm for the machine, as if the one
could balance the other.[30] Thus an implicit rejection of modernity
was evident in the widespread middle-class enthusiasm for imitation
Colonial furniture and architecture. Made first for the mass market in
the 1880s and going strong through the 1920s, the colonial style offered a comforting security in the face of rapid change. Meanwhile,
for the antiques collector, able to purchase the real thing and not
merely the reproduction, antiques were a symbol of old and glorious
spiritual and political values, now lost in an age of mongrel designs
and shoddy machine-made goods: "We love the earliest American
forms," Wallace Nutting wrote chauvinistically in his catalogue, *Period Furniture*, "because they embody the strength and beauty in the
character of the leaders of American settlement. . . . We carry on their
spirit by imitating their work."[31] The case of Henry Ford was only the

most visible of a host of smaller acts of piety toward the idealized past. Was it bewilderment at what the new technology had wrought that prompted Ford to create, at his Dearborn museum in the late 1920s, a dream of the preindustrial past? Or was it an urge to preserve the presumed perfection of an earlier time in order to hedge a bet against the dreamed perfection of the technological future? "When we are through," Ford said simply, "we shall have reproduced American life as lived."[32] Like many Americans, Ford was looking in the rearview mirror while driving full speed ahead, not fully content with the direction in which things were heading.

Elements from both of these extremes—looking backward to an idealized American past of craft and essential forms, and forward to a future of mechanized efficiency—composed the synthesis that Lewis Mumford was articulating during the 1920s and 1930s. Mumford was writing for a wide range of periodicals and audiences—from the liberal *New Republic* to the the elitist *New Yorker*, from the pungently iconoclastic *American Mercury*, to the dryly professional architectural journals. With his ubiquitous contributions to annuals and collections of essays, and with his own books reaching a wide general audience as well as an audience of designers, Mumford was arguably the most important design critic of the time.[33] And his effort to define a design tradition that would embody an authentic "American" ethos, a way of accommodating the machine to contemporary mass culture while preserving the values of a creative and politically sound society, can serve as an axis around which to fix various other positions during the period between the wars.

Mumford, along with many others at the time, was inspired by Van Wyck Brooks's effort to reclaim an American past that was "usable" and that would demonstrate the country's maturity and independence from Europe.[34] Scorning the middle-class taste for department store Colonial counterfeits, Mumford went back to the more complex source of the popular icons: the New England village of the seventeenth and early eighteenth centuries, where he found an ideal balance between common land and private development, between individual and community, between structure and materials, between work and leisure, an ideal that was an American equivalent, for Mumford, of the medieval urban synthesis in European civilization.[35] This would serve him as a touchstone against which to measure contemporary values and practices. One of the earliest evidences of this attitude was in his review of the Metropolitan Museum's period rooms, which were opened in 1924 as a regular display of American decorative arts. Mumford celebrated the chests, gateleg tables, windows, and other features of the seventeenth- and early eighteenth-century interiors, admiring their austerely functional designs, their essential forms. After the mid-eighteenth century, however, "good taste" supplanted "decent necessity"; and he feared now, with the installation of these rooms, that we would use the machine to imitate the worst of the past—reproducing artifacts that have no real connection with contemporary life—rather than build upon the tradition of good design that was part of the earlier, functional ethos.[36]

While Mumford thus used the organic community of the seventeenth-century New England village as a standard against which to measure the subsequent stages of industrialization, he was by no means fixed on the past, or on reproducing it through slavish imitation or nostalgic recreation. In fact, he was emerging, during the 1920s, as a thoughtful advocate of the machine and of its potential for creatively transforming American culture, yet one who was also extremely wary of its equal potential for distorting individual lives and social forms. To Mumford, there were two kinds of *reproduction*, as he observed while excoriating museums that fill their rooms with the "scraps of other cultures" (and collectors who do likewise, like Isabella Gardner): "One has to do with the results of bringing together two different individualities which mingle and give birth to a third, unlike either and yet akin to both. In contrast to this is mechanical reproduction, which takes a certain pattern, and repeats it a dozen, a hundred, a million times. *Cultures flourish in the first kind of living contact; and so far as the museum serves this end, it exists for a worthy and rational purpose.*"[37] It was the mechanical reproduction, the mere imitation, of past models (especially European) that would stultify American culture and that must be avoided. The goal was "not to counterfeit handicraft, but to produce its equivalent by another method"—a method that exemplified the right use of the machine.[38] And the role of the cultural critic was to define that use.

For Mumford, right use of the machine meant exploiting its virtue—the greater goods it affords mass society—and accepting its logic and aesthetic, which Mumford defined on a number of occasions as a purification of form according to the principle of economy. Modern technics "strips off from the object all the barnacles of association, all the sentimental and pecuniary values which have nothing whatever to do with esthetic form, and it focuses attention on the object itself," as he put it in his major work of the 1930s, *Technics and Civilization*. The new values were "precision, calculation, flawlessness, simplicity, economy."[39] In the early 1920s, Mumford had hailed the new subways and lunchrooms of Manhattan as models of contemporary design, praising their accuracy and fine finish, and their decent respect for the requirements of urban life.[40] Writing ten years later, Mumford articulated in more subtle detail the new facts of aesthetic experience based on technology—the lightness and strength in steel cranes, the boundaries and spaces in skyscrapers, the forms and colors of the world seen through the microscope, the rows of manufactured goods, exhibiting endless repeating patterns, etc. "There is an esthetic of units and series," he declared, "as well as an esthetic of the unique and the non-repeatable."[41] (Mumford saw the camera as a primary vehicle for and symbol of this new aesthetic.)

If models from the past were needed for the contemporary designer, they would be found not in the exotic architectural styles from the world's storehouse of types, which Mumford assailed as romantic and irrelevant, but from shapes wrought by necessity in the industrial landscape: "A grain elevator here, a warehouse there, an office building, a garage—there has been the promise of a stripped, athletic, classical style of architecture in these buildings which shall embody all that is good in the Machine Age: its precision, its cleanliness, its hard illumination, its unflinching logic."[42] And Mumford was not alone in thus confirming the artistic value of engineering design. Sheldon and Martha Cheney, writing in the 1930s, affirmed that "Today's modernist knows the Crystal Palace, Sir John Paxton's 'temporary contrivance' in iron and glass, as belonging with the great nineteenth-century monuments of engineering; and as creative forerunner, with the Eiffel Tower and Brooklyn Bridge, of the age of steel construction."[43]

It was a question of what was usable. And while the Crystal Palace did not represent for Mumford much more than a "magnified conservatory," the Cheneys' last example—the Brooklyn Bridge—would have been particularly dear to Mumford, for John Augustus Roebling and his son Washington, who built it, were representative of what was most valuable in the nineteenth-century past, and the bridge was a central icon in America's engineering tradition.[44] And Mumford would likewise have endorsed designer Walter Teague's enthusiasm for the "superlative rightness of certain modern airplanes, power plants and machine tools, parkways and bridges," with their integration of parts "achieved by the pressure of necessity." But the usable past included not only the great works of civil engineering and industrial architecture; it also included the tradition of American designers. And here it was Louis Sullivan and Frank Lloyd Wright who most importantly stood out.[45]

Throughout the 1920s and 1930s, Mumford had been finding in the writings and buildings of both men the most significant models for contemporary practice. (Mumford paid little attention to Gustav Stickley during the 1920s and 1930s, although by the time he published his autobiographical *Sketches from Life* [1982] he had come to see Stickley, in his role of editor of *The Craftsman*, as having done more than anyone before World War I to "open the windows to the fresh currents that were stirring in architecture.")[46] Both Sullivan and Wright had figured briefly in Mumford's second book, *Sticks and Stones* (1924), as exemplars of the artistic adaptation of functional design to good social purpose; but it was not until his subsequent study of the previously largely overlooked nineteenth-century heritage—*The Brown Decades* (1931)—that Mumford articulated more fully their value to American culture.

Mumford saw Sullivan as a crucial link between Richardson's earlier effort at a style that respected the vernacular traditions and local character of place and Frank Lloyd Wright's subsequent career. Yet Sullivan's contribution lay not so much in his buildings. (Mumford was queasy about the skyscraper in general, and also about Sullivan's ornamentation, which he saw as an expression of individuality in what ought to be a more collective art.) Rather, it lay in his thought: "Sullivan was the first American architect to think consciously of his relations with civilization"; and he cited Sullivan's keystone belief that architecture was " 'a *social manifestation*,' " expressing, as Mumford put it, "the forces at work in society, in industry, in the human personality."[47] And Sullivan's fundamental premise was Mumford's as well—that the whole problem of building needed to be rethought in terms of modern society. Mumford was sympathetic too with Sullivan's respect for the engineer's mentality and its relevance for the twentieth-century: engineers, Sullivan had written enthusiastically, are " 'the only men who could face a problem squarely; who knew a problem when they saw it. Their minds were trained to deal with real things, as far as they knew them, as far as they could ascertain them, while the architectural mind lacked this directness, this simplicity, this singleness of purpose.' "[48]

"One might call him the Whitman of American architecture," Mumford wrote of Sullivan, on account of his absorptive powers and the largeness of his vision.[49] An apt comparison, for Sullivan in fact was deeply impressed by Whitman when he read the poet while working on the Auditorium Building in Chicago, and sent him an adoring letter, together with a copy of a prose-poem, "Inspiration." In fact, Sherman Paul has affirmed that everything Sullivan wrote "from the time of 'Inspiration,' and much that he built, is an elaboration and enrichment of Whitman's gospel, transmitted with renewed vitality in the utterance of word and stone."[50] (Paul reads Sullivan's whole career in Whitmanesque terms, structuring his biography as a kind of analogue of Whitman's writings.) Moreover, like Whitman himself, Sullivan was largely neglected, except by a small coterie, and his commissions were few after 1905.

It was through his writings that Sullivan kept alive his influence, for despite the decline in his practice, Sullivan continued to publish his "Kindergarten Chats," and other occasional essays and talks (seeking a wider audience, he printed several in Stickley's *The Craftsman*) in which he addressed problems in the culture that were reflected in architecture, but went beyond building art. In "What is Architecture: A Study of the American People Today" (1906), which was published first in *American Contractor* and reprinted later the same year in *The Craftsman*, Sullivan formulated a position that would anticipate Van Wyck Brooks's critique of the division within American culture between highbrow and lowbrow. For Sullivan contrasts the university graduate, "with no consummate ability to interpret things," with the "active-minded but 'uneducated' man." Both, Sullivan says, believe they are "dealing with realities, but both in fact [are] dealing with phantoms." They need to study "the real hearts" and "the real thoughts" of the people. The problem, as Sullivan diagnosed it, was that our minds deal with words, not things. We must "escape slavery to WORDS and be at liberty, in the open air of reality, freely and fully to deal with THINGS."[51] Sullivan thus answered in his writings the central problem of the machine age—the problem of man's alienation from the concrete world of experience.

In exhorting us to have contact with real things, Sullivan was clearly offering himself as a Whitman Redivivus, yet behind that program lay experiences ingrained in his own life and education, as he so artfully explained in *The Autobiography*. There, Sullivan recalled his experience as an eight-year-old (in 1864), pleading with his grandfather to take him along on a visit to see the waterfalls at Lyons Falls, New York. "Grandpa, I have never seen a waterfall, only in pictures, and in pictures they don't move and they don't roar; I want to live with a *real* waterfall; . . . you know, Grandpa, pictures don't give you any real idea; why Grandpa, a picture of a tree isn't anything at all when you see a real tree, like our great Ash at Cowdry's."[52] (Stickley had made the same observation about the detached quality of American education.) And it is tempting to see in this basic habit of thought the germ of Sullivan's whole approach to architectural problems as a thinking through things, a discovery of form in function, rather than in the picture or style of a given time or fashion: "For words in themselves he had come to form a passing aversion, since he had noted their tendency to eclipse the vibrant values of immediate reality. Therefore, he preferred to think and feel and contemplate without the use of words."[53]

As an outgrowth of his scientific studies early on in his career, Sullivan tells us in *The Autobiography*, came the great discovery of the relationship between form and function: "And amid the immense number and variety of living forms, he noted that invariably the form expressed the function, as, for instance, the oak tree expressed the function oak, the pine tree the function pine, and so on through the amazing series. And, inquiring more deeply, he discovered that in truth it was not simply a matter of form expressing function, but the vital idea was this: That the function *created* or organized its form." This was the "universal law admitting of no exception" that Sullivan had sought from his student days. Yet, as Sullivan suggests in the *Autobiography*, there was a major disjunction between natural law and human behavior, and understanding social codes meant becoming educated in a process of reading, of deciphering appearances that concealed some hidden reality, for within the social organism were "mask-forms, counterfeit forms, forms with protective coloration, forms invisible except to those in the know."[54] Like Edith Wharton, looking back on the same decades of the late nineteenth century, Sullivan was living in a "hieroglyphic" world, seeking in architectural form a more solid reality.

Sullivan's work can, in fact, be read as an attempt to come to terms with the contradictions between form and social habit. He devised the skyscraper as a fulfillment of the various functions of the large office building; and he would conceptualize the form of a building together with its surface ornament "at the very beginning of the design," making it specific to each structure.[55] But insofar as they were heavily ornamented, Sullivan's buildings were an effort to elevate their purpose. (For he scorned the business civilization that required such concentrations of power and regimentation of persons). And we might regard the ornament on his towering buildings as an effort to create an ideal synthesis—between the function of the building and the beauty of its surface, between its materials and its spirit, to use Whitmanesque terms.[56] In a way, he was engaged in his own masking of functions by counterfeit forms—one of the reasons for Mumford's disapproval of the ornamentation. Put more posivitely, Sullivan, like Stickley, was fashioning a material environment that would ideally bring about more perfect social conditions.

Sullivan was in eclipse when Mumford featured him in *The Brown Decades*, but in the following years he would be universally credited by modern designers of the 1930s with the keystone principle of functionalist design—Form Follows Function.[57] And along with Sullivan, Frank Lloyd Wright was consistently coupled: the two were the twin progenitors, or better, the Father and Son, of the Modern Spirit.[58] (Mumford considered Wright a greater architect than Sullivan—although Wright himself always referred to Sullivan as *his* own master.) It was the moderns, Hugh Ferris declared in 1931, and not the traditionalists with their facades of Gothic and Renaissance, "who are faithful to the real traditions of Architecture."[59] The circle was coming round: as in the early years of the century the Chicago school had influenced European designers, so were they now influencing Americans, who were discovering in their own past (and present) the grounds of a native tradition in functional architecture.

The tradition that Mumford traced in *The Brown Decades*, from the steel and stone bridges of Roebling, through the flowing interiors and locally derived materials of Richardson to the office buildings of John Wellborn Root and of Sullivan, culminated in Frank Lloyd Wright. And the characteristic he was isolating in these American examples was a quality of design that is expressive while being austere, a quality Mumford called *Sachlichkeit*, borrowing the word from the postwar

Louis Sullivan, Wainwright Building, St. Louis, Missouri, 1890–91
(Courtesy of Museum of Modern Art, New York)

movement in German painting, *Neue Sachlichkeit*, with its effort to grasp things objectively, in their immediate reality. Adapting the term to his own purposes, Mumford meant by *Sachlichkeit* a "thingness," a structural honesty that is "one of the distinguishing marks of modern civilization: first appearing in the engineer, it has made its way, step by step, into every other department of life."[60] Though he uses the word sparingly in *Brown Decades*, *Sachlichkeit* is a core term for Mumford at this time, summing up the qualities that inhere in functionalist design based on the machine. (The term was extended by Mumford to discussions of photography as well, as we shall see.) In Frank Lloyd Wright, Mumford found its chief architectural exponent.

The significance of Frank Lloyd Wright lay, for Mumford, in his having come to terms with the machine and hence with the necessities of modern life and art. In fact, Wright's speech at Chicago's Hull House—delivered in 1901 before the Chicago Arts and Crafts Society—was for Mumford "the first whole-hearted word" that was said in favor of the machine, "the first hint that the results which Morris hoped to achieve by going back to the Middle Ages might be attained by going forward to a new destination."[61] Not the medievalism of Ruskin and Morris, but a technologically based design philosophy that was aggressively of its own time was what Wright exhorted his Arts and Crafts audience to follow. Wright may have persuaded few of his listeners at the time, but "The Art and Craft of the Machine" (with its pointedly paradoxical title) has become a touchstone for the modern movement.

Wright's talk, delivered at the juncture of the nineteenth and twentieth centuries, in fact looked both ways, backward to the handicraft tradition, and forward to an as yet unformulated mode of architectural creation that placed the architect-artist at the center of the design and engineering process. Examining present practices, Wright declared himself to be against all wood carving—the hallmark of the artisan labor that Arts and Crafts practitioners esteemed—for it was, he said, "apt to be a forcing of the material."[62] (He preferred the clean cuts of the machine, which revealed the natural grain and color of the wood.) Standing before the Arts and Crafts Society of Chicago, Wright assaulted its dearest assumptions about the value of hand labor. "Joy in mere handicraft," for example, which was a fundamental value deriving from Ruskin and Morris, Wright dismissed as so much self-indulgence—"like that of the man who played the piano for his own amusement—a pleasurable personal accomplishment without real relation to the grim condition confronting us." In fact, Wright takes the cautious, if not hostile, attitude toward the machine held by the Arts and Crafts societies, and turns it on its head, declaring at the outset of his talk, in roundly prophetic tones, that "in the Machine lies the only future of art and craft—as I believe, a glorious future; that the Machine is, in fact, the metamorphosis of ancient art and craft." And the function of the artist in the Machine Age is to make plain the meaning of the machine. Rather than an enslaver, the Machine was, for Wright, the "Forerunner of Democracy."[63]

At the bottom of Wright's thinking was a fusion of science and art that would become a hallmark of the early twentieth-century synthesis that so many artists and intellectuals in America were seeking, the basis of a unified vision designed to bridge the polarities of American life. (We shall see it again in the rhetoric and practice of the photographic and literary arts during the first several decades of the twentieth century.) Estimating future needs—fulfilled in his own later Taliesen studios—Wright declared in his talk at Hull House that "not one educational institution in America has as yet attempted to forge the connecting link between Science and Art by training the artist to his actual tools, or, by a process of nature-study that develops in him the power of independent thought."[64]

The link between Science and Art, between the Machine and the Artist, was indeed slow to form. Writing a quarter of a century later, Wright found it necessary to make the same points over again. The machine had not yet been mastered as a tool, it had not yet been used to make living things. Instead our "technique" consisted of "reproduction, imitation, ubiquity." The millions of Usonians—Wright had coined a word to distinguish the United States from Canada and South America—had profited by the quantity production of our machine economy, but the quality of that mass life was another matter: "One may live on canned food quite well—But can a nation live a canned life in all but the rudimentary animal expressions of that life? Indefinitely? Canned Poetry, Canned Music, Canned Architecture, Canned Recreation. All canned by the Machine."[65] There was clearly a right use and a wrong use of the machine; standardization by itself was "no detriment to art or artist," Wright declared. "It has always existed. And like any principle has its uses and its abuses." What was necessary was that the thing have life in it, "that quality of it or in it which makes it perfectly *natural*—of course that means organic."[66] And it was just that quality that Mumford evidently identified in Wright's own designs, for the architect's delight in "mechanical techniques" was "not merely a passive adaptation to the machine age," Mumford observed; rather, it was a "reaching toward a more biotechnic economy," grounded in the "permanent realities of birth, growth, reproduction, and the natural environment."[67]

At the center of Wright's design philosophy was the concept of "Abstraction," derived perhaps from his earliest experiences with Froebel's learning blocks, which taught him to look for the inner essence of the form rather than the outer appearance. For it was necessary for the architect to *abstract* from nature the structural form of good design. (Not surprisingly, Japanese architecture and graphic design was always a strong influence on Wright.)[68] Interestingly, Wright puts the issue as a distinction between "Realism" and "Reality"; in a characteristically apodictic chain of assertions, walking backward to prior premises, Wright explained the necessary logic:

> Realism—sub-geometric,—however, is the abuse of this fine thing. The 'fine thing' is Reality.
> Reality is spirit, the Essence brooding just behind the Aspect.[69]

Wright's distinction—between "realism," which is a literal rendering of form, imitative of nature; and "Reality," which captures in the purer forms of geometry the essential spiritual dimension of the form—is a paradigmatic formulation of the changed motivation in the arts between the nineteenth century and the twentieth, and we shall encounter it again in terms of the visual and literary arts.

If we think of the Johnson Wax Building, with its core tower standing like a tree; or if we think of the Guggenheim Museum, built like a chambered nautilus, we have simple examples of this embodiment of "Reality" in an abstraction from nature; but the more complex formulations of the domestic architecture, from the first Prairie houses in the early 1900s to the Usonian designs of the 1930s, reflect a similar sense of abstract form derived from the necessities of the particular project—its use, its site, the restraints of climate, the available building materials, the allowable cost of construction, and so forth. Wright's houses were organic in the sense that they seemed to live in the spaces they inhabited, adjusting their lines and volumes to the landscape, becoming indeed a part of the landscape. "His houses

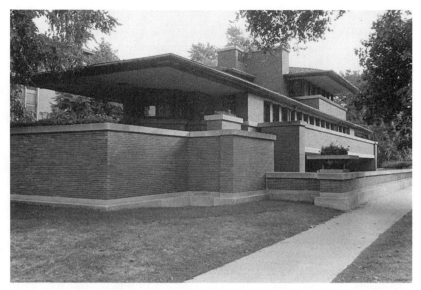

Frank Lloyd Wright, Frederick C. Robie Residence, Chicago, 1906,
photograph by Patricia Evans
(Courtesy of University of Chicago)

seem to grow out of the ground as naturally as the trees," Harriet
Monroe (the editor of Chicago's *Poetry Magazine*) wrote, and we
think of the many times he incorporated trees, or waterfalls, rocks, or
other existing natural features into the design.[70] "Bring outside world
into house and let inside go outside," as he put it in the *Autobiography*.[71] Wright broke open the form of the house—declaring war on
attics, cellars, columns, pilasters, window placements—the way the
new poets of the century declared war on the constraining conventions of genteel poetry, opening up the form of the poem to the materials of the real world. In all of this, Wright was going against the very
different (and influential) practice of Le Corbusier, who featured a
clean geometry of form and smooth surfaces, regardless of locality, as
if a building were, like Stevens's jar in Tennessee, the maker of its
context; Wright (and Mumford) inveighed against this colder homage
to technology, this *imitation* of the machine, rather than the adaptation and humanizing of it.[72]

Almost thirty years after Wright had called for a building and industrial art founded on the machine, the keynote speaker at a 1929 meeting of the American Management Association could finally declare that the best things no longer were handmade, but were made by machine.[73] But the question remained to be answered: what would the new, machine-made world look like, and what values would it embody? The problem was articulated clearly in an essay by Mumford, "Culture and Machine Art." Writing in 1931, Mumford saw a choice between standardization at a low level of design (producing servile imitations of debased rococo furniture) or at a high level, which would accept the virtues and canons of machine production. Although modernist design was superficially enamored of the machine, the studios produced essentially a luxury art; what was needed was industrial design with an ethical orientation toward mass culture, confirming what Mumford believed was the tendency of the machine to contradict the standards of bourgeois society. Machine designs "are cheap; they are common; they fulfill their peculiar function. . . . Whatever the politics of a country may be, the machine is a communist!" Mumford saw the machine as doing away with "industrial slavery" and creating an "equal share in the essentials of life" for everyone.[74]

Something of this same vision lay behind the earlier efforts of John Cotton Dana, the influential director of the Newark Museum, to encourage community production, based on the machine, at a high aesthetic level. Mumford had criticized the bourgeois home because it aspired to the false prestige of the museum; Dana took the museum and turned it into a showroom for the home. Believing that the European treasures and aristocratic standards of art in museums could paralyze the contemporary craftsman-artist, Dana redefined the museum's role to be patron of pots and pans as well as the fine arts.[75] Dana argued that the museum, after surveying the industrial and artistic life of the city, should carefully select the best manufactured objects—both useful and decorative—and including, ideally, paintings and moving pictures. For the function of the museum was to teach us about the practical and fine arts, thus increasing the pleasure of our daily lives and improving the quality of our own production. Where Duchamp had brought hardware items into the museum in order to startle our eyes and our aesthetic categories, Dana wanted to evoke a different act of revaluation on the part of the museum visitor—an appreciation of standards of design in everyday objects, a crossing of boundaries between "high" art and the real world not in order to shock the world of high art (as had Duchamp) but to elevate the world of the common person. (Dana once mounted a sign at the conclusion of an exhibition of plumbing, pottery, etc.: "All the objects in this collection were bought in the local five and ten cent stores, no single object costing more than twenty-five cents.")[76] Rooted in the life of the community, Dana's museum was the epitome of the democratic institution.

The goal of all this, as Richard F. Bach of the Metropolitan Museum put it in 1923, was to achieve "Americanism in our industrial art." "It will free us from our present dependence upon European sources for all of our inspiration and over half of our designs."[77] The call for "Americanness" in the industrial arts was central to the design community's thinking in the 1920s and 1930s, the expression of a longstanding urge for cultural independence that had already been felt in the other arts of the twentieth century, an urge voiced by the editor of the *Annual of American Design 1931* in tones that inevitably recall the exhortations of Walt Whitman seventy-five years earlier: the American designer must "emancipate himself from European masters."[78] The emancipation, once begun, was soon judged to be complete: in 1934 the annual show of the National Alliance for Art and Industry had as its purpose "to CELEBRATE THE EMERGENCE OF AN AMERICAN STYLE."[79]

In fact the early years of the 1930s saw the development of a number of new product lines, reflecting not only a flowering of cultural nationalism, but also simple economic self-interest, for the condition of the economy during the Depression forced on many businesses the task of refashioning goods in the hopes of creating markets where none had previously existed; more simply, not to "modernize" might be to lose the competitive edge in a tight market. And so the idioms of high design in the 1920s were gradually translated to the mass market in the 1930s.[80]

Ironically, another catalyst in the Americanization of modern design was the influence of European trends, which rippled through the American design community following key exhibitions such as the display of four hundred objects from the famous 1925 International Exposition of Modern Decorative and Industrial Arts in Paris, which traveled to Boston, New York, and Chicago in 1926; and the 1931

Installation view from the exhibition Machine Art, *March 5 through April 29, 1934, Museum of Modern Art, New York*
(Courtesy of Museum of Modern Art, New York)

"International Style" exhibit at the Museum of Modern Art (with a catalogue by Philip Johnson and Henry Russell Hitchcock), which confirmed the new direction. (When the Bauhaus group came to America later in the 1930s to teach a generation of designers, that influence was of course much extended.)[81] The example of the European models did for architecture and design what they did as well for painting, photography, literature, and music: they offered the freedom of a new formal vocabulary to artists who were searching for ways to connect with native traditions. The result, for American high design in the late 1920s, was a fetishism of the machine that transformed the look of everything from skyscrapers to toasters, evident in a vocabulary of electric angularities and zigzag designs connoting the *excitement* of the machine. And this gave way, in the 1930s, to the smooth curves and the aura of precision and exactitude of the streamlined style with its signification of the *power* of the machine.

Henry Dreyfuss, 20th Century Limited *locomotive, 1938*
(Courtesy of Dreyfuss Archive, Cooper-Hewitt Museum of Design,
Smithsonian Institution, New York)

Virtually everyone during the 1930s who tried to account for the streamlined style invoked Sullivan and Wright as sources, without, however, observing the difference between streamlined "functionalism" and the design philosophies of Sullivan and Wright. (Nor, for that matter, did they observe how very different Sullivan and Wright were from one another: where Sullivan, for example, designed for all materials alike, Wright studied the unique properties of each; where Sullivan's decorative impulse moved from simple shapes to more elaborate, Wright sought always the abstract essence; where Sullivan's ornamentation clothed his structures, Wright's was more integral to the form.)[82] What was important was to have a lineage within the American tradition that connected the new practices with older values.

Walter Dorwin Teague, whose own work included everything from Kodak cameras, Texaco gas stations, and Pullman day coaches to the Ford Exposition at the 1939 World's Fair, and whose memoir, *Design This Day*, is the most thoughtful and scholarly of the manifestos or memoirs produced by the great industrial designers of the 1930s, was one of those invoking Sullivan and Wright. For Teague, the essence of the new Machine Age functionalism was a "visible rightness" in things.[83] But what was "visible rightness"? Teague's theoretical foundation could in practice support a variety of structures, based on a belief that beautiful form was "the outward revelation of inward soundness and rightness, the aspect of a perfectly functioning order." This harmony of function and form Teague took to be a universal law for all time; for there was "but one standard of rightness"—continuous from Greek and Gothic culture through to contemporary design, although every age produced a type peculiar to its own conditions.[84]

Others were even more flexible in their formulation of the functionalist ethos. Norman Bel Geddes, who began his career as a theatrical designer, and moved to commercial store window displays, developed a practice during the 1930s that encompassed stoves, metal bedroom furniture, factories, ocean liners, and—at the '39 Fair—the spectacularly successful General Motors Building and Futurama exhibition; Geddes scorned the "applied decoration" of artificial machine style, advocating instead a "sincere style" that was "the direct result of the problem to be solved, of the materials involved, and of the sensitiveness of the artist." Yet given the individuality of the designer, Geddes admitted no single solution to his problem: "While function once arrived at, is fixed, its expression in form may vary endlessly under individual inflection."[85]

An even more casual approach was taken by the flamboyant Raymond Loewy, who designed everything from pencil sharpeners to ocean liners, including the Sears Coldspot refrigerator, the Greyhound bus, and the Pennsylvania railroad locomotive. "I believe that when a given product has been reduced to its functional best and still looks disorganized and ugly, a plain, simple shield, easily removable, is aesthetically justified. This shield accomplishes something, and it becomes functional, the specific function being to eliminate confusion."[86] At this point we have clearly left behind the essence of functionalism—that form follows function—save in the clever rhetoric of Loewy's rationale. Certainly the functionalism of Stickley's Craftsman furniture—based on the pleasure of our seeing the design reveal the structure—has been buried beneath the greater complexity of the machinery Loewy is working with. The machine has become a value in itself, replacing the synthesis of craft and tool that lay behind the earlier goal of authenticity; design has become subterfuge, a "style" applied to the object or building. And all we can add in Loewy's defense is that if he was on occasion pandering to the public's new taste for the streamlined look, he knew well what he was doing.[87]

Yet Loewy's concealing designs were a response to a problem in the way people thought about the machine, a problem made even more clear by designer Paul T. Frankl, when he declared that the curved lines of streamlined design "cover up the complexity of the machine age," and "direct our attention and allow us to feel ourselves master of the machine."[88] Master of the machine: what was crucial here, in an era when the economy seemed deranged, was the need for some control over powerful, possibly redemptive forces; and the streamlined style—with its clean lines and simplified forms joined together by powerful curves and massive shapes—can itself be seen as a celebration of technological force and a representation of the fiction of man's mastery over technology and over nature.[89] In this, there was an unacknowledged and fundamental contradiction between Sullivan and Wright on the one hand—who built according to canons of nature—and the streamlined designers, whose designs evoked the efficiency of the machine: smooth surfaces, geometric shapes, imagery of speed and power.

The views of Stickley and Mumford were expressed with somewhat

closer approximation in the self-consciously American styles evolved
by Russel Wright, which were widely marketed and extremely popular during the 1930s and 1940s. Wright had begun as a designer of
elite objects, but over the course of the 1930s had developed a more
populist attitude, aiming for products that would answer the needs of
a mass consumption society. Wright's "Modern Living" furniture line,
developed in the mid-1930s, encompassed sectional sofas and other
versatile pieces suited for smaller apartments, featuring hidden storage areas and coordinated units. Shifting from his earlier use of ve-
neer, Wright now exploited the beauty of the structural material itself—maple wood in a reddish tone and in an unstained blonde finish.
The design was essentially rectilinear, with rounded corners; fabrics
were simple and sturdy. There was an open and functional look to the
pieces—chair arms were open, joints were overlapping—recalling
the Stickley aesthetic of the early twentieth century.[90] In 1937, Wright
shifted his concerns to dinnerware, creating in the "American Modern" line what would prove to be extremely popular sets of ceramics,
glass, and woodenware. Forms were rounded and functional (like the
furniture), smoothly finished; the effect was geometric without being
mechanical, for the shapes were modeled on "life forms," with all
of the elements of the table coordinated to dramatize the service.
Wright's furnishings were keyed to the middle class (within the income range of $2,000 to $5,000) in order to "relate production to
consumption in a hitherto woefully disintegrated branch of endeavor."[91]

Russel Wright's designs represent a perfect accommodation to
mass taste in being at the same time comfortably familiar yet excit-
ingly new: both traditionally American and progressively modern.
Wright had been strongly influenced by the Bauhaus, both in design
and social philosophy; but, proclaiming his intention that "American
design should spring from native sources,"[92] he had consciously
strived to adapt European ideas to the American market, embodying
the values of authenticity in his designs: the functional simplicity of
form, the affirmation of natural materials, the allusion to American
design traditions—Colonial, Shaker, Mission. (Wright had, significantly, grown up with Mission furniture in his own home.)[93] In his
hands, the Arts and Crafts tradition underwent a transmogrification
aimed at the mass market: the furniture used wood in "full, hardy,
craftsmanlike forms," designed, as the promotional literature put it,

*"Modern Living," furniture line designed by Russel Wright, 1935
(Courtesy of George Arents Library, Syracuse University,
Syracuse, New York)*

to "continue and modernize a century-old tradition of American furniture design."[94] The restyling of the American thing was explicitly
seen by Wright as a solution to the problem of developing an "American" art of design, and to the implicit problem posed by the machine
in the twentieth century. Yet if we judge Wright's success not only by
the marketplace but also by the objects themselves, we must find his
solutions not always happy. Thus, for example, the ceramic furnishings he designed for the Bauer Pottery Company in the early 1930s
use machine production to fashion objects that look like "art pottery"
made by hand; such *imitations* of authenticity betray a confusion in
Wright's practice deriving from the same effort at synthesis that more
usually produced designs at once biomorphic and unabashedly machine made.

　　The culmination of Russel Wright's efforts was the cooperative of designers named, with a chauvinism that reflects its founding in 1940, "The American Way"; initiated with great fanfare at Macy's (Eleanor Roosevelt opened the displays), "The American Way" folded within a couple of years, a victim of logistical problems, wartime shortages, and weak quality control. Although Wright's combination of practicality and idealism remained unabated—he moved toward the end of his career into environmental and park design—his influence waned, his heyday had passed.

What remains of great interest in Wright's thinking is how one of the leading designers of the 1930s—certainly the most popular—conceived of the place of design within the totality of American material culture. Wright defined his own understanding of American design most clearly (and proudly) in a speech to the New York Fashion Group in 1938, when he related the story of an encounter with a German acquaintance at the Museum of Modern Art Bauhaus exhibit a few days before. The German had accused American designers of merely copying designs done years earlier by Europeans, and Wright's reaction was to confirm what he saw as the uniquely American virtues: the grand scale, the bold, vital form, distinctive colors. And he offered as examples of American genius the great engineering achievements that have marked the urban landscape since the end of the nineteenth century—"Our bridges. Our roads. Our factory machinery. Our skyscrapers." He took pride as well in the work of Frank Lloyd Wright. (The two met later on, in the 1950s, and admired each other's work, but were not close.) And in the technological marvels of the kitchen and bathroom, in business machines and gas stations, in movie theatres and cafeterias. "No matter how vulgar they are." In all of these manifestations of America's industrial and commercial energy, Russel Wright, whose own career had begun with stage and theater design, thought, "there is a distinct American character of design," and "our home furnishings *tie in to this character* [ital. orig.]."[95]

As Russel Wright implies here, the objects the designer creates are not a means of elevating popular American taste, particularly, but a way of confirming it; designed goods become a part of the larger set of American things that encompasses bridges and skyscrapers as well as shooting galleries and barber shops. ("No matter how vulgar.") In eliding the differences between engineering and architecture, between vernacular and high culture, Wright may have found the key to popular acceptance. One can see in his designs, moreover, a material embodiment of the program of cultural synthesis Van Wyck Brooks had, earlier in the century, articulated. And he had done so in an affirmation of collective and somewhat disorganized energies that Mumford, say, with his more utopian visions of American possibilities, had never dreamed of.

With Russel Wright's affirmation of the whole of American culture, lock, stock, and barrel, we have come a long way from Stickley's great educational and reform effort, and a long way too from Frank Lloyd Wright's effort to design a world he deemed fitting (and fittingly elevating) for his fellow Usonians. The older Wright, as had Sullivan, connected himself with the prophetic strain in Whitman, taking the poet as a model for his own romantic individualism, and seeing himself—as did the poet—as the representative, the voice, of the common man, yet separate from him;[96] Russel Wright might be seen as the Whitman who was brother in arms to the common man, his comrade on the ferries and omnibuses of New York City. Mumford saw Frank Lloyd Wright as *outside* his culture, in the way Whitman was;[97] Russel Wright clearly was *inside* of his. And of the two perhaps it was Russel who best exemplified Louis Sullivan's dicta that "the desire at once to follow and to lead the public should be the critical attitude of our profession toward the formation of a national style," and that "no architectural style can become a finality, that runs counter to popular feeling."[98]

But was Russel Wright's catholicity, his populist embrace of the wide range of American vernacular culture from the Brooklyn Bridge to the "trick cocktail gadget" really the direction in which America was going? Wright had asked, "Why can't someone, a Museum of Modern Art or a New York World's Fair, put on an exhibit in which they would dramatize all design that is American?"[99] As it happens, the 1939 New York World's Fair was close to being exactly that, a celebration of American vitality and productivity, and it yields a telling image of the designer's America in the 1930s by virtue of its intended orientation toward the future. There were, in the amusement areas, the usual alligators, dancing girls, and exotic natives; but the official spaces of the fair were dominated by a streamlined vision of the future in which major corporations (General Motors, Chrysler, Ford) had assumed the leading position of power—above states, principalities, and nations—a world, in other words, where power was wielded by business rather than polis. It was a world where the spontaneous and quirky qualities of the culture—qualities that Russel Wright had celebrated and that had come through in that other major collective effort of the 1930s, the state and local guidebooks of the Federal Writers Project—had been largely submerged; in its place was put an ideal vision of static harmony—Democracity—viewed from balconies installed within the center of the Perisphere. It was a world designed with reverence for efficiency, where efficiency meant stimulating desire and controlling its expression through the purchase of goods and experiences; a world of conveyor belts and revolving platforms that moved products and people, of crowds that flowed around ramps and up escalators like so many bottles moving through the conveyor belts of a beverage factory. It may not have been what Russel Wright had in mind exactly, but it was, in important ways, a microcosm of the consumer society, and it crystallized changes that had been underway since 1900.

For one, the fair embodied in its architecture a frank and enthusiastic acceptance of the role of the machine in modern life, evident in the "sincerity" of the building designs: there was, after all, a world of difference between the Columbia Exposition of 1893, with its elegant ersatz replications of the Roman Empire, and the 1939 fair, in which "There was an absolute conviction that buildings must be made to look what they are—temporary exhibit structures. No imitations of historic architecture or imitations of permanent materials were permitted."[100] And the startling shapes of the fair—the trylon and perisphere, the flowing geometries of scores of other buildings—were all tacit evidence of the imaginative power of the famous designers of the day—Geddes, Loewy, Teague, Dreyfuss—each of whom had major responsibilities. Physically the fair thus carried a major political message, for the designer was the embodiment of man's desired control over the machine.

And yet the figure of the designer, looked at closely, was not without overtones that seem, in retrospect, somewhat threatening. Mumford had been among the first to propose the architect as an important new synthesizer for the culture as a whole, embodying the contrary ideologies of craft and machine, when he wrote: "Cut off though he is from the actual processes of building, he nevertheless remains the sole surviving craftsman who maintains the relation towards the whole structure that the old handicraft workers used to enjoy in connection with their particular job." At least that was Mumford's hope, for, as he added, it was impossible to say at the time whether architects would be "extruded by mechanism, or whether they will have the opportunity to restore to our machine-system some of the freedom of an earlier regime."[101] And that freedom was certainly the goal of the industrial designers who became prominent in the 1930s, among them Teague, who praised the craft technologies of the preindustrial age and saw in the products of the machine "the revival of the ancient pride in skill and joy in things skillfully made. . . . We are seeing around us a rebirth of the intuitive, unself-conscious spirit of craftsmanship," a new Machine Age craftsmanship, "aiming again at rightness in things and in living conditions."[102]

By fiat, as it were, the problem of the machine was solved: the designer was the surrogate Craftsman, only larger than life, of heroic proportion. Sheldon and Martha Cheney had put it well when they wrote of the industrial designer, a few years before the fair, in language borrowed from Elie Faure's description of Cézanne: "He is in accord with the secret rhythm of his century; he is urged on . . . by profound forces of which he is no more conscious than were the masons of the last Romanesque churches whose nave was suddenly to leap, lighten, elongate, and hover like a wing over the generation that was arising."[103]

The designer's role in the production process was emblematic of the way planning and reason could govern the political process as well. One sees this technocratic faith in Geddes's conviction that the expert manager would prevail over the confusion of human needs: "Tomorrow, municipal governments embodying the brains of the community will plan their cities in the light of the city's needs."[104] And it is visible as well in Teague's similar vision of a society that would function with the "serene harmony" of the perfect machine, and yet still—paradoxically—would allow the individual "full scope to exercise whatever capacity for enjoyment of life and for fruitful activity he possesses. [Society] will have the perfect integration of parts we see today in some of our products and that machine production makes possible in all of them."[105] What passed unnoticed in this notion of the designer was the subversion of the democratic premises of Whitman, Sullivan, Stickley, and Mumford; the one true and remaining Craftsman was also, it seems clear in retrospect, being celebrated as Benevolent Despot.

*Industrial designer's office designed by Raymond Loewy and Lee Simpson
for Contemporary American Industrial Design, museum exhibition at
Metropolitan Museum of Art, 1934
(Courtesy of Metropolitan Museum of Art)*

The rhetoric of the World's Fair was misleading on several other counts as well: if the designer embodied man's vicarious control over the machine, and over society, where did that leave the worker? Earlier in the decade, Richard F. Bach, of the Metropolitan Museum of Art, had envisioned that the designer would make "of technology a skilled laborer in the cause of design and of industry the well-managed servant of industrial art."[106] Real factory workers on assembly lines seem to have disappeared in this representation; instead we have abstractions like "technology" and "industry" serving in some vague way the "art" of production. Bach's rhetoric conceals, of course, the effects of Taylorization on factory organization, which segmented the work of production into discrete jobs at the lowest possible skill level, thus turning the worker into a cog in the machine process.

Similar populist rhetoric suffuses the official *Guidebook* to the fair, beginning on the first page ("This is *your* Fair, built for *you* and dedicated to *you*") and continuing through the descriptions of the various exhibits. (The Perisphere's "Democracity" was climaxed by a symphonic poem with a "chorus of a thousand voices" singing a hymn to the farmers and mechanics who all "must work together to make possible the better life" of tomorrow.)[107] Concealed beneath the promise of human mastery of technology and the cooperation of all elements in society was the brute reality of factory labor, with its maximum of efficiency—in the understanding of the time—achieved by the transformation of the worker into a part of the great production mechanism. And while General Motors seemed to promise a future filled with luxury automobiles and freedom of travel, it neglected to make clear that the taxpayer would be paying for the highways. As the narrator's father explains in Doctorow's *World's Fair*, "So General Motors is telling us what they expect from us: we must build them the highways so they can sell us the cars."[108]

The fair argued, moreover, that society was on the brink of perfection (it was in fact the eve of World War II) and that we—the viewer, the spectator, the worker—had only to choose this world in order to bring it about. After all, if perfection could be achieved at the World's Fair, why not in the world at large? The Futurama exhibit embodied precisely this logic when it directed spectators to exit from the scale model of the future city into a life-size replica of the same urban intersection they had just looked down on in miniature—only now with real cars rolling by beneath the pedestrian traffic. And Mumford's script for the movie, *The City*, shown at the 1939 fair, insisted that the viewer must choose the kind of world he would have—urban chaos or garden city utopia—as if all that was needed was the citizen's approval. Viewers looked down at the static geographic and social hierarchies of Geddes's model city of 1960 at the fair as if it were a great shining goal of harmony just ahead of them; but really it was as remote as a Chinese vase in a museum case, removed from the actualities of free market forces and history.

In some ways, however, the World's Fair was only too representative of the world at large. Not only did it mirror the ideal of a consumer society, tracking its desires through endless corridors and displays; it also reflected the power structure that lay behind the smoothly turning wheels, a structure in which the industrial designer may not have had quite the all-powerful role he imagined. As Jeffrey Meikle cogently put it, "However much designers like Teague or Geddes preferred to see themselves as social engineers designing and controlling a machine-age environment, their control extended only to areas conceded by corporate patrons."[109] The mastery over the machine that the architect and designer had achieved was limited, at best, within a larger context of political and economic forces that would defy even the best intentions of the corporations.

By the end of the 1930s, the machine had become fully integrated into American life, although the intimate mastery that Stickley had promoted, uniting the head and hand of the worker, was becoming ever more scarce in the workplace; the vestigial remains of the craft tradition Stickley espoused were being relegated to the hobbyists' workbench and the Sunday afternoon. As for the structural integrity of Craftsman designs, with their restrained ornament and visible authenticity of materials, those values had undergone considerable modification, but they survived still, as a catchword at least—that form must follow function, whatever that might mean in practice. And the craft ideal survived as well, to some degree, in the mass-market designs of Russel Wright, later to be replaced by a taste for Scandinavian Modern. But the main trend of design in the marketplace during the 1930s and again after the war, was a restless changing of styles, devoid of functionalist stability, designs that were a function of the marketplace and planned obsolescence rather than of any

*Armchair visitors to City of 1960 designed by Norman Bel Geddes, at
Futurama, New York City World's Fair, 1939
(Courtesy of Harry Ransom Humanities Research Center,
University of Texas at Austin)*

enduring design purpose. Only in the great structures of engineers, in the highways and bridges, did the functionalist tradition in its purer forms survive. Meanwhile, Geddes's observations of Coney Island architecture were prescient of a growing commercial design ethos that would eventually culminate in the facsimile environment of Disneyland and its many imitations.

But as America moved into a world of larger and larger scale, so did nostalgia for a simpler pace grow; Colonial Williamsburg in the 1920s was only the first of many subsequent acts of restoration, turning the preindustrial folk world into a museum of crafts and social harmony for the edification of the industrial urban public. The Federal Arts Project's *Index of American Design*, which sought to connect the integrity of traditional design with modern functionalism, was a culminating expression of a culture trying to take stock of its past before it was too late.

Stepping back to view the early decades of the century as a whole, one can see repeated efforts to achieve unity in a single, fixed "American" style, but in reality there was an increasing fragmentation of design modes. Mumford's exhortations during the 1920s, that we adapt the machine to the needs of the community and to those of the biological organism, were replaced, in the 1930s, by his sense that in the massive scale of a technological society we were increasingly passing the point of control. Meanwhile, Frank Lloyd Wright's Usonian houses—an effort to design for the great middle class—were attractive (and affordable) mainly to the upper-middle professional, while the mass market bought the builder's stylistic bastardizations, whether of Wright or ranch, Colonial or Tudor. Striving to develop an authentically American style while coming to terms with the machine, the designer would seem, all too often, to be making utopian gestures in a marketplace governed by big money.

But the effort at cultural invention and renewal in the twentieth century was of course not limited to architects and designers; and the artist who could afford to take a stand somewhat off center from the marketplace might be less vulnerable to changing fashion and the client's patronage. In photography and literature some of the same themes examined in this chapter work themselves out quite differently: there, the pursuit of "authenticity" as a moral and aesthetic goal was less trammeled by the exigencies of traffic and commerce. When Mumford concluded *The Brown Decades*, he wrote of Stieglitz the photographer in terms that he had previously used to describe Sullivan and Richardson and Roebling, and that I have quoted before: "In Stieglitz's photographs one has the *Sachlichkeit* that Roebling was the first to express firmly in the Brooklyn Bridge. This quality is one of the distinguishing marks of modern civilzation: first appearing in the engineer, it has made its way, step by step, into every other department of life. Stieglitz's uniqueness was to embody this *Sachlichkeit* without losing his sense of the underlying human attitudes and emotions. He did not achieve objectivity by displacing humanity but by giving its peculiar virtues and functions and interests the same place that he gives to steam engines, skyscrapers, or airplanes."[110] In the maker of images, then, Mumford, along with many other intellectuals and artists, would find society's best example of the master of the machine and restorer of objectivity.

The Camera and
the Verification
of Fact

*T*o the nineteenth century, the camera was an unwieldy machine to be overcome by a combination of stamina and subtlety; to the twentieth century, the fact that the camera was a machine became its most exalted characteristic, guaranteeing the authenticity of its productions and forming the basis of its appeal, among artists and intellectuals, as a model for the synthesis of science and art. As I argued in an earlier chapter, the impact of the camera in the nineteenth century was based on its powers of description and generalization: it summed up experience, presenting a normative vision of the world that could enter the common memory as a facsimile of reality, an imitation founded on typological representation; it extended the individual's power of vision, and it provided models—images ready to the mind's eye—for thinking about the world. This function continued into the twentieth century in a good many forms, most notably in the practice of photojournalism, which was taking over from print more and more of the burden of communication during the early decades of the century. ("All the world sees with the same eyes," as one writer put it, "and what it sees often multiplied, must influence the whole of its life.")[1] Yet beginning around the turn of the century a new approach to the camera evolved, initiated in the work of Alfred Stieglitz, whose influence on the vocabulary of photography was profound over the next several decades.

This approach emphasized the photographer's eye, his particular angle on the subject, whether detailed close-up or aerial view; it emphasized the idiosyncrasy of the camera's way of seeing as a function of its mechanical character, rather than its capacity to reproduce a facsimile of "normal" vision. For the authenticity of the camera, it was believed, was the authenticity of a machine that was accepted as a machine. And the photograph functioned not as a surrogate for experience, or as a memory device, but as an instrument of revelation, changing our way of thinking about, and seeing the world. In proclaiming its duality as a way of seeing that was at once scientific and artistic, photography assumed a special importance in twentieth-century culture, becoming a symbol of a kind of vision that is central to the culture of authenticity.

And yet, the first four decades of the twentieth century saw a distinct shift in the practice and theory of photography from an aesthetic to a social orientation, from a mode of observation that was scientific and optical to a mode (in the 1930s) that was rooted in the "objectivity" of social science. But significantly the rhetoric of photographic discussion remained surprisingly consistent, revolving around the persistent goal of representing some more intense, more authentic reality, beyond mere replication, something closer than "realism" to "the real thing" itself. I will be attending, in this discussion, as much to the verbal discourse surrounding photography as to the photographs themselves, for the cultural significance of the camera lies not only in the images it produced, but in how people thought about it.

What did Stieglitz symbolize? (For his importance was as much symbolic as anything else.) When Edward Weston was asked in 1923 to contribute an article to a volume on pictorial photography, he explained why he was no longer a pictorialist by invoking the example of Stieglitz. Pictorialism was "illustrative," it was "genre" work, a "little byproduct of literature"; instead, Weston had placed Stieglitz at the center of his thoughts, not least for his exploitation of the camera's mechanistic qualities. Weston quoted a number of recent articles on Stieglitz to explain his disaffection from pictorialism, among them a piece by the critic Paul Rosenfeld that had appeared in *The Dial* in 1921. "Never, indeed, has there been such another affirmation of the majesty of the moment," Rosenfeld had written. "No doubt, such witness to the wonder of the here, the now, was what the impressionist painters were striving to bear, but their instrument was not sufficiently swift. For such immediate response, a machine of the nature of the camera was required." And Weston added: "Good reason, indeed, for photography's existence."[2] The key to Stieglitz's meaning, and the key to the cultural meaning of photography in the early twentieth century was an affirmation of the camera as a machine that was tuned to the new age.[3]

Rosenfeld's article had appeared, along with a spate of others confirming Stieglitz's significance, following the major retrospective exhibition of Stieglitz's work at the Anderson Galleries in 1921, and it indicates clearly the degree to which photography had moved to the center of cultural discourse in the early decades. Rosenfeld had clarified Stieglitz's cultural importance by placing him in the context of America's machine civilization. "For a century," he wrote, machines "have been impoverishing the experience of humanity," enslaving people to the repetitive work of the manufacturing process, numbing "their desire for improving themselves through improving their crafts," forcing them to think only in terms of cheaper production. The result was a deprivation of experience and a deadening of the soul. In language that echoed Van Wyck Brooks, Rosenfeld wrote that "the whole of society was in conspiracy against itself, eager to separate body and soul, to give the body completely over to the affairs of business while leaving the soul straying aimlessly in the clouds."[4] To Rosenfeld, Stieglitz's greatness lay in his using the machine to demonstrate "the unmechanicalness of the human spirit." He had made the camera "a part of his living, changing, growing body"; he had used it like a craftsman working with chisel and brush. And in doing so, Stieglitz had met the environment—the world of "complex modern mechanisms"—on its own terms, and had affirmed the values that industrialism had denied him.[5]

This notion of the camera as a part of Stieglitz's own body was a prime element in the mythmaking surrounding the photographer. Indeed, at times Stieglitz seemed to undergo a kind of Ovidean metamorphosis, as in this description by Stieglitz's friend, the writer Horace Traubel, which takes off on the issue of whether a machine can produce works of art: "You edge up to me and ask me whether I'm aware that the camera's a machine. Certainly. And I'm also aware that Stieglitz is another machine. And I'm a machine. And the man who kicks is a machine. But Stieglitz is also a man. And when I look at these pictures I think somehow that the machine is also a man.... I can't tell where the machine in either case stops and where the man begins." Traubel, who as a young man had sat with the ancient Walt Whitman, recording meticulously his conversations and asides (photographing them, we might say), saw in photography an art as defensible, and as significant, as free verse.[6]

To Traubel, as to others, the merging of the individual and the machine in Stieglitz and his camera was cause for celebration. In the enthusiasm of the moment, the Frankenstein myth—with its warning against our perfect technologies taking on a life of their own beyond human control—became grist for the Dadaist mill. With whimsy and fantasy the monster could be subdued and caressed and transformed into a Galatea. "We are living in the age of the machine," said the photographer and writer Paul B. Haviland in *291*. "Man made the machine in his own image. She has limbs which act; lungs which breathe; a heart which beats; a nervous system through which runs electricity. The phonograph is the image of his voice; the camera the image of his eye." This bionic female creation is superior to man in efficiency, yet needs man's direction. The fantasy ends in an incestuous symbiosis: in their mating, man and machine "complete one another . . . Photography is one of the fine fruits of this union."[7] Or, as critic and artist Marius De Zayas put it around the same time, Stieglitz "married Man to Machinery and he obtained issue."[8] Behold, Photography.

But the more serious point of Stieglitz's significance was elaborated carefully in an essay by the young Paul Strand, whose work had been featured in the final two issues of *Camera Work* (in 1916 and 1917). To Strand, Stieglitz was the exemplary photographer, whose handling of the camera symbolized man's mastery over the machine. In his important 1922 article, "Photography and the New God," Strand argued that "creative control of one form of the machine, the camera," was symbolically countering the general sense of the machine's domination of man. Building on his discussion of Stieglitz, Strand constructed an image of the artist who "has seized upon the mechanism and materials of a machine, and is pointing the way. He it is who is again insisting, through the science of optics and the chemistry of light and metals and paper, upon the eternal value of the concept of craftsmanship." And Strand, like Rosenfeld, offered the camera as a means to effect a fusion of the split in American culture between a destructive materialism and "anemic phantasy," between technology and art: "Must not these two forms of energy converge before a living future can be born of both?"[9] To some extent this is a return to a way of thinking about photography—as both science and art—that was common among amateur photographers in the nineteenth century.[10] But the twentieth-century renewal of this idea was at a higher level of synthesis, regarding the photographer not as a strange hybrid (part chemist, part artist), but as the user of a modern machine capable of confronting the modern world. Through his mastery of the machine, the photographer carried forward the nineteenth-century craft tradition in the same way that the modern architect and industrial designer were thought to carry the craft tradition into the twentieth century.[11]

But we must place this central point in a larger historical context. In the latter decades of the nineteenth century, the camera had been dismissed by many as an artistic instrument because it was *merely* a machine; the extreme reaction of the Photo-Secession group promoted by Stieglitz around the turn of the century had been to manipulate the photographic plate in dozens of ways to achieve a "handmade" rather than a mechanical effect. But beginning in the second decade of the new century the camera was celebrated precisely because it *was* a machine—a machine that a person could manifestly control. It was not simply, as Traubel had said, that it was all right if the camera was a machine; in the 1920s and 1930s the mechanical nature of the instrument was essential to the whole mystique of photography in America.[12] And this notion would remain a part of the Stieglitz legacy, reiterated again by Lewis Mumford in his tribute to the photographer in the 1934 celebratory volume, *America and Alfred Stieglitz*, where the photographer represents *right use* of the machine—"subordinate to his human direction."[13]

It seems only fair to note, in retrospect, that the significance attributed to the camera rested on something of a conceptual legerdemain. For there are, after all, several distinct kinds of "machines," and the discourse on photography during the teens and 1920s elided these distinctions. There are, for example, machines or artifacts that are unique and sublime in their conception and scale (for example, the big Corliss Engine at the Centennial, or the Brooklyn Bridge, which Hart Crane was to celebrate in *The Bridge* [1930]); as such they stand as feats of achievement, remarkable icons of a technological civilization. But there are also, at the other extreme of technological production, machines that are reduplicated endlessly (as in a factory) and that in turn endlessly perform repetitive tasks—echoed by the laborer—to the end of producing endlessly identical objects for mass consumption. This of course is the "machine" that Rosenfeld and the others were speaking about as the force that deprives people of their humanity. The camera is yet a third kind of technological artifact, the machine as instrument, as hand tool; and in the right hands, it could lend itself to artistic control. The camera thus became, during the first decades of the century, an almost magical object within the artistic and intellectual community, representing symbolic control over technological forces that otherwise were felt to be out of control. In the logic of modernist thought, the camera was a David that would counteract the Goliath force of the giant machine.

Central to the new aesthetic of the camera was its scientific character, which was a function of its speed and, consequently, its power of analysis. "Photography is the most modern of the arts," the photographer A. L. Coburn had written in *Camera Work* in 1911; "it is more suited to the art requirements of this age of scientific achievement than any other." For the camera, in the hands of a Stieglitz, could match the pace of urban life and record "an impression in the flashing fragment of a second."[14] Or, as Hart Crane wrote to Stieglitz, "speed is at the bottom of it all—the hundredth of a second caught so precisely that the motion is continued from the picture infinitely: the moment made eternal."[15] To be modern was to comprehend reality in a new way, in accord with the new discoveries about space and time that were flowing from science.[16] The painter and poet Marsden Hartley, who was an intimate in the Stieglitz circle, drew a distinction between the old assumptions and the new, when he wrote, in 1921, "Art these days is a matter of scientific comprehension of reality, not a trick of the hand or the old-fashioned manipulation of a brush or tool." And Stieglitz, who eschewed such manipulations in his photographic practice, was the exemplary figure for Hartley: in diagnosing a problem he is "scientific first and whatever else afterward, which is the hope of the modern artists of all movements, regardless."[17]

Yet the enthusiasm for the scientific method in the Stieglitz circle was tempered, significantly, by a reaffirmation of the transcendent spirit of art. Thus, Marius De Zayas declared in 1913 that "modern art is analytical. It wants to know the essence of things; and it analyses them in their phenomena of form, following the method of experimentation set by science, which consists in the determination of the material conditions in which a phenomenon appears";[18] but he also said, in the same essay, that, "taking the world as it is," the camera artist would nevertheless find "the eternal in it."[19] Here was a definition of the middle ground between science and art that responded to the need to bridge the split cultures of America that Van Wyck Brooks was simultaneously writing about. And standing behind this conception of photography (and behind the other arts as well), was Whitman, who was increasingly invoked as the great precursor of modernism, the artist who had first assimilated modern experience in an original form, who had vivified facts, whose transcendent vision was rooted in materiality.[20] And if Whitman was a central inspiration to American artists during the years between the wars (including writers), Stieglitz himself was Whitman Reborn.

"Save for Whitman there has been amongst us no native-born artist equal to this photographer," Paul Rosenfeld declared.[21] Rosenfeld cannot help sounding like Whitman himself as he describes Stieglitz's subjects—"the navel, the *mons veneris*, the armpits, the bones underneath the skin of the neck and collar"; and he borrows Whitman's own trope in describing Stieglitz's organic aesthetic, in which a circuit is created between the world and the eye: "Clothes-lines and hands, white shirts and leafing trees, . . . have all been taken into the photographer and issued again, suffused utterly with his own law and revelatory of it."[22] And Mumford confirmed the connection in the 1930s, stressing the discovery of art in real things themselves: "He does not look for subjects—'aesthetic' subjects, or *'photogénique'* subjects—because his subject is life, and for him, as for Whitman, a blade of grass is a miracle."[23] Stieglitz, in the 1930s, was regularly being placed in the lineage of original American artists, the great pantheon of organic functionalists: a contributor to the celebratory volume, *America and Alfred Stieglitz*, wrote that he was "a continuator in our time of the tradition launched by Emerson and Whitman and Louis Sullivan" in their times. "These men also strove to create the tradition of the American thing. They tried to visualize the unique indigenous American person, and through multitudes of him, the honest creative America."[24]

From the earliest years of his practice, Stieglitz's photographs revealed a factual and objective approach to "the American thing," even while he was strongly supporting—through exhibitions and as editor of *Camera Work*—the pictorialist fashion in art photography, which leaned toward allegorical subjects, soft-focus treatments, and manipulated surfaces. In the early issues of *Camera Work*, with photographs by Gertrude Kasebier, Edward Steichen, and Clarence White, A. L. Coburn, and others, figures are posed and mannered, sometimes costumed or surrounded by objets d'art; landscapes are romantically suffused with dawn, twilight, or artificial moonlight; titles are allusive and literary. Meanwhile, Stieglitz was experimenting with a whole range of available modes beyond the conventions of pictorialism, including, for example, street photography. The street photographs taken during this period, both in Europe and New York, exhibit the character types favored by photographers working in the realistic mode at the time—ragpickers, vagrants, peasants—but Stieglitz's treatment is always distinctive. The youth in "Venetian Boy" (1887), for example, is strikingly ragged, but he confronts the camera with a seriousness and dignity nowhere present in Stieglitz's contemporaries, who tended to turn the subject into a more pathetic type.

During the 1890s Stieglitz was already concentrating on the urban subjects that would attract so much attention from artists and writers outside the camera club circles and that would come to mark his peculiarly "modern" vision. The city had of course been a major subject for photographers throughout the nineteenth century, but the rhetorical mode had been either promotional (with a focus on static scenes, buildings, vistas, panoramas), or else voyeuristic (with an emphasis on "low-life" subjects who were deemed "interesting").[25] Stieglitz followed neither of these modes, developing instead a style of apprehending urban life that raised it to the level of a personal artistic vision. His urban images were marked by an impressive technical virtuosity or by a daring choice of subject—and sometimes both. Consider, for example, the shimmering play of streetlights on a rainy plaza in "The Savoy Hotel, New York, 1898"; or the blizzard in "Winter, Fifth Avenue, 1893," with its horse-drawn carriage moving down the center of a snow-filled street, for which Stieglitz said he waited hours, in order to capture exactly the right moment. These were the kinds of images that Charles Caffin might have had in mind when he wrote of the combination of scientific and artistic virtues in Stieglitz that resulted in the "realization of a vivid mental conception."[26]

But Stieglitz was also, during the period around the turn of the century, experimenting with subject matter of a more aggressively urban, quotidian nature, the opposite of the "poetic" subjects that were considered appropriate for art photography. In these photographs the sense of America as a changing place was emphasized, with buildings and streets, machinery, transportation, and industrial subjects, yet still with an eye to the special weather and atmosphere of particular moments. Commercial photographers during the latter decades of the nineteenth century had specialized in industrial subjects and railroads as part of a regional catalogue of sights that would interest the tourist or represent regional features. Stieglitz's industrial and urban subjects were not topographical in this way; they captured the drama of urban street life, the excitement of technological change, but their purpose was not description, it was the evocation of a moment in the life of the city.

Several of these earlier images were deliberately anti-heroic, affirming the value of the mundane, the anti-poetic, most particularly, "The Street Paver" (1893) and "The Asphalt Paver" (1892). In others, the coupling of the machine and natural energies interested Stieglitz, especially when the natural force was that of the horse. "The Terminal" (1892), for example, captured the steam rising off the horses' bodies as they were washed down at the end of a car line, still harnessed to the heavy omnibus behind them; while "Excavating—New York" (1911) featured a confusion of horses and derricks and carts in the pit of a building site. (Stieglitz loved horses, and horse-racing, from his boyhood days, and the harnessed animals of the city had a particular significance for him.)

Yet as the new century began, Stieglitz's imagery began to evoke the heroic technological forces at work in industrial America and the city, anticipating a growing aesthetic interest in the machine during the postwar era. Smoke billows powerfully out of a locomotive at the center of a landscape of gently curving railroad tracks, offering a contrast between the textures of smoke and steel. Called "The Hand of Man" (1902), the title suggests an attempt to assimilate the industrial imagery to a Romantic perspective somewhat at odds with the actual subject. A similar subject done in the next year ("In the New York Central Yards" [1903]) is grittier. The skyscraper also figures importantly in these years, with the famous Flat-iron building, the tallest structure at the time, pictured in a snowstorm ("The 'Flatiron'" [1903]), looming up—like an ocean liner, Stieglitz thought—above the park, a tree in the foreground providing a contrasting natural tower. However much Stieglitz set himself in opposition to the commercial civilization of the United States and its money values, he was enthralled by the energies it expressed, and several photographs of the first decade picture the rising skyscrapers of Manhattan as dynamic structures, looming above the water's edge, material symbols of modern technology.

Alfred Stieglitz, Excavating—New York, *1911*
(Courtesy of Philadelphia Museum of Art)

Stieglitz had been enlarging the vocabulary of photography for nearly two decades when, in 1910, his work, and the journal *Camera Work*, took a decisive turn toward modernism. The October 1911 issue contains several images already mentioned here, but some others that are new in a way that brings to photography the laws of composition that were being promulgated by the post-impressionists and cubists. And with this issue what we might call Stieglitz's second phase of development becomes evident. Subjects are clearly recognizable— the New York harbor, ferryboats, skyscrapers, wharves, smoke—but now the shapes within the picture frame form rhyming patterns, as if the surface were a two-dimensional abstraction. This is evident, for example, in "The Ferry Boat" (1910), where the population of piles on the wharf in the foreground mirrors the passengers about to disembark the ferry, and where the curving shape of the wharf and the curve of the ferry also form a repeating pattern.

Perhaps the most famous of all Stieglitz shots, "The Steerage" (1907), which also appeared in the same issue of *Camera Work*, exhibits this new quality of composition most clearly.[27] With the picture

Alfred Stieglitz, The Steerage, *1907*
(Courtesy of Philadelphia Museum of Art)

plane divided in half, cut by the gangplank across the middle, and with the crossing line of the funnel on the left echoed by the ladder on the right, the image has an overall abstract organization that is enriched by other rhyming shapes—the crossed suspenders, the circles of hats, etc. With a hindsight that may have brought to the surface what had been only vaguely intuitive, Stieglitz described his own fascination with the composition in the moment of its making: "I stood spellbound for a while. I saw shapes related to one another—a picture of shapes, and underlying it, a new vision that held me: simple people; the feeling of ship, ocean, sky; a sense of release that I was away from the mob called 'rich.' "[28] The progress of Stieglitz's thought in the last phrases suggests that the new vision was also bound up with a feeling for the greater authenticity of the lower classes, a feeling that may have been carried with him on board as part of the baggage of realism. (It also reflects Stieglitz's need to escape from the confines of his first marriage and the luxury of their first-class appointments.)

To Stieglitz's contemporaries, "The Steerage" had, above all, that quality of objectivity that came to symbolize the machine aesthetic. When *291* reprinted the image as a feature of its September–October 1915 issue, Marius De Zayas wrote, "In 1907, Stieglitz, in the photograph which we publish in the present number of *291* under the title 'The Steerage,' obtained the verification of a fact. The desire of modern plastic expression has been to create for itself an objectivity. The task accomplished by Stieglitz's photography has been to make objectivity understood for it has given it the true importance of a natural fact."[29] It is as if De Zayas is announcing a major scientific discovery—the first electron, the invention of penicillin, the "verification of a fact."

Paul Strand, writing an appraisal of Stieglitz following his death, also looked back on "The Steerage" as a major achievement, with the runway in the image seen as "fact and symbol separating those who were able to travel to America in the clear air of the upper deck and those who had to come in the darkness of the hold."[30] But Strand's interpretation, although plausible enough, only indicates how far from fact Stieglitz's "verification of a fact" could go once it entered the world as symbol; for Stieglitz's own report reveals that the photograph was taken on a ship bound toward Europe, not America, and that the people pictured were therefore returning to their homelands

Alfred Stieglitz, The City Across the River, *1910*
(Courtesy of Philadelphia Museum of Art)

after whatever disenchantment they had experienced in the promised land. Moreover, the separation of classes that Strand presumes is illusory; until 1920 or so ocean liners had only two classes—first and steerage—and so Stieglitz, traveling in first class, was looking at a section of the ship that was most likely all "steerage," encompassing working-class and middle-class passengers. Still, this image is as good as any to sum up Stieglitz's second phase, when the goal of art photography was the production of the single image that would compete with any other work of the imagination. But it does not anticipate the new direction Stieglitz would take in the late teens and in the decades beyond, when, increasingly, he thought not in terms of single images but in terms of the series.

The production of a single image that would stand against a Picasso embodied a belief in the power of the camera to render a representative moment, to penetrate the instant and render it timeless in its aesthetic perfection. Underlying the concept of the series is a rather different assumption: that the camera can be used as a recording instrument to render repeatedly the reality of time as an experience of changing phenomena. The individual photograph in a series is always modified by the other members of the series, which qualify its uniqueness and imply analogies of structure and purpose, yet also allow for the finer discrimination of singularity. Together, the members of the series compose a totality whose sum is greater than its parts. Stieglitz simultaneously worked on three major series during the 1920s and 1930s: a collective portrait of Georgia O'Keeffe (actually begun in the late teens); a series of cloud studies; and a series of urban vistas taken from the windows of Manhattan buildings.

The O'Keeffe series began in 1917, shortly after the two had met, when the painter was 29. "His idea of a portrait was not just one picture," O'Keeffe wrote in retrospect. "His dream was to start with a child at birth and photograph that child in all of its activities as it grew to be a person and on throughout its adult life. As a portrait it would be a photographic diary."[31] Stieglitz wrote to Sadakichi Hartmann in 1919 that he had had in mind to do such a portrait—"heads & ears—toes—hands—torsos"—for many years, and in fact he had begun a diary of his daughter Kitty, picturing her at various times of the day, some years earlier.[32] Over three hundred photographs eventually formed the final core of the O'Keeffe series (many more were shot), exhibiting an enormous range of emotions and attitudes—from pensive sadness to mischievous gaiety, from proud aloofness to frank openness, from vulnerability to austerity.

Stieglitz had always experimented methodically with his prints, making dozens before he might be satisfied; now he experimented with his subject, shooting plate after plate of different aspects of the same thing, exploring the formal possibilities of abrupt framing and cropping, of close-up examinations of skin texture, of abstract shapes of the torso. The whole added up to a kind of Whitmanesque catalogue, an anatomy or composite essence of the body. Stieglitz achieved, as Lewis Mumford put it, "the exact visual equivalent of the report of the hand or the face as it travels over the body of the beloved," restoring a reality and authenticity to nudity that had been missing in the "halo of arcadian romanticism" that had marked the pictorialists' treatment of the nude.[33] In his 1922 volume, *Civilization in the United States*, Harold Stearns had argued that the intellect must establish contact with the body, and that the "dignity" of thought can be reached only when it functions in a full relationship with "the more clamorous instincts of the body."[34] That joining of mind and biology —a part of the healing fusion of opposites that was sought in the culture at large, replacing the dislocations of the genteel tradition and Puritanism—was also a goal of Mumford's synthesis, and Stieglitz had achieved it in his O'Keeffe series.

The O'Keeffe series must be seen as the expression of intimacy between the photographer and his subject, in which the camera itself becomes an instrument of love. The cloud series and the Manhattan series are altogether different. Stieglitz had begun photographing buildings while he was still at "291" (his Fifth Avenue gallery) in the 1910s, and he continued to point his lens out the windows of the American Place gallery and of his living quarters in the Shelton Hotel during the 1920s. There are no people in these photographs. And no trees. Instead, we see the city as an artificial construction, a world of buildings—walls, bricks, windows, girders, tubes, and towers. The changing time of day is apparent in gradations of light in the background, ranging from nighttime to broad daylight, with the play of shadows on the buildings forming a major subtheme in a number of the images. Looking at the Manhattan pictures in the context of the Depression, Mumford saw them as studies of "the ultimate result of putting nature at a distance and subordinating all the values of living to the paper routine of pseudo-work and profit-pyramiding. These skyscrapers of Stieglitz's last photographs might be the cold exhalations of a depopulated world."[35] Stieglitz was indeed hostile to the commercial world, but Mumford was unable to see that his series on the city turns the machine-made urban environment into an exhibition of formal possibilities, inexhaustible variations on a single theme. Taking the extreme challenge of the genre—using only the window out of which you are looking, make as many photographs having different qualities as you can—Stieglitz demonstrated the richness of restraint and the virtuosity of the camera as a machine to see with. The Manhattan landscapes borrow the hard-edged vocabulary of the precisionists, but they turn the shapes of the city into a series of cubist explorations, the triumph of a machine-art.

With the cloud series we are in another world entirely. The technical challenge here was not to overcome the fixed position of the camera as it faced a finite landscape, but precisely the opposite: to work under an infinitely changing sky from a potentially infinite number of vantage points. Here the subject is change, but purely within the natural realm. Some of the early images of the 1920s show edges of land, an occasional building, a tree, but the later studies of the 1930s eliminate any possible human or artifical context: we are looking at a framed area of clouds, a window into the sky overhead.[36] The technical qualities of the prints are of course impressive—detailed cloud textures are revealed under varying lighting conditions—but they serve an aesthetic end larger than description, looking back to Turner's clouds and forward to the meditations of Sol LeWitt. Stieglitz called them "Equivalents," meaning that they were pictures of inner states of mind, feelings, thoughts. (The idea stimulated Minor White's whole aesthetic theory, but is at best somewhat cloudy.) Stieglitz had his Emersonian moods, and nature surely did wear the colors of the spirit for him; but we might just as well regard the cloud studies as part of a scientific catalogue of chance meteorological formations, a kind of sequel to Muybridge's studies of animal locomotion. But perhaps they are best placed somewhere in between science and transcendentalism, a demonstration of the representative possibilities of natural facts.

Two things must be said finally about the series of clouds and skyscrapers. First, the subjects are utterly different in character, the one organic and natural, the other utterly artificial. (These extreme purifications of subject matter were typical of modernist art in the 1920s.)[37] Second, how similar Stieglitz's approach was to both subjects, despite the difference: for in each case, he is conducting an exploration of formal possibilities, a set of variations that exploits the full range of his subject matter. In setting himself these problems, Stieglitz was pursuing habits of seeing and categorization that were developing among the photographic community in general during the 1910s and 1920s.

From the standpoint of the mid-1930s, Paul Strand wrote of Stieglitz: "These amazing portraits, whether they objectify faces or hands, the torso of a woman, or the torso of a tree, suggest the beginning of a penetration of the scientific spirit into the plastic arts."[38] Strand's observation identifies Stieglitz's value for the next generation of photographers, and it also invites us to draw some distinctions between Stieglitz's eye and the vision of those who learned from him. What Strand apparently had in mind as evidence of the "scientific spirit" were Stieglitz's close-ups, especially in the O'Keeffe series, where the photographer's studied attention to parts of the body reveals details of texture and shape that are otherwise invisible to the lens that politely stays back, details that are even less visible to the pictorialist soft-focus lens, with its idealizing intent. Yet in many ways Stieglitz's eye retains its normal range: he comes close, but not to the point of distortion; objects usually retain their expected weight and size; the angle of vision is not sought out for its strangeness; there are no abrupt compressions of foreground and background. All of which is to say that although Stieglitz represents the indispensable "beginning of the penetration of the scientific spirit into the plastic arts," he accommodated the spirit of the twentieth century to an eye that had its prior shaping in the nineteenth century. For Strand and the photographers after him, the eye was formed in the different world of the twentieth century, and the difference is visible, for one, in how the object is framed.

By and large, during the nineteenth century and continuing through the first decade and a half of the twentieth century, photography had followed the proportions and perspectives of normal vision. The image was a representation of the world more or less the way we might see it if we ourselves were where the camera had been placed, which was typically in a carefully selected but accessible location;

objects appeared in relation to other objects in a space that was governed by the same gravity that governed our own movements. This "normal" vision dominated photography until Strand dramatically closed the distance between the eye and the thing seen, with an impact on art photography that was immediate. Strand had arrived at his own early experiments with the close-up in the mid-teens, through his exposure to cubism and his effort to adapt its principles to photography. By moving close to the object, he could obtain an image that decontextualized it, fragmenting the whole form so as to obscure its identity. Working with common objects, he produced images whose experimental nature was clearly announced, yet whose tie to the real world of things was also clear: "Abstraction, Bowls"; "Abstraction, Porch Shadows." But after these early experiments Strand maintained a close attention to the object as a recognizable form. In 1922, delighted with his new ownership of an Akeley motion-picture camera, he did a series of close-ups of machines that brought together abstraction and mechanical form. "Lathe," "Gears," "Drilling Machine," "Akeley Motion Picture Camera," and "Double Akeley"—all showed with luminous clarity the textures of metal, the abstract shapes of machine parts, the intricate association of one component with another, and all were taken so close to the object as to eliminate context and with it any sense of scale. We are inside the world of the machine in these images, and it is, in Strand's vision, a world of pure aesthetic form.

A decade later the painter Fernand Léger was to articulate the power of the fragmented object in a piece that appeared in *The Little Review* in 1926, "A New Realism—The Object: Its Plastic and Cinematic Value." The "new realism" he advocated was based on the power of the camera—he was referring to motion-picture cameras, but his point is valid for the still camera as well—"to isolate the object or the fragment of an object and to present it on the screen in close-ups of the largest possible scale. Enormous enlargement of an object or a fragment gives it a personality it never had before and in this way it can become a vehicle of entirely new lyric and plastic power."[39] Strange effects could result from such close-ups, as the work of early modernists like Ralph Steiner would prove: seen up close, the manufactured object—a typewriter keyboard, for example—might appear to negate the logic of technology by giving a kind of individuality to the mass-produced object, while the effect of a close-up image of the

Paul Strand, Akeley Motion Picture Camera, New York, 1922, *Copyright
1971, Aperture Foundation, Inc., Paul Strand Archive
(Courtesy of Paul Strand Archive)*

Ralph Steiner, Typewriter as Design, *1921–22*
(Courtesy of Worcester Art Museum)

human body might be just the opposite—to rob the individual of his or her uniqueness and reduce the subject to an abstract and impersonal configuration of skin and bones.

Strand's interest in the machine as subject was yet another declaration of the modernity of the new god, Photography. There had of course been many photographs of manufacturing machinery and of industrial engineering projects in the nineteenth century, made on the order of companies and agencies, to record, or celebrate, their products. Such images, relatively straightforward in technique, aimed at supplying certain essential information about the object. And Stieglitz had, a few years before Strand, approached the machine in a new spirit of aesthetic enthusiasm: in "The Dirigible" and "The Aeroplane" (both 1910) the objects are pictured as abstract silhouettes against a space of sky and clouds. But Strand himself must be credited with the first expressive photographic close-ups of mechanical objects, beginning with "Automobile Wheel" (1917), which followed shortly upon the first paintings of abstract mechanical forms being done by Duchamp and Picabia. "Automobile Wheel" was new not only in that its emphasis was on the abstract form of the subject; it was new by virtue of the subject itself, the mechanical forms of the wheel, the spokes, the spring, which stood out in the marked contrasts of light and shade. It was, in short, a picture of the modern world.

Earlier, in 1915, while the pictorialists were out looking for poetic brooks at dawn, Strand had photographed telegraph poles in Texas, the wires and timbers outlined against the sky; at Fifth Avenue and 42nd Street he had looked down onto an intersection filled with pedestrians, automobiles, a horse-drawn hansom. It was as if Strand were responding directly to Sadakichi Hartmann's earlier call, in *Camera Work*, for new works based on new laws of composition that are appropriate for the modern world: "The main thoroughfare of a large city at night, near the amusement center, with its bewildering illumination of electrical signs, must produce something to which the accepted laws of composition can be applied only with difficulty. Scenes of traffic, or crowds in a street, in a public building, or on the seashore, dock and canal, bridge and tunnel, steam engine and trolley, will throw up new problems."[40] Strand's solutions to these new problems were printed in the last two issues of *Camera Work*—scenes of New York taken from positions on high, looking down onto the street, or into backyards, or down onto pedestrians in a park or in front of an ominously shadowed building. (The new organization of the picture, Strand had written, "is evolved either by movement of the camera in relation to the objects themselves or through their actual arrangement.")[41]

Where Strand, during the teens and early 1920s, significantly advanced Stieglitz's initial efforts at abstraction, Edward Weston, during the 1920s and 1930s, developed a clarity of vision that just as significantly intensified the "objectivity" of Stieglitz's photographic realism. "The mission of the photograph," Mumford wrote in *Technics and Civilization*, "is to clarify the object. To see as they are, as if for the first time, a boatload of immigrants, a tree in a Madison Square Park, a woman's breast, a cloud lowering over a black mountain—that requires patience and understanding."[42] Mumford was describing Stieglitz's photographs here, but his general point would apply as well to Weston, who, like Strand, derived his first principles (after he abandoned pictorialism) from Stieglitz. In a letter to his friend Johan Hagemeyer, following his initial meeting with Stieglitz, Weston wrote enthusiastically, " 'A maximum (amount) of detail with a maximum of simplification.'—with these words as a basis for his attitude towards photography—Alfred Stieglitz—talked with Jo and me for four hours —rather he talked *to* us . . . Brilliantly—convincingly."[43] Weston did not mind the maximum of Stieglitz's afflatus. For the truth he came away with was the truth of his own work: a maximum of detail with a maximum of simplification. The camera is "best in close-up," Weston wrote, "taking advantage of this lens power: recording with its one searching eye the very quintessence of the thing itself rather than a mood of that thing."[44] The closer to the object, the more real, the more authentic, the thing.

Yet Weston's use of the close-up was different from Strand's. Strand had favored, in addition to the studies of machinery, natural forms— rocks, plants, toadstools, spider webs, roots. (Again, the two extremes of the organic and the mechanical.) But with either natural or artificial subject matter, his approach was the same: he moved close enough to the object to present only a fragment of its total form, and he viewed it from an angle or placed it off-center in the frame. Exploiting the camera's capacity for detailed revelation of surfaces and for the organization of form in shades of black and white, Strand filled the picture frame from edge to edge. Weston more often gives us a full view of the object, isolated against a neutral background, or, if less than the whole is seen, it is usually presented symmetrically so as to reveal its structure. Shells, cabbages, toadstools, rocks, tree stumps, kale, peppers, radishes—these were Weston's subjects, and the photographer would often devour them after he had immortalized them on film. With the camera "the physical quality of things can be rendered with utmost exactness: stone is hard, bark is rough, flesh is alive, or they can be made harder, rougher, or more alive if desired."[45] This was exactly the quality the painter Diego Rivera saw in the photographs. Weston recorded in his diary that Rivera, whom Weston knew and much admired in Mexico, pleased him enormously by his response to an exhibit of his images: "Looking at the sand in one of my beach nudes, a torso of Margrethe, he said, 'This is what some of us "moderns" were trying to do when we sprinkled real sand on our paintings or stuck on pieces of lace or paper or other bits of realism.'"[46] A disjunction within the medium—as in the felt difference between sand and paint—was far from Weston's intention, but Rivera's appreciation of the intensity of *thingness* was exactly what the photographer was after.

Harder, rougher, more alive. Weston's realism moves inevitably toward super-realism, a word Weston himself used, in 1939, to describe the camera eye's "heightened sense of reality—a kind of super realism that reveals the vital essences of things." And from there it is but a short step to declaring, in a daring reversal of Plato, that the "recreated image" may seem "more real and comprehensible than the actual object."[47] (Stieglitz had admitted to Sherwood Anderson a similar intention: "There is a reality—so subtle that it becomes more real than reality. That's what I'm trying to get down in photography.")[48] Weston was simply admitting what anyone looking at a Weston and then looking at an ordinary artichoke, radish, or pepper would realize: the intensity of the photographed object, taken out of its normal context, enlarged so as to reveal hitherto invisible details of structure and surface, surpasses our unaided vision of the real thing.

The authenticity Weston was after was based on the literal mimetic power of the camera, a capacity that he associated with the nineteenth-century documentary photographers, as against the pictorialists Rejlander and Robinson, whose artificiality he scorned. Yet Weston's own authenticity was after all, an artificial contrivance, in which

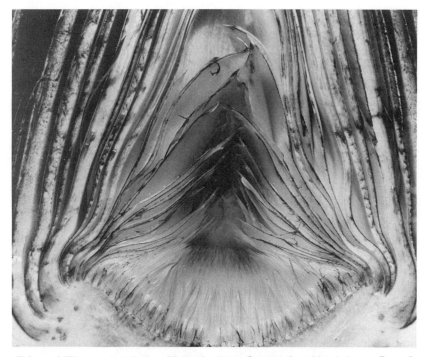

Edward Weston, Artichoke, Halved, *1930, Copyright 1981 Arizona Board
of Regents, Center for Creative Photography
(Courtesy of Museum of Modern Art, New York)*

the subject was fully posed and controlled by the photographer and in
which the print was enhanced to the point of its perfection. In fact,
Weston was fascinated by artifice, and did a series during the late
1930s on the MGM studio in Hollywood, featuring mannequins, false
facades, trompe l'oeil landscapes, and props. Here Weston's own artifice served the exposure of a false artifice, demonstrating pictorially
what he was shortly to write in an encyclopedia article on photography: "the camera lens sees too clearly to be used successfully for
recording the superficial aspects of a subject. It searches out the actor
behind the make-up and exposes the contrived, the trivial, the artificial, for what they really are."[49]

The social function of modernist photography was most clearly
(and optimistically) articulated by Lewis Mumford: "Restoring to the

eye, otherwise so preoccupied with the abstractions of print, the stimulus of things roundly seen as things, shapes, colors, textures, demanding for its enjoyment a previous experience of light and shade, this machine process in itself counteracts some of the worst defects of our mechanical environment. . . . Photography—and perhaps photography alone—is capable of coping with and adequately presenting the complicated, inter-related aspects of our modern environment."[50] And Mumford noted what some of the aspects of this new world might be—the vast mechanisms, "gigantic steel birds," unloading ships on the waterfront; a microscopic view of a hair, a leaf, a drop of blood; a warehouse filled with "a row of bathtubs, a row of siphons, a row of bottles, each of identical size, shape, color, stretching away for a quarter of a mile."[51]

Mumford's examples aptly suggest a movement that was already underway, an expansion of the vocabulary of the camera, a discovery of new ways of looking at objects of all sizes, going well beyond the conventions of industrial photography that were practiced at the time —the "mundane realism," as David Nye calls it, that emphasized "sharp focus, the avoidance of special effects, and a factual style of presentation."[52] What was needed was a dislocation of the "normal" vision of nonphotographic seeing, and certain techniques that achieved such effects, many of them developed during the 1920s in Europe, soon had wide currency. Léger's emphasis on the fragment, mentioned earlier, was one way that photography could move away from the norm; the wide-angle lens made possible a move in the opposite direction, allowing the eye to encompass more than would normally be seen at once. This was an effective technique in capturing large areas of landscape (often from towering structures); it was also useful in accentuating the repeated forms and large quantities of things that are endemic to mass production. Thus were pictured rows upon rows of shoes, bowls, wheels, sewing machines, buildings, generators, bottles, and sewing needles. Modern skyscrapers too were often pictured in this way, shot from below or from above as a single monolithic image, filled with a multiplicity of windows. (An early example is A. L. Coburn's New York photograph, "The House of a Thousand Windows" [1912], although it did not become common until more than a decade later.) The patterned-repetition shot, if we can give it a name, is based upon an aesthetic of multiples that emphasizes the redundancy of units in modern industrial or architectural processes. Such images of artificial structures emphasized their identical features, thus creating a pattern that seemingly arbitrarily closed off the potential infinity of reproductions that existed outside the picture space. The effect produced amounted to a contemporary version of the technological sublime.[53]

Not surprisingly, the industrial and manufacturing corporations of the 1920s and 1930s found in photography a stylish way of dramatizing the magnificence of modern technology and the skyscraper. Contrary to Mumford's quite different vision of the social power of photography, the camera was lending itself in a variety of ways to the development of industrial capitalism: it was of course an instrument for analysis and record; it was also an instrument for promoting an *image* of the product that would stamp it in the public mind. The three great modernist photographers, Stieglitz, Strand, and Weston, had, in their different ways, all viewed photography primarily as an art form, one that was as demanding aesthetically as any other art, and as expressive; they specifically eschewed the commercial and advertising applications of the medium. Yet, as Edward Steichen shrewdly observed, the Stieglitz aesthetic—the "frank objectivity of the photograph," with its "meticulous detail [and] biting precision"— was irresistible to the businessman and the public.[54] The camera's intense rendering of the thing that was the essence of the artist's vision of authenticity when applied to an anonymous automobile fender was, paradoxically, of equal use in creating an image of almost magical intensity when focused on a handbag or pair of shoes. (Not surprisingly, the contemporary museum has a hard time drawing the line between art and advertising in the photography from the 1920s and 1930s; without the social context and purpose, the differences may be few.) And as such it became the basis for the fashionable advertising photograph, whose most successful practitioner was Margaret Bourke-White; her emphasis on power and movement—using the latest techniques of dramatic angling and patterned-repetition— served to glamorize modern industry and the city, transforming the mundane into the sublime and making her the most sought after commercial photographer of her time.[55] Bourke-White's genius was to adapt the freer and more dramatic technique of the European photographers without losing sight of the utilitarian context of the image and its ultimate base in a precise rendering of reality.

The scientific spirit that Strand had attributed to Stieglitz, and that was evident in his own work, and in Weston's, had at its base the pursuit of a more intense, a more penetrating, a more authentic engagement with the object in an effort to understand the underlying geometry and organic form of things. But the scientific spirit of abstraction had penetrated the work of several other photographers of the 1920s and 1930s in an even more marked way, leading them, however, away from the object and toward an almost mathematical construction of the photographic image. This movement toward photographic abstraction is evident in the careers of such photographers as Edward Steichen, Man Ray, and Francis Bruguière, all of whom were active during the 1920s and 1930s; but for our own purposes, the most interesting of these artists is Paul Outerbridge, whose radical experiments add a dimension to the exploration of photographic authenticity otherwise not available.

Outerbridge started from the commonly held assumption about the special modernity of photography, although he stated the point in extreme terms, holding that "most of the best art of the world in painting and sculpture had been done, and that this newest form was more related to the progress and tempo of modern science of the eye."[56] Outerbridge's most characteristic experiments of the early 1920s featured the transformation of everyday objects into pictures that exploit the flattening power of the picture plane to set up a tension between the three-dimensionality of the object and the two-dimensionality of the picture. Technological artifacts are isolated and distorted through aerial perspective and through hard-edged shadows (for example, "Telephone" and "The Dragon Fly's Wing" [both 1922]); common commercial products—an H.O. oats box, a saltine box—are muted into a subtle harmony of shapes and shadows; a saw and square are softened into a study of angles, while a pitcher and pie plate compose a study of "Rhythmic Curves" (1923). Also during these early years, Outerbridge began the photographing of still-life arrangements that would quickly lead to his becoming a master commercial photographer. Early studies of eggs in a bowl, of eggs and a milk bottle, of a common pail, allow the object its own clear identity and presence, while placing it within an abstract composition; given the commercial goal of picturing a manufactured object, Outerbridge's compositional clarity served him well, as in the famous "Ide Collar" ad (1922), in which Outerbridge positions the curve of the collar against a black and white checkerboard background, with everything sharply in focus. (Marcel Duchamp cut it out of a magazine to hang on his studio wall.)

But Outerbridge went even further than these austere abstractions, exploring ingeniously the formal nature of the controlled photographic illusion that was accepted at its face value in the public world of advertising. That the photographer was a kind of magician, for example, was amply evident from a close inspection of "Leavenings" (1931), in which a globe of indeterminate substance floats on the peak of a pyramid of indeterminate substance, with two additional globes suspended in air behind this structure; in "Consciousness" (1931), two eggs appear to stand before an acutely angled cone, while the substance of one egg and the side of the cone melt imperceptibly into nothingness. In "The Triumph of the Egg" (1932), Outerbridge surpasses Steichen's study of an egg by the same title, offering a perfect egg perched miraculously on top of a perfect pyramid, over which is fitted an echoing artist's triangle, while in the background a photographer's reflecting lamp echoes the rounded egg form. Here, as in later color works like "Images de Deauville" (1936) and "Kandinsky" (1937), Outerbridge juxtaposes pure geometric solids and everyday objects (a bottle, a die, a shell), exploring the opposition between flat plane and depth, between pure form and useful form, all in a Constructivist vein.

More philosophical yet in their motivation are the still-life compositions in which the opposition between artifice and reality is explicitly explored. Thus, in the late 1920s, Outerbridge did a series of mannequin portraits which occcupy the border between the living and the dead. In the next decade, he went in the other direction, turning art back into reality by posing models to look like famous paintings. (See especially "Dutch Girl" [1938] and "Odalisque" [1936], which are modeled on Picasso's "The Dutch Girl" and Velazquez's "Rokeby Venus," respectively.)[57] Here the extraordinary verisimilitude of the color photographs, and of the flesh tones especially, restores a shocking sexuality to images that have been otherwise aesthetically neutralized. In still other photographs of the late 1930s, Outerbridge carries artifice to the limits of hyper-reality by making plain the greater "authenticity" of the photographic image when compared with the framed painting. Carefully positioning a showgirl model before an ornate frame in "Backstage at the Follies Bergère" (1937), Outerbridge makes the point very simply; more effective are the two studies, "Nude with Frame, Frontview," and "Nude with Frame, Rearview" (both 1938), in which the vividly fleshy nude model has seemingly stepped out of the huge frame beside her, an otherwise plain background for her pictorial incarceration. The climax in this genre, combining the trompe l'oeil investigations of a Peale with the surrealist juxtapositions of a Magritte, is "Still-Life with Fruit and Lithograph" (1938), in which Outerbridge has recreated a Currier and Ives chromolithograph directly in front of the print, testing, and demonstrating, the superior illusion of the photographed fruit as against the flatter rendering of the chromo. Outerbridge makes explicit in these works the hidden formal premises of objectivist practice that underlay modernist photography.

In the glossy world of advertising, as well as in the relatively self-contained world of modernist art, the beauty of the object was paramount, separating it from the real world of dust, grease, and bank accounts. Yet beginning in the early 1930s, as the effects of the Depression grew steadily more apparent, the discrepancy between this imaged world and the real world outside the magazines and galleries became painfully obvious. Writing from the perspective of Europe, which was undergoing a parallel economic transformation together with a political mutation into fascism, Walter Benjamin observed critically that the creative or fashionable principle was capable of masking the underlying social relations governing a society dominated by big business. The "motto" of the creative photographer is "the world is beautiful," and his work "raises every tin can into the realm of the All but cannot grasp any of the human connections that it enters into, and which, even in its most dreamy subject, is more a function of its merchandisability than of its discovery." And Benjamin quotes Brecht's observation that "less than ever does a simple *reproduction of reality* express something about reality."[58]

"Reality" came more and more, during the Depression, to mean the new facts of deprivation, dislocation, and suffering. Looked at more closely, the world was not so beautiful. A good many photographers—along with a good many writers, of course—underwent a radical shift in their sensibilities and in the nature of their work, but none so dramatically, perhaps, as Margaret Bourke-White. Flying out west on assignment for TWA airlines (and doubling her commission by shooting pilots smoking Chesterfields), Bourke-White was appalled at the effects of the dust storm on the Midwest. Cattle were dying, farmers were hopeless; in the dust that was everywhere, even scratching her camera lenses, Bourke-White began to undergo a change of consciousness that would place her, by 1936, in the vanguard of socially concerned photographers. In that year, she helped enlist other photographers for the First Artists Congress (at which she herself delivered a somewhat naive paper on the Soviet Union as an artist's utopia); she renounced her career as the country's most successful advertising photographer; she signed a contract with the new *Life* magazine as a feature photographer working on stories involving economic and social change. And she began work with Erskine Caldwell (whom she subsequently married) on what would become a prototype of documentary photojournalism during the 1930s, *You Have Seen Their Faces*, a work that was intended to create a vivid image of rural southern poverty and suffering, thus lending a seemingly unassailable authenticity to the fictional cartoon world Caldwell had created in *Tobacco Road*.[59]

You Have Seen Their Faces was symptomatic of a basic reorientation in American photography. The authority of the camera as an instrument for persuasion had been established in the late nineteenth century, most dramatically in the photographic volumes of Jacob Riis; and Lewis Hine, in the early years of the twentieth century, had extended its use in an activist photojournalism that would set a powerful example for the 1930s. But during the 1920s—as the camera's persuasive power helped establish the credibility of the advertised world of perfect consumer goods—the social motivation grew nearly extinct in America. With the new orientation toward society that resulted after the Depression, the rhetorical power of photography to expose the present state of things and thus point toward the need for action, was rediscovered. A textbook example of this appropriation of the camera was Charles Cross's *A Picture of America: The Photostory of America—As It Is—And As It Might Be. Told by the News Camera.*[60] Using montage and collage techniques borrowed from European experiments, this volume was a primer on the Depression (however elementary), explaining the evil of big business profits and unemployment, and arguing for the need to spread available work. The camera itself is used as an overt symbol of the revelation of reality: it opens the book, like a giant eye looking down at America; and at the end the camera is "closed." Norman Thomas, in the introduction, elaborates the metaphor at even greater length: "This book appeals to the eye in order to change the mind. These pictures, ripped out of the chaotic album of American life, and provided with the bare bones of explanation, play a terrible searchlight upon a crumbling economic order and light up the path to something better."[61]

Bourke-White was only the best known of a younger generation of photographers—Walker Evans, Dorothea Lange, Ben Shahn, Russell Lee, Arthur Rothstein, Berenice Abbott—who, beginning in the mid-1930s were to exploit the documentary power of the photographic image. In some ways the modernist sensibility that had developed in the teens and 1920s, with its commitment to photography as an *art* form, albeit a uniquely modern one, was at odds with the documentary mode. Stieglitz, who by the 1930s was already an old man, was virtually immune to the changes in the world below his hotel window. But even Strand, who had become involved in left-wing documentary filmmaking during the 1930s, reviewed Dorothea Lange's *An American Exodus* from the standpoint of earlier aesthetic standards: "If books like this are to have their maximum value, then it is clear that their basic material, the photographs, must be more than documentary records."[62] What the younger generation shared was a sense of urgent need that pervaded the whole discourse of the documentary culture of the 1930s. The immediacy of the image superseded, for many, the problem of aesthetic form. Yet the reverence for the objectivity of fact, the conception of the camera as a technological artifact peculiarly in tune with the modern age, the effort to render the exact feel and reality of things—all articles of firm belief on the part of the modernist photographers—were adapted as part of the foundation for a new generation of photographers who began working in the late 1920s and 1930s and for whom an overt description of the geographical and industrial and social landscape was a defining purpose.

The younger generation of Farm Security Administration (FSA) photographers, working under the direction of Roy Stryker, took a direct approach to the problems of the Depression, picturing scenes that would predispose the viewer toward needed legislation and social change. For it was clearly understood that the very purpose of the photographic information unit that Stryker headed was to supply pictures that would promote the government's programs. The individual photographers working for Stryker all inevitably (and deliberately) possessed a unique style and point of view, but their role as government workers was to gather information, and not to be *artists*. And to the extent that they were following instructions from Washington, fulfilling stated needs for specific kinds of pictures (erosion, floods, parched lands, FSA rehabilitation projects, etc.), the pictures seem at times interchangeable. There were some images that were reminiscent of classic modernist photography, where an abstract design captured the viewer's attention, but the overwhelming majority of documentary photographs of the 1930s feature *people*, not things— ordinary farmers, migrant workers, the urban poor, some industrial laborers. And the power of the photographs often derived from the uncanny effect of seeing people in situations that simulated normal activity but yet conflicted sharply with implicit norms: here are children reading a book in a living room papered with newspaper; here is a family gathered around a kitchen table for a meal that seems foodless; here are a mother and child in rags. By their facsimile representation of "normality" the photographs almost mock their subjects, although in no personal way. Technology is a recurrent theme, but its treatment is not celebratory; instead, factories appear ominous on the horizon, tractors stand menacingly in farm fields, evidence of the mechanization of farming that, during the 1920s and 1930s, hastened soil erosion and the displacement of farmers from the dust bowl. The question raised earlier in the century, of whether people would succeed in mastering the machine, seemed to be answered in the negative in these photographs of unemployment lines and idle factories.

Yet the mystique of the camera, a mystique born amid the cultural uncertainties induced by rapid technological change in the early twentieth century, survived the Depression. Indeed, the new uncertainties about technology gave to the camera, once more, a kind of salvational role. If it could no longer be taken as a symbol of man's mastery of the machine, it could still serve as a symbol of truth, of moral responsibility, of a commitment to "the fact" that would yet result in a victory over irrational economic forces. As Stryker himself put it, "By the precision of their instrument, by the very mechanical limitations of shutter, lens, and film, they [photographers] are invested with credibility; simple honesty will render to their pictures the dignity of fact; feeling and insight will give their fraction of a second's exposure the integrity of truth."[63] And the passage from Francis Bacon that Dorothea Lange had posted on her darkroom door for years might serve the whole group as a motto: "The contemplation of things as they are, without substitution or imposture, without error or confusion, is in itself a nobler thing than a whole harvest of invention."[64]

But the emphasis on fact over invention would seem at times more a matter of style than substance. The problem, as Stryker put it, was that the "documentary photographer feels obliged to bring home more than a cold record. Somehow he has to incorporate into that rectangle which he has cut out from the surrounding therefore formless reality, what the real thing sounded like, what it smelled like— and most important, what it felt like."[65] In achieving that goal—what the real thing felt like—the documentary photographers developed a style that, ironically, returned to the nineteenth-century mode of typological representation, where the particular stands for the larger category of experience. Documentary style during the 1930s ranged from the presentation of stark particulars, as in the Federal Writers' Project guidebooks, to the representation of allegorical types, as in the Federal Theater's Living Newsreels; somewhere in the middle zone, where the particular became universalized, were the FSA photographs.[66] The photographer's skill was to capture the subject at the moment of maximum drama or pathos, the sum of FSA imagery constituting a typology of theatrical gesture. Consider the range of postures: Ben Shahn's image of a sharecropper's wife, hands crossed in front of her, gripping her arms, her face contorted in suffering; or the more leisurely gravity of a couple on their porch in a Russell Lee photo; or the pensive dignity of Dorothea Lange's famous "Migrant Mother," her children clustered about her, one hand poised delicately at the corner of her mouth; or Lange's quite different shot of a plantation owner, his knee aggressively and possessively perched on the fender of a car, a huddle of black workers behind him.[67] These are all images of "what it felt like," studies of human posture as an expression of a state of mind. We can feel the presence of the photographer in these images, the tacit delight in the ironies of juxtaposition, the use of a real-life stage setting which could not be better if the photographer had deliberately placed the props there.

Which is exactly what the photographer, in many cases, was in fact doing. Arthur Rothstein's cow skull, posed several times on the parched mid-Western earth, is the most flagrant example (it caused a political brouhaha when the posing was uncovered by the *New York Herald Tribune*, no friend of Roosevelt), but there are many others.[68] Rothstein explained how he directed one of the most famous of all

Depression shots, "The Duststorm": "The little boy was asked to drop back and hold his hand over his eyes. The farmer was asked to lean forward as he walked. Finally the whole scene was made to take place in front of the shed."[69] If documentaries of the 1930s often look stagy, like still shots from a Hollywood movie, it is because they were indeed so often staged. Rothstein's rationale was simply to enhance the effect, to focus attention on the significant: "Provided the results are a faithful reproduction of what the photographer believes he sees," Rothstein wrote with unimpeachable self-qualification, "whatever takes place in the making of the picture is justified."[70] FSA documentary was conceived, in short, as a probable fiction, a credible facsimile.

Stryker's best-known photographer, the one whose work would stand out as the definitive codification of Depression America, was Walker Evans, who was fond in later years of picturing his year with the FSA as essentially a tour of the United States at the government's expense. Stryker and Evans must be seen, finally, in opposition to one another, but to a large degree Evans shared with Stryker, even anticipated, the latter's broad goal of creating a visual bank of information about the United States. Evans had written in 1931, several years before the formulation of the government's photography unit, of the need for a new application of the camera. Reviewing several books on photography for the little magazine, *Hound and Horn*, Evans called for a fresh exploration of the photographic medium, making little distinction between scientific and artistic approaches. He was most enthusiastic about August Sander's portrait-catalogue of German society, *Antlitz der Zeit* (Face of our time), the first of his volumes in the "Man in the Twentieth Century" series: "This is one of the futures of photography foretold by Atget. It is a photographic editing of society, a clinical process; even enough of a cultural necessity to make one wonder why other so-called advanced countries of the world have not also been examined and recorded."[71] In other ways too there was a congruity between Evans and Stryker, for in each case small-town and rural America represented values they wanted to preserve. Stryker would construct shooting scripts for his photographers in the field that would convey the direction of his curiosity and the slant of his imagination: "Bill posters; sign painters—crowd watching a window sign being painted; sky writing; paper in park after concert; parade watching, ticker tape, sitting on curb."[72] Evans's pictures of such places would stir Stryker's sense of nostalgia for an America that was "safer and more peaceful," "before radio and television."[73]

Moreover, both Stryker and Evans aimed at creating what in effect was a response to the Van Wyck Brooks challenge of the teens—to create a cultural expression that would bridge the highbrow and low-brow elements of the society, that would synthesize the best elements of the intellectual tradition and the best elements of the practical tradition, and fuse them in an art that would represent the energies of twentieth-century America. And both were at bottom constructing an elaborate response to the values of an economy built on social division and slick advertising, a response made up out of the visual evidence of popular culture.

But despite the shared vision uniting the director and his star photographer, there were also irreconcilable differences that would make Evans's tenure at the FSA a short one. For one, the purpose of the FSA photography unit was at bottom propagandistic, while Evans's goal was to create, with the camera, "pure record not propaganda." He was thus at odds with the constraints of government work—the need to "make photographic statements for the government or do photographic chores for gov or anyone in gov"; the need to turn over his negatives to the government office for printing; the need to compromise his pure aesthetic goals with the collective and practical demands of a Washington bureaucracy.[74] And where Stryker prided himself on the FSA photographs being positive in tone ("there is no picture in there that in any way whatsoever represents an attempt by a photographer to ridicule his subject, to be cute with him, to violate his privacy"),[75] Evans took a more aloof, ironic, witty stance toward his subjects, as suggested by some notes he made in a 1934 letter regarding a project to photograph the "typical" American city: "Architecture, American urban taste, commerce, small scale, large scale, the city street atmosphere, the street smell, the hateful stuff, women's clubs, fake culture, bad education, religion in decay."[76] Evans had studied America through the satiric slant of E. E. Cummings and T. S. Eliot; he had fashioned his artistic persona on the irony and aloofness of Baudelaire, the objectivity and coldness of Flaubert. Put simply, Stryker's *sentimentality* was anathema to Evans, along with the inevitable tendency toward melodrama that was part of FSA sensibility. Whatever else we may say about the two most famous FSA shots—Lange's "Migrant Mother" and Rothstein's "Duststorm"—they came out of a sensibility that was alien to Evans.

In the afterword to his friend Evans's *American Photographs*, Lincoln Kirstein described the function of photography as Evans understood and practiced it: "The facts of our homes and times, shown surgically, without the intrusion of the poet's or painter's comment or necessary distortion, are the unique contemporary field of the photographer, whether in static print or moving film. It is for him to fix and to show the whole aspect of our society, the sober portrait of its stratifications, their backgrounds and embattled contrasts. It is the camera that today reveals our disasters and our claims to divinity, doing what painting and poetry used to do and, we can only hope, will do again."[77] What Paul Rosenfeld had done for Stieglitz, interpreting his symbolic role within the culture, naming his intellectual universe, Kirstein does for Evans in this essay. Only where Rosenfeld had made Stieglitz into a kind of lyric poet of modernism, expressing through the camera a special sensibility, Kirstein's Evans is more objective—a surgeon, a doctor of society, an analyst, a revealer of truths. Some years later, Evans himself defined the function of photography in similar terms, echoing Gustav Stickley and Louis Sullivan in their complaint against the abstractness of American education, seeing in the camera an instrument that could restore reality, as Mumford earlier had seen Stieglitz's function: "Our overwhelming formal education deals in words, mathematical figures, and methods of rational thought, not in images. This may be a form of conspiracy that promises artifical blindness. It certainly is that to a learning child. It is this very blindness that photography attacks, blindness that is ignorance of real seeing and is perversion of seeing. It is reality that photography reaches toward."[78] Evans's social role was to restore authenticity to the American vision.

What gives Evans's images the illusion of objectivity is the quality of direct confrontation, of a head-to-head meeting with his subjects that grants them the full respect of their own presence and character. And this is as true for his architectural studies as for his human portraits. With his large-frame, tripod camera, Evans captures in detail the grain of wood, the warping of planks, the textures of corrugated tin; his approach is to shoot head on, allowing the symmetry of the buildings and their fragile solidity to meet the viewer with full force. The portraits are even more striking, with the subjects looking usually right into the lens, their faces sober, guileless, dignified. Partly, our impression of Evans's objectivity is a function of his simply approaching his subjects frontally, framing them square: compare Dorothea Lange's usual approach, which takes the subject from an angle, creating a typically diagonal composition; or look at Ben Shahn, who often uses asymmetry and dramatic conflicts between foreground and background, with figures coming into the edges of the print, as if the photo continued on past the frame; or look at Margaret Bourke-White, whose favorite position was shooting up from the ground or down from on high, thus giving her subjects distorted, Mannerist figures. Evans, in this context, seems direct, unmanipulative, objective. Yet he was careful, in his later years, to call his approach a "documentary style" as opposed to the creation of "documents," and the qualification is important: "This style does seem honest. It isn't always so, but it seems so."[79] The recent argument that Evans actually moved furniture around in the houses he photographed in Alabama only confirms what he was already in principle admitting. Evans was aware of the degree to which he was manipulating his subjects, even when not appearing to do so; he was aware that the objectivity of the camera is a matter of degrees, of winning assent to a probable fiction.[80]

Evans had worked his way toward the objective approach of the 1930s through an apprenticeship in modernism (in the late 1920s) which included skyscraper abstractions in the precisionist style of early Strand and Sheeler, industrial abstractions that recall A. L. Coburn's Vorticist phase, and aerial views modeled on the European modernists.[81] These experiments in eccentric angles and distorted vision gave way in the early 1930s to what would become the characteristic symmetry and rectangular approach of his documentary style. But in certain of Evans's early photographs one can discern a more idiosyncratic interest in materials that would ultimately become the core of his work: candid snapshots of people on the street in New York and at Coney Island, storefronts, close-ups of neon signs in New York City, Victorian architecture in small towns, and itinerant street photographers at work in city streets. Here are the beginnings of Evans the social historian, the photographer as recorder of everyday society, of vernacular culture.

Evans located his own particular viewpoint on American society by taking a position as ironic spectator, an American Atget, staring di-

Walker Evans, Window Display, Bethlehem, Pa., *1935*
(Courtesy of Library of Congress)

rectly at the popular culture of the American twentieth century. Against the glossy advertising world of glittering consumer products, of an all-powerful technology with immense powers of mass production, against the world created by a Bourke-White or a Steichen (of the latter, Evans wrote, "his general note is money, understanding of advertising values, special feeling for parvenu elegance, slick technique"),[82] Evans recorded the antiworld of folk commerce—country stores stocked with general goods, pawnshops, roadside tire stores, street vendors. Against the modernist elevation of the beautiful technological artifact into an icon of abstract perfection, Evans showed us the humble object in its natural surroundings—towels worn thin with use, a broom angled against a wall; chairs, bowls, silverware—yet objects that had a certain dignity in the simplicity of their shape and their adaptation to human need. Against the towering skyscraper and the latest streamlined engineering marvel, Evans offered the intricacies of Victorian Gothic houses, or the simple rows of workers' cottages in industrial towns, or the lone shack in the rural South, or the disheveled elegance of a run-down Southern plantation.

Evans stepped outside the world of advertising by recording advertisements themselves, in situ, as they appear surrounding our lives— as signs in the street; as hand-painted barn decorations; as commercial signs hanging outside country stores; as theatrical and minstrel posters, half torn, posted on brick walls; as movie billboards, advertising the glamour of Hollywood in working-class neighborhoods; as magazine advertisements, cut out to serve as wall decorations; as stand-up store displays, used as cardboard insulation for unheated shacks. Street advertisements had appeared as the subject of photographs as early as the teens in some of Paul Strand's cityscapes and, treated as elements in an abstract composition, in Paul Outerbridge's "42nd Street El" (1923).[83] In a somewhat more self-conscious affirmation of the aesthetic worth of popular culture, invoking the spirit of Whitman, Robert Coady's little magazine, *The Soil*, had published a two-page photographic spread featuring the mannequin-filled windows of the Monroe Clothes Shop on Broadway.[84] Evans, who had reacted against the romantic mysticism and aestheticism of Stieglitz, might be seen as picking up where Coady and *The Soil* had left off. But Evans was adding to the American Dadaism of Coady a sense of irony and pathos that had been unimagined earlier—a sense of the deeper juxtapositions of modern American life, the contrasts between

Walker Evans, A Miner's Home, Vicinity Morgantown, West Virginia, *1935*
(Courtesy of Library of Congress)

glamour and poverty, between advertised life and real life, a sense of
how people live within a world of signs and symbols.

Evans's consciousness of visual signs extended, not surprisingly, to
the photograph itself as a ubiquitous presence in society, and a leit-
motif throughout his work of the 1930s is the role of the professional
maker of pictures—the itinerant street photographer, the small-town
commercial studio. A major theme of *American Photographs,* as Alan
Trachtenberg has shown, is the process of photography as a making-
over into images or pictures, a process that has its echoes and re-
duplications in other images of graphic representation throughout
the volume.[85]

Evans's own portraits are deliberately different from the typical
studio or commercial or passport photograph that he liked to sub-
sume within his own photographic world. They are different in two

quite opposite ways: on the one hand, Evans liked to position his subjects close to the camera lens, inviting them to stare directly at the machine before them in a way that often produced startlingly direct, serious, somewhat vulnerable images. One feels the subject has let down his guard, not knowing whether to trust or mistrust the camera. (Despite the often wildly different social status of his subjects, Evans's portraits often have a uniform quality.) The result is a portrait that is quite different from the typical smiling face or otherwise theatricalized portrait: Evans captures an almost existential confrontation with the Camera as Other, a moment when, one feels, his subjects are looking into themselves as well as into a lens. Yet on the other hand, Evans recorded faces that were totally *unaware* of the camera's presence, in an effort to achieve an utterly natural, unguarded expression, an authentic bit of life lifted from the stream of everyday social interaction. Evans had been fascinated by Strand's experiments in the teens with a fake lens on the front of his camera, allowing him to shoot from the side, and up close, at persons on the street who were unaware of being photographed ("Blind Woman" [1916], was a favorite). Evans updated Strand's unobtrusive recording of society by fitting himself with a hidden camera and riding the subway in the late 1930s, photographing every rider who sat opposite him.[86]

As Stieglitz was the representative photographer of the early decades of the twentieth century, so Evans was the representative image-maker of the 1930s. And as Stieglitz had been celebrated earlier as the Romantic Whitman, who had used the camera as a tool for embracing twentieth-century America, Evans may be seen as the Ironic Whitman, both in and out of the game, aloof, cold at times, detached, working against the grain, against the commercial values that had come to dominate the twentieth century. Evans was not the celebrator of American optimism, he was the pessimist. Like Whitman he was an omnivorous collector of images, an accumulator of particulars, with a particular affection for the meanest of things. But Evans was colder than Whitman, colder than Stieglitz. If Stieglitz had made the camera a part of himself, turning it into an extension of the body, Evans had worked the opposite magic, making himself into a part of the camera, developing an eye that was more purely photographic than any other of his time, more purely attuned to the incongruities visible through the camera's lens. Evans saw with the eye of a camera, and with more than a little of its clinical detachment.

Using the machine in the full range of its capacities, from the large and obtrusive view camera to the unobtrusive, hidden 35 mm, Evans recorded an America in which the machine had largely transformed social life. As Kirstein put it, "The eye of Evans is open to the visible effects, direct and indirect, of the industrial revolution in America, the replacement by the machine in all its complexities of the work and art once done by individual hands and hearts, the exploitation of men by machinery and machinery by men."[87] Strand's hope that the camera could serve as a model for man's mastery of the machine would seem, from the standpoint of Evans's 1930s, to have been a pipe dream; Evans was under no such illusions. He took his position outside the mainstream of commercial society, outside even the benevolent purposes of the FSA. His commitment was to a way of seeing that was honest and anti-authoritarian, that embodied, above all, a kind of authenticity grounded in the independence of the photographer's eye. The irony is that although Evans had defined himself against Stieglitz (the latter "was artistic and romantic. It gave me an aesthetic to sharpen my own against—a counteraesthetic"),[88] Evans shared with the older photographer a personal quality of independence (if not orneriness) that must have found in the camera a perfect instrument for the observing eye—an instrument with a capacity for objective treatment of the visible world.

Mediating between the world and the brain, the camera during the years between the wars was a powerful instrument of revelation, changing our sense of the world by its power to shock the sensibilities or move the viewer emotionally; restoring our sense of touch by stripping the eye of its encrusted conventions, its visual habits, its mental habits. As such, it was in harmony with the authenticity of structure and materials that was basic to the rhetoric of architecture and design in the early twentieth century; and as such it was a prime symbol for a way of seeing, and imagining, that the writer too was seeking in the first half of the twentieth century.

SEVEN

Not "Realism" but

Reality Itself

*I*n his deliberately disordered obituary on the old art (and manifestation of the new), *Spring and All* (1923), William Carlos Williams wrote, "up to now shapes and meanings but always the illusion relying on composition to give likeness to 'nature.'" Rhyme, meter, perspective, symbolism—all the tricks of representation and verisimilitude that stand between people and nature, all the "lies" of art, to use a phrase of Anatole France that Williams quotes, are to be jettisoned: "now works of art cannot be left in this category of France's 'lie,' they must be real, not 'realism' but reality itself—."[1] Reality itself? The phrase must stop us. Frank Norris and the other realist writers around the turn of the century had said what sounds like the same thing: we want life not literature. But what they in fact meant was blood, sex, money, grime, garbage, immigrants, and killing snowstorms—a recognition of areas of experience previously excluded from polite literature. And despite the resistance of the genteel establishment, those people who held to a notion of literature as an uplifting moral art unsullied by the basics or the baseborn, the once-forbidden subjects gradually entered the mainstream of American writing.[2] What Williams meant by "reality itself" was, however, quite different; it was a quality of authenticity that was held to be missing from a literary "realism" that had itself grown conventional.

Realism, it was believed, had lost contact with reality, and modernists like Williams were seeking, through the work of art, somehow to restore that contact. On the face of it, modernism seemed to shift the focus of the arts away from the thing signified, as we would say nowadays, to the signifier itself, the medium of the artwork, whatever that might be—words, sounds, paint, wood, movement; for the serious writer after World War I, it was the form of the literary work—its language and shape—that was being reinvented as part of a more general response in all of the arts to a world whose materials and underlying laws of construction were all seen to be changing, a world that was being experienced in new ways. This was a revolutionary effort, but it was also restorative, and Williams reminds us that the goal was not to escape reality, but somehow, through the work of art, to restore it. Making the artwork real and making it new meant overhauling the language of description and breaking open the closed forms of literature in a way that was consonant with the new facts of modern life, but it also meant restoring what was thought to have been taken away—contact with reality. By inventing works that asserted the artist's moral and aesthetic power of clarification, yet works that remained in contact with the soil, with local materials, the writer was answering implicitly Brooks's call in the teens for a literature that bridged the growing gap in American culture between the practical and the spiritual spheres.

The problem with realism was described precisely in the carefully nuanced repetitions of Gertrude Stein, whose sensibility, in the beginning of the century, was undergoing a profound change as a result of her exposure to European art, a change that would be experienced repeatedly after Stein by scores of other writers and artists, as the French spirit in modern art spread its influence in the United States. Looking back on those years, Stein recalled that while still in San Francisco, collecting etchings reproduced in magazines, seeing oil paintings at local exhibitions, she had come across a painting by Cazin of a wheat field whose realism, so impressive and fascinating at first, ultimately disturbed her: "One does not like to be mixed in one's mind as to which looks most like something at which one is looking the thing or the painting."[3] Later, in Spain, a similar experience occurred with paintings by Velásquez: "they were too real and yet they were not real enough to be real and not unreal enough to be unreal."[4] With Cézanne, Stein began to develop an appreciation of a kind of representation that does not conceal its medium in an excess of verisimilitude; with Cézanne, an oil painting, whatever else it was, was also just that—an oil painting. There *was* a relation between the thing represented and the painting of it, but gradually Stein realized that "the relation between the oil painting and the thing represented was really nobody's business."[5] Stein was learning from modern French painting a principle that would lend support to her own experiments: the writer must be free to cut loose the word from its strict reference, free to treat words as things in themselves, not merely representations of things.

Although what they were ultimately reaching toward was a far greater freedom than the earlier American romantics had claimed, the American modernists were standing on the shoulders of the nineteenth-century giants. Thus Emerson had created for the twentieth-century poet the essential mythology of language, a concept of historical devolution that posited a fall from wholeness to brokenness, from innocence to corruption. In the beginning, according to Emerson's organic philosophy of language, man's word was in harmony with the world—"words are signs of natural facts"; but in the contemporary world the putative simplicity of character has been broken up by "the desire of riches, of pleasure, of power, and of praise"; "old words are perverted to stand for things which are not, a paper currency is employed, when there is no bullion in the vaults."[6] The poet's function, in this fallen world, is to reattach words to visible things, making use of the material world in imagery, and thereby restoring the full value to the debased currency. Here is the essence of the American modernist's vocation: to rebuild the ruined words.

Yet the twentieth-century writer would stand not only on the shoulders of Emerson but also on Whitman's. For Whitman, who had himself been inspired by Emerson, went beyond the Concord poet in anticipating more closely the modernist assumption about language as an autonomous resource; although Whitman assumed a link between the word and the world, words had for him an independent existence and were within the imaginative power of the writer to use *as things* (and not merely, as Emerson would be likely to say, as images or emblems of things). "A perfect user of words uses things— they exude in power and beauty from him. . . . A perfect writer would make words sing, dance, kiss, bear children, weep, bleed, rage, stab, steal, fire cannon, steer ships."[7] Whitman created an American world by creating a language that was isomorphic with America, a linguistic melting pot, a plurality of tongues, slang, neologisms, inventive usages, all rolled together into a surging, relentlessly cumulative rhythm, all an expression of a confident stance toward the world outside the self. The modernist lacked Whitman's confidence, but shared his sense of the autonomy of language. As Williams put it, "The only real in writing is writing itself."[8]

In arriving at this sense of language, in starting again from where

Whitman had left off, Gertrude Stein had been of prime importance. If language had been burdened by religion, science, philosophy, law, etc.—"Little more than fetishes of unspeakable abhorrence"—Stein had unburdened it. A rose is a rose is a rose: accept the separation of words from conventional association and exploit that separation; use words as the painters were using the pigments, as an abstract medium. Words were not transparent, they were densely material, things in themselves. Stein's words, Williams said, were "like a crowd at Coney Island, let us say, seen from an airplane."[9] (It is a wonderful image of units divisible yet nearly indistinguishable, separate yet amalgamated, words that are ready to go for a swim.) And Marianne Moore had performed an equally essential cleansing of language, though words with her were seen not from an airplane, but through a microscope. "With Miss Moore," Williams wrote, "a word is a word most when it is separated out by science, treated with acid to remove the smudges, washed, dried and placed right side up on a clean surface."[10]

The simplification the poets aimed at was also a goal of fiction writers during the 1920s and 1930s. Willa Cather, writing in the early 1920s, put it in terms of furnishings, observing that fiction had for too long been "overfurnished." Yet, as she continued in "The Novel Dé-meublé," "there are hopeful signs that some of the younger writers are trying to break away from mere verisimilitude, and, following the development of modern painting, to interpret imaginatively the material and social investiture of their characters; to present their scene by suggestion rather than by enumeration. The higher processes of art are all processes of simplification."[11] In poetry and fiction, as in the visual arts and material culture, form was repeatedly to be reconceived along the lines of abstraction and simplification: Stieglitz and Frank Lloyd Wright were running along lines that were parallel to the modernist writers.

The larger premises of the new writing were clearly stated by Gertrude Stein when she wrote, in "Composition as Explanation," "The only thing that is different from one time to another is what is seen and what is seen depends upon how everybody is doing everything. . . . Nothing changes from generation to generation except the thing seen and that makes a composition."[12] And her experience was shared by a generation of writers who were describing "the thing seen" in new terms, inspired by the visual environment of the twentieth century. For a part of the peculiar synthesis that was literary modernism was in fact an openness to the formal implications of the very things that were changing "how everybody is doing everything"—an openness to popular culture, to science and technology, above all an openness to the forms of visual representation that were evident in photography, advertisements, and cinema. Thus Vachel Lindsay describes excitedly the new world of the artist in the early twentieth century as a kaleidoscopic environment of visual stimuli, an environment that we have long since taken for granted: "American civilization grows more hieroglyphic every day. The cartoons of Darling, the advertisements in the back of the magazines and on the billboards and in the streetcars, the acres of photographs in the Sunday newspapers, make us into a hieroglyphic civilization far nearer to Egypt than to England."[13]

But there was even more involved in the changed environment of twentieth-century technology than Lindsay had noted—a panoply of artifacts that were in a variety of ways supplementing the available information about the world. Jean Epstein surveyed these new apparatuses in *Broom* in 1922 and called them "deformations"—meaning not necessarily errors, as he was at pains to point out, but simply distortions, in the way that glass will curve a line that might otherwise appear straight to the naked eye.

> The machine technology of civilization, the innumerable instrumentations that encumber laboratories, factories, hospitals, photographic studies, and electrical shops, the engineer's table and the architect's drawing-board, the aviator's seat, the moving picture theatre, the optician's show window and even the toolkit of the carpenter permit an infinite variety of angles of observation.... And all these instruments: telephone, microscope, magnifying glass, cinematograph, lens, microphone, gramophone, automobile, kodak, aeroplane, are not merely dead objects. At certain moments these machines become part of ourselves, interposing themselves between the world and us, filtering reality as the screen filters radium emanations. Thanks to them we have no longer a simple, clear, continuous, constant notion of an object.... The world for people today is like descriptive geometry, with its infinite planes of projection.[14]

All of these changes in the perception of the world had influenced modern French literature, as Epstein noted, but they were of course having a profound effect on American literature as well, causing a fundamental reexamination of literary form. Implicit in the modernist revolution was the understanding that language mediated between us and the world, and that writing was itself an instrument of observation.

For the late nineteenth-century realist committed to a literature of verisimilitude, the camera's presumed objectivity had served as a model of seeing and representation. And, I must stress again, the popular literature of the twentieth century continued to be written, and read, within what I have called the mainstream middle-class culture of replication established by the nineteenth century, a culture that accepted the writer's medium as a transparent one. My subject here is how the new writing in the early twentieth century challenged the comfortable assumptions of the past, raising fundamental questions about form and representation: What was the material of the literary work? the reservoir of established speech, or a new language to be invented by the poet, rebuilt by the novelist? And how much of "reality" in the form of "found language" could be brought into the artwork? How far could words go in embodying the reality of experience? Was there a correspondence between word and thing? How does the writer achieve aesthetic authenticity, how does one reproduce "reality itself" in a world in which modes of vision have been radically affected by technologies of perception? What was the overall form of the literary work to be? And these questions apply across the literary genres, for the reinvention of writing was taking place within fiction and drama as much as within poetry, and included hybrid forms in between as well. Wallace Stevens, T. S. Eliot, Marianne Moore, E. E. Cummings; Eugene O'Neill and Elmer Rice; William Faulkner, Ernest Hemingway, Willa Cather, Sherwood Anderson—all were dealing with the problem of representation, posing different solutions to the challenge of going beyond realism, beyond the traditional epistemological assumptions of a culture of imitation.

I want to focus here on three writers—William Carlos Williams, John Dos Passos, James Agee—who seem to me particularly interesting in this context because they were all especially conscious of problems of representation. Moreover, each was aiming at an original and authentic representation of reality that would serve as a model of how an artist in a technological society might function. They are useful for several other reasons as well: for one, they represent a generational response to the problem of writing—Williams (1883–1963) beginning seriously in the teens, Dos Passos (1896–1970) in the 1920s, and Agee (1909–1955) in the 1930s—thus offering an overview of the progress of modernism during the early decades of the century. For another, they offer complementary views of the transformation of genres in the twentieth century, for each began with a different major mode of the time—poetry, fiction, documentary—and ended by subverting the traditional assumptions of the genre.

If the problem was, as Williams put it in *Spring and All* (1923), that "There is a constant barrier between the reader and his consciousness of immediate contact with the world," then the aim of poetry was to bring the eye into fresh contact with reality.[15] Not realism—with its weight of stale conventions, its merely copied exhibitions of life—but the thing itself. "You do not copy nature," Williams advised the writer, "you make something which is an imitation of nature—read your Aristotle again."[16] But how do you *make* a natural object? How do you render its vital touch? How does the artist rival nature's processes?

First of all, for the modernist, it meant clearing the ground of previous assumptions and starting with a clear feeling for the thing itself, and a clear sight of it. "Things" and "real things" figure in much of the rhetoric of this period as an expression of the concreteness and vividness aimed at. Looking back on his early years Williams wrote, "I was interested in discovering about life, I put down daily impressions. Certain poems are very real because I was touched by real things."[17] Hemingway too uses the phrase when he contrasts the kind of writing he was doing for the newspapers, in which the timeliness of the subject inevitably conveyed a certain emotion, with the peculiar literary effects he was aiming at: "But the real thing, the sequence of motion and fact which made the emotion and which would be as valid in a year or ten years or, with luck and if you stated it purely enough, always, was beyond me and I was working very hard to get it."[18] And Gertrude Stein makes the same point in recalling her own advice to Hemingway: "If you keep on doing newspaper work you will never see things, you will only see words and that will not do, that is of course if you intend to be a writer."[19]

What they all meant by "things" and "real things" was, in part at least, quite simply, things. As Amy Lowell had put it in an essay on the new poetry in the 1910s, "We are materialists in a strange, joyful way—loving the things we can see, and hear, and taste, and touch, and smell. So these verses are full of scenes and objects, of beauties— Nature's, Art's—of preoccupation with the things all about us."[20] Lowell was thinking of Vachel Lindsay, William Rose Benet, and H. D. in these years, but her description of the sheer delight in things and in the senses would be entirely congenial to Williams too, and to Marianne Moore. Real toads, Moore wanted in her imaginary gardens, and for Williams she had succeeded in placing them there, along with apples and much else: "To Miss Moore an apple remains an apple whether it be in Eden or the fruit bowl where it curls. . . . One is not made to feel that as an apple it has anything particularly to do with poetry or that as such it needs special treatment."[21] What it does have to do with is creating a space within the poem where things can be named and given reality, and it is an impulse that has remained a dominant one in American poetry, continuing through the Objectivist writings of George Oppen, Louis Zukofsky, and Charles Reznikoff, and still strong in the work of such later poets as Charles Olson, Charles Simic, and Louis Simpson. (As Simpson wrote in "American Poetry," "Whatever it is, it must have / A stomach that can digest / Rubber, coal, uranium, moons, poems.")[22]

As I have argued in previous chapters, this effort to embody the authenticity of things was at the core not only of modernist poetry, but of the other arts as well. As the painter Marsden Hartley wrote, "the thing must be brought clearly to the surface in terms of itself, without cast or shade or the application of extraneous ideas."[23] And Mumford had expressed a similar value in the term borrowed from German art, *Sachlichkeit*, which he applied to Roebling, to Sullivan, and to Stieglitz. Williams shared this sensibility, even taking the engineer as a kind of model for the artist, who must likewise start with a firm contact with the thing itself: "It has been by paying naked attention first to the thing itself that American plumbing, American shoes, American bridges, indexing systems, locomotives, printing presses, city buildings, farm implements and a thousand other things have become notable in the world."[24] One visual artist who had thus paid attention to the thing itself was Williams's friend Charles Sheeler, and the poet's admiration for him was based partly on the solidity and precision of Sheeler's renderings: "It is the real world, the world of things with which the artist has to do, this cannot ever be too strongly emphasized."[25]

Given the emphasis on the thing itself, it is not surprising that modern photography was of such importance as a model of direct, objective seeing to Williams, and to the Objectivists generally. (In his introduction to the 1931 issue of *Poetry* devoted to the Objectivists, Zukovsky would make the inspiration of optics explicit: "An Objective: [Optics]—The lens bringing the rays from an object to a focus.")[26] Williams's tribute to Stieglitz in the 1934 celebration, *America and Alfred Stieglitz*, places the importance of the camera within a cultural context that indirectly explains the importance of the new poetry as well: "The photographic camera and what it could do were peculiarly well suited to a place where the immediate and the actual were under official neglect."[27] And photography would function throughout Williams's career as a touchstone for the quality of freshness in visual representation: thus, for example, he marvels at the "vitality of touch" in Rembrandt and Holbein, and in "the older daguerreotypes" (*Camera Work* had celebrated these as precursors of "straight photography"); he reads Whitman as if for the first time under the influence of a set of photographs illustrating *Leaves of Grass*, images that show us the world "as Whitman saw it."[28]

Williams's poem, "Young Sycamore," inspired by Stieglitz's photograph of a lone tree growing on a New York sidewalk ("Spring Showers"), is only the most obvious instance of the camera's influence; many other poems show a more oblique but no less important sense of the photographic object (as it was understood then)—the object directly portrayed, without decoration, without metaphor, the object captured in a seemingly still moment and recorded by the eye of the artist intent on the real thing before him. Williams's most famous poem, "The Red Wheelbarrow" exemplifies this quality with a pointed simplicity, offering too a sense of the enigma that might reside in the "thingness" of the object clearly seen and simply described.

> so much depends
> upon
>
> a red wheel
> barrow

glazed with rain
water

beside the white
chickens[29]

The writer, then, must start with a fresh sense of the thing itself. But words too were things, and often, in Williams, the poem could become an exhibition of words *as things*.[30] Thus one might import into the poem a list of ice cream flavors, or window signs, or whatever, in the same way that Stuart Davis might import words into the composition of a painting. (Not surprisingly, Davis was a favorite of Williams.) Words taken from the street or from commerce were attractive as well because they were ostensibly antipoetic material (like a piece of broken glass, the subject of another short poem); their presence as words in a poem were interestingly alien and focus the attention on the substance and color of the language itself. (The word "SODA" appears framed by asterisks—like an electric sign—in "The Attic Which Is Desire.")[31] Like the prose sections of *Paterson*, as Benjamin Sankey points out, such samples of American speech and colloquial writing give Williams something to work against, a context— rhythmically and idiomatically—for poetic speech.[32]

One strategy Williams used to achieve contact with the world was thus to reveal the thing objectively. But another strategy, evident as early as the major writings of the twenties, took a deliberately opposite approach, emphasizing the burden of the imagination in *transforming* the thing before it into a work of art. The artist works with things, as Williams put it in *Spring and All*, "Things with which he is familiar, simple things—at the same time to detach them from ordinary experience to the imagination." Things thus seen are still real, still as if "photographed," but now also are seen "in some peculiar way—detached." As he put it in summary, "The only realism in art is of the imagination."[33]

The "detachment" Williams speaks of is depicted strikingly in some lines from *Paterson*, not least because of the blatantly "unpoetic" subject matter constituting the "thing" the poet starts with.

Things, things unmentionable,
The sink with the waste farina in it and

> lumps of rancid meat, milk-bottle tops: have
> here a tranquility and loveliness
> Have here (in his thoughts)
> a complement tranquil and chaste.[34]

What is depicted is the transmutation of dross into gold: Here are some things. Here is the poem I have made. And here (in the poet's mind) is the means of poetic production, the imagination that starts with things and ends with poems. It is a passage that enacts its own theory of poetry: the things unmentionable are first mentioned, called into existence, then brought into the poet's, and the reader's, thoughts in the lilting rhythm of the last three lines especially. The peculiar mimesis that is poetry rests precisely, for Williams, on the difference between things "out there" and things "in the poem"; the artful bridging of the gap between world and word is the poem itself. The act of the imagination is thus an act of fresh perception, an artful distortion; it is the act of making poems that take on the freshness of original things, of "reality itself." "You no longer copy, but *make* a natural object."[35]

Thus at the center of Williams's poetic is a tension, if not indeed a paradox, illustrated, on a small scale, by the abrupt transition that occurs between the first and second section of the final unit, XXVII, of *Kora in Hell*: in the first section Williams writes that the "particular thing," even a sharpened pencil, "dwarfs the imagination" (there are echoes of Whitman here) and constitutes the "gist of poetry"; but the very next section begins, "There is no thing that with a twist of the imagination cannot be something else." The imagination is dwarfed by the thing; it also has the power to transform it. The freshness Williams sought, the recreation of reality that would shock the senses and focus the attention, takes place within a field defined at one end by the thing itself and at the other by the imagination. In short, not *things* alone, and not *ideas* alone. Rather, *no ideas but in things*.[36]

The "twist of the imagination" working on the thing before it might take any number of forms. At the simplest level, it might involve a syntactic twist, the ordering of words (as in "The Red Wheelbarrow") so that the image is framed with an implied question (*What* depends on the red wheelbarrow, etc.?). Other poems in *Spring and All* begin with simple statement and move toward some more elaborate conceit (see, for example, XII: "The red paper box / hinged with cloth" and

XXVII: "Black eyed susan / rich orange / round the purple core").[37] And the suite of fifteen short poems called "January Morning," to give another example, features fifteen vignettes, some of which stop with the bare statement of fact (for example, XIV: "—and the flapping flags are at / half mast for the dead admiral"), while others offer the rudiments of metaphor in a simple comparison (for example, VII: "—and the worn, / blue car rails [like the sky!] / gleaming among the cobbles!").[38] The poem allows the object to stand forth clearly in the reader's eye; but it is also a gathering point for the mind's eye, a nexus for the imagination and the thing.

Another way to effect the "twist of the imagination" is through a visual image of the thing that explicitly evokes the vocabulary of Cubist art. (Juan Gris is a presence throughout *Spring and All.*) Thus, for example, the elusive image in "The rose is obsolete" (from *Spring and All*) does what it starts out to say: it shows the obsolescence of the conventional image of the rose and a way of exciting the eye by the verbal equivalent of the synthetic collage of concrete fragments and abstractions. Or consider this description of a hibiscus plant in "This Florida: 1924":

> those varying shades
> of orange, clear as an electric
> bulb on fire
>
> or powdery with sediment—
> matt, the shades and textures
> of a Cubist picture[39]

Another example is the lesson in painting that Williams gives in "To a Solitary Disciple" (disciples were hard to come by in the early years) in which the moon and the steeple become objects in a composition (reminiscent of a Charles Demuth), the actual things being subsumed by the imagination's geometry:

> See how the converging lines
> of the hexagonal spire
> escape upward—
> receding, dividing!
> —sepals

that guard and contain
the flower!

Observe
how motionless
the eaten moon
lies in the protecting lines[40]

As these poems suggest—and it has been amply demonstrated elsewhere—Williams's eye was profoundly affected by the new currents
in art that were present in New York during the teens and twenties.[41]

Williams was not alone in thus altering normal vision, estranging
our senses so as to achieve, in the literary work, a fresh perception of
reality.[42] Even the popular Dashiell Hammett, describing his hero at
the start of *The Maltese Falcon* sketched a cubist abstraction: "Samuel
Spade's jaw was long and bony, his chin a jutting v under the more
flexible v of his mouth. His nostrils curved back to make another,
smaller, v. His yellow-grey eyes were horizontal. The *v motif* was
picked up again by thickish brows rising outward from twin creases
above a hooked nose."[43] But in Williams the transformation of the
visual world is a constant preoccupation. And it resulted not only
from the influence of the new art, but from a scientist's sensitivity to
artifacts of vision that were not necessarily new, but that the modern
artist—for Dr. Williams was both scientist and artist—might now feel
free to respond to.

The camera had pointed the eye to a closer contact with the object.
But a variety of other optical technologies served as models for Williams of ways of twisting the imagination and freshening the vision.
Thus, for example, an entry in Section 18 of *Kora in Hell* depicts a
montage of images, including "a vague cinema lifting its black moon
blot all out," followed by a commentary that, "*In the mind there is a
continual play of obscure images which coming between the eyes and
their prey seem pictures on the screen at the movies* [ital. orig.]."[44] A
later entry in *Kora*—foreshadowing the mirror dance of "Danse Russe"
—affirms that "*The simple expedient of a mirror has practical use for
arranging the hair, for observation of the set of a coat, etc. But as an
exercise for the mind the use of a mirror cannot be too highly recommended. Nothing of a mechanical nature could be more conducive to
that elasticity of the attention which frees the mind for the enjoyment of*

its special prerogatives."[45] And shortly after, Williams is watching the world turn under his feet, sending the eye aloft in an airplane in a way that looks forward to the aerial views of *Paterson*. The very cover of *Kora*—it was Williams's idea—featured a drawing of an ovum being penetrated by a sperm cell, a vision of things seen under a microscope. It was also, of course, an image of *contact* at the most basic level, suggesting that poetry itself was beginning freshly again, *ab ovo*.

Like Whitman, Williams saw himself as an inventor, picking up where the earlier poet had left off, designing forms that were consonant with the technological and scientific processes of the day. He defined the enterprise of the modern writer in these terms in an essay on Whitman written in 1955: "By paying attention to detail and our telescopes and microscopes and the reinterpretations of their findings, we realize that man has long since broken from the confinement of the more rigid of his taboos," and that our efforts—building on Whitman's original effort to make room within the line of the poem—would be to go in, "into the cell, the atom, the poetic line, for our discoveries."[46] The notion that the writer is making "discoveries," that he is an originator of new forms yet is working within the context of a given culture, marks the modernist enterprise and focuses our attention on problems of structure, style, and substance.

But it is precisely in matters of structure and form that Williams is most different from Whitman. Where the earlier poet was constructing a large container equal to the whole of America, a single large poem that gathered poems as it grew, sweeping them into an integrated whole, Williams's affinity was, on the contrary, for fragments, *broken forms*. "By the brokenness of his composition the poet makes himself master of a certain weapon which he could possess himself of in no other way," Williams wrote in the 1918 "Prologue" to *Kora in Hell*, thus setting himself conspicuously against the example of Wallace Stevens, whose letter to him he has just included on the page before, as if to demonstrate in the very structure of his own text the discontinuity and miscellaneousness that Stevens has just argued against.[47] The text would be made more "difficult," but also more sensational. Thus would the act of reading, of perception, be prolonged; thus would our awareness of form and construction be heightened. The work's texture was, in any case, a response to the necessity of achieving, as Williams put it, an "intense vision of the facts" ("the only human value of anything"), in a world that all too easily cheapens the meaning of words. "The difficulty of modern styles," he wrote in *The Descent of Winter*, "is made by the fragmentary stupidity of modern life, its lacunae of sense, loops, perversions of instinct, blankets, amputations, fullsomeness of instruction and multiplications of insanity."[48]

From the early imagistic poem "Between Walls" ("broken / pieces of a green / bottle") to the massively broken forms of *Paterson*, Williams's aesthetic, based on the tension between the actual thing and the twist of the imagination, found its strongest expression in the assimilation of fragments of reality to an overall design that favored abrupt juxtapositions of unlike materials. In *Kora in Hell* (1920), for example, prose improvisations alternate with italicized sections that present a more reflective meditation, a second-order consideration obliquely related to the first-order spontaneity of the automatic writing. In *Spring and All* (1923), prose discussions on a wide range of topics—including the art of poetry—alternate with sections of one or more poems in such a way that to read the poems *out* of context, as they are printed, say, in the *Collected Poems* or in anthologies, is to miss the peculiar resonance individual poems have been given by their surroundings. And, another instance, *The Descent of Winter* (1928), is a diary, with some of the entries as poems, others as prose. The technique was carried as well into the prose variorum, *In the American Grain* (1925), which consists of whole extracts from printed historical sources, as well as Williams's imaginative recreations of archaic styles. "In letters, in journals, reports of happenings I have recognized new contours suggested by old words so that new names were constituted. Thus, where I have found noteworthy stuff, bits of writing have been copied into the book for the taste of it."[49] But *Paterson* is the great example of broken form, a discontinuous epic—unending, Williams finally realized—in which actual personal letters, prose excerpts from existing texts, and of course the lines of verse, all compose the "poem."

The dialectic between word and thing, between the imagination and the world, is thus the engine behind the machine that is the poem. And the opposing energies of word and thing create, one might say, the broken forms that Williams returns to again and again, as if, in brokenness, in stress, in tension, lie a greater authenticity than could otherwise be got into literature. These points are illustrated thematically in two of Williams's most sustained works—*The Great American Novel* and *Paterson*—and I want to discuss them both briefly before concluding this discussion of Williams. Each dwells on the question we started with: How does one create a language to deal with contemporary experience?

The Great American Novel (1923) treats this question jocoseriously, with a comic extravagance befitting the pseudo-grandiose ambitions of the title. "One must begin with words if one is to write. But what then of smell? What then of the hair on the trees or the golden brown cherries under the black cliffs."[50] The referential capacity of language, its power to recall to the memory the sensations of experience, is at odds with its purely inventive, purely fictive, factitious quality. "But can you not see, can you not taste, can you not smell, can you not hear, can you not touch—words?" (*GAN*, 159). We are prevented from looking through the language to the world; we are stopped at the window, or are somewhere between language and the world, not sure whether we are suspending our disbelief or focusing our attention on it: "The words take up the smell of the car. Petrol. Face powder, arm pits, food-grease in the hair, foul breath, clean musk. Words." (*GAN*, 159). The writer is the maker of language, the maker of words. Why not, then, allow him full mastery over the building blocks of his materials? "Break the words. Words are indivisible crystals. One cannot break them—Awu tsst grang splith gra pragh og bm—Yes, one can break them. One can make words" (*GAN*, 160).

But given the extraordinary self-consciousness of the book, there is hardly chance for Williams in *The Great American Novel* to move his work forward. ("If there is progress then there is a novel," the book begins. But there is no progress.) Plotless, characterless, *The Great American Novel* is a miscellany of conversations and scenes about a writer who is writing a novel, ending with a seemingly random note on rag merchants who specialize in producing "shoddy" and other fakes: "You've seen this fake oilcloth they are advertising now. Congoleum. Nothing but building paper with a coating of enamel" (*GAN*, 227). It is a fitting conclusion to a "novel" about the problems of authenticity.

"We have no words," Williams complained in *The Great American Novel*. "Every word we get must be broken off from the European mass." Our American words are "plastered with muck out of the cities" (*GAN*, 175). *Paterson*, a poem about a city who is also a man, takes this as its starting point and provides, in the Falls at the center of the poem-city-man, a metaphor for speech that is clean, resounding, and expressive of the place. Here, in the Falls, is the *thing* as *word*. If only we could touch it, make contact between the mind and the thing. (For it is the failure of language that is the failure of society, as Williams sees it.)

> The language, the language
> fails them
> They do not know the words
> or have not
> the courage to use them
> —girls from
> families that have decayed and
> taken to the hills: no words.
> They may look at the torrent in
> their minds
> and it is foreign to them.   . (*P*, 20–21)

The failure of language is at the root of the two historical incidents that resonate throughout the poem—the disappearance of Mrs. Sarah Cumming into the Passaic Falls and the disappearance of Sam Patch into the Genessee.

Both Mrs. Cumming and Patch are "silent, uncommunicative" (*P*, 31). Mrs. Cumming stands before the raptures of the scene, her husband the Rev. Cumming beside her, and in a moment she is gone, claimed "without minister" by the "stupendous works of nature around them" (*P*, 24). The story is mysterious, suggestive, but opaque. Was it the "laughter" of the Falls that drew her in, away from her husband? Or was it an "emptiness," as an early version, omitted from *Paterson*, poses the problem. The Patch story also is in the end unclear, although Williams implies a closer connection between the Falls and Patch's expressive leap; for his leap is preceded by a speech: "A speech! What could he say that he must leap so desperately to complete it?" But Patch wavers in the air. "Speech had failed him. He was confused. The word had been drained of its meaning" (*P*, 27). The stories in *Paterson* are drawn from history, they are bits of stuff woven into the poem, but they exemplify the problem of the poet: how to be reconciled with the world when "the language is worn out" (*P*, 103). How to leap successfully over the chasm between word and thing?

Language and place, word and thing, remain in Williams dialectically conjugal, yet unresolved, a relationship to be reconciled in the act of the poem itself. He had written in the early *Contact* about the need for the poet to establish "the essential contact between words and the locality that breeds them," and he had gone on, in the prose and poetry of the next several decades, to do just that—in poems that captured the spoken word, and in stories that featured closely heard dialogue, the slang of his patients; in the poet's own speaking voice, dramatized in tracts, addresses to solitary disciples, messages left on refrigerators, etc.[51] If the poem was, for Williams, its own self-contained universe—

> When the sun rises, it rises in the poem
> and when it sets darkness comes down
> and the poem is dark   . (*P*, 122)

it was also a bulwark against the chaos of the world, part of a poet's moral program. As Williams put it in a 1950 letter to Robert Creeley: "To write badly is an offence to the state since the government can never be more than the government of the words. If the language is distorted crime flourishes."[52] Or, as Williams put it more simply in "To Elsie," without the anchor of local traditions and a language with which to speak the world around us, "The pure products of America / go crazy"; without a meaningful *contact* with the concrete particulars of experience, things are out of control—"No one / to witness / and adjust, no one to drive the car."[53]

For Williams, finally, poetry was a social act, a way of giving voice to feeling, which was a condition for being rooted in a society. The contact created in the poem derived from local experience, but its significance was as a representative model for the larger cultural life of the nation. Williams began small, but he ended with the epic of the local—*Paterson*. If Williams is thus the exemplary modernist poet, John Dos Passos is the exemplary modernist novelist, attempting on the grand scale of his *U.S.A.* trilogy, to contain the whole of twentieth-century American experience, yet starting, as Williams had, with the word, with the speech of the country.

The poet's wish to be the unacknowledged (or better yet, the acknowledged) legislator of the world dies hard, and Williams was not alone in investing the highest moral and political importance in the writer's function. It is central as well to John Dos Passos's trilogy of the 1930s, *U.S.A.*, a work that succeeds as well as anything else in its time in being what Williams had jokingly essayed to write a decade earlier—The Great American Novel. I should say that the Dos Passos I am concerned with here is the writer who first gained recognition in the 1930s as America's greatest proletarian writer—a distinction that the anti-Communist, patriotic conservative of the later years was sometimes at pains to live down. Dos Passos was always cantankerously independent and grew increasingly impatient after World War II with a generation he thought ruined by television; but leaving aside questions of consistency or inconsistency between the earlier and the later work, Dos Passos's 1965 formulation of the writer's task, which he attempted in a speech at his alma mater, the Choate School, is an apt statement of the general principles that guided him in the 1920s and 1930s as well: the writer has an obligation to "choose for himself what is true and what is not true, what is real and what is not real in the picture of society established for him by his elders."[54] For Dos Passos, the established picture he was defining himself against was in large part the product of the technological media that had supplied the inescapable environment in the early decades of the century. "Mass culture is the screen through which we see reality and the mirror in which we see ourselves," the critic Robert Warshow wrote in 1947, in words that could define precisely the climate of *U.S.A.* "Its ultimate tendency is even to supersede reality."[55] Given this condition, Dos Passos's ultimate purpose in *U.S.A.* was to reclaim reality, to affirm a kind of moral and aesthetic authenticity against the confusion of mass culture and the betrayals of history. "I can't think of good writing in any other way than as reality," he wrote to his friend Robert Cantwell, though he prudently added, "I'd hate to have to define what I mean by that term."[56] What he meant by the term can at least be described, if not defined, by Dos Passos's own fictional practice, by the writing of what he called the "contemporary chronicle."

What Dos Passos was after in *U.S.A.* was in many ways a reinvention of *Leaves of Grass*. As Whitman was a model for Williams, so was he also, from the very beginning, for Dos Passos. In his first professional publication—a 1916 essay in *The New Republic* called "Against American Literature"—Dos Passos lamented the absence of passion and color in American literature, its lack of profound thought or deep connection with nature. Whitman was, however, the exception; and he asked in a tone that was too public to be anything but private,

"Shall we pick up the glove Walt Whitman threw at the feet of posterity?"[57] The identification with Whitman would only grow stronger until, in the final chronicle, *Century's Ebb*, the nineteenth-century poet is present in his own voice, in a passage quoted from *Democratic Vistas*, lamenting that America has had few or none among "our geniuses and talented writers" who have "yet really spoken to this people, created a single imagemaking work for them or absorbed the central spirit and the idiosyncrasies which are theirs and which thus in highest ranges so far remains entirely uncelebrated, unexpressed."[58] This was, of course, Whitman's way of talking about himself; and it was also Dos Passos's. The chronicle was Dos Passos's ongoing, never-ending *Leaves of Grass*.

The structure of *U.S.A.* was as synoptic, as omnivorous in its appetite for the whole of American life, as was *Leaves of Grass*. Something of Dos Passos's intention was visible embryonically in the earlier *Manhattan Transfer* (1925), and D. H. Lawrence, reviewing that work in 1927 described it in terms that would apply as well to the later trilogy. "If you set a blank record revolving to receive all the sounds," Lawrence wrote, "and a film-camera going to photograph all the motions of a scattered group of individuals, at the points where they meet and touch in New York, you more or less get Mr. Dos Passos's method."[59] Or, as Dos Passos wrote, the chronicler uses *everything*: "the fragments of talk he overhears in the subway or on a streetcar, the letter he picks up on the street addressed by one unknown character to another, the words on a scrap of paper found in a trash basket, the occasional vistas of reality he can pick out of the mechanical diction of a newspaper report."[60] Dos Passos was hugely assimilative, indulging an impulse to *collect* that was unstoppable. (The later chronicles following *U.S.A.* continue the basic technique established in the 1920s.) All of it would add up to Whitman's "single imagemaking work."

U.S.A. is as original an invention as was *Leaves of Grass*, yet like the earlier work, it is thoroughly rooted in the total aesthetic culture of its day and was the result (in part) of changes in the arts and communication media that had been visible in the United States at least since the 1913 Armory Show. In fact, the trilogy is as much a visual construction, relying on a simultaneity of effect, as it is a linear work. And it is the spatial quality of the novel especially—derived from cubism and synthetic collages, as well as from the cinematic montages of

Eisenstein that so impressed Dos Passos on his trip to Russia in the late 1920s—that is initially most striking about it. With its abrupt shifts from one section to another, *U.S.A.* often *looks*, on the page, like a synthetic construction—especially the Newsreel passages. If Dos Passos was turning the novel into a verbal/visual montage (as his friend E. E. Cummings was turning poetry into a kind of typographical painting), he was responding to a broadly shared sense of a change in the culture: "In the last fifty years," he wrote, "a change has come over the visual habits of Americans as a group. . . . From being a wordminded people we are becoming an eyeminded people."[61]

Maybe the best formulation of the range of influences on *U.S.A.* was written by Dos Passos himself in 1931, when he introduced the volume of poems by Blaise Cendrars that he had translated. Because it was composed at the same time he was immersed in the trilogy, and because Dos Passos is speaking from the center of the new modernist aesthetic, reaching out to the whole spectrum of changes in the avant-garde and popular arts, it is worth quoting at length:

> The poetry of Blaise Cendrars was part of the creative tidal wave that spread over the world from the Paris of before the last European war. Under various tags: futurism, cubism, vorticism, modernism, most of the best work in the arts in our time has been the direct product of this explosion, that had an influence in its sphere comparable with that of the October revolution in social organization and politics and the Einstein formula in physics. Cendrars and Apollinaire, poets, were on the first cubist barricades with the group that included Picasso, Modigliani, Marinetti, Chagall; that profoundly influenced Maiakovsky, Meyerhold, Eisenstein; whose ideas carom through Joyce, Gertrude Stein, T. S. Eliot (first published in Wyndham Lewis's "Blast"). The music of Stravinski and Prokofieff and Diageleff's Ballet hail from this same Paris already in the disintegration of victory, as do the windows of Saks Fifth Avenue, skyscraper furniture, the Lenin Memorial in Moscow, the paintings of Diego Rivera in Mexico City and the newritz styles of advertising in American magazines.[62]

Dos Passos's evident openness to the new structures of experience in the early twentieth century—encompassing as part of the same revolution the various changes in the arts, as well as in advertising, politics, and science—is manifest in the form and substance of *U.S.A.*, which has that "classic" connection to its own time, marking it as unmistakably a product of the years between the wars.

Novelistic precedents of various sorts have been mustered by Dos Passos and by his critics, from *Tristram Shandy* and *Vanity Fair* to *Ulysses*, yet none seems close to the real quality of *U.S.A.* Poetic models seem closer, not only Whitman, but Dos Passos's contemporaries—Williams, Cummings, Moore, Pound; all were incorporating "anti-poetic" materials—quotations, documents, letters, signs and other bits of authenticity—into structures that were as much spatial designs as traditional literary formulations. Thinking of *U.S.A.* as a whole, one thinks of visual metaphors: it is a panorama, a vast survey of American characters and places in the early twentieth century; it is a collage of incongruous materials which yet interrelate thematically; it is a montage sequence of images blending into one another; it has the ragged, angular rhythm of a Vorticist construction, the seemingly ad hoc arrangement of a newspaper. Or, to use a metaphor Dos Passos most invites, it is a photograph. A selection from *U.S.A.* (drawn particularly from *The Big Money*) appeared in *Esquire* in April 1936, under the title, "The Camera Eye," and labeled "semi-fiction" (a nice compromise), "treatment: a verbal photomontage." Arnold Gingrich wrote an "Editor's Note" introducing the piece which Dos Passos urged his publisher's book salesmen to "read and digest." ("Every one of the half million readers of *Esquire* is a potential buyer of the book," he wrote.)[63] Gingrich wrote: "First, do not insist upon making consecutive sense of every phrase and sentence as you go along. The effect is as cumulative as that of music or painting. Second, remember that this is the verbal equivalent of the inclusive technique of photography, registering apparently irrelevant and even distracting detail for the sake of achieving a complete atmospheric approximation of reality."[64] Dos Passos's endorsement of the note, not to mention his use of the phrase "Camera Eye" as the title for this excerpt from the book, makes plain the centrality to his own thinking of the photographic metaphor, which aptly suggests the "objectivity" of the tone and the seemingly passive, all-inclusive recording of the social background in the trilogy.

Another way of thinking of *U.S.A.* is as a machine. Williams had written that "A poem is a small (or large) machine made of words," meaning that there is no part that is redundant, that it is functional rather than sentimental, that its movement derives from the energy of its speech.[65] But it was *U.S.A.*, more than any other work of its time, that best exemplified that notion. With its architectonic structure, its four interacting elements—fictional narratives dealing with several principal characters; Biographies of actual historical figures; Newsreel sections consisting of a collage of actual headlines and songs; and Camera Eye vignettes of an autobiographical nature—and above all with its fictional engine driven by *speech*, *U.S.A.* was the exemplary novel of the machine age. In the same way that Frank Lloyd Wright affirmed the aesthetic value of the machine when properly used, and in the same way that Stieglitz had come to stand for the mastery of the machine, Dos Passos was constructing a novel that implicitly confirmed the rational economy and the aesthetic of the machine at the same time that it explicitly attacked the American corporate capitalism that was built on the base of the industrial machine.

What is a chronicle? What is its relationship to conventional fiction on the one hand, and to "history" on the other? Though Dos Passos called the novelist a "sort of second-class historian," and though his own work has served as a kind of model for later professional historians, we should not confuse the Dos Passos chronicle with the many things it resembles.[66] There is no confusion of fact and fiction, as in the historical novel or in the fictionalized biography or in that contemporary monster, the docudrama. Despite its heterogeneous nature, the novel's purpose is always clear to the reader. One knows when the material is based on fiction and when nonfiction (which is not always the case, for example, in Doctorow's contemporary hybrids); and in the nonfiction sections (the Biographies and Newsreels) Dos Passos's tone is sufficiently ironic to make his purpose in using history clear. Though he resorted to the Biographies in order, as he put it, to "get something a little more accurate than fiction," his aim in the work as a whole "was always to produce fiction."[67] Where the reader may legitimately claim confusion—as in the autobiographical Camera Eye sections—the effect is minimal. Dos Passos used his own life in these segments, distorting certain facts to match the needs of the fiction, but the Camera Eye does not purport to be historically accurate, merely accurately suggestive, in a representative, impressionistic sense.[68]

The Dos Passos chronicle is different from the conventional novel in yet another respect: the character of the reader's experience. The fictional narratives carry the burden of *U.S.A.* and to them we return repeatedly after the "interruptions" of the other sections. In fact, it is easy to become immersed in the stories of Mac, of Janey, J. Ward Moorehouse, Eleanor Stoddard, Joe Williams, Richard Ellsworth Savage, Eveline Hutchins, Ben Compton, Charley Anderson, Mary French, Margo Dowling; and our immersion in the narratives, our suspension of disbelief when we are reading them, gives them an authority and authenticity the other sections lack. Lulled into the stories, we resent the intrusions of the Camera Eye sections, the Newsreels, the Biographies. Just as we have become involved in the unceasing drama of the lives, the fast-paced clip of the narrative, Dos Passos cuts the flow. It is disturbing. We want to find out what happens next. The dream of fiction has been interrupted, sometimes without ever properly rounding off the story that was unfolding. In effect, Dos Passos is constantly distancing us from these stories, fracturing the plate-glass transparency of the narrative, making us pay attention to something that seems extraneous: a set of headlines, a biography. And there precisely is Dos Passos's genius. The interpenetration of fact and fiction in *U.S.A.* (like the interpenetration of spaces in the towers of Eiffel or Tatlin that Siegfried Giedion observed, or like the interpenetration of nature and artifice in a Frank Lloyd Wright construction) creates a new experience for fiction. The interrupted form, the openness of the structure of *U.S.A.*, compels a new kind of attention from the reader, it removes us from the fiction to a point where we can survey the whole of it at once as an emotional and an intellectual construct. And one cannot really describe the effect as a shuttling between fiction and non-fiction, for the non-fiction sections—Newsreels and Biographies—have been shaped carefully by Dos Passos in a way that gives them a quality of intention, an effect of purpose not unlike the purely fictional lives. What is real in *U.S.A.*? We suspend our disbelief and the fiction is real; we read the newsreels and the events alluded to are real; we read the lives of historical figures and they are real. Each segment qualifies the previous one and sets us up for a jolt when we enter the succeeding one. It is an aesthetic of perpetual qualification, of perpetual motion, that we can grasp as a whole only by standing back and seeing the sum of the parts, the way we look at a skyscraper. Williams's *Paterson*, which is likewise composed of discontinuous elements, fuses what Dos Passos keeps separate: Williams's presence pervades the poem—the mind of the poet is the mind of Dr. Paterson which is the city itself and its history. Dos Passos restricts his own subjective presence to the Camera Eye. Where *Paterson*, like the mind, is layered with memory and history, *U.S.A.* is a serially unfolding whole, a continuous present tense, moving in time from the turn of the century through the first three decades to the Crash.

Let us look more closely at the individual generic components of the trilogy, each of which contributes to that "complete atmospheric approximation of reality" Gingrich speaks of. As I have said, the most immediately engaging parts of *U.S.A.* are the fictional lives, which occupy by far the bulkiest portion of the composition as well. They are the traditional stuff of the novel, and Dos Passos uses the sequential portraits to good effect—immersing us in one after the other, rounding out the picture of American society by thus giving us exemplary lives at various social levels. He also allows the characters to stray into one another's narrative segments, so that when a character who has received full treatment in an earlier section makes an appearance in a subsequent sequence having a different focus, we feel a multiplied richness in the interwoven texture of the fiction: we know the "minor" characters as well as the "major" ones. Yet because of the sheer numbers of characters and the lack of any real center (Moorehouse extends through all three volumes and is thematically central, but he does not fully enlist our sympathies) we feel the absence of the kind of coherent drama we are used to in the traditional novel.

Nevertheless, the narratives are in fact filled with dramatic incidents, told in a rapidly moving, tersely sketched manner; what distinguishes the Dos Passos narrative is the absence of strong lighting, the consistently understated treatment of events that might in other fictions be momentous. There is a ticker-tape sameness to the lives, as they move on their plotted ups and downs across the geography of the states and Europe. For example:

> In Washington [Mary French] fixed herself up a little apartment in a house on H Street that was being sublet cheap by Democratic officeholders who were moving out. She often cooked supper for George there. She'd never done any cooking before except camp cooking, but George was quite an expert and knew how to make

Italian spaghetti and chiliconcarne and oysterstew and real
French bouillabaisse. He'd get wine from the Rumanian Embassy
and they'd have very cozy meals together after long days working
in the office. He talked and talked about love and the importance
of a healthy sexlife for men and women, so that at last she let
him. He was so tender and gentle that for a while she thought
maybe she really loved him. He knew all about contraceptives
and was very nice and humorous about them. Sleeping with a
man didn't make as much difference in her life as she'd expected
it would.[69]

The effect is additive, as Jean-Paul Sartre observed, with the author
taking a position both inside and outside the character's head, shifting easily within a fluid discourse that is doubtless more precise than
his character's, yet expresses thoughts and feelings the character
would have had himself.[70] Flaubert was Dos Passos's god, and not
surprisingly there are parts of *U.S.A.* that remind one of Flaubert, and
vice versa: there is in both authors the same distance from the action,
the same understatement, the same detachment and objectivity. The
characters seem to *show themselves*, with only the assistance of the
author.[71]

The Biographies, which Dos Passos said were inspired by his fascination with thirteenth- and fourteenth-century tableaux "with large
figures of saints surrounded by a lot of little people," are in another
key entirely.[72] The twenty-seven portraits in the trilogy, sorted evenly
throughout the volumes and providing a resonant historical person-
age for the given thematic moment, are clearly shaded images: we
know which are the heroes (for example, Eugene Debs, Bill Hay-
wood, Bob La Follette, Thorstein Veblen, Frank Lloyd Wright) and
which are the villains (for example, Minor Keith, Andrew Carnegie,
William Randolph Hearst, Frederick Winslow Taylor). There are also
figures who are more complexly portrayed—their fates are mixed,
their successes slightly ambiguous—like Isadora Duncan or Rudolph
Valentino or Charles Steinmetz. The portraits add literal reality to the
trilogy, they are "real people," part of the background against which
the swirling fictional action takes place; and each stands for a larger
historical process in the evolution of American culture in the twentieth century—labor, capital, management, public relations, science,
architecture, etc. But in all of the Biographies one knows what to

make of the life before us: Dos Passos's tone is clear in its irony, or its sarcasm, or its celebration.

The Newsreels, like the Biographies, add real toads to the imaginary gardens of *U.S.A.* Here, history is comedy: headlines, snatches of songs, and news stories, the major events of the era, all are given equal notice with the day's trivia. Dos Passos had already incorporated newspaper clippings less systematically into the texture of *Manhattan Transfer* (1925), inspired probably by the 1923 Paris production of the ballet *Within the Quota*, which employed stage sets designed by Dos Passos's friend, Gerald Murphy—the two talked often in Paris during this time—featuring nonsense headlines as part of the backdrop. (The cubists too were incorporating newspapers into their collages.) Also, of course, the early movie newsreel itself provided a model for the presentation of current events in a popular rhythm.[73]

Dos Passos uses the Newsreels not only to import "reality" into the fiction and add a documentary texture to the trilogy, but also to comment ironically on the issues and actions of the period. The headlines and stories are sources of background information, but they are also often blatantly propagandistic, thus betraying the discrepancy between the news media and reality. In thus exploiting the ironic possibilities of the form, Dos Passos is more nearly related to the Dadaist spirit of irreverence than he is to the documentary spirit of the 1930s. (Steinbeck's use of documentary inter-chapters in *The Grapes of Wrath* serves the similar purpose of supplying a general background for the fictional action, but Steinbeck's discursive, explanatory tone has a quite different effect from Dos Passos's expressionistic rhythm.) But the random juxtapositions of the newspaper and the typically heterogeneous mix of the movie newsreel only *seem* to shape the logic of Dos Passos's Newsreels. In fact, the sequences are carefully structured bits and pieces, grouped usually around a central theme or two (for example, war, labor strikes, Sacco and Vanzetti, the economy) and designed to exploit the incongruities of tone and sentiment within the given sequence.

Not infrequently the Newsreels open with a connection to a preceding fictional segment and close with a lead-in to a following narrative, thus providing threads of continuity within what is otherwise a discontinuous structure. For example, the story of Eleanor Stoddard closes at one point with her decorating business in disarray, while her romantic attachment to Moorehouse is growing; misty-eyed, she witnesses Moorehouse's announcement to his wife that he is going off to serve in the war. "'I'll join the Red Cross,' she said. 'I can't wait to get to France.'" Newsreel XIX then immediately begins:

> U.S. AT WAR
> UPHOLD NATION CITY'S CRY
> *Over there*
> *Over there*
> at the annual meeting of the stockholders of the Colt Patent Firearms Manufacturing Company a $2,500,000 melon was cut. The present capital stock was increased. The profits for the year were 259 per cent[74]

And so forth. Through such juxtapositions Dos Passos knits together the fragments of *U.S.A.* into a web of interconnections.

The fourth type of segment in *U.S.A.* is the "Camera Eye," which numbers fifty-one distinct units of one or two pages each, and which diminishes in frequency as the trilogy progresses. Dos Passos intended the Camera Eye to drain off the subjectivity of the novel, to gather the impressionistic view of the author, leaving the rest of the narrative free to be "objective." The author in fact uses his own life story closely (but not literally) throughout the segments, allowing his authorial persona to develop in step with the century. Dos Passos was four years old in 1900—just old enough to begin to have memorable sensations, and the Camera Eye units move from early childhood to young manhood in World War I and on to an increasingly radical point of view on America through the 1920s, culminating in the Sacco and Vanzetti case. Dos Passos had used an impressionistic prose style in the headings of chapters in *Manhattan Transfer* to set a mood for the chapter to follow (for example, the opening, "Ferryslip": "Three gulls wheel above the broken boxes, orangerinds, spoiled cabbage heads that heave between the splintered plank walls . . .") but the *U.S.A.* Camera Eye sections are different.[75] The headings in the earlier novel have an almost Stieglitzian quality to them ("Tracks," "Steamroller," "Fire Engine," are some of the titles), capturing moods of the city in various locales and at various times; in *U.S.A.* the prose is equally impressionistic but the "I" of the eye is emphatically present. The images and vignettes are frankly records of experience and the emphasis is as much on nonvisual sensations and feelings as on visual ones—for example, "and I felt itchy in the back of my neck

would I be struck by lightning eating the bread drinking the commu-
nion me not believing or baptized or Presbyterian and who were the
Molly Maguires?"[76] And the witnessing Eye becomes increasingly
resolute and ethically firm as the trilogy progresses, until the final,
pessimistic conclusion following the Sacco and Vanzetti execution—
"all right we are two nations."[77]

The Camera Eye sections also provide the implicit theoretical basis
for the construction of the whole of *U.S.A.*, for they place at the center
of the panoramic novel the creative consciousness of the artist. In so
naming these autobiographical units Dos Passos was doubtless attempting to capitalize on the aesthetic authority of the still camera
during the early decades of the century as an instrument for objectively registering the visual world; and probably too he was borrowing the political authority of the moving picture camera that was a
part of the influential Soviet documentary cinema movement (Kino-
Pravda) anchored by Dziga Vertov. But Dos Passos's view of photography was more complex than I have yet suggested, and the objectivity
of the camera was only part of its meaning. His early notes for the
Camera Eye suggest he was thinking of using the sections as a kind of
snapshot collection, a personal memory bank: "Newspaper photographs of old / photographs in a trunk the pathetic / enthusiasm—
. . ."[78] But behind the Camera Eye is another, more significant meaning: that the eye is prior to the word, that vision is a prelude to
speech. The key passage is in Camera Eye 47: "from the upsidedown
image on the retina painstakingly out of color shape words remembered light and dark straining."[79] The implied sense of vision itself as
something that must be turned right side up, interpreted, was a persistent part of Dos Passos's epistemology: "Your two eyes are an accurate stereoscopic camera, sure enough," he wrote in "Satire as a Way
of Seeing" (1937), "but the process by which the upsidedown image
on the retina takes effect on the brain entails a certain amount of
unconscious selection. What you see depends to a great extent on
subjective distortion and elimination which determines the varied
impacts on the nervous system of speed of line, emotions of color,
touchvalues of form. Seeing is a process of imagination." The artist is
thus constructing his vision, his eye formed by the climate of visual
stimuli in the culture at large: "the visible arts shape the way we see
just as the audible arts shape the way we hear." The conventions of
the visual arts "furnish the frame of reference by which we invent
nature as we look at it."[80]

The objective qualities of *U.S.A.*—its weight of facts and trivia, its scraps of headlines and biographic portraits, all the elements that make it a "chronicle" of early twentieth-century America, thus are crucially balanced against the Camera Eye, which provides a representative focal point, an ego, creating its own vision out of these elements: "we invent nature as we look at it." But the Camera Eye also embodies the act of articulation, of making sense, of arriving at an ethical point of view, and as such it offers the example of an education in political and moral sensibility. In this sense, *U.S.A.* is as much Bildungsroman as chronicle. And what the Camera Eye provides as well is a center for the *speech* of the novel, a voice that allows us to measure the other voices against its own. It is as much a verbal construction, therefore, as a visual one; and *U.S.A.* as a whole—like *Paterson*—may be read as an essay on the relationship between the world and the word.

Both Williams and Dos Passos begin with the assumption that the poet uses language to invent the world, to bring it into being within the space of the poem. But where Williams enacts this process of discovery and invention over and over again, Dos Passos accepts it more or less as a given, incorporating the function of the imagination in the Camera Eye sections. For Dos Passos, the Camera Eye—the writer—exists in a world already teeming with speech, already filled with the language of the tribe; as the prologue to the trilogy puts it, "mostly U.S.A. is the speech of the people." Yet the speech has grown unreal, inauthentic. It is the age of the demagogue—a William Jennings Bryan, a Woodrow Wilson, a William Randolph Hearst, a J. P. Morgan; and against the hollowness of their political speech, there are the relatively powerless, like Randolph Bourne, or Paxton Hibben, or Thorstein Veblen, or the journalist-revolutionary, Jack Reed. ("Reed was a Westerner and words meant what they said.")[81] The speech of the people is, it slowly develops, at the heart of the problem of Dos Passos's America, and this major theme affords a concluding perspective on the trilogy.

Much of the satire in *U.S.A.* is aimed at professions that are new to the twentieth century, professions that trade in words and images, where the goal is precisely to use words so that they don't mean what they seem to say. And Dos Passos exposes the incongruity between word and reality on several interrelated levels—the news media, public relations, advertising, and Hollywood, to name only the most obvious. ("MARKET SURE TO RECOVER FROM SLUMP," a 1929 headline assures us.)[82] Dos Passos measures his characters by how they use words, and one of the few honorable characters in the trilogy—Jerry Burnham—quits his newspaper job precisely because he cannot stand the lies. The separation of word and thing that was the basis of the modernist insight took on a new urgency in the Depression, when political rhetoric was continually being tested by the visible reality of urban breadlines, Dustbowl migrants, and labor strife. Dos Passos saw the writer in the 1930s to be living in a time of "confusion and rapid change," as he put it in his talk before the American Writers' Congress in 1935, "when terms are continually turning inside out and the names of things hardly keep their meaning from day to day."[83]

Two characters who do not mind compromising themselves in *U.S.A.* are J. Ward Moorehouse (a failed songwriter) and his protégé Richard Ellsworth Savage (a failed poet), who are pioneers in what is called "public relations." (Public relations can also become private, the art of insincerity spilling over into personal life, as when Savage confesses his feelings of love to Eveline Hutchins, only to think, "It sounded phony in his ears, like something he'd say to a client.")[84] Moorehouse, the central character in the trilogy, is the chief exhibit. Beginning his climb to success in the metals business, Moorehouse fills his mind with "augerbits, canthooks, mauls, sashweights, axes, hatchets, monkeywrenches. . . . Jolting in the straphanging crowd on the way downtown, staring at the headlines in the paper without seeing them, chainlinks and anchors and ironcouplings and malleable elbows and unions and bushings and nipples and pipecaps would jostle in his head."[85] Moorehouse is successfully turning himself into a man of his times, a spokesman for the business civilization of the United States, a mental counterpart to the factory, stock exchange, and office building. Given such a metamorphosis, one is not surprised to find that Moorehouse's sleep is troubled: "words, ideas, plans, stock quotations kept unrolling in endless tickertape in his head."[86]

But if the business mind of America is dominated by things—bushings and nipples and pipecaps—and denied its own private dreams, it can at least partake of the mass dreams supplied by the Hollywood film factories. One of Dos Passos's finest scenes shows us such Hollywood image making in action, as Sam Margolis directs Rodney Cathcart in a love scene with the newborn star, Margo Dowling: "They all feel they are you, you are loving her for them," Margolis intones persuasively, "the millions who want love and beauty and excitement, but forget them, loosen up, my dear fellow, forget that I'm here and the camera's here, you are alone together snatching a desperate moment, you are alone except for your two beating hearts, you and the most beautiful girl in the world, the nation's newest sweetheart.... All right ... hold it.... Camera." (Incidentally, Margolis proudly displays a lionskin trophy at home, which he has garnered at the zoo.)[87]

Given such a world of factitious images, of mock sentiments and mocking falsehoods, given the vast linguistic reservoir of American speech, the writer, as Dos Passos said in a 1935 essay—at least ide-ally—"molds and influences ways of thinking to the point of changing and rebuilding the language, which is the mind of the group."[88] That purpose—to rebuild the language—is central to *U.S.A.* and appears, most importantly, in the forty-ninth Camera Eye as an exhortation to the self and to the reader: "rebuild the ruined words worn slimy in the mouths of lawyers districtattorneys collegepresidents judges without the old words the immigrants haters of oppression brought to Plymouth how can you know who are your betrayers America."[89] Whatever else it is, the trilogy is a polemic against the society of the elders: "America," Dos Passos begins his peroration in Camera Eye 50, "our nation has been beaten by strangers who have turned our language inside out who have taken the clean words our fathers spoke and made them slimy and foul."[90]

And the crystal around which this point of view forms is the Sacco and Vanzetti case of the 1920s, in which Dos Passos himself became intensely involved. It is in the context of the murder trial of the two Italian immigrants that the theme of the novel as a whole is made explicit. Sacco and Vanzetti "made the old words new before they died"; the new immigrants of the twentieth century thus restored, in Dos Passos's logomachy, the language of the earliest immigrants— "the roundheads the sackers of castles the kingkillers haters of op-pression."[91] Thus Dos Passos reverses the roles of insiders and out-siders, turning the execution of the accused murderers and pre-sumed anarchists into a martyrdom, and giving to their lives the significance of an act of piety toward the earliest immigrants.

For all its exuberance, for all its exhilarating kaleidoscopic move-ment, *U.S.A.* is a sad work. Concluded in the midst of the Depression, it ends on a picture that was an almost archetypal image of America in the 1930s—the vagabond on the road, hungry, unemployed, thumbing a ride somewhere, anywhere. (And Dos Passos includes a final contrasting irony—an anonymous complacent passenger in an airplane overhead, vomiting into his food container.) Dos Passos's effort to restore authenticity to America by restoring the meaning of the old words would continue after World War II, but by then his image of the storybook democracy of America was growing increasingly out of touch with contemporary pluralistic sensibilities, his critique of America was falling on fewer and fewer ears. *U.S.A* was his finest work, the one in which the writer's sensibility was most in tune with the contemporary aesthetic; in it, he had transformed that aesthetic, and the deepest concerns of the times, into an act of representation that was at once a powerful analysis of the growing distance between the word and the world and a strenuous effort toward closing the distance and restoring authenticity.

With James Agee's *Let Us Now Praise Famous Men* we reach the limit of the writer's effort to arrive at a total reproduction of reality, the logical conclusion of the modernist drive to produce "Not 'realism' but Reality Itself." Starting with an assignment from *Fortune* magazine to do a story on the plight of southern farmers during the Depression, Agee spent the summer of 1936 traveling through Alabama looking for material, ultimately settling down for several weeks on a farm in the heart of the cotton belt. With him was Walker Evans, whose photographs Agee knew and admired enormously. (Evans was on loan from the Farm Security Administration.) What resulted from their sojourn in the South was an account of things that proved unacceptable to *Fortune* (as Agee knew it would be), and the volume that took shape through endless revisions over the next few years was eventually published in 1941 as *Let Us Now Praise Famous Men*.[92] While the popular press was largely puzzled (or offended) by the book's extravagant prose, its disruptive form, and its tortured meditations, a few reviewers (including Lionel Trilling) celebrated its moral depth. But soon, with America on the verge of a war, what was to be the first volume of a trilogy called *Three Tenant Families* slipped without fanfare into oblivion, from which it rose to fame only on its republication in 1960, five years after Agee's death. Like Dos Passos, Agee was aspiring to a representation of American reality that would have the illusion of completeness. But where Dos Passos achieves his effect by the vastness of his scheme—ranging across the entire continent (and Mexico and Europe), across social classes, across three decades, and encompassing the industrial growth of the country, its media and popular culture—Agee essays a kind of completeness at the other extreme, burrowing into his subject, recording his personal experience in one particular corner of the South with an exhaustiveness that borders on the compulsive, "with no detail, however trivial it may seem, left untouched," as he proclaims.[93]

Behind *Famous Men* is not only an experiment in writing (of which more later) but a deeply personal experience for Agee. Educated at Harvard, working in Manhattan's Chrysler Building, on assignment for *Fortune* magazine, Agee was worlds away from the unsophisticated tenant farmers he was observing, yet his stay with them represented to him a return, vicariously, to his own family roots in Tennessee. Agee was enacting in his personal life what had become by the 1930s almost an archetypal pattern in modern literature, a radical response to the anomie of contemporary urban life—the world of figures, desks, offices, giant buildings, clocks, and mechanical entertainments. Agee in Alabama was restoring the wholeness of body and mind, for himself and for the reader, in the same way that Sinclair Lewis's Babbitt had gone to the Maine woods; or Hemingway's Nick Adams had gone fishing in the wilderness of northern Michigan; or Faulkner's Ike McCaslin had sought the missing thing in the woods of Yoknawpatawpha; or T. S. Eliot had sought it in the Dry Salvages of the New England coast; or Steinbeck had found it in his celebrated zygote, the cellular beginning of social life; in the same way that Williams had found it in the round of the seasons. For Agee, the restoration of self was in the soil of Alabama.

Yet it was an experience that, perhaps because of its depth, Agee could not easily express, or would not make easily accessible to his reader. The structure of *Famous Men* is a defiant puzzle, a confusion of false starts and premature endings, a trunk full of fake bottoms. Agee's own set of compositional strategies and techniques, embedded in the text as "On the Porch: 2," offers a suggestive guide to his intentions, as does his Guggenheim application (1937), which lists dozens of projects, seemingly unrelated, yet many of which found their way into the final version of *Famous Men*.[94] My own preference is to view the volume more simply in its broadest structure, taking lightly Agee's own table of contents. The descriptive heart of the book is, then, the two hundred pages or so dealing with Money, with Shelter,

with Clothing, Education, and Work; the hundred pages before and
the hundred pages after this central core comprise a reflexive frame,
a narrative about the trip down South, about locating suitable living
arrangements, about relationships with various individuals, together
with a more analytic, equally self-conscious commentary on the process of writing the book itself. It is that process—the act of representation that encompasses seeing the thing and writing about it—that I
want to dwell on here; and I want to place *Famous Men* not simply in
the context of Depression documentary but in the broader movement
of modernist prose in the first four decades of the twentieth century.

At the outset of Agee's volume the author announces disconcert-
ingly, "If I could do it, I'd do no writing at all here." Instead: "fragments of cloth, bits of cotton, lumps of earth, records of speech,
pieces of wood and iron, phials of odors, plates of food and of excrement" (p. 13). This is only in part a kind of introductory bravado; for
at the center of Agee's attempt to render the lives of the three families
is a disturbing premise: that the effort itself is doomed to failure, that
any literary reproduction must pale before the fact of the real thing.
Thus, with respect to George Gudger (his host during the weeks in
Alabama), Agee declares "somehow a much more important, and dignified, and true fact about him than I could conceivably invent,
though I were an illimitably better artist than I am, is that fact that he
is exactly, down to the last inch and instant, who, what, where, when
and why he is." And the writer's abasement before his subject expands even further, with Agee arguing that "everything in Nature,
every most casual thing, has an inevitability and perfection which art
as such can only approach" (p. 233). All of this is unsettling, leading,
as it does, to a question that would stop cold the artist's whole enterprise: Why bother? Why not just exhibit the raw stuff, Gudger himself? Agee considers doing exactly this, but he imagines the critics
would then murmur, "yes, but is it art." Agee, who liked to position
himself at the Circean borderland between art and life, was thus the
mirror image of Marcel Duchamp; where Duchamp expanded the
likeness between art and non-art, Agee was fixed on the *difference*, in
fact on the absolute superiority of the real thing to the artwork.[95]

On the one hand, such a view must result finally in silence on the
part of the artist, and that is indeed close to where Agee leaves us
(and himself) at the conclusion of *Famous Men*—listening intently to

the sound of two foxes calling to one another, and at last falling asleep.[96] But on the other hand, an immense respect for "actuality," a sense that "the centrally exciting and important fact . . . is: that was the way it was" (p. 241), can also compel the artist to get as close to the real thing as possible, provoking an enormous imaginative effort. And therein lies the motivation behind *Famous Men.*

Agee, like Williams and Dos Passos before him, strove for authenticity by first clearing away the weight of literary convention, taking nothing for granted, reinventing the process of writing. His starting point was a suspicion of language itself, for words are "the most inevitably inaccurate of all mediums of record and communication"; they falsify through "inaccuracy of meaning as well as inaccuracy of emotion," and through their "inability to communicate simultaneity with any immediacy" (pp. 236–37). (Agee's work, dense with such doubts, seems to have been written by someone who has just read C. K. Ogden and I. A. Richards's *The Meaning of Meaning*; and in fact Richards was one of Agee's instructors at Harvard, where the critic's thought and personality had made an enormous impression on the young writer.)[97] Thus given the intention, say, of reproducing a certain street, Agee ruminates, one might detail every object as impersonally as possible, yet the whole lengthy effort in prose adds up to a "time and weightiness which the street does not of itself have" (p. 235).

Agee's efforts to overcome the problem of description take many forms, among which are his use of two contrary modes—exaggerated hypotaxis (elaborate syntactical subordination) and parataxis (the simple addition of phrase to phrase). Both devices are a deliberate subversion of "normal" prose syntax. Consider, for example, Agee's description of a typical tenant farmer's house from the section on "Shelter." The two opposite modes are employed, the first a single sentence, suspended over the length of a paragraph:

Here I must say, a little anyhow: what I can hardly hope to bear out in the record: that a house of simple people which stands empty and silent in the vast Southern country morning sunlight, and everything which on this morning in eternal space it by chance contains, all thus left open and defenseless to a reverent and cold-laboring spy, shines quietly forth such grandeur, such sorrowful holiness of its exactitudes in existence, as no human consciousness shall ever rightly perceive, far less impart to another. . . . (p. 134)

and on it goes for several more lines. The second, opposite mode is of an extreme, unadorned simplicity:

At the exact center of each of the outward walls of each room, a window. Those of the kitchen are small, taller than wide, and are glassed. Those of the other rooms are exactly square and are stopped with wooden shutters. (p. 138)

And so on for several more paragraphs.

Agee's opposite extremes of hypotaxis and parataxis attempt to overcome, by their contrasting eccentricities, the anesthesia of "normal" prose; with Agee we see the object first from a distance, set in a cosmic context, and then up close, at a microscopic distance.[98] What Agee avoids is the middle range of the syntactical spectrum, which might be illustrated by the following passage from a contemporaneous government report, also describing living conditions:

The house in which they live is a 4-room structure in such a state of dilapidation that the condition of the floors allow only 2 rooms to be used. The floors of the 2 habitable rooms have been repaired with that part of the flooring which was serviceable in the remainder of the house. A rain driving from the southeast is certain to result in a leaking roof. The house itself has never been painted. Its rooms are papered with newspapers. There are no screens and only one small pane of window glass, so that flies are a constant pest.[99]

Here the author—L. S. Dodson—has confidence in his observations, and a kind of omniscience concerning his subject: the house is situated in the history of its repairs, in the predictable effects of climate and weather; it is portrayed in its typicality, not its uniqueness. It exists in a particular county (of Kentucky), not in any universal space or time. Where Agee offers the house as an object of religious and aesthetic grandeur, Dodson takes a straightforward social reformer's approach. Where Agee's prose is elaborately controlled, ranging from the nuances of subjectivity to the barest of facts, Dodson speaks in a no-nonsense, conversational tone, casual and to the point. Where

Agee calls attention to his style by the extremes of his rhetoric, Dodson writes an invisible prose, formulaic but serviceable.

Agee's experiments in description take place within an overall theoretical context that argues the ultimate difficulty, if not impossibility, of achieving through language his goal—an authentic representation of the thing itself, "an illusion of embodiment" (p. 238). But if language must inevitably sag beneath the weight of naturalistic description, the visual image, in its wordless immediacy, could avoid that problem. Hence the camera became, for Agee, of primary significance as a model for verbal representation. "One reason I so deeply care for the camera is just this. So far as it goes (which is, in its own realm, as absolute anyhow as the traveling distance of words or sound), and handled cleanly and literally in its own terms, as an ice-cold, some ways limited, some ways more capable, eye, it is, like the phonograph record and like scientific instruments and unlike any other leverage of art, incapable of recording anything but absolute, dry truth" (p. 234). The camera's greater objectivity, as Agee saw it, its passive mechanical registering of what lay before the lens, made it capable of reproducing appearances without the intervention of subjectivity.

But Agee's qualifications are important: he does not assume that the camera is, in everyone's hands, a recorder of "truth." The *misuse* of the camera, for example, is represented by the work of Margaret Bourke-White. Thus, in an appendix to *Famous Men*, Agee reprints a magazine interview with the most popular photo-journalist of the age (with whom, in fact, Agee collaborated on occasion for *Fortune* magazine), which, by implication, makes clear her abuse of the medium and her disdain for her subjects. For example, of the rural black southerners she photographed for her pictorial documentary (with Erskine Caldwell), *You Have Seen Their Faces*, Bourke-White says—in the fully reprinted interview—"They seem to live on snuff and religion—which has no real relation to religion—and patent medicine" (p. 452). And an examination of the Bourke-White volume itself reveals fictitious captions that patronize the people pictured, camera angles that distort the body to the disadvantage of the subject, and—despite the author's good intentions—a generally condescending, grotesque treatment of rural southern poverty. If Bourke-White, with her characteristic overstatement, her melodrama, her exploitative use of the camera, was at one extreme, Walker Evans was at the other. What Agee valued in Evans—and it is a quality he found as well in vernacular photography (documents, snapshots, unaffected scientific photographs) as well as in the early daguerreotypes of Brady and the street photographs of Atget—was its straightforward quality, its being handled "cleanly and literally in its own terms" (p. 234). Agee was not naive about the camera's potential for distortion. "It is doubtful whether most people realize how extraordinarily slippery a liar the camera is," he wrote in the 1946 introduction to Helen Levitt's photographs.[100] Yet he felt strongly that, in good photography, "the actual is not at all transformed; it is reflected and recorded, within the limits of the camera, with all possible accuracy." The camera seemed to him unique, he went on, in allowing the artist (one must still be an artist, despite having the magical instrument) to "perceive the aesthetic reality within the actual world" without altering it.[101]

One way Agee emulated the effects of the photographic medium was simply by evoking Evans's images directly, as when he supplements his verbal description of Mrs. Gudger's eyes by saying, "you may meet them, with all the summoning of heart you have, in the photograph in this volume of the young woman with black hair" (p. 321). Or, in describing the Woods's kitchen, he adds, ostensively, "and on the walls, what you may see in one of the photographs" (p. 192). In addition to the still camera, Agee was of course enormously interested in moving pictures (after *Famous Men*, he wrote several screen plays, including *African Queen*, and his movie reviews are now considered classics) and at other times he will use the motion picture camera as a reference point for the kind of seeing he evoked in his prose: "and here a moving camera might know, on its bareness, the standing of the four iron feet of a bed, the wood of a chair, the scrolled treadle of a sewing machine" (p. 149; also see p. 251).

On a number of other occasions, Evans's photographs and Agee's text provide competing reproductions of the same object, raising implicitly one of the key questions in *Famous Men*: What are the relative virtues of camera and prose as documentary media? Or, as Agee put it on his Guggenheim application of 1937, the Alabama project was, among other things, "a skeptical study of the nature of reality and of the false nature of recreation and of communication," including "a strict comparison of the photographs and the prose as relative liars and as relative reproducers of the same matters."[102] Agee never quite undertook a systematic comparison along these skeptical lines in *Fa-*

mous Men, but he does afford a number of occasions for the reader to inquire into the relationship between text and image.[103] Evans photographed, and Agee described, the same houses, mantelpieces, washstands, overalls, shoes, faces, and bodies. I want to explore the similarities and differences further, but first a disclaimer is necessary: one cannot, with any real accuracy, compare a photograph and a verbal description, any more than one can compare the color red and the odor of a rose, or the word rose and any picture of it. Representations of the same subject in different media are, it might be argued, simply incomparable by virtue of their offering differing concrete sensory experiences for the viewer.

Having said as much, and allowing for the necessarily general level of the comparison, examining Evans and Agee side by side is essential if we are to illuminate some of the central issues of representation that the book raises. Take, for example, the Gudger mantelpiece and wall, which are described verbally under a section called "The altar" (pp. 162–65) and pictured visually in the first section of photographs, devoted to the Gudger family. Avoiding the extremes of hypotaxis and parataxis, Agee's prose is, for the most part, clean and literal: "in front of the fireplace, not much more than covering the full width of its frame, the small table: and through, beneath it, the gray, swept yet ashy bricks of the fireplace and short hearth, and the silent shoes." But there are occasional surprises: "gray, swept yet ashy bricks"; "silent shoes." Occasionally, Agee will bring our attention to something we might have overlooked in the photograph, a locket that is swinging open on a nail, for example; and sometimes an observation will carry a trace of amusement: "At the right of the mantel, in whitewash, all its whorlings sharp, the print of a child's hand." Elsewhere, the objects will be related to their human context and given an emotional history of sorts, as when the girl Louise's fluted saucer is mentioned as having been given to her "to call her own and for which she cares more dearly than for anything else she possesses." Finding words to describe what is before him, Agee inevitably colors our sense of the objects, but in no way more obviously than in the added sense of time with which he endows the word-pictures: "Pinned all along the edge of this mantel, a broad fringe of white tissue pattern-paper which Mrs. Gudger folded many times on itself and scissored into pierced geometrics of lace, and of which she speaks as her last effort to make this house pretty" (p. 163).

In Evans's photograph of the same wall, virtually everything Agee mentions is visible, but it is hard to say what one will notice. The simultaneity that Agee despaired of creating in a prose description is more or less inherent in a visual image, yet we may or may not be aware of what we are looking at, unless we force the eye to move from point to point over the image. And even then, we may miss the tonal and emotional and historical dimensions that a prose description may supply. (How would we know Louise's or Mrs. Gudger's feelings, for example?) The Evans photo, like so many of his images in *Famous Men*, is in sharp focus, revealing textures and details usually overlooked by the seeing eye. And like nearly all of the Alabama shots, it is taken head on, and features a basically rectangular arrangement of forms, within an overall symmetrical pattern. We are looking at the subjects in an Evans photograph, but we are also aware of how the picture frame has been filled, how the space has been composed by the photographer's eye so as to fill the frame.

If we move to the level of general characteristics, then, what becomes apparent in a comparison of Agee and Evans is that they were markedly different in their stylistic approach. Agee's complexity stands opposed to Evans's relative simplicity; Agee's extreme self-consciousness stands opposed to Evans's seeming withdrawal from the image, as if a camera took the pictures on its own. (Agee is constantly bringing himself into the composition, so that *Famous Men* is really as much about the author as about his subjects; he thus makes a virtue of Heisenberg's uncertainty principle, which declares that the observer himself is an inevitable function in the calculus of observation, that the eye of the seer makes the thing seen.) And if we step back to view the overall contexts in which the photo and description respectively appear, we discover yet another difference: Agee's whimsical, baroque structure is opposed to Evans's rational organization. This last point is worth expanding on.

The three-page description of the mantelpiece and wall is printed under the heading, "The altar," making the whole of the verbal description a kind of metaphor, as if the objects and their arrangement had a central religious function in the household. And the text is part of a larger section called "The front bedroom," which in turn is part of a larger segment called "The Gudger House," which is part of the larger unit called "Shelter," which, if we look at the "Design of Book Two," turns out to be a subsection of "Part Two: Some Findings and Comments." Book Two is virtually the whole of the text of *Famous*

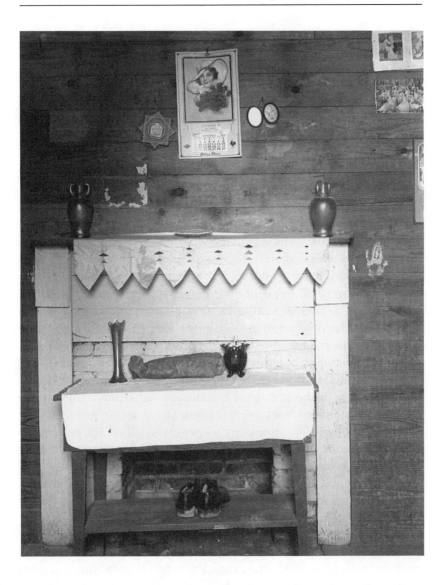

Walker Evans, Fireplace and Objects in a Bedroom of Floyd Burroughs's
Home, *Hale County, Alabama, 1936 (Agee changed
"Burroughs" to "Gudger" in the text of* Famous Men)
(Courtesy of Library of Congress)

Men, as it happens, with Book One occupying only a few pages of miscellaneous preliminaries—epigraphs, dramatis personae. In short, the text is a bewildering nest of compartments within compartments, within a gigantically lopsided enveloping structure.

Evans's photographs, by contrast, exist within a deliberately ordered space. The thirty-one images in the original 1941 edition fall into four subject areas (in the 1960 edition Evans inserted a blank page between these sections, which were somewhat altered in content): one section for each of the three families, and a concluding section of three images (expanded to nineteen in the 1960 edition) dealing with the geographical context of their lives—Hale County and the surrounding Alabama towns. Within each family unit there are individual portraits of husband and wife (except for the third, which features only the husband), followed by group portraits and individual portraits of the children; in addition, Evans placed an occasional study of the interior of their homes—a bedroom, a kitchen, a mantelpiece, a kitchen wall, a view looking into a house from the porch, some family snapshots nailed to a wall. (Only in the 1960 edition did Evans mitigate the intensity of this interior examination by adding photographs of house exteriors and surrounding yards.) The Gudger mantelpiece photo, to return to our starting point, comes approximately in the middle of the Gudger series, and is joined by another mantelpiece from another room on the facing page, inviting the viewer to both discriminate and generalize. The differences between Evans and Agee, in spite of Agee's announced effort to emulate the camera, are clearly very many.

And yet Wright Morris is correct, I think, in saying that the conflict between words and images in *Famous Men* "is more fruitful than if the words and images were on the same plane."[104] They are independent, structurally separate presentations of the Alabama experience, but they are complementary, adding a richness to each other the more we turn from one to the other. The effect is quite different from that of *An American Exodus*, the famous photodocumentary by Dorothea Lange and Paul Schuster Taylor that appeared (in 1939) while Agee's writing was in progress. Lange and Taylor's purpose had been to present words and images in a coordinated whole, as if the text, the captions, and the photographs were, as they put it, the three legs of a tripod. And the layout of the book integrated words and images on many of the pages. Agee and Evans deliberately kept the photographs separate from the text, claiming their mutual independence. And no captions at all influence our interpretation of the photographs. There is, as Morris says, a fruitful conflict between image and text, but there is also, it seems important to add, a definite complementarity, even harmony, of approach.

The congruity of text and photographs in *Famous Men* is largely, I think, a matter of tone and attitude, resulting, it seems safe to assume, from the reciprocal influence of Evans on Agee and of Agee on Evans. One way to judge the influence of Agee on Evans, is to compare Evans's work *outside* the Alabama project with the photographs that went into *Famous Men*. *American Photographs*, for example, has material that overlaps with the southern work, but the overall tone of the photographs in that volume, which had no other creative force to accommodate, was witty and ironical, and the images were structured so that one "spoke to" another in terms of themes and visual patterns. These characteristics are not obviously present in *Famous Men*. Instead, Evans's treatment accords his subjects the utmost dignity: they are pictured as serious, sad, but proud. Their lives have a kind of heroic stature. The structure of the images is systematic and expository.

This is not to say that the image Evans presents in *Famous Men* is a false one; only that it is one of several possible ways of picturing their lives and seems the product of deliberate selection. The proof of Evans's deliberation is evident in the record of the total number of photographs taken in Alabama, which have been reprinted in the volume of Evans's Farm Security Administration images. (Evans was technically on loan from the FSA during his field research with Agee, and the *Famous Men* images are part of the overall FSA collection.)[105] What we see when we look at that larger set of images is a variety of shots that were taken but not used. (In fact, a few that were not used in *Famous Men* were used by Evans in *American Photographs*.) These rejected images reveal his subjects in various degrees of undignified or informal posture, including several candid shots taken with a 35 mm camera, that show them priming themselves, preparing to have their photographs taken by the larger view camera. Other rejected images show their subjects as too happy, or else as somewhat undignified—surrounded by watermelons, for example. We are so used to the portraits in *Famous Men*, with their respectful presentations of a subject who is looking directly into the camera, that we forget that

Evans was given to taking a wide range of quite different images. (The subway shots taken at the end of the 1930s were done with a hidden camera.) The 1960 edition of *Famous Men*, which expands the number of photographs from thirty-one to sixty, does not significantly change our view of the subjects pictured, but it does round it out by the inclusion of more photographs of their homes, including outside views and several pictures of the farmers at work. These images, together with the much enlarged section featuring the local towns, supply a broader context for their lives, in a way that is parallel to Agee's textual breadth; but the greater number also dilutes somewhat the intensity of the original edition, with its fewer images and its consequently starker statement.

Briefly, what Evans gives us in the original photographic section of *Famous Men* is really a relative lie, to use Agee's phrase. Yet Evans's lie is consistent with Agee's own relative lie. For Agee too is at pains to celebrate the dignity of his subjects and the honor of their lives, and his treatment of their material furnishings likewise emphasizes the simplicity and beauty of their forms. Like Evans, Agee has selected his materials, emphasizing universals—tables, houses, clothing—and the representative qualities of the farmers' conditions rather than any individual idiosyncrasies. Both writer and photographer probe the intimate living conditions of their subjects, yet they do so with a keen awareness of the delicacy of their situations as "spies" (as they conceived it) from the intellectual world of Manhattan, who were infiltrating a corner of the South.

Evans and Agee together tread the line between respectful observation and unwanted intrusion, though it is Agee who leaves us the more vivid evidence of their violations of privacy, both in his own acts of snooping and in Evans's photographing of their hosts. For Agee is fully aware that the taking of a picture is a violation of privacy, and he empathizes with Mrs. Ricketts's victimization, "addressing" her as he recalls her standing "naked in front of the cold absorption of the camera in all your shame and pitiableness to be pried into and laughed at" (pp. 363–64). And when Evans stoops beneath the black hood of his tripod camera he is "a witchcraft preparing, colder than keenest ice, and incalculably cruel" (p. 364). Agee shares that guilt ("It is not going to be easy to look into their eyes," he writes, after nosing around in the Gudgers' house one day [p. 189]), but that does not prevent him from bending every effort to recording what is there. Yet finally we are brought back to one last quality that Agee and

Evans share, and that is an enormous respect for their subjects, together with a sensitivity in reproducing their lives for public consumption that translates into a responsibility for the act of recording, in all its ambiguities.

The doubts expressed in *Let Us Now Praise Famous Men* about the nature of the whole enterprise only raise to the level of extreme self-consciousness Agee's drive toward "Reality Itself." At the center of his work was a respect for actuality that was also, as I have been arguing, the basis for the new art of the twentieth century. *Famous Men* sums up not only the documentary impulse of the 1930s, with its urge to encompass the social reality of life in Depression America, but also the modernist urge to invent forms that would reflect the new scientific and technological conditions of knowledge and that would embody our consciousness of the *thing* that is at the bottom of experience. And Agee's sense of the significance of the camera and of the effects of science generally on the artist was not far distant from the attitudes of other artists during the 1920s and 1930s, including Williams and Dos Passos. Out of the artist's complex sensibility and his attunement to the age would arise, in Agee's words, "the beginning of somewhat new forms, call it art if you must, of which the still and moving cameras are the strongest instruments and symbols. It would be an art and a way of seeing existence based, let us say, on an intersection of astronomical physics, geology, biology, and (including psychology) anthropology, known and spoken of not in scientific but in human terms" (p. 245). Whatever else he may have had in mind, Agee was probably thinking of the book he was at that moment writing; but the feeling among a good many writers was that art was remaking itself in a world that was itself being remade by science and technology.

For the writers between the wars whom we have been considering—Williams, Dos Passos, and Agee—as well as for others, Whitman was the presiding genius; and his call for American writers to create "the poems of materials"—a call seconded by Waldo Frank in *Our America* (1919)—had been answered by them in a variety of ways. The materials out of which poems are made are finally words, and so the writer in pursuit of Reality Itself brought into the work of art a collection of verbal artifacts, made in America, that were normally kept safely outside in the street—signs, newspapers, documents, lists, calendars, advertisements. The writer might test his construction materials, pushing them to the breaking point ("Awu tsst grang splith gra pragh og bm"—Williams); and he might then, with Dos Passos, rebuild "the ruined words worn slimy in the mouths of lawyers districtattorneys collegepresidents judges"; and certainly he would need, with Agee, to clean and rectify language in order to achieve a more exact representation of our consciousness of things.

This effort to reconstruct literature from the ground up placed the modernist in the middle of his culture, and in each of the writers we have been examining, the function of the artist was conceived along the lines established by Van Wyck Brooks earlier in the century. Whether or not they were gaining an audience commensurate with their goals, the modernist writers were defining in their works a literature that would span the contrary impulses that Brooks had identified—the practical and the aesthetic, the spiritual and the material. When Dos Passos spoke to the American Writers' Congress in 1935 he defined the process of writing as "not very different from that of scientific discovery and invention. The importance of a writer, as of a scientist, depends on his ability to influence subsequent thought. In his relation to society a professional writer is a technician just as much as an electrical engineer is."[106] Dos Passos was trying hard, in the midst of his democratic enthusiasm, to demystify the writer's art, but the terms of his formulation are revealing: in depicting the artist as an engineer, Dos Passos not only borrows the new mystique of science, he brings together in the single person of the writer the sundered components of American culture Brooks had worried about —the technical and the theoretical, the scientific and the artistic, the practical and the spiritual. Williams and Agee may have been less explicit, but they too shared the general terms of the formulation— defining the poem as a machine, or the writer as a camera—along with many other writers of the period. And while Whitman's and Brooks's dream of a national culture worthy of America's potential would inevitably remain a dream, the impulse behind it inspired, for several decades, a literature where fundamental questions about the relationship of person, thing, and language could be explored in a society that otherwise tended to avoid fundamental questions. The work of the American modernists accepted the challenge of defining authenticity in a culture that was coming more and more to thrive on caricatures of itself.

The Dump Is
Full of Images

*G*iven the way so much of our aesthetic and material culture has been conditioned by the tension between imitation and authenticity, and given the definitional problems that arise inevitably at the threshold between the two, it is not altogether surprising to find a strong undercurrent of fascination with junk. What is junk? Junk is the antiworld of the technological civilization, the stuff that is useless, discarded, utterly lacking in appeal, the unadvertised object. We are aware of junk as a symptom of disorder, of things gone wrong, of waste, a negative in the balance sheet of civilization. Yet junk is also raw material for the artist intent on making it new by starting with something old; it is the object found and rescued, reclaimed, reworked, reintegrated, the thing with a history, the mass-produced object become individualized, the object to be collected. The history of junk, including our aesthetic awareness of junk, is obviously too vast a subject to do justice to here, but I would like to provide a final perspective on the problem of authenticity in our culture by at least a brief look at a subject that is, inevitably, at the edge of a concern with the real thing.

A good place to begin is the first year of the depression, with the recently founded nexus of money, journalism, and art, Henry Luce's new business magazine, *Fortune*. In an issue otherwise devoted to stories about gold and wine, Macy's and the Vanderbilts, the *New York Times* and the International Paper Company, was an article called "Vanishing Backyards," an article on junk. In the hands of *Fortune*, junk is a multivalent sign—a sign of disorder, but also of vitality. On the one hand, America is likened to a child that recklessly "hurls its refuse out the window, and doesn't care how high are piled the tin cans in the backyard." Yet on the other hand, the process of creating garbage is a sign of America's health, especially as compared with a more mature and tidier country like England, which is cautious but moribund and crowded: "Essentially, the English scene is sad and the American scene is happy. It is smelly, but it is also exuberant and vigorous to strew the country with things worn out and left over. Every garbage dump, every row of ramshackle houses lining the railroad track, is evidence of our boundless wealth. This is space we do not need. We have so much." The article concludes with the fond expectation that as the country grows more crowded, cities will deal with our need for order by creating exquisite Garbage Parks (on the model of one in California), thus welding "esthetics and sanitation and economics into an irresistible force on the side of tidiness." Thus will even garbage, according to the propitious laws of nature and capitalism, be changed into money.[1]

The editors of *Fortune* asked the painter Charles Burchfield and the photographer Ralph Steiner to depict visually the process being described in "Vanishing Backyards." "Together they have assembled a record—not of the new America, its skyscrapers, its airplanes, its dynamos—but of the America which remains unregenerate, its back porches and backyards, its ugliness and its waste."[2] But the reader might be puzzled by these visual records. Burchfield's illustrations of life along the edges of the city, of Victorian houses and trees, have a picturesque, almost a nostalgic quality. The photographs by Steiner are at least as puzzling: here is the photograph, now classic, of a wicker rocking chair on a pleasant porch, casting its broken shadow on the wall behind it, a beautiful image of lines and shadows; and here is an abstract treatment of a car fender and wheel—old, but far from a wreck (in fact it shows the influence of Steiner's master, Paul Strand); and here a dramatic, abstract treatment of a fence post with barbed wire. Where's the junk? Other images do explicitly feature trash—some refuse in front of a movie poster; some old milk cans; a trash barrel in front of a Nehi sign—but these are all well-composed, witty photographs; aesthetically speaking, they are gold.[3] *Fortune's* illustrators seem caught between an ideology of progress that pushes the past from our view as fast as possible, and a contrary, deep attachment to things as they were, to old things, to junk.

That attachment is especially evident in Walker Evans (also a *Fortune* photographer from time to time), whose photographic meditations on the antiworld of the "new America"—the world not of airplanes and dynamos but of roadside debris, the detritus of civilization —have entered the aesthetic tradition of twentieth-century culture.

Ralph Steiner

Ralph Steiner

If, suddenly, the new church and the new school and the new apartment house spring up beside the tin cans, it is easy to cart them down the road a mile or so. Or across the river. Or down by the railroad tracks. Back go the fringes of the city, the deadlines of order. Back into the open country where fields are dedicated by billboards to liver pills or pop or hotels with rooms at $1.50 and up. Here one may make a mess. No one cares.

Thus young America. But England, like a nurse or a mother, prudently tidies up. Neat are the rosebushes and the

cabbage patches in her back yards, and infinitely neat the hedges which bound them. The fringes of her cities recede into an ordered countryside. It is a sign of age and forethought and caution.

Essentially, the English scene is sad and the American scene is happy. It is smelly, but it is also exuberant and vigorous to strew the country with things worn out and left over. Every garbage dump, every row of ramshackle houses lining the railroad track, is evidence of our boundless wealth. This is space we do not need. We have so much. Actually,

Ralph Steiner

Ralph Steiner

· 78 ·

Page from *"Our Vanishing Backyards,"* Fortune, *May 1930,*
photographs by Ralph Steiner

Evans's 1938 volume, *American Photographs*, is filled with the things
that litter the public spaces of rural landscapes and small towns,
things that Evans depicts not with any sense of criticism but with a
strong affection tinged with irony. The automobile carcasses in "Joe's
Auto Graveyard, Pennsylvania, 1936," huddle together like sheep in a
mechanical-pastoral landscape, their boxy forms sharply detailed
against a flat background; "Torn Movie Poster, 1930," like so many
other peeling Evans billboards, takes the fake drama of the original
image and reveals it in a new light, as an object suffering the indigni-
ties of fortune on the wall to which it is stuck; the Cherokee Garage
(1936) shows us tires and inner tubes suspended on a building facade
like elements in a surrealist collage; and the tin relics that begin and
end Part 2 of the volume show the sheer beauty of the stamped metal
artifacts, devoid of their original ambitions of elegance, featured now
as richer systems of shadow and light, designs that have been shaped
by accident as much as intention.

Evans's photographs picture the world *Fortune* was relegating to
the scrap heap; yet what his camera found in this disavowed world
was the poetry of the discarded thing, the sense of layered time that is
inherent in things which have passed from use and have entered, in
the artist's hands, the realm of aesthetic irony. Evans took the mass-
produced thing, identical with its thousandth mate off the assembly
line, and restored its individuality, the product of its implied history.
He took the reproduction that, as Benjamin would have it, was lacking the charisma of an original "aura," and endowed it with originality. He took the thing that, as junk, no longer speaks to us in its
original voice, and gave it a new voice in a larger context of dissident
values. Often in the field Evans would "take" these objects twice: first
as photographs, then as souvenirs, to be rescued from the junk heap
and brought back to his own home. As he confessed in a 1971 interview, "I'm an incurable and inveterate collector. Right now I'm collecting trash, literally. I've gotten interested in the forms of trash, and
I have bins of it, and also discarded ephemera, particularly in printing." These are things that belong, he said, "in some kind of collage."[4]

We can see in a remark like this how close was Evans's sensibility
to that of James Agee, for Agee too was deeply attracted to those
discarded things that are given a fresh existence by their users' invention. *Let Us Now Praise Famous Men* details meticulously the calendars and photographs and other graphic decorations that grace the

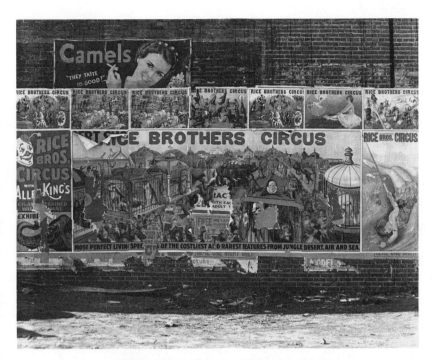

Walker Evans, Posters, Alabama, *1936*
(Courtesy of Library of Congress)

mantelpieces and walls of the tenant farmers' houses; at one point
the inventory turns the printed page of the book into the image of
a collage, featuring the scissored newsprint in its exact state of
amputation:

GHAM NEWS
hursday afternoon, March 5, 1936
Price: 3 cents
   in G
   (else

and so on, for several pages.[5] We are witness here to time and accident. Elsewhere, Agee could render the commonplace objects of the
farmers' experience—their clothing and accoutrements—within a
context of permanence and even holiness, as when he describes
Gudger's worn shoes: "like many other small objects they have great

massiveness and repose and are, as the houses and overalls are, and the feet and legs of the women, who go barefooted so much, fine pieces of architecture."[6]

Agee's stay with the tenant farmers in Alabama provided the occasion for these observations. He was not otherwise habitually in peoples' homes, looking at the common things that are their intimate possessions. But William Carlos Williams, the physician who made house calls, was, and in a piece written around 1937 called "Effie Deans," Williams discourses on the paraphernalia of people's lives. "I mean not pictures alone but all sorts of things, furniture, fabrics, books, letters even, occasional pieces of jewelry such as my own mother's filigree earrings, all of greatest interest."[7] Why not have a show of such things? he proposes, detailing from memory the various chairs, clocks, dolls, flutes, medallions, that have come his way or that he would recruit. What's involved is a reevaluation of things from a fresh perspective, a recognition of their intensity as things, their "reality": "That's right, the Early Americana—my Lord! Stuff they threw away. Glazed paper decorations in black frames. Pictures of fruit . . . They used to call them ugly and put them up in the attic when the golden oak craze came in . . . Stuart has a lifelike peach, I saw just two weeks ago, lying beside a small pool of water and reflected there. Amazingly real."[8] These are all things we might recognize from Williams's poems, but in a poem they would be transformed by the imagination, whereas here they are simply things, containers of association, objects of human devising and use, that need only reframing—or an exhibition—to take on the special aura of Reality.

Reframing, or simply framing, is the crucial point here, the key to the transformation of everyday objects and ephemera into works of vitality, and nowhere is that process better illustrated than in the work of Joseph Cornell. Beginning with montages in the early 1930s that resembled those of Max Ernst (whom Cornell may or may not have known when he first started), Cornell quickly moved to the construction of boxes—three-dimensional picture frames that are like self-contained windows inviting our inspection—containing an assemblage of mysterious objects.[9] Cornell's vocabulary, the objects out of which he assembled his constructions, included everyday manufactured objects of a geometrically simple form, like bottles, thimbles, wine glasses, dolls, pipes, balls, and springs; natural objects, like eggs and stuffed birds; and printed materials, like maps, charts of constellations, photographs, playbills, graphic illustrations, reproductions of paintings. The Cornell object was seldom unique or handcrafted; rather, it was typically mass-produced and was placed in combination with identical (or similar) objects in an arrangement that repeated elements within a theme and variation structure. Like Evans, Cornell endowed mass-produced objects with an original aura; but Cornell was of course far more manipulative than Evans, creating within the theatrical space of the box a world of his own devising, discovering in the commonplace a quality of mystery. Beginning with objects that were already old, Cornell's constructions were freighted with memory and indistinct associations. Yet the simple everyday objects —a ball, a shell—seldom appear without some graphic context, whether a reproduced image from a theatrical or dance bill, or a map, or marbled endpaper, stamps, or picture postcards; and the effect of the cloistered atmosphere of the box is to lift the assemblage into its own aesthetic sphere.

Cornell's whimsy, his sense of irony, his apparent theoretical interest in the reproduction as a *thing* in our culture, are surely signs of his modernity; yet in other respects he reminds us of a previous age. His was the Victorian world of bric-a-brac, of philosophical toys, of replications, of bell-jar juxtapositions of artifice and nature; of framed collages containing hair, shells, curled paper, etc. Cornell miniaturized the assortment of things in the overstuffed interior, composing an order not of comfort or conspicuous display, but of hidden associations and startling juxtapositions. In this he may remind us too of another strain in American art that had European affinities—the late-nineteenth-century still life of William Harnett, of John Haberle, of John Frederick Peto. Peto, especially, comes to mind, for like Cornell, he too was using objects that were well worn and weighted with associations—candlesticks, inkwells, knives, books, tankards, vases, pipes; and both artists would arrange their materials in violation of normal expectations, experimenting with the limits of physical and metaphysical disorder. And, most relevant to the present context, both were involved in operations of salvage and transformation, taking the detritus of contemporary civilization and raising it to the level of a kind of rebus poetry.

The fascination with common things, whether junk or simply elements of the unregenerate everyday life, remains a strong element in the contemporary poetic sensibility, but in a way that often carries us

back to an earlier time, as the thing itself is a record of earlier time.
Thus Robert Lowell pictures Hawthorne:

> Leave him alone for a moment or two,
> and you'll see him with his head
> bent down, brooding, brooding,
> eyes fixed on some chip,
> some stone, some common plant,
> the commonest thing,
> as if it were the clue.[10]

Fascinated by mute, everyday objects that might serve the ends of
some higher speech, or reveal some higher mystery, or offer clues to
an unspecified crime, Hawthorne meditates, in Lowell's poem, on the
commonest objects, the most palpable things of *this* world. Lowell
describes an attachment to things, yet a going beyond them, that suggests an almost talismanic quality in objects.

Hawthorne is an appropriate figure for Lowell thus to meditate
upon, but the more likely origin of this strain was Whitman, who had
established the most influential model in America for the transaction
between the self and things. Whitman had taken as his subject the
whole of industrial civilization as he knew it at the time, and had
celebrated the tally of the self with this world. Yet the created self was
not complete; all the catalogues and boasting had left something out,
the poet felt in the late 1850s. And so Whitman pictured himself in "As
I Ebb'd with the Ocean of Life," walking the seashore, seeking types
of the self, and finding them, ironically and dismally, in "Chaff, straw,
splinters of wood, weeds, and the sea-gluten, / Scum, scales from
shining rocks, leaves of salt-lettuce, left by the tide." Yet finally Whitman embraces this flotsam jetsam as a part of himself:

> You friable shore with trails of debris
> You fish-shaped island, I take what is underfoot,
> What is yours is mine my father.[11]

We are very distant, here, obviously from Whitman's more optimistic
identification with gasometers and kitchen ware. In the salvaging of
junk, Whitman set a precedent for a recurring effort by the modern
artist who would reject the glossy world of the consumer's Republic
in pursuit of a grittier reality.

One sees this modern rejection of the vanities of consumption, together with an attempt to approach an aesthetic reality beyond the devices of realism, in the abstract clarity of Wallace Stevens. Approaching the dump with a purist's appetite for absolutes, Stevens's "Man on the Dump" finds there a heap of worn-out poetic devices— "the floweriest flowers dewed with the dewiest dew"—that must be rejected if one is to get to a more intense contact with reality. "The dump is full / Of images"; but in a moment of "purifying change," a striking renewal is effected:

> Everything is shed; and the moon comes up as the moon
> (All its images are in the dump) and you see
> As a man (not like an image of a man),
> You see the moon rise in the empty sky.

For Stevens in the late 1930s the final truth is stripped of adjectives and metaphors and similes and comes down to the basic particles of language: "Where was it one first heard of the truth? The the."[12] In Stevens's quest for "The Thing itself" we see the modernist preoccupation with authenticity in its purest form: the "Thing" is always about to be articulated, never fully embodied. Stevens takes us to the wall of language ("The the"), beyond which, we might say, lies postmodernism.

At the dump, we are at the limit, the fringe of the city, the rough and worn edge of the machine-made world. The modern artist—Agee, Williams, Cornell, Evans, Stevens, Lowell,—walking out beyond the borders of the technological civilization, might find in some worn-out object the gist of authenticity for which he was looking. But for many artists after World War II, the whole quest for authenticity that marks the first half of the twentieth century had reached its end. At least for those post–World War II artists whom we have called postmodernists, culture is a department store in which one can shop for usable pasts, with full credit at one's disposal; the junk heap is a mountain of resources—discarded images and styles—out of which to fashion a whole new vocabulary. In this new frame of mind it is not authenticity that is sought, but just the opposite—an exaltation in artifice and allusive irony. The locus classicus here is in Donald Barthelme's *Snow White*, when one of his characters declares, "And there can no longer be any question of 'disposing' of it [trash], because it's all there is, and we will simply have to learn how to 'dig' it—that's slang, but peculiarly appropriate here. . . . It's that we want to be on the leading edge of this trash phenomenon, the everted sphere of the future. . . ."[13]

One artist definitely in the vanguard of the trash phenomenon is Claes Oldenburg, who has been able, as much as anyone, to handle the images in the dump with the peculiar mix of affection and satire that often distinguishes that leading edge.

> I am for an art that embroils itself with the everyday crap & still comes out on top.
>
> . . . .
>
> I am for the art of cheap plaster and enamel. I am for the art of worn marble and smashed slate. I am for the art of rolling cobblestones and sliding sand. I am for the art of slag and black coal. I am for the art of dead birds.
>
> . . . .
>
> I am for the art of things lost or thrown away, coming home from school.[14]

Oldenburg sounds Whitman's note in this excerpt from an exhibition catalogue ("Environments, Situations, Spaces" [1961]), but a Whitman who has gone to school with Duchamp and the surrealists. His comic bravura, his sense of wild incongruity, his impiety toward "the tradition," his love of what disgusts him, his sophisticated self-understanding, all contribute to the postmodernist tone of complex irony that marks Oldenburg's sketches, sculptures, and notebooks.

For Oldenburg, "city nature comes canned in images," and his strategy is to "liquify" the otherwise hard-edged thing—eraser, electrical appliance, plug, telephone, lipstick, clothespin, plumbing element—softening it up, making it more vulnerable, changing its scale and substance.[15] His earlier works took pieces of scrap wood, found objects, and turned them into constructed "flags," a strategy that quickly evolved into the more complex "scrap method" underlying the elaborate collection of transformed objects in a work like "The Store" (1961).[16] One of his most complex projects, done in the mid-1960s, is based on the 1935 Chrysler Airflow—an icon of the streamlined era, and an object Oldenburg has an additional fondness for because of its commercial failure; in a variety of media, including drawing and sculpture, and in varying sizes, Oldenburg transmutes the inner workings and outer frame of the car into an exploded model

Claes Oldenburg, Giant Soft Fan, *1966–67, construction of
vinyl filled with foam rubber, wood, metal, and
plastic tubing; fan, 10' x 58⅞" x 61⅞", variable;
plus cord and plug, 24' 3¼". The Sidney and Harriet Janis Collection,
Museum of Modern Art, New York
(Courtesy of Museum of Modern Art, New York)*

of machine design, a sad dissection of an automobile that was considered too advanced for its time. There is undoubtedly a nostalgia and poignance in Oldenburg's various recreations of industrial artifacts that connect with the modernist effort to find in junk the ultimate text for our culture; but finally Oldenburg's metamorphic comic imagination makes his work representative of a new sensibility that develops after 1950 and that finds its literary parallel in such writers as Max Apple and Don DeLillo.[17]

But the artists, writers, and intellectuals before the war had not yet reached the end-zone of American civilization that the postwar sensibility would inhabit. Though the prewar artist would meditate in various ways on junk, the examination was at bottom a critical one. "City nature"—with its abundance of discarded things—could not yet be accepted, as it was for Oldenburg and others, as simply a given of reality. The intellectual between the wars could still wish to renovate the spaces we inhabit; the city—and junk—was only half of a vision, the other half of which was nature. Such at least was the sentiment behind the effort by the economist and semanticist Stuart Chase to take stock of American civilization and to argue for the necessity of a renewal of society. Writing at the start of the decade in a volume called *Mexico: A Study of Two Americas*, Chase looked at the excesses of North America's industrial civilization and recommended destructive measures borrowed from the Aztec rituals of renewal, which included destroying household goods every fifty-two years: "Such an epoch, terminating, say, in 1879, with black walnut, red plush, ball tassels, china shepherdesses, crayon portraits in gilt frames, bustles, pot hats and whatnots on the propitiating pyre, would have provided a spectacle almost as rewarding as the midnight ceremony itself."[18] Chase's modest proposal for the dismantling of the nineteenth century's culture of imitation would have cleared the way for a new round of consumption. (The follow-up ritual cleansing presumably would then occur in 1931, the year *Mexico* was published.)

Chase was interested in renewal, not merely destruction, and he was advocating for both South and North America a *via media* between the two extremes represented by the United States and by Mexico. His best-selling study, based on anthropologist Robert Redford's analysis of Tepoztlan, advised Middletown *and* Mexico to take the best of both worlds, believing they were not mutually exclusive.[19] The Mexicans should adapt our electricity, our sanitation, and our decentralized industry, but hold onto their handicrafts and philosophy of craftsmanship. ("Flowers are more important to Mexicans than are motor cars, radios, and bathtubs combined," Chase wrote with just a little escapist fancy.)[20] Meanwhile, Middletown should eliminate money changers, sales talk, and the regimentation of large-scale industrial processes. Chase's synthesis recalls the challenge of Van Wyck Brooks earlier in the century to create a culture of the middle between theory and practice, between poetry and business, a culture that would also serve to bridge the gap in social classes that Charles Dudley Warner had identified as a grave problem in the 1870s.

In Chase's synthesis of a machine civilization and a craft civilization, as in the various efforts by artists to devise a culture of authenticity, as in the efforts noticed here to reclaim the real thing from the junk heap of civilization, we see the persistence of an idea that can only seem, from our present pluralistic perspective—aware as we are of limits and suspicious as we are of single solutions—poignantly hopeful. The modernist pursuit of authenticity met its demise, we might say, in the war that in so many ways broke apart the assumptions of the first several decades of the century. And while the postmodernist artists who came afterward found high coin and comedy in pop art and K Mart fiction, the pursuit of authenticity and The Real Thing would in other ways become democratized in the counterculture strain of the popular culture that begins in the 1960s—in a taste for crafts, house plants, natural foods, earth shoes, fringed leather jackets, camping, flea markets and collectables, and the other means whereby the factitiousness of the industrial world is at least partially mitigated. That all of these "naturals" could be reproduced, mimicked, adulterated, and otherwise manufactured for mass consumption, should come as no surprise in a culture forever wedded to a dialectic between authenticity and imitation.

NOTES

INTRODUCTION

1. For a recent survey of modernism, see the special issue, "Modernist Culture in America," *American Quarterly* 39 (Spring 1987), especially Singal, "Towards a Definition of American Modernism," pp. 7–26. Also see Kenner, *A Homemade World*; and Bradbury and McFarlane, eds., *Modernism*.

2. Wheelright, *Metaphor and Reality*, pp. 171–72.

3. Lawrence, *Studies in Classic American Literature*, p. 8.

4. Benjamin, "The Work of Art in the Age of Mechanical Reproduction," p. 222. See also Benjamin, "Paris, Capital of the Nineteenth Century," "The Author as Producer," and "A Short History of Photography."

5. See Trachtenberg, *The Incorporation of America*; Wiebe, *The Search for Order*; Chandler, *The Visible Hand*.

6. See Kern, *The Culture of Time and Space*; Schwartz, *The Matrix of Modernism*; Bullock, "The Double Image," pp. 58–70.

7. Schwartz, *The Matrix of Modernism*, p. 36.

8. Adams, *The Education of Henry Adams*, p. 451.

9. Marcuse, *The Aesthetic Dimension*, p. 9.

10. Geertz, "Art as a Cultural System"; also see Geertz, "The Impact of the Concept of Culture on the Concept of Man," pp. 33–54.

11. Harris, "Iconography and Intellectual History," p. 209. Also see Veysey, "Intellectual History and the New Social History," p. 15; and Mechling, "Mind, Messages, and Madness," pp. 11–30, esp. p. 16.

12. Arthur Danto has described a parallel shift in aesthetics from the "Imitation Theory of Art," in which the artist was understood to be imitating real forms, to "Reality Theory," in which the artist was aiming not at imitation but at a "non-imitation"; such a work was not a real object and not a facsimile but a new entity occupying the space in between. Though Danto offers Reality Theory as a way of understanding contemporary art, he is setting out a logical rather than a historical theory. See Danto, "The Artworld," pp. 571–84.

13. Bell, "Modernism Mummified," p. 125.

14. Owens, "The Discourse of Others," p. 66.

15. Morris, "Photographs, Images, and Words," p. 466.

16. Boorstin, *The Image*.

17. MacCannell, *The Tourist*.

18. Eco, *Travels in Hyperreality*.

19. Baudrillard, "The Precession of Simulacra," p. 254.

CHAPTER 1

1. On the catalogue form, see Coffman, "'Crossing Brooklyn Ferry,'" pp. 225–32; Buell, "Transcendentalist Catalogue Rhetoric," pp. 325–39; Chari, "The Structure of Whitman's Catalogue Poems," pp. 3–17; Mason, "Walt Whitman's Catalogues," pp. 34–49; Reed, "First Person Persona and the Catalogue in 'Song of Myself,'" pp. 147–53.

2. Emerson, *The Selected Writings of Ralph Waldo Emerson*, ed. Atkinson, pp. 323, 327.

3. Whitman, *Leaves of Grass*, 2d ed., pp. 378–79. On Tupper's influence, see Stovall, *The Foreground of "Leaves of Grass*," pp. 255–57.

4. Whitman, "A Backward Glance O'er Travel'd Roads," p. 566.

5. See Beaver, *Walt Whitman*; Rubin, *The Historic Whitman*; Stovall, *The Foreground of "Leaves of Grass*."

6. Whitman, Preface (1855), *Leaves of Grass: A Norton Critical Edition*, ed. Bradley and Blodgett, p. 728.

7. Whitman, "A Backward Glance O'er Travel'd Roads," pp. 566–67.

8. Saisselin, *The Bourgeois and the Bibelot*, pp. 21–23.

9. Whitman, *Leaves of Grass: A Norton Critical Edition*, ed. Bradley and Blodgett, p. 711.

10. Whitman would later, in *Democratic Vistas*, celebrate the artist's "image-making faculty, coping with material creation, and rivaling, almost triumphing over it." He would use the image of photography at that time derogatorily as a symbol of merely literal creation and warn the artist to make "no useless attempt to repeat the material creation, by daguerreotyping the exact likeness by mortal mental means." Instead, he urged the poet to work by "analogies, by curious removes, indirections." Photography by then had come to stand for a kind of limited seeing, for the literalism of "realism" that Whitman associated with the materialism and commercialism of the country. We should note too the disappointment Whitman had expressed in *Specimen Days* that existing portraits of Lincoln—including photographs—had failed to capture the greatness of the inner man. All this is true, but the camera had by then already served its purpose. (*Leaves of Grass*, ed. Kouwenhoven, pp. 510, 623.)

11. Sontag, *On Photography*, pp. 27ff.

12. Whitman, "Notes on the Meaning and Intention of 'Leaves of Grass,'" 9:10.

13. See Orvell, "Reproduction and 'The Real Thing,'" pp. 49–64.

14. Emerson, "The Poet," p. 340. Whitman does use the mirror in the 1855 Preface to conduct a self-examination, inviting the reader to do the same ("You shall stand by my side and look in the mirror with me"). Whitman, Preface (1855), in *Leaves of Grass: A Norton Critical Edition*, ed. Bradley and Blodgett, p. 719.

15. Whitman, "Notes on the Meaning and Intention of 'Leaves of Grass,'" 9:21.

16. [Hale], Review of *Leaves of Grass*, *North American Review* (January 1856), in Murphy, ed., *Walt Whitman*, p. 45.

17. The daguerreotype process itself resulted in a unique image on a copper plate, but paper was also used in early photographic experiments and would dominate the market in the late 1850s as the wet-plate collodion process replaced the daguerreotype.

18. Whitman, "There Was a Child Went Forth," p. 364. Future references to Whitman's poems will be to *Leaves of Grass: A Norton Critical Edition*, ed. Bradley and Blodgett, and will be incorporated in the text.

19. See Beaver, *Walt Whitman*, pp. 68–70, who takes these lines as a reference to the ether of interstellar space.

20. Whitman, *Walt Whitman: Notebooks*, ed. Grier, 1:58.

21. Review of Whitman's *Leaves of Grass*, *Brooklyn Eagle*, September 15, 1855.

22. This strategy of converting a mechanical process into an organic one has been observed by Roy Male with respect to typography, whereby Whitman uses type to regain the oral tradition. See Male, "Whitman's Mechanical Muse," pp. 35–43.

23. Whitman, *Walt Whitman: Notebooks*, ed. Grier, 1:233.

24. Traubel, *With Walt Whitman in Camden*, 3:553. The passage was cited by Alan Trachtenberg, "The Photographic Portrait as Cultural Artifact," American Studies Association Convention (Minneapolis), September 28, 1979.

25. Newhall, *The Daguerreotype in America*, pp. 80–81; Rudisill, *Mirror Image*, pp. 164–66. Also see Trachtenberg, "Brady's Portraits," pp. 230–53.

26. See Reisch, "Poetry and Portraiture in Whitman's *Leaves of Grass*," pp. 113–25.

27. Root, *The Camera and the Pencil*, p. 165.

28. Furness, ed., *Walt Whitman's Workshop*, p. 65. Whitman clearly knew what the conventions were and in 1890 gave us a good generalized portrait of the genteel poet in his normal habitat: "Longfellow, reminiscent, polish'd, elegant, with the air of finest conventional library, picture-gallery or parlor, with ladies and gentlemen in them, and plush and rosewood, and ground-glass lamps, and mahogany and ebony furniture, and a silver inkstand and scented satin paper to write on." (Whitman wrote this during his Camden years, when visitors to his Mickle Street house would be struck by the extraordinary clutter of manuscripts, books, newspapers, magazines, and photographs, littering his simply furnished rooms.) Whitman, *Specimen Days*, ed. Stovall, 1:285.

29. *New York Tribune*, July 23, 1855, reprinted in Adimari and Holloway, eds., *New York Dissected*, p. 154.

30. From the *Critic* (London), in Murphy, ed., *Walt Whitman*, p. 58.

31. From the *London Leader*, in Murphy, ed., *Walt Whitman*, p. 62.

32. Allen, *A Reader's Guide to Walt Whitman*, p. 49.

33. Whitman, *Leaves of Grass: A Norton Critical Edition*, ed. Bradley and Blodgett, p. 712.

34. Erikson, *Childhood and Society*, p. 285.

35. *Leaves of Grass* was first sold at Fowler and Wells, a phrenological bookstore, which coincidentally was located in the same building as the country's largest seller of photographic supplies, Edward Anthony. Whitman's own exhortation to the reader—"Undrape! you are not guilty to me, nor stale nor discarded" (35)—went beyond such phrenological tracts as George Combe's *The Constitution of Man* (1834), which counseled that we must exercise our bodily organs and external sense.

36. Zweig, *Walt Whitman*, pp. 88–100. See also Hungerford, "Walt Whitman and His Chart of Bumps," pp. 350–84; Wrobel, "Whitman and the Phrenologists," pp. 17–23; Krauss, "Tracing Nadar," pp. 117–34.

37. Lavater, *Essays on Physiognomy*, 1:20.

38. From "The Toilet," *Godey's Lady's Book*, pp. 460–61. Quoted in Halttunen, *Confidence Men and Painted Women*, p. 83.

39. See Halttunen, *Confidence Men and Painted Women*, pp. 48–50.

40. See Arnheim, "On the Nature of Photography," 2:149. "The I was fully authorized to stare at the Thou as though it were an It."

41. Rodgers and Black, eds., *The Gathering of the Forces*, 2:113–14.

42. Nye, *Society and Culture in America*, p. 166.

43. Rudisill, *Mirror Image*, pp. 156–57.

44. Whitman, *Walt Whitman: Notebooks*, ed. Grier, 1:277; see also "I Was Looking a Long While" (1860), in Whitman, *Leaves of Grass: A Norton Critical Edition*, ed. Bradley and Blodgett, pp. 387–88.

45. Grimsted, "Melodrama as Echo of the Historically Voiceless," p. 94.

46. Justin Kaplan has remarked on the similarity between "Pictures" and the repeated cover illustration for Orson Fowler's *American Phrenological Journal*—a "gallery" containing thirty-nine "vignettes of people, animals, birds, and familiar objects . . . displayed within a profiled human head." (*Walt Whitman*, p. 153.) And Rudisill has interestingly connected the poem with similar responses to the daguerreotype at the time, especially the theories of geologist Edward Hitchcock, who lectured widely during the 1840s on the universe as a vast, cosmic gallery of impressions, formed out of *"our words, our actions, and even our thoughts"* (ital. orig.). (Rudisill, *Mirror Image*, pp. 89–93.) See also Zweig, *Walt Whitman*, pp. 174, 204.

47. On the invention of the panorama by Robert Barker in Edinburgh (1788), see Sternberger, *Panorama of the 19th Century*, pp. 185ff. Also Altick, *The Shows of London*; Bergmann, "Panoramas of New York," pp. 119–37; Marsh, "Drama and Spectacle by the Yard," pp. 581–90; Rinhart and Rinhart, *The American Daguerreotype*, pp. 233ff.

48. Rudisill, *Mirror Image*, p. 139.

49. Kouwenhoven, *The Columbia Historical Portrait of New York*, p. 194. Quoted in Kaplan, *Walt Whitman*, p. 113.

50. Christman, *Walt Whitman's New York*, p. 19.

51. See Marsh, "Drama and Spectacle," p. 588.

52. Novak, *Nature and Culture*, p. 27.

53. Whitman, *Leaves of Grass: A Norton Critical Edition*, ed. Bradley and Blodgett, pp. 711, 713. Although we have no record of Whitman's having seen panoramas, there are abundant references to them in his writings. See Zarobila, "Walt Whitman and the Panorama," p. 59.

54. Bode, *The Anatomy of American Popular Culture*, pp. 130–31; Nye, *Society and Culture*, pp. 280–81; Rosenberg, *Technology and American Economic Growth*, chaps. 1–4.

55. Whitman, *Leaves of Grass: A Norton Critical Edition*, ed. Bradley and Blodgett, pp. 714, 738–39.

56. Emerson, *Journals and Miscellaneous Notebooks*, ed. Gilman, pp. ix, 498. Quoted in Kasson, *Civilizing the Machine*, p. 131.

57. Whitman, *Leaves of Grass: A Norton Critical Edition*, ed. Bradley and Blodgett, pp. 279, 713.

58. Murphy, ed., *Walt Whitman*, p. 31.

59. Silliman and Goodrich, eds., *The World of Science, Art, and Industry*, pp. 10, 15–16.

60. Holloway and Schwarz, eds., *I Sit and Look Out*, pp. 129–30.

61. Quoted in Zweig, *Walt Whitman*, p. 171.

62. Benjamin, "Paris, Capital of the Nineteenth Century," p. 82.

63. Whitman, *Prose Works 1892*, ed. Stovall, 2:681. Quoted in Allen, *The Solitary Singer*, p. 120.

INTRODUCTION TO PART TWO

1. Whitman, *Uncollected Poetry and Prose*, ed. Holloway, 2:250; also see Holloway and Schwarz, eds., *I Sit and Look Out*, p. 133.

2. Whitman, *Leaves of Grass: A Norton Critical Edition*, ed. Bradley and Blodgett, p. 198. Elsewhere Whitman warned his countrymen of the mortal dangers of excessive materialism; see *Democratic Vistas* and "Thou Mother."

3. Platt, "Invention and Advancement" (1891), p. 39.

4. See Ewbank, *The World a Workshop*; "Effects of Machinery," *North American Review* 34 (January 1832): 220–46, reprinted in Hughes, ed., *Changing Attitudes Toward American Technology*, pp. 123ff.; Walker, "A Defense of Mechanical Philosophy," *North American Review* 33 (July 1832): 122–36, reprinted in Pursell, *Readings in Technology and American Life*, p. 68. And see the excellent critical discussion in Marx, *The Machine in the Garden*, pp. 150–69. On Walker, see Segal, *Technological Utopianism in American Culture*, pp. 81–87.

5. Quoted in Harris, *Humbug*, p. 40.

6. Thayer, "The New Story-Tellers and the Doom of Realism," in Current-Garcia and Patrick, eds., *Realism and Romanticism*, p. 158.

7. Quoted in Allwood, *The Great Exhibitions*, p. 84.

8. Cawelti, "America on Display," p. 345.

9. See Applebaum, *The Chicago World's Fair of 1893*, p. 95; also see

Benedict, who views the Midway as a parody of the main exhibition areas, in "The Anthropology of World's Fairs." Trachtenberg points out that to Daniel Burnham, the fair's master-planner, the classically modeled Court represented the "real and the original," while the Midway was seen as the realm of fantastic "reproductions." [Trachtenberg, *Incorporation of America*, p. 212; on the fair as corporate alliance, see pp. 212–17.] On the origins of the Midway and on its implicit racism, see Rydell, *All the World's a Fair*, pp. 62–68.

10. Kasson, *Amusing the Millions*, pp. 71–72. On the fair as sham spectacle, see Trachtenberg, *Incorporation of America*, pp. 230–31; also see Snow and Wright, "Coney Island."

11. Fielding, "Hale's Tours."

12. Arrangements of flowers or other decorative objects were especially popular, including, for example, skeleton leaves, which were ghostly dried plant structures bleached to a bone white, arranged with or without funereal overtones. See Earle, ed., *Points of View*, p. 49; Darrah, *The World of Stereographs*.

13. Howells, *A Hazard of New Fortunes*, p. 79. See Sundquist, "Country of the Blue," p. 16.

14. See Cronin, "Currier and Ives"; Marzio, *The Democratic Art*; Trachtenberg, *The Incorporation of America*, p. 150.

15. Beecher and Stowe, *The American Woman's Home*, p. 94.

16. Marzio, *The Democratic Art*, p. 104.

17. Kimball, "Machinery as a Gospel Worker," p. 320.

18. *Atlantic* (March 1869); quoted in Marzio, *The Democratic Art*, p. 96.

19. Godkin here anticipates Walter Benjamin, in this facet of his argument, at least. Twain had in turn anticipated Godkin when he perversely and gleefully noted, in *Innocents Abroad* (1869), that he preferred the copies of European masters to the originals; Henry James would note, with greater detachment, that the neophyte Christopher Newman preferred Mlle. Nioche's copies of oil paintings to the originals in *The American* (1877).

20. Godkin, "Chromo-civilization"; also see Marzio, *The Democratic Art*, pp. 1–3.

21. Twain, *A Connecticut Yankee in King Arthur's Court*, pp. 46–47.

22. Twain to Andrew Lang, in Smith, ed., *Popular Culture and Industrialism*, pp. 400–401.

23. Bruce, *The Century*, p. 20.

24. Ibid., p. 159.

CHAPTER 2

1. Wharton, *The Age of Innocence*, p. 42. Cf. the earlier satire of duplicity in an 1845 play called *Fashion*, in which a virtuous rural character, Trueman, says, in exasperation at the state of manners, "Everything is some-

thing else from what it seems to be." Quoted in Halttunen, *Confidence Men and Painted Women*, p. 154.

2. See Hendrickson, *The Grand Emporiums*; Boorstin, *The Americans*; Harris, "Museums, Merchandising, and Popular Taste." On the department store as fusion of economic and cultural values and as representation of the world, see Trachtenberg, *The Incorporation of America*, pp. 131–39. Also see Barth, *City People*, p. 122; John Maass, *The Glorious Enterprise*, pp. 113–14; Benedict, *The Anthropology of World's Fairs*, pp. 27ff.; Rydell, *All the World's a Fair*, p. 21.

3. Wanamaker, "On the Department Store," p. 658.

4. This fundamental shift in middle-class habits has been discussed by Susman in *Culture as History*; and by Lears, "From Salvation to Self-realization," pp. 1–38; and Lears, "Some Versions of Fantasy."

5. See Marcus, *The American Store Window*, p. 12.

6. See "Man on the Sidewalk," and "Suicide," in Pizer, ed., *Theodore Dreiser*.

7. Dreiser, *Sister Carrie*, p. 17. See Fisher, "Acting, Reading, Fortune's Wheel"; "Merchandise flirts with the shopper just as the actress does with her audience," p. 268; also see Bowlby, *Just Looking*, pp. 62ff.

8. Ginger, *Age of Excess*, p. 39.

9. Barth, *City People*, p. 138.

10. On the importance of the "wish book," see Potter, *People of Plenty*, p. 80.

11. On the widespread availability of house-plans, see Garvin, "Mail-Order House Plans and American Victorian Architecture," pp. 309–34.

12. See Douglas, *The Feminization of American Culture*.

13. Lowe, *History of Bourgeois Perception*, p. 71. Also see Saisselin, *The Bourgeois and the Bibelot*, pp. 29, 42–48.

14. Whitman, "Wicked Architecture," p. 92.

15. See Hayden, *Grand Domestic Revolution*; Handlin, *The American Home*, especially chapter 1; Cohn, *The Palace or the Poorhouse*. Meanwhile, art critic Jarves warned of the excesses of domestic fetishism—that it causes "negation of public liberality" and distraction of the individual "too much from mankind at large" in *The Art Idea*, p. 251.

16. Downing, *Victorian Cottage Residences*, p. ix.

17. Beecher, "A July 4 Oration," p. 72. Also see Trachtenberg, *Incorporation of America*, p. 146.

18. Somewhat earlier, Beecher had recognized that a man's house is necessarily "a compromise between his heart and his pocket." Beecher, "Building a House," p. 286.

19. Pizer, *Theodore Dreiser*, p. 190.

20. Praz, *An Illustrated History of Interior Decoration*, p. 25. Also see Green, *The Light of the Home*.

21. The plurality of styles was noted by Ames, "Notes toward a Theory of Style."

22. Ames, "Renaissance Revival Furniture in America," p. 252; also see Ames, "Grand Rapids Furniture at the Time of the Centennial."

23. See Ferebee, *A History of Design from the Victorian Era to the Present*, pp. 25–26.

24. Howells, *A Hazard of New Fortunes*, pp. 49–50.

25. See Harris, "The Drama of Consumer Desire," p. 194.

26. The more complex operations of production were still done by hand well into the 20th century, according to Ettema, with the general savings on labor estimated at about 15 percent. See Ettema, "Technological Innovation and Design Economies in Furniture Manufacture," pp. 199, 205. Also see Earl, "Craftsmen and Machines."

27. See Giedion on the imitation of the "ruling taste" in middle-class furniture: *Mechanization Takes Command*, pp. 344–45.

28. Baudrillard, *Le Système des Objets*, p. 80.

29. See, e.g., trade catalogues of the Pettyjohn Company, Terre-Haute, Indiana (1912); Johns Manville, "The Book of Roofs."

30. E.g., Beecher, *A Treatise on Domestic Economy*; and Beecher and Stowe, *The American Woman's Home*.

31. Morse, "About Furnishings," p. 181. On the whole movement, see McClaugherty, "Household Art."

32. Praz, *An Illustrated History of Interior Decoration*, p. 25.

33. From *The Housekeeper's Quest*, pp. 3–4; cited in Fennimore, "Fine Points of Furniture, American Empire," p. 47.

34. Henry T. Williams and Mrs. C. J. Jones, *Beautiful Homes, or Hints on House Furnishings* (1878); cited in Ames, "Renaissance Revival Furniture in America," p. 77; also see McClaugherty, "Household Art," p. 6.

35. Downing, *Country Houses*, p. 225. In a similar vein, a writer in *The Crayon*, an art journal, complained on October 17, 1855, of the large number of art reproductions on the streets of New York: "Each has its own peculiar means for deceiving the eye," p. 248.

36. Cahan, *The Rise of David Levinsky*, p. 95.

37. Dreiser, *Fine Furniture*. Also see Kwolek-Folland, "The Elegant Dugout," pp. 21–37.

38. Quoted in Struik, *Yankee Science in the Making*, p. 181.

39. Twain, *Life on the Mississippi*, p. 236.

40. Quoted in Hower, *History of Macy's of New York: 1858–1919*, p. 53.

41. Hower, *History of an Advertising Agency*, p. 296.

42. Sears, Roebuck and Co., *Catalogue No. 117, The Great Price Maker*, pp. 231, 672.

43. Ibid., pp. 259, 1047.

44. Benedict, *The Anthropology of World's Fairs*, p. 5.

45. Cf. the positing of a hypothetical "nature": "It is only by virtue of the imitation that the popular classes have the illusion of *having* at all.... This imitation marks the final wresting of the market away from the place we think we know, firsthand, as nature." Stewart, *On Longing*, p. 169.

46. Beecher and Stowe, *The American Woman's Home*, p. 98.

47. See, for examples, Seale, *The Tasteful Interlude*, passim, especially

p. 132; and Lisa Taylor et al., *American Enterprise*, pp. 52, 53; Giedion, *Mechanization Takes Command*, pp. 432ff.

48. Spofford, *Art Decoration Applied to Furniture*, p. 208.

49. Norris, *Vandover and the Brute*, pp. 70–71, 80.

50. See Kuhlmann, *Knave, Fool, and Genius*. Also see Halttunen, *Confidence Men and Painted Women*.

51. See Green, "The Ironies of Style," pp. 17–34.

52. Benson, *Appleton's Journal*, cited in Kouwenhoven, *The Arts*, p. 88.

53. Johnson, *Great Exhibition of the Industry of all Nations, 1851*, p. 96.

54. See Girouard, *Sweetness and Light*.

55. Richard Guy Wilson, "The Decoration of Houses and Scientific Eclecticism," pp. 193–204.

56. Wharton and Codman, *The Decoration of Houses*, p. 195.

57. Ibid., pp. 27, 186, 26.

58. Baudrillard, *Le Système des Objets*, p. 108.

59. See Pilgrim, "Decorative Arts," p. 146; and Pach, *The Art Museum in America*, p. 65.

60. Herrick, *The Common Lot*, p. 168.

61. Duncan, *Culture and Democracy*, p. 417.

62. Horowitz, *Culture and the City*, p. 77.

63. Richard Guy Wilson, "Architecture and the Reinterpretation of the Past in the American Renaissance," p. 73.

64. E. L. Godkin, "The Expenditure of Rich Men," pp. 495–501.

65. See Pilgrim, *The American Renaissance*, 146; and Richard Guy Wilson, "Architecture and the Reinterpretation of the Past," pp. 69–87.

66. Wharton and Codman, *The Decoration of Houses*, p. 191.

67. Norris, *The Pit*, pp. 154–55.

68. Alexis de Tocqueville, *Democracy in America*, 2:53.

69. Lawrence, *Studies in Classic American Literature*, p. 48.

70. Lawrence, "Things," 3:844–53.

71. McDonald, ed., *Phoenix*, p. 90.

72. One of the few works making the connection between James and the consumer world, with an emphasis on *The Golden Bowl*, is Jean-Christophe Agnew's "The Consuming Vision of Henry James," in Fox and Lears, eds., *The Culture of Consumption*, pp. 65–100.

73. Henry James, *Portrait of a Lady*, pp. 172–73.

74. *Portrait of a Lady*, pp. 219, 290; see discussion of *Portrait* in Anderson, *Person, Place, and Thing in Henry James's Novels*, especially pp. 92–117; and Veeder, *The Lessons of the Master*, pp. 98–99. Cf. Walter Pater, in *Gaston Latour*: "It might be that . . . things, as distinct from persons, such things as one had so abundantly around one, [had] come to be so much, that the human being seemed suppressed and practically nowhere amid the objects he had projected from himself." Quoted in Praz, *History of Interior Decoration*, p. 65.

75. Henry James, *The Art of the Novel*, p. 123.

76. Henry James, *The Spoils of Poynton*, pp. 7–8.

77. Ibid., p. 104.
78. Ibid., p. 24.
79. Ibid., p. 35.
80. Ibid., p. 106.
81. Nietzsche, *A Cultural History of the Modern Age*, cited in Hughes, *Consciousness and Society*, p. 40. Also see Lears, *No Place of Grace*, on the "yearning for more 'authentic' experience" at the turn of the century [p. 5].
82. Fuller, *With the Procession*, p. 59. Fuller's point is made in a slightly different way in Norris's *The Pit*, as well, where the onward movement of the Jadwins toward greater and greater wealth (with its consequent pressures) generates in Curtis and Laura, the husband and wife at the center of the novel, dreams of their respective simple, happy childhoods, culminating in their contempt for possessions and their final rejection of "things."
83. Ibid., p. 60.
84. Mumford, *Technics and Civilization*, pp. 201–2.
85. See McClaugherty, "Household Art."
86. Marden, *Little Visits with Great Americans*.
87. Cf. Slater: "Our economy depends upon our willingness to turn to things rather than people for gratification—to symbols rather than our bodies"; *The Pursuit of Loneliness*, p. 93.
88. Fitzgerald, *The Great Gatsby*, p. 173.

CHAPTER 3

1. Cf. Benjamin: Photography has, "since the middle of the century, enormously expanded the scope of the commodity trade by putting on the market in unlimited quantities figures, landscapes, events" not previously available. "Paris, Capital of the Nineteenth Century," in *Reflections*, p. 151.
2. Loftie, *A Plea for Art in the House*, p. 66. Also see Root, *The Camera and the Pencil*, p. 28.
3. Halstead, introduction to *Camera Mosaics*. On the growth of spectatorship and vicarious experience in the nineteenth century, see Trachtenberg, *The Incorporation of America*, pp. 122–25.
4. Buel, *The Magic City*.
5. Holmes, "Sun-Painting and Sun-Sculpture," p. 15.
6. Holmes, "The Stereoscope and the Stereograph," p. 112.
7. Ibid., pp. 113–14. Also see Sekula, "The Traffic in Photographs," pp. 22–23.
8. Ibid., p. 113; Ivins, *Prints and Visual Communication*, p. 180.
9. For a discussion of the conservative positions of Beaumont Newhall, Helmut Gernsheim, and John Szarkowski, see Jonathan Green, *American Photography*, pp. 147–48.

10. Brewster, *The Stereoscope*, pp. 181, 204ff.; also see Eagleson, *Trick Photography*; and Woodbury, *Photographic Amusements, Including a Number of Novel Effects Obtainable with the Camera*.

11. Coleman, "The Directorial Mode," pp. 480–91.

12. Shear, *Panorama of the Hudson*.

13. Two of the most esteemed geographical and scientific photographers of the late nineteenth century had at least brief interests in creating models: William Henry Jackson and Eadweard Muybridge. Jackson, one of the great recorders of the western landscape, constructed a model replica of a southwest pueblo for the Philadelphia Centennial, where he served as "tourguide" for the visitors. Some years later, Eadweard Muybridge, who had returned to England after earning a reputation as the world's greatest scientific student of animal motion, was building a scale model of the Great Lakes in his backyard at the time of his death. It was as if the camera were merely one possible tool by which to achieve the ultimate goal—the replication of reality.

14. Bassham, *The Theatrical Photographs of Napoleon Sarony*, pp. 20–21, 26–27.

15. Taylor, A. A. E., *Philadelphia Photographer*, 3, no. 29 (May, 1866): 130, 131.

16. For a general discussion of Robinson, see Vertrees, "The Picture Making of Henry Peach Robinson," pp. 78–101.

17. Robinson, *Pictorial Effect*, p. 75; *The Elements of a Pictorial Photograph*, p. 15.

18. On composite imagery and combination printing, see Sobieszek, "Composite Imagery and the Origins of Photomontage" and "New Acquisitions"; Borcoman, "Notes on the Early Use of Combination Printing"; Sally A. Stein, "The Composite Photographic Image and the Composition of Consumer Ideology."

19. Robinson, *Pictorial Effect*, p. 109. Richard Avedon, speaking of his portraits in the American West, has recently stated his aims in terms that strongly recall Robinson: "But if this kind of candor is what any ambitious portrait photographer is after, I suspect it can only be achieved through contrivance, and it's in trying to direct the traffic between Artifice and Candor, without being run over, that I'm confronted with the questions about photography that matter most to me" (*New York Times*, December 27, 1985, C-27).

20. Robinson, *The Elements of a Pictorial Photograph*, pp. 18–19. By 1901, when, under the influence of Alfred Stieglitz, Charles Caffin published his *Photography as a Fine Art*, Robinson's pictorialist aesthetic could be archly scorned as a crude crowd-pleaser: contrasting Stieglitz's actual pictures of moonlight with the merely pretty studio ersatz, Caffin wrote, "So these 'moonlights' pleased, and the discovery that they were faked lent a further zest. The 'Who'd have thought it?' followed on the 'Oh! my, how pretty!' and that curious trait of human nature, recognized by Barnum, was satisfied" (Caffin, *Photography as a Fine Art*, p. 30).

21. Root, *The Camera and the Pencil*, p. 445.

22. Ibid., p. 449.

23. Sobieszek and Appel, *The Spirit of Fact*, p. xxiii. Even earlier, S. F. B. Morse had viewed photography as a complementary merging of the artistic and the scientific visions: "Nature, in the results of Daguerre's process, has taken the pencil in her own hands, and she shows that the minutest detail disturbs not the general repose." Morse to Washington Allston, in Samuel I. Prime, *The Life of Samuel F. B. Morse* (New York, 1875), quoted in Rinhart and Rinhart, *The American Daguerreotype*, p. 248.

24. Bartlett urges the photographer to develop his powers of natural observation, but also to study the Dutch masters. And he quotes George Eliot's *Adam Bede* on the need to enlarge subject matter so as to encompass the whole range of society: "Paint us an angel, if you can, with floating violet robe, and a face paled by the celestial light; . . . but do not impose on us any aesthetic rules which shall banish from the region of art those old women scraping carrots with their work-worn hands . . . " (Bartlett, "On the Choice of a Subject Suitable for a Photographic Picture," p. 262). Yet only ten years later Lewis Hine would stand before a conference on charities and argue the value of photography to social uplift, speaking on behalf of a realism that would seek not a studio version, but the old woman herself of Eliot's quotation. In fact, he quotes the very passage from *Adam Bede* at the conclusion of his talk (Hine, "Social Photography: How the Camera May Help in the Social Uplift").

25. Robinson, *The Elements of a Pictorial Photograph*, pp. 102, 94–100.

26. Jussim, *Slave to Beauty*, p. 7. I am indebted to Jussim's study for the basis of the discussion of Day that follows.

27. *British Journal of Photography*, p. 702; quoted in Jussim, *Slave to Beauty*, p. 134.

28. See Tibbetts, "The Real Thing." Tibbetts argues correctly that Emerson and Robinson both favored the type as subject, though he then suggests, mistakenly I think, that "both these attitudes seem more scientific than artistic. The scientist's business, after all, is to classify and categorize" (p. 167). Artists, too, classified and categorized. On the nineteenth-century photographer's assumption of a harmonious nature, see Jeffrey, "Photography and Nature," p. 27.

29. Jussim and Lindquist-Cock, *Landscape as Photograph*, p. 45.

30. Root, *The Camera and the Pencil*, p. 143.

31. See, for example, Rev. H. J. Morton, "Photography Indoors."

32. Experimentation with instantaneous photography was urged in the early 1870s. See, for example, Pearsall, "Instantaneous Portraiture."

33. Vogel, "Photography and Truth," pp. 262, 264.

34. Ames, *Renaissance Revival Furniture in America*, p. 212.

35. For examples of early portraits, see Rudisill, *Mirror Image*. Also see Gernsheim, *Creative Photography*, pp. 70, 72; Hillier, *Victorian Studio Photographs*, p. 32.

36. Crihfield, "Relation of Backgrounds to Subjects," p. 55.

37. Bigelow, *Artistic Photography and How to Attain It*, p. 13.

38. Holmes, *Soundings from the Atlantic*, p. 259.

39. Sobieszek and Appel, *Spirit of Fact*, see example on pp. 44–45.

40. Galton, *Inquiries into Human Faculty and Its Development*, pp. 222–23.

41. Peirce, "How to Make Our Ideas Clear," p. 133.

42. Iles, *Flame, Electricity and the Camera*, p. 319. Also see Stoddard, "Composite Photography"; Bowditch, "Are Composite Photographs Typical Pictures?"

43. Flinn, ed., *Official Guide to the World's Columbian Exposition in the City of Chicago*, p. 38.

44. Norris captures some of the windy vacuity of the notion when he presents his heroine Laura Jadwin in *The Pit* ruminating on the "duty" of doing one's work amid life forces that can overwhelm the individual: " 'The individual—I, Laura Jadwin—counts for nothing. It is the type to which I belong that's important, the mould, the form, the sort of composite photograph of hundreds of thousands of Laura Jadwins. Yes,' she continued, her brows bent, her mind hard at work, 'what I am, the little things that distinguish me from everybody else, those pass away very quickly, are very ephemeral. But the type Laura Jadwin, that always remains, doesn't it?' " (Frank Norris, *The Pit*, p. 193). Laura's thoughts are a consolation to her but also a form of irresponsibility, sanctioning the escapism of her life.

45. Snyder, in Snyder and Munson, *The Documentary Photograph as a Work of Art*, pp. 21–22.

46. Quoted by John Baskin, in Morgan and Brown, *Prairie Fires and Paper Moons*, p. viii.

47. Gardner, preface to *Gardner's Photographic Sketch Book of the Civil War*.

48. See Frassanito, *Gettysburg*. On the ideology of Civil War photos, see Trachtenberg, "Albums of War."

49. For the former position, see Snyder, "Documentary without Ontology"; for the latter, see Hales, *Silver Cities*, pp. 163–217. Also see Orvell, review of *Silver Cities*.

50. See reviews by Eldridge T. Gerry and A. F. Schauffler, in Riis, "Commendations," in *The Children of the Poor*.

51. For a discussion of Krausz, together with examples of his work, see Hales, *Silver Cities*, pp. 224–33.

52. Riis, *How the Other Half Lives*, pp. 64–67.

53. Edward S. Curtis, *The North American Indians*, 1:xii–xiv.

54. Lyman, *The Vanishing Race and Other Illusions*. See also Scherer, review of Lyman, *Studies in Visual Communication*, which emphasizes the frequency of ethnographic inaccuracies in anthropological photography of the period; Curtis's reconstruction of the past was "then accepted practice among anthropologists" (p. 80). See Jacknis, "Franz Boas and Photography."

55. Dingus describes a wide variety of manipulative techniques in *The Photographic Artifacts of Timothy O'Sullivan*; see especially pp. 31–64. And see Naef and Wood, *Era of Exploration*, pp. 68–69.

56. Sandweiss, *Masterworks of American Photography*, pp. 6–10.

57. Krauss, "Photography's Discursive Spaces." And the same held true for news photography, when that genre developed as a mass form in the 1890s. Writing in 1892 on "Some Phases of Contemporary Journalism," a commentator observed that illustrations sell newspapers, but that "pictorial veracity" was "absolutely unessential" (Cockerill, "Some Phases of Contemporary Journalism," p. 701). And more than a decade later another writer, after noting the widespread use of faked pictures to depict news events, nevertheless confirmed the value of photography in making vivid the news of the day and in teaching us "that imaginative view of history in the making which means so much for social enlightenment and brotherhood" (Richards, "Pictorial Journalism," p. 852). Such practices, and a similar rationale, remained acceptable through the 1930s. Yet clearly not all photographers approved the flexibility of the medium as it was often practiced, an attitude indicated by the scrupulous distinction drawn by Lewis Hine in 1909, when he said that "while photographs may not lie, liars may photograph" (Hine, "Social Photography," pp. 356, 357). On the magazine editor's use of photography, see Christopher Wilson, "The Rhetoric of Consumption," pp. 39–64.

58. King, *Mountaineering in the Sierra Nevada*, p. 126.

59. See Bartlett, "Has the Brain a Photographic Function?"

60. See Crawford on the influence of photographic technology on aesthetic "syntax" in *The Keepers of Light*, pp. 1–16.

61. See Muybridge, *Animals in Motion*, pp. 10–11.

62. See Warren and Brandeis, "The Right to Privacy," and William James, "The Hidden Self." Also see A. A. E. Taylor, "Photographic Views of the Inner Man." Along with the hidden self, some tried to capture the bidden spirit; see Gettings, *Ghosts in Photographs*.

63. Quoted in Hendricks, *The Photographs of Thomas Eakins*, p. 9.

CHAPTER 4

1. See Baym, *Woman's Fiction*.

2. Warner, "What Is Your Culture to Me?," pp. 344, 339. On culture as antidote to rebellious impulses, see Trachtenberg, *The Incorporation of America*, pp. 144–47.

3. Warner, "Modern Fiction," p. 464.

4. Maurice Thompson, *The Ethics of Literary Art*, pp. 87, 88.

5. Garland, *Crumbling Idols*, p. 133.

6. See Berthoff, *The Ferment of Realism*, pp. 3–4, and Tomsich, *A Genteel Endeavor*, p. 23.

7. Darrow, "Realism in Literature and Art," p. 109.

8. Ibid., p. 111.
9. Riis, preface to *Children of the Poor*, p. v.
10. See Schiller, *Objectivity and the News*.
11. Stanley, "The Passion for Realism and What Is to Come of It," p. 240.
12. Ibid., p. 239.
13. Mabie, "The Interpretation of Idealism," p. 93.
14. Editor and teacher Charles Eliot Norton was one of the chief proponents. See Horowitz, *Culture and the City*, pp. 16ff.; and Roger Stein, *John Ruskin and Aesthetic Thought in America, 1840–1900*.
15. Howells, "Editor's Study," p. 973.
16. Howells, "James's Hawthorne," p. 236.
17. Howells, "The Man of Letters as a Man of Business," pp. 305, 307–8.
18. Trilling, "William Dean Howells and the Roots of Modern Taste," pp. 76–103.
19. See Lynn, *William Dean Howells*, p. 301.
20. Howells, *A Hazard of New Fortunes*, p. 23.
21. Ibid., p. 57.
22. Ibid., p. 73.
23. Ibid., pp. 332–33.
24. Ibid., p. 353.
25. Ibid., pp. 355–56.
26. See Lynn: "Caught between tragic theme and comic outlook, *Hazard* fails to come to grips with" the meaning of life in the city (*William Dean Howells*, p. 299).
27. Howells, *A Hazard of New Fortunes*, pp. 200–201.
28. Ibid., pp. 334–35.
29. Ibid., p. 533.
30. Howells's preface to *A Hazard*, p. xxiv.
31. Howells, "Problems of Existence in Fiction," pp. 336–37.
32. Ibid., p. 338.
33. Ibid., p. 339.
34. Garland, *Crumbling Idols*, p. 135.
35. Howells, "A Case in Point," p. 13.
36. Ibid., p. 14.
37. Norris, "Novelists of the Future," p. 13.
38. "A Rough Novel," p. 38–39.
39. Norris, "An Opening for Novelists," p. 30. On Norris's fears of being too "feminine" and his distrust of his own literary vocation, see Lears, *No Place of Grace*, pp. 129ff.
40. On Norris's ironic style, see Michael Davitt Bell, "Frank Norris, Style, and the Problem of American Naturalism," p. 93.
41. Norris, *Vandover and the Brute*, p. 351.
42. See McElrath, "Frank Norris's *Vandover and the Brute*," p. 192.
43. Norris, *Vandover*, p. 354.
44. See Pizer, "Evolutionary Ethical Dualism in Frank Norris's *Vandover and the Brute* and *McTeague*"; Ziff, *The American 1890s*, p. 264. Warren

French takes a more psychological view: Vandover's trouble "is not that he degenerates, but that he fails to grow." *Vandover* is "a lament for lost childhood" (French, *Frank Norris*, p. 59). Meanwhile, to Don Graham *Vandover* is a tragedy of imperception; hence the causes are rooted within the character rather than in "forces greater than the self" (Graham, *The Fiction of Frank Norris*, p. 42).

45. Norris, *Vandover*, p. 225.

46. Ibid., p. 311.

47. Ibid., p. 314. For a discussion of art and self-representation in *Vandover*, see Michaels, "The Gold Standard and the Logic of Naturalism."

48. Norris, *Vandover*, p. 143. See McElrath, "Frank Norris's *Vandover and the Brute*," pp. 189–90.

49. Howells, "Editor's Study," p. 155.

50. On trompe l'oeil painting in America, see Frankenstein, *After the Hunt*; and Gerdts, *Painters of the Humble Truth*, especially pp. 153–205.

51. Mark Twain, writing in a humorous vein, was an exception here: his explanatory note at the beginning of *Huck Finn* claims the extreme authenticity of his southwestern dialects, done "painstakingly and with the trustworthy guidance and support of personal familiarity with these several forms of speech." But Twain had no embarrassment about entertaining his reader, and his universality was built upon such specifics.

52. Fuller, "Dr. Gowdy and the Squash," p. 349.

53. Norris had made a similar point (with a similar lion) in a satiric detail in the description of Ida Wade's home in *Vandover*: over the mantelpiece "hung a large and striking picture, a species of cheap photogravure, a lion lying in his cage, looking mildly at the spectator over his shoulder. In front of the picture were real iron bars, with real straw tucked in behind them" (Norris, *Vandover*, p. 71). In his essays and journalism Norris repeatedly distinguished the writer's work from a literal description of actuality: "Fiction is what seems real, not what is real" (Norris, "Fiction Is Selection," p. 51).

54. Fuller, "Dr. Gowdy," p. 331.

55. Henry James, *Selected Short Stories*, p. 130.

56. The photographer Eadweard Muybridge, in his studies of human movement, obliquely confirmed James's artist on the use of models: Muybridge avoided artist's models because of their ungraceful movements, preferring to use society women and dancers. In photographing motion he *needed* the real thing, whereas in painting from a posed position James's artist needed the more flexible model. On Muybridge's models, see Haas, *Muybridge*, p. 149. On James and models, and on the importance of the "type" to late nineteenth-century painting and literature, see Banta, "Artists, Models, Real Things, and Recognizable Types," pp. 9–15.

57. James's late story, "Paste" (1899), which is concerned with the discrimination between true and false pearls, also clearly connects with this issue: as one character says, speaking of tableaux vivants, "Our jewels, for historic scenes, don't tell—the real thing falls short." Something

"larger than life" is needed ("Paste," p. 459). James had made a similar point with respect to Whitman in reviewing the poet's *Drum-Taps*: Whitman was no poet, James declared, because he lacked the larger ideal. "He is not a poet who merely reiterates ... plain facts *ore rotundo* ... for the poet, although he incidentally masters, grasps, and uses the superficial traits of his theme, is really a poet only in so far as he extracts its latent meaning and holds it up to common eyes" (*Portable Henry James*, p. 423). Later in life James came to appreciate Whitman.

58. *The Turn of the Screw* may be the most obvious example of this kind of narrative control and is in some ways akin to a magic trick. James's connections with impressionist painting have been explored extensively, but his affinities with the world of magic, which was an enormously popular entertainment form in the late nineteenth century, may well be worth exploring.

59. In choosing photographs, James specifically wanted to avoid any painted illustrations that might *compete* with his own scenic imagination; Coburn's elegance and refinement appealed to James, along with the fact that photography was, as compared to prose, in "as different a 'medium' as possible." James's detailed directions to Coburn were with the goal of supplying complementary metaphors, subjective impressions, relating to the scenes of his fiction. See James, "Preface to the Golden Bowl," in James, *The Art of the Novel*, p. 333; and Coburn, *Alvin Langdon Coburn*, pp. 52–60.

60. Warner, "Modern Fiction," p. 464. The whole question of photography's impact on literature is treated in a different context in Orvell, "Reproduction and 'The Real Thing,'" pp. 49–64.

61. Burroughs, *Indoor Studies*, p. 253.

62. Kirkland, "Realism versus Other Isms," p. 101.

63. Howells, "A Case in Point," p. 15. Norris was glad to receive Howells's encouragement, but he himself had a more skeptical view of photography's objectivity: something was not necessarily "true," he wrote, "even when narrated with the meticulous science of the phonograph or pictured with the incontestable precision of the photograph" (Norris, "Frank Norris's Weekly Letter," p. 5; reprinted in *The Literary Criticism of Frank Norris*, ed. Pizer, p. 73). For a discussion of Norris's use of photographic imagery, see Mottram, "Frank Norris and Photographic Representation."

64. Howells, pp. 1, 35. For a catalogue of Howells's references to photography in *London Films*, see Arms, "Howells's English Travel Books."

65. Salzman, ed., *Theodore Dreiser, The Critical Reception*, pp. 2, 3, 10, 15.

66. See Kwiat, "Dreiser and the Graphic Artist"; Moers, *Two Dreisers*, pp. 10–13, 39–40; Leonard, "Alfred Stieglitz and Realism," pp. 277–86.

67. Dreiser, "A Remarkable Art," p. 430.

68. Dreiser, *Sister Carrie*, p. 342.

69. Ibid.

70. Norris, "Stephen Crane's Stories of Life in the Slums," p. 13; re-

printed in *Literary Criticism of Frank Norris*, ed. Pizer, p. 164. See also the unsigned review of *Maggie* in the *New York Times*, which said that the stages in the girl's career were shown "with such vivid and terrible accuracy as to make one believe they are photographic" (*New York Times*, May 31, 1896, p. 31; reprinted in *Stephen Crane*, ed. Weatherford, p. 42). To Bergon, Crane's style is "cinematic" rather than "photographic." See Bergon, *Stephen Crane's Artistry*, p. 13.

71. Crane, *Maggie*, ed. Gibson, pp. 139–40.

72. Frederic, *New York Times, Supplement*, January 26, 1896, p. 22; cited in introduction to *Stephen Crane*, ed. Stallman, p. xviii.

73. Crane, *Red Badge of Courage*, p. 518. Cf. Gardner's description, accompanying O'Sullivan's image (plate 36): "A battle has been often the subject of elaborate description; but it can be described in one simple word, *devilish!* and the distorted dead recall the ancient legends of men torn in pieces by the savage wantonness of fiends. Swept down without preparation, the shattered bodies fall in all conceivable positions" (Gardner, *Gardner's Photographic Sketch Book of the Civil War*, n.p.).

74. Crane, "Joys of Seaside Life," ed. Bowers, pp. 510–14.

75. Cited in Wogan, "Crane's Use of Color in 'The Red Badge of Courage,'" p. 172.

76. Crane, "Coney Island's Failing Days," ed. Bowers, p. 324.

77. Studies of Crane have recently begun to explore in detail the epistemological basis of his work, especially Nagel, *Stephen Crane and Literary Impressionism*. More concerned with the act of perception itself is Holton, *Cylinder of Vision*. Also see Solomon, *Stephen Crane*.

78. Garland, "An Ambitious French Novel and a Modest American Story," in *Maggie*, ed. Gullason, p. 144.

79. Crane, *Maggie*, ed. Gibson, p. 154.

80. Ibid., p. 163.

81. Grimsted, "Melodrama as Echo of the Historically Voiceless."

82. Crane, *Maggie*, ed. Gibson, pp. 164; 163.

83. Ibid., p. 151.

84. Norris, "A Plea for Romantic Fiction," p. 77. Cf. Paul Leicester Ford: "There is more true romance in a New York tenement than there ever was in a baron's tower—braver battles, truer loves, nobler sacrifices" (*The Honorable Peter Stirling*, cited in Bremner, *From the Depths*, p. 86).

85. Howells, in *Stephen Crane*, ed. Weatherford, p. 39.

86. At least one reviewer objected to the unrelieved pessimism of Crane's treatment of the slums: "It is too hopeless, too full of misery, degradation and dirt" (*Nashville Banner*, August 15, 1896, in *Stephen Crane*, ed. Weatherford, pp. 50–51).

87. Crane, *Maggie*, ed. Gibson, p. 158.

88. Traubel, *With Walt Whitman in Camden, April 8—September 14, 1889*, ed. Gertrude Traubel, p. 131.

89. Crane, *Red Badge of Courage*, in *The Red Badge of Courage and Selected Prose and Poetry*, p. 414.

90. Ibid.

91. Whitman, *Specimen Days, Leaves of Grass and Selected Prose by Walt Whitman*, ed. Kouwenhoven, pp. 587, 588.

92. See Pease, "Fear, Rage, and the Mistrials of Representation in *The Red Badge of Courage*," in *American Realism: New Essays*, ed. Sundquist, pp. 155–75.

93. Crane, *Red Badge of Courage*, p. 538.

94. Ibid. This passage from the manuscript was not in the originally published version of the novel.

95. Ibid. If Crane had written, "Through the hosts of leaden rain clouds came a golden ray of sunlight," we would perhaps have a different interpretive problem: either (a)—surely he is emphasizing the sun, hence Fleming is approved; or (b)—surely he is using sentimental imagery parodically, hence Fleming is being satirized.

96. Crane, "The Blue Hotel," in *Red Badge of Courage*, p. 388.

97. Ibid., p. 407.

98. Crane, "An Experiment in Misery," in *Stephen Crane: Stories and Tales*, ed. Stallman, p. 27.

99. Crane provides a model for the whole tradition of costumed reporters who would infiltrate alien populations in an effort to discover "first hand" what things are "really" like. See, for example, the sociologist Walter Wyckoff's record of his sojourn across the country living and working the life of the laborer, *The Workers*.

100. Crane, "An Experiment in Misery," p. 31.

101. Ibid., p. 33.

102. Ibid., p. 27.

103. Ibid., p. 38.

104. Ibid. For a detailed discussion of "An Experiment in Misery," see Trachtenberg, "Experiments in Another Country," pp. 138–54. Trachtenberg argues that the experiment does transform the youth, but only "provisionally" (see p. 153).

105. Crane, "An Experiment in Misery," p. 27.

106. Crane, "The Open Boat," pp. 274–75.

107. Crane, "Manacled," p. 162.

108. See Michelis, "Aesthetic Distance and the Charm of Contemporary Art," p. 33.

109. Crane, "Fears Realists Must Wait," in *Red Badge of Courage*, p. 652.

INTRODUCTION TO PART THREE

1. See Wilson, Pilgrim, and Tashjian, *The Machine Age in America, 1918–1941*, especially pp. 23–29.

2. See Presbrey, *The History and Development of Advertising*; Lears, "Some Versions of Fantasy."

3. Steichen, "Commercial Photography."

4. Marcus, *The American Store Window*, p. 19. Also see the photographs grouped under the heading, "Communities of Objects," in Kepes, ed., *The Man-made Object*.

5. See *McClure's Magazine*, May 1908. I am indebted to Philip F. Mooney, Manager, Corporate Archives, The Coca Cola Company, Atlanta, Georgia, for providing me with information regarding the history of the "Real Thing" ad campaigns.

6. *Colliers* (September 28, 1907); *Colliers* (October 7, 1911); *Colliers* (March 22, 1913); *Colliers* (March 20, 1915); *Colliers* (April 4, 1931); *Colliers* (October 26, 1935); *Life* (May 24, 1937); *Life* (May 31, 1937); *Life* (October 6, 1941).

7. Thorne Smith, "Advertising," p. 392. For a more complete discussion of advertising and the consumer during this period, see Lears, "From Salvation to Self-Realization," in Fox and Lears, eds., *The Culture of Consumption*, pp. 1–38; also Lears, "Some Versions of Fantasy," pp. 349–405; and Harris, "The Drama of Consumer Desire," pp. 189–216.

8. Spitzer, "American Advertising Explained as Popular Art," pp. 145, 121.

9. Sinclair, *The Jungle*, pp. 78–79.

10. Edmund Wilson, "Mr. and Mrs. X," pp. 434, 436. See also Merz, *The Great American Bandwagon*, p. 130; and Chase and Schlink, *Your Money's Worth*, pp. 1–26.

11. Henry Miller, *Tropic of Capricorn*, p. 205.

12. Hopkins, *Magic, Stage Illusions and Scientific Diversions*, p. 404.

13. Howells, "A Sennight of the Centennial," p. 86.

14. Marcuse, *One Dimensional Man*, p. 9.

15. William Carlos Williams, *In the American Grain*, p. 177.

16. West, *The Dream Life of Balso Snell*, p. 14.

17. Mumford, "The City," pp. 9, 8.

18. Dos Passos, *The Big Money*, in *U.S.A.*, p. 132.

19. Lindsay, *The Art of the Moving Picture*, p. 229.

20. Lee, *Crowds: A Moving-Picture of Democracy*, p. 13.

21. Elmer Rice, *A Voyage to Purilia*, p. 289.

22. Lippmann, *Public Opinion*, pp. 54, 100, 61. A perfect dramatization of Lippmann's political psychology was Elmer Rice's *The Adding Machine* (1923), in which the pleasant socializing of the characters, their minds saturated with advertising slogans, movie romances, and newspaper xenophobia—culminates in this orgiastic chant of the "mass mind": "Damn foreigners! Damn dagoes! Damn Catholics! Damn sheenies! Damn niggers! Jail 'em! Shoot 'em! Hang 'em! Lynch 'em! Burn 'em! My country 'tis of thee, Sweet land of liberty!" (Rice, *The Adding Machine*, p. 19).

23. Farrell, *Judgment Day*, p. 59.

24. Santayana, "The Genteel Tradition in American Philosophy," pp. 39–40.

25. Frank, *Our America*, p. 72.

26. Brooks, "America's Coming-of-Age," pp. 17–18. On Brooks's early

influence, see Nelson, *Van Wyck Brooks*, especially pp. 100–108; Dow, "Van Wyck Brooks and Lewis Mumford," pp. 238–51; and May, *The End of American Innocence*, pp. 322–26.

27. Brooks, "America's Coming-of-Age," p. 35.

28. See Tashjian's study of the avant-garde, *Skyscraper Primitives*.

29. Rugg, "The Artist and the Great Transition," p. 196.

CHAPTER 5

1. Lee, *Crowds*, p. 37.

2. See Cathers, *Furniture of the American Arts and Crafts Movement*, p. 55; and Boris, *Art and Labor*, p. 28. General interest in Stickley and in his milieu was spurred by the 1972 exhibition and catalogue, *The Arts and Crafts Movement in America, 1876–1916*, ed. Robert Judson Clark. For an updated survey of the movement, see Wendy Kaplan, *"The Art That Is Life."*

3. For an overview of *The Craftsman*, see Sanders, ed., *The Craftsman*.

4. Stickley, "Als Ik Kan," p. 689.

5. Stickley, "Thoughts Occasioned by an Anniversary," p. 114.

6. Background on Stickley is drawn from Mary Ann Smith, *Gustav Stickley*.

7. Yet there were differences rooted in class preferences: although middle-class reformers advocated the simple order of the Arts and Crafts style in settlement houses and domestic-science classes, the working classes and recent immigrant groups tended to remain fixed on the more elaborate, European-derived styles, possibly because they were symbolic of their aspirations and traditions; also, no doubt, they were the available trade in used furniture. See Cohen, "Embellishing a Life of Labor." Also see Cohen, "Respectability at $50.00 Down, 20 Months to Pay!," pp. 238–39.

8. Spofford, *Art Decoration as Applied to Furniture*, p. 222; quoted in Gwendolyn Wright, *Building the Dream*, p. 111.

9. Stickley, *Craftsman Homes*, p. 158.

10. Stickley, "Ornament," p. 104.

11. Stickley, "The Use and Abuse of Machinery, and Its Relation to the Arts and Crafts," *The Craftsman*. Where the Arts and Crafts Movement appealed to the individual on these grounds—as maker, rather than as consumer—it tended to attract relatively sophisticated persons, many of them women, particularly in the ceramic arts, for whom the goal of unifying the hand and the brain was intellectually derived.

12. Ibid., pp. 107, 108.

13. Stickley, "The Old Crafts and the Modern Factories," p. 231.

14. Stickley, *Craftsman Homes*, p. 156.

15. Stickley, "Als Ik Kan," p. 687.

16. On the craft movement and reform, see Gilbert, *Work Without Sal-*

vation, pp. 83–118; and Lears, *No Place of Grace*, pp. 66–96. On the communitarian experiment at Rose Valley, Pa., which was contemporaneous with Stickley's projected plan, see Boris, *Art and Labor*, pp. 162–65.

17. Ashbee's book, *Where the Great City Stands*, takes its title from Whitman's "Song of the Broad Axe," evidence that Whitman was assuming renewed importance to turn-of-the-century reformers, who were seeking an overall cultural program. Also see Lambourne, *Utopian Craftsmen*, pp. 32–33.

18. The manual-training movement can be seen as part of the general enthusiasm for object-teaching in America—the system of teaching from concrete things rather than signs of things, thus leading the child from the object to the abstraction—which began in Europe with Johann Heinrich Pestalozzi and Friedrich Froebel and continued through John Dewey and Maria Montessori. Adler: "By manual training, we cultivate the intellect in close and inseparable connection with action" (Adler, "The Influence of Manual Training on Character," pp. 275–76). John Dewey on Froebel: "The imaginative play of the child's mind comes through the cluster of suggestions, reminiscences, and anticipations that gather about the things he uses. . . . The materials, then, must be as 'real,' as direct and straightforward, as opportunity permits" (*School and Society*, pp. 118–19). Frank Lloyd Wright traced his own imaginative training to his childhood use of Froebel's play blocks.

19. Triggs, "The New Industrialism," p. 104.

20. Triggs, *Chapters in the History of the Arts and Crafts Movement*, p. 187.

21. Veblen, "Arts and Crafts," pp. 108, 109, 110.

22. "The Work of L. & J. G. Stickley [,] Fayetteville, New York," in *Stickley Craftsman Furniture Catalogues*, p. 3.

23. Stickley, "The Old Crafts and the Modern Factories," p. 233, and "Waste," p. 91.

24. Crosby, "Democracy," p. 125; Cranston, "Guild of Dames of the Household—One Practical Solution to the Servant Problem."

25. Cited in Cathers, *Furniture of the American Arts and Crafts Movement*, p. 37. On the internal contradictions of the movement, see Anscombe and Gere, *Arts and Crafts in Britain and America*, p. 41; Ross, "The Arts and Crafts"; and Batchelder, "The Arts and Crafts Movement in America," pp. 544–49.

26. Stickley, "The Ethics of Home Furnishing," p. 412.

27. On the engineer as cultural symbol, see Tichi, *Shifting Gears*, pp. 97–170.

28. Vos, "Art and Machinery," pp. 17, 18.

29. Heap, editor's introduction, *Little Review*, pp. 36, 37.

30. Cf. Warren Susman's contrast between Williamsburg and the Pentagon, in Susman, "Culture and Commitment," pp. 208–10.

31. Nutting, *Period Furniture*, p. 5, quoted in Stillinger, p. 190. Stillinger suggests that for many old families, collecting antiques was a means of

creating distance between themselves and the new immigrants (Stillinger, *The Antiquers*, p. 51).

32. "Henry Ford's Great Gift to the American People," cited in Stillinger, *The Antiquers*, p. 261.

33. Mumford's *Technics and Civilization* was called "The most important background book for industrial-design students, treating the whole complex of social and technological factors historically and analytically" (Cheney and Cheney, *Art and the Machine*, p. 302–3). Of course during the 1920s Mumford was also writing several influential and seminal works on American literary culture—*The Golden Day* and *Herman Melville* among them. For an overview of Mumford's early career, see Donald L. Miller, "Lewis Mumford, Master of Many Arts."

34. See Trachtenberg, "Mumford in the Twenties," pp. 28–42.

35. See Duffey, "Mumford's Quest," p. 66.

36. Mumford, "American Interiors."

37. Mumford, *The Golden Day*, p. 214.

38. Mumford, "American Taste," p. 403. Mumford was not absolutely uniform in his attitude. His most pessimistic assessment came in *Sticks and Stones* (1924), where he inveighed·against the values of the marketplace that dominated our use of technology, arguing instead (long before we had the term) for a kind of "appropriate technology" based on smaller-scale uses of the machine, designed in conformity with biological and community needs. The problem was, "The machine has stamped us; and we have not reacted." During the next decade, Mumford considerably revised his tone, finding more positive possibilities for a culture wedded to technology (Mumford, *Sticks and Stones*, p. 85). In the introduction to the 1955 Dover edition, Mumford attributed his negativity to the influence of Patrick Geddes, whom he had just met. Later on, Mumford would again grow pessimistic.

39. Mumford, *Technics and Civilization*, pp. 353, 350.

40. Mumford, "Machinery and the Modern Style," p. 264.

41. Mumford, *Technics and Civilization*, pp. 333–34.

42. Mumford, "The City," in Stearns, ed., *Civilization in the United States*, pp. 11–12. Walter Pach, writing the essay on "Art" in the same collection, affirmed in conclusion a similar signficance for industrial expression: "The steel bridges, the steel buildings, the newly designed machines, and utensils of all kinds we are bringing forth show an adaptation to function that is recognized as one of the great elements of art" (p. 241). See also Mumford, *The Brown Decades*, pp. 176–77. And see Stilgoe, "Moulding the Industrial Zone Aesthetic."

43. Cheney and Cheney, *Art and the Machine*, p. 44.

44. See Mumford, *Sticks and Stones*, pp. 38–39.

45. The importance of Sullivan and Frank Lloyd Wright is acknowledged, for example, in Teague, *Design This Day*, p. 53.

46. Mumford, *Sketches from Life*, p. 423.

47. Mumford, *Sticks and Stones*, pp. 79, 84–85.

48. Mumford, *The Brown Decades*, pp. 155, 162–63.
49. Ibid., p. 143.
50. Paul, *Louis Sullivan*, p. 3.
51. Sullivan, "What is Architecture," pp. 231, 230.
52. Sullivan, *The Autobiography of an Idea*, p. 129.
53. Ibid., p. 199.
54. Ibid., pp. 290, 291.
55. Sullivan, "Ornament in Architecture," p. 188.
56. See Paul, *Louis Sullivan*, p. 130. Robert Twombly has recently argued that the high point in Sullivan's design represents a fusion of the male (structural mass) and the female ("poetic" ornaments); in Sullivan's later work the "female" component overwhelms the "male." See Twombly, *Louis Sullivan*, pp. 400–402.
57. Paul points out that the Western Association of Architects championed "organic form" before Sullivan and that "many of the ideas usually attributed to Sullivan ... were the common property of the Chicago School" (*Louis Sullivan*, pp. 29–30).
58. In his recent history, *American Design Ethic*, Pulos continues to stress the continuity of functionalist principles in American architectural and industrial design practice. Kenneth Ames has argued against Pulos's monolithic functionalism and for a more plausible notion of design pluralism in America. See Ames, review of *American Design Ethic*, pp. 226–29.
59. Ferris, "The Real Traditions of Architecture," p. 107.
60. Mumford, *The Brown Decades*, pp. 136–37, 234–35.
61. Ibid., p. 171.
62. F. L. Wright, "The Art and Craft of the Machine," p. 65. David Hanks observes, however, that even Wright's own designs, which may appear to be made entirely by machine, were in fact finished by hand; Wright did design for the machine, but it was an ideal of sorts ("Frank Lloyd Wright," p. 211). Eileen Boris sees Wright's advocacy of the machine as part of a current in Chicago's intellectual world, including Veblen's enthusiasm for the engineer as restorer of "the instinct of workmanship" (*Art and Labor*, p. 47).
63. F. L. Wright, "The Art and Craft of the Machine," pp. 70, 55, 73.
64. Ibid., p. 69.
65. F. L. Wright, "The Architect and the Machine," p. 132.
66. F. L. Wright, "Standardization, the Soul of the Machine," p. 136.
67. Mumford, *The Brown Decades*, pp. 168–69.
68. See F. L. Wright, *The Japanese Print*.
69. F. L. Wright, "Principles of Design," p. 101.
70. Monroe, "In the Galleries," p. 112.
71. F. L. Wright, *Autobiography*, p. 515.
72. Twombly, *Frank Lloyd Wright, His Life and His Architecture*, p. 203.
73. Pulos, *American Design Ethic*, p. 330. On the signs and significance

of the new machine age, see Richard Guy Wilson et al., *The Machine Age in America, 1918–1941*, pp. 23–40.

74. Mumford, "Culture and Machine Art," pp. 9, 10. Mumford would, in the 1950s, considerably revise his views, seeing the economics of mass production as imposing on society "a terrible new burden—the duty to consume," with a corresponding debasement of a culture devoted to reproductions of every type ("Standardization, Reproduction and Choice," p. 55).

75. Dana, *A Plan for a Useful Museum*, pp. 31, 42, 57. Also see Harris, "Museums, Merchandising, and Popular Taste," pp. 140–74.

76. Kingdon, *John Cotton Dana*, p. 104. Cf. Richard F. Bach, of the Metropolitan Museum of Art, who similarly argued that the museum should collect everything—"the whole range of production from the extreme of the manual craftsman to the other pole of the items of cheap jewelry and ribbons, pasteboard boxes and wrappers, stock chairs, cottonfrocks, or apartment home lighting fixtures" (*Museums and the Industrial World*, p. 2).

77. Bach, "What Is the Matter with Our Industrial Arts?," p. 49.

78. Glassgold, "Design in America," p. 174. Complaints had been widely voiced in the design field at the beginning of the century. A writer for *House Beautiful* in 1904, for example, inveighed against the taste of the rich, whose furniture, tapestries, and hangings are all "real," yet "false" nevertheless: in emulating past European models, "they are untrue to American life, to American thought, to American ideals" ("The Poor Taste of the Rich," pp. 20ff.), p. 114. Also see Kouwenhoven, *The Arts in Modern American Civilization*, p. 44.

79. Cited in Meikle, *Twentieth Century Limited*, p. 181.

80. Among those making the shift to mass-market designs were George Sakier, in glassware designed for the Fostoria Company; Lurelle Guild, in aluminum utensils for Wear-Ever; and the bedroom and living room suites of Gilbert Rohde made for Herman Miller, Inc.—all beginning around 1934. For illustrations, see Greif, *Depression Modern*, pp. 180–81, 174–75, 156–57.

81. See James Sloan Allen, *The Romance of Commerce and Culture*, passim.

82. See F. L. Wright, *Autobiography*, p. 526; also see Hanks, *The Decorative Designs of Frank Lloyd Wright*, pp. 5, 7.

83. Teague, *Design This Day*, p. 15.

84. Ibid., pp. 15, 39–40.

85. Geddes, *Horizons*, pp. 186, 223. See the excellent discussion of functionalist theory in Meikle, *Twentieth Century Limited*, especially pp. 135–40.

86. Loewy, *Never Leave Well Enough Alone*, p. 219.

87. Ibid., pp. 220–21.

88. Frankl, *New Dimensions*, p. 17, cited in Gebhard, "The Moderne in

the U.S., 1920–1941," p. 15. By 1931, Frankl had seemingly given up on mastery, declaring that "true modernism no longer holds aloft the banner of the defunct handicrafts and peasant arts, but acknowledges its allegiance to the benevolent despotism of the machine" (Frankl, "The Home of Yesterday, Today, and Tomorrow," p. 26).

89. Compare streamlined design with the visually separated forms of the "International" style of the twenties, championed by Philip Johnson at the Museum of Modern Art, where the articulation of parts was more pronounced, suggesting a more complicated rendering of the functional aspects of the object. See Gebhard, "The Moderne in the U.S.," p. 11.

90. Hennessey, *Russel Wright, American Designer*, p. 35. Also see Greif, *Depression Modern*, pp. 44–45.

91. "Russel Wright's 'American Way,'" p. 627.

92. R. Wright, cited in Cheney and Cheney, *Art and the Machine*, p. 188.

93. Hennessey, *Russel Wright, American Designer*, p. 35.

94. Ibid., p. 31.

95. Cited in Greif, *Depression Modern*, p. 43, from an address given to the New York Fashion Group in 1938.

96. See Abernethy, "Frank Lloyd Wright and Walt Whitman," pp. 46, 51.

97. Mumford, "Frank Lloyd Wright and the New Pioneers," p. 153.

98. Sullivan, "Characteristics and Tendencies of American Architecture," p. 180.

99. Quoted in Greif, *Depression Modern*, p. 43.

100. The state buildings at the fair were a noted exception to this rule. See *Official Guide Book of the New York World's Fair, 1939*, p. 31.

101. Mumford, *Sticks and Stones*, pp. 106–7.

102. Teague, *Design This Day*, pp. 15, 34.

103. Cheney and Cheney, *Art and the Machine*, p. 95. Another source for this notion is Walter Gropius, whose First Proclamation of the Weimar Bauhaus (1919) embodied the ideal of the composite artist-craftsman-architect-engineer.

104. Geddes, *Horizons*, p. 285. Teague evinced a similar faith in the power of expertise because, given the enormous engineering problems of mass society, "only the ablest minds can cope with them" (Teague, *Design this Day*, p. 37).

105. Teague, *Design this Day*, p. 97.

106. Bach, "Industrial Design," p. 81.

107. *Official Guide Book of the New York World's Fair*, pp. 7, 45.

108. Doctorow, *World's Fair*, p. 366. Here and elsewhere in the novel, Doctorow evidently makes use of Warren Susman's essay, "The People's Fair: Cultural Contradictions of a Consumer Society," in *Culture as History*, pp. 211–29.

109. Meikle, *Twentieth Century Limited*, p. 133.

110. Mumford, *The Brown Decades*, p. 234.

CHAPTER 6

1. Chase and Schlink, *Men and Machines*, pp. 269–70. Chase is citing the editor of the *London Evening Standard*.

2. Weston, "Letter Regarding Pictorialism and the Work of Alfred Stieglitz," p. 33. On the connections between Stieglitz, realism, and impressionism, see Leonard, "Alfred Stieglitz and Realism," p. 282.

3. Cf. Solomon-Godeau, "Back to Basics," who emphasizes Stieglitz's subjectivity and intuition, in distinction to the objectivity and technological orientation of European photographers. Stieglitz did have a subjective orientation, but this view ignores the photographer's own way of thinking of the camera as a machine, and, more importantly, it submerges the symbolic cultural significance of Stieglitz.

4. Rosenfeld, "Stieglitz," p. 212. Stieglitz himself had earlier used similar terms in describing his sense of the modern city as a place without a soul, though his mood is at once paradoxical and optimistic. "It fascinated me for years because of that lack," he wrote in a 1916 letter to Georgia O'Keeffe. "I thought that the huge machine would eventually discover its soul—Will it? Machines have great souls.—I know it.—Have always known it.—But they must be given a chance to show them.—People interfere too much and have no faith. . . . " Whatever he might have meant by the last paternalistic phrase (the need to respect the autonomy of the "machine-child"—i.e., the canons of precision?), Stieglitz is hinting at an intentional synthesis of machine and man of exactly the sort that he was about to become identified with (Stieglitz to O'Keeffe, October 7, 1916, in Stieglitz, *Alfred Stieglitz*, ed. Greenough and Hamilton, p. 201).

5. Rosenfeld, "Stieglitz," pp. 215, 214. On Stieglitz as a force for cultural renewal, see Abrahams, *The Lyrical Left*, pp. 93–203.

6. Traubel, "Horace Traubel on Photography," p. 49. Shortly after Traubel's piece appeared in *Camera Work*, the French artist Francis Picabia drew a cartoon of Stieglitz for the newly founded magazine *291* (a short-lived magazine of the arts published by Stieglitz admirers)—*Ici, c'est ici Stieglitz*—which shows the metamorphosis complete: it consists of a bellows camera stretching upward toward the word "Ideal" (in Gothic print) just beyond the lens. But the bellows itself curves flaccidly off to the side—whether by intention or by defect of strength is not clear—before reaching its goal. For an illustration, see Homer, *Alfred Stieglitz and the American Avant-Garde*, p. 191; Homer sees the drawing as a symbol of "the photographer's declining energies in the struggle for modern art after the Armory Show" (p. 190). If so, it was only temporary, as his spirits were shortly to be invigorated with the arrival of Georgia O'Keeffe in his studio.

7. Haviland, *291*; quoted in Tashjian, *Skyscraper Primitives*, pp. 43–44.

8. De Zayas, *291*; in Green, ed., *Camera Work*, p. 324.

9. Strand, "Photography and the New God," pp. 139, 143, 144. In the late 1930s this idea was still much alive: Elizabeth McCausland, who collabo-

rated with Berenice Abbott in her New York book, and who had a long-standing interest in photography, wrote, "Actually, man has a better chance of being a God—or rather being a human being in control of his destiny—with machines than without them" ("Documentary Photography," p. 11).

10. See Panzer, *Philadelphia Naturalistic Photography, 1865–1906*, pp. 10–12, 18.

11. One of the most prominent industrial designers of the 1930s, Norman Bel Geddes, confirmed this view of the camera: "Artists are fast mastering the camera, which is purely a machine. The camera will develop into the perfect instrument of the artist. It automatically attends to the obvious and literal for him. It reacts instantly to his sensitiveness and creative imagination." Geddes, *Horizons*, p. 293.

12. On attitudes toward the machine among the avant-garde communities during the 1910s and 1920s, see Tashjian, *Skyscraper Primitives*, passim.

13. Mumford, "The Metropolitan Milieu," p. 47.

14. Coburn, "The Relation of Time to Art," p. 216. During the nineteenth century, by contrast, photography was "harnessed to serve a view of Nature as ideal, harmonious, and purposeful" (Jeffrey, "Photography and Nature," p. 27).

15. Hart Crane to Stieglitz, April 15, 1923, in *Stieglitz Memorial Portfolio, 1864–1946*, ed. Norman, p. 48.

16. On the modern understanding of time and speed, see Kern, *The Culture of Time and Space, 1880–1918*, pp. 10–35, 109–30. On the concept of "modernity," see Calinescu, *Faces of Modernity*, especially pp. 86–92.

17. Hartley, *Adventures in the Arts*, pp. 106, 110–11. Among the earliest critics to establish Stieglitz's importance as a symbol of the fusion of art and science was Charles Caffin, who emphasized the photographer's possession of the "scientific and the artistic temperament," arguing moreover that his scientific background was indispensable to his artistic achievements. (Stieglitz had discovered the camera while in Berlin to study engineering, and his initial experiments were rigorous explorations of photographic technique.) (Caffin, *Photography as a Fine Art*, pp. 28–30)

18. De Zayas, "Modern Art—Theories and Representations," p. 14.

19. Ibid.

20. On Whitman's importance to artists like Marsden Hartley and Abraham Walkowitz, see Homer, *Alfred Stieglitz and the American Avant-Garde*, pp. 140, 149–50, 175. On the importance of Whitman generally during the 1910s and 1920s, see Tashjian, *Skyscraper Primitives*, passim. On Whitman and the film *Mannhatta*, made by Strand and Sheeler in 1921, see Hammen, "Sheeler and Strand's 'Mannhatta,'" pp. 6–7. In addition to these examples of inspiration and influence, there was as well a direct connection with the poet through two intimates of Stieglitz, both of whom knew Whitman personally and both of whom wrote enthusias-

tically about photography—Horace Traubel and Sadakichi Hartmann. (Traubel's report of Whitman's conversation in his later years, *With Walt Whitman in Camden,* came out in three volumes in the first decades of the century; Hartmann too, as a youth, had sought out the poet and recorded his brief meetings in a slim but vivid volume, *Conversations with Walt Whitman.*)

21. Rosenfeld, "Stieglitz," in Newhall, *Photography,* p. 215. Also see Dijkstra, *Cubism, Stieglitz, and the Early Poetry of William Carlos Williams,* p. 103.

22. Rosenfeld, "Stieglitz," in Newhall, *Photography,* pp. 209, 210.

23. Mumford, "A Camera and Alfred Stieglitz," p. 30.

24. Rugg, "The Artist and the Great Transition," p. 196. The shift toward an "objective" photography found an explicit parallel in the Craftsman movement, which throughout its existence carried many articles on photography. One article makes the point specifically that both photography and design were turning from an art of the exotic to an art "found in the present or in real things." The more conventional art photography of the 1890s is associated with the deceptions of "machine made woodwork . . . made to look like hand carving," while praise is given the "new kind of beauty" that results from accepting, and exploiting, the mechanical nature of the photographic art (See "A Vital Expression in German Photographic Art," pp. 26–33). The point is discussed also by Doty, *Photo-Secession,* p. 57, and by Conn, *The Divided Mind,* p. 284.

25. See Hales, *Silver Cities,* pp. 69–130, 163–217.

26. Caffin, *Photography as a Fine Art,* p. 49.

27. An earlier photograph, "A Street in Sterzing, the Tyrol" (1890), anticipates "The Steerage" in its dense play of repeated forms (the windows on the houses of the narrow street), and in the complexity of the intersecting angles of walls and shadows. But where the camera frame arbitrarily creates the subject in "The Steerage," the street in the earlier photograph provides a kind of interior frame and coherence for the picture. On Stieglitz's framing and cropping, as it develops from his earlier phase to the cloud photographs, see Krauss, "Stieglitz / *Equivalents,*" pp. 129–40.

28. Norman, *Alfred Stieglitz,* p. 76.

29. De Zayas, *291.*

30. Strand, "Stieglitz," p. 94.

31. O'Keeffe, introduction to *Georgia O'Keeffe, a Portrait.*

32. Stieglitz to Hartmann, April 27, 1919, in Stieglitz, *Alfred Stieglitz,* ed. Greenough and Hamilton, p. 205.

33. Mumford, "The Metropolitan Milieu," p. 57.

34. Stearns, "The Intellectual Life," p. 148.

35. Mumford, "The Metropolitan Milieu," p. 51.

36. See Krauss, "Stieglitz / *Equivalents.*"

37. See Brown, *American Painting from the Armory Show to the Depression,* p. 119.

38. Strand, "Alfred Stieglitz and a Machine," p. 285.

39. Léger, "A New Realism—The Object," p. 231. Also see Deborah Irmas's essay on the treatment of the object in the exhibition catalogue, *Signs of the Times: Some Recurring Motifs in Twentieth-Century Photography* (San Francisco: San Francisco Museum of Modern Art, 1985); and Benjamin on the close-up, with its power to reveal new structures in the object ("The Work of Art in the Age of Mechanical Reproduction").

40. S. H. [Sadakichi Hartmann], "On the Possibility of New Laws of Composition," p. 200. Also see Pultz and Scallen, *Cubism and American Photography, 1910–1930*, p. 3.

41. Strand, "Photography," p. 326.

42. Mumford, *Technics and Civilization*, p. 339.

43. Weston, "Weston to Hagemeyer, November 1922," p. 35.

44. Weston, "Photography—Not Pictorial," p. 155.

45. Ibid.

46. Weston, *Daybooks of Edward Weston*, 1:26.

47. Weston, "Seeing Photographically," p. 163.

48. Stieglitz to Anderson, August 15, 1923, in Stieglitz, *Alfred Stieglitz*, ed. Greenough and Hamilton, p. 206.

49. Weston, "Photographic Art," 1:99.

50. Mumford, *Technics and Civilization*, p. 340.

51. Ibid., p. 334. The designer Norman Bel Geddes also noted his admiration for photographs of multiple objects. See *Horizons*, p. 13.

52. Nye, *Image Worlds*, p. 49.

53. Such techniques could also be applied to the depiction of the masses themselves, with more sinister intention. Writing during the 1930s, Walter Benjamin made a point, in "The Work of Art in the Age of Mechanical Reproduction," of the political significance of the mass shot, featuring rallies and parades, in which "the masses are brought face to face with themselves." Thus aesthetics are introduced into political life and the masses, through propaganda films, are violated (p. 333).

54. Steichen, "Commercial Photography," p. 157.

55. See Silverman, *For the World to See*.

56. *Coronet* (March 1940), p. 24; cited in Howe and Markham, *Paul Outerbridge, Jr.*, p. 9.

57. See Dines, ed., *Paul Outerbridge*, pp. 22–23.

58. Benjamin, "A Short History of Photography," pp. 213, 215. Before the Depression, Franz Roh had noted with equanimity in the influential *Photo-Eye* catalogue in 1929 that the camera has broad appeal to the common man, who uses it on his Sunday excursion, but it also "serves the capitalistic upper classes by its steadily increasing insertion into advertisement" (*Photo-Eye*, p. 15).

59. Silverman, *For the World to See*, pp. 76–81. Also see Andre, "The Rhetoric of Power," pp. 6–7.

60. Cross, *A Picture of America*.

61. Ibid., p. 2.

62. Paul Strand, *Photo Notes*, p. 2. Stieglitz had occasionally voiced an egalitarian enthusiasm over the possibility of mass-producing affordable copies of fine photographs, but his practice remained wedded to the superbly crafted individual print, thus leaving him aloof from the visual culture of the magazines. As for Weston, he had stayed away from commercial photography, only to resent the penurious consequences of his choice, and found that his own essentially autonomous aesthetic *almost* harmonized with the collective requirements of the moment. Weston was featured by the leftist *Experimental Cinema* in 1931 as "Left-wing American Photographer," a label that caused him considerable mirth, but which he also attempted to justify on the grounds that he had done his part toward clarity of vision and solidarity by revealing "to others the living world about them, showing to them what their own unseeing eyes had missed: I have thus cleared away the haze of a futile romanticism, allowing identification with all things by those who had been drifting apart." And Weston insisted that the artist, while not being a propagandist or social reformer per se, must still relate his work to "present needs, or to future hopes" (Weston, *Daybooks*, 2:210–11).

63. Stryker, "Documentary Photography," 4:1369.

64. Lange to Nancy Newhall, April 13, 1958, in *Photographers on Photography*, ed. Lyons, p. 67.

65. Stryker, "Documentary Photography," 4:1365.

66. For a broad-ranging examination of documentary genres during the 1930s, see Stott, *Documentary Expression and Thirties America*.

67. I have drawn these illustrations from those available in *In This Proud Land*, ed. Stryker and Wood. See pp. 178, 17, plate ix, 48, 8.

68. See "Fargo Fakery," p. 36.

69. Rothstein, "Direction in the Picture Story," 4:1360. Rothstein's later claim that he had not posed the shot does not in any case affect the more general point that such staging was general practice. See Rothstein, "Setting the Record Straight," pp. 50–51.

70. Rothstein, "Direction in the Picture Story," 4:1357.

71. Evans, "The Reappearance of Photography," *Hound and Horn*, p. 128.

72. Wood, "Portrait of Stryker," p. 13.

73. Ibid., p. 15.

74. Evans, "Handwritten Draft Memorandum Re Resettlement Administration Job, Spring 1935," p. 112.

75. Stryker, "The FSA Collection of Photographs," p. 351.

76. Evans, "Unfinished Letter to Ernestine Evans, February 1934," p. 98.

77. Kirstein, "Photographs of America," p. 186.

78. Evans, "Photography," p. 646.

79. "Walker Evans, Visiting Artist," p. 320.

80. Curtis and Grannen, "Let Us Now Appraise Famous Photographs," pp. 1–23. On Evans's touching up an image to improve it, see White, "Vernacular Photography," p. 58.

81. For example, see Evans, *Walker Evans at Work*. Also see Evans's review of *Photo-Eye*, pp. 125–28.

82. Evans, "The Reappearance of Photography," p. 127.

83. Also, during the 1910s and 1920s painters—e.g., Stuart Davis and Charles Demuth—incorporated commercial signs and billboards into their works.

84. For an excellent discussion of Coady and the effort to frame an American aesthetic during the 1910s, see Tashjian's *Skyscraper Primitives*, pp. 71–84. Also see *New York Dada*, ed. Kuenzli.

85. Trachtenberg, "Walker Evans's America," pp. 56–66.

86. Evans, *Walker Evans at Work*, p. 161.

87. Kirstein, "Photographs of America," p. 188.

88. Evans, in Katz, "Interview with Walker Evans," 1:124.

CHAPTER 7

1. William Carlos Williams, *Spring and All*, p. 117.

2. See Sedgwick, "The American Genteel Tradition in the Early Twentieth Century," pp. 49–67.

3. Gertrude Stein, "Pictures," p. 66.

4. Ibid., p. 73.

5. Ibid., p. 79.

6. Emerson, "Nature," pp. 14, 17.

7. Whitman, *An American Primer*, pp. 70, 71.

8. William Carlos Williams, *The Embodiment of Knowledge*, p. 13.

9. William Carlos Williams, "The Work of Gertrude Stein," p. 116. Also see Dijkstra, *Cubism, Stieglitz, and the Early Poetry of William Carlos Williams*, p. 140; and Kenner, *A Homemade World*, p. 81. There was an American precedent for Gertrude Stein's act of liberating language from the encrustations of habit in the remarkable early nineteenth-century philosopher Alexander Bryan Johnson, who anticipated logical positivism by defining the fallacies concealed in words. Johnson's argument was, put simply, that the names of things are distinct from objects: "instead of contemplating creation through the medium of words, men should contemplate creation itself" (*A Treatise on Language*, p. 299). But where Stein would accept the word as the basis for an evocative poetry, Johnson would take the separation of word from world as the justification for silence: "When a child ... asks me what is a rose: I reply, it is a word with which we name an associated sight, feel, and smell. For the sensible existence itself, I refer him to his sense, as alone able to communicate the information:—words being unable to perform the functions of our senses" (*Treatise on Language*, p. 54).

10. William Carlos Williams, "Marianne Moore," p. 128.

11. Willa Cather, "The Novel Démeublé," pp. 43, 48.

12. Gertrude Stein, "Composition as Explanation," p. 513.

13. Lindsay, *The Art of the Moving Picture*, pp. 21–22.

14. Epstein, "The New Conditions of Literary Phenomena," pp. 6–7. For a discussion of Epstein in the context of the *Broom* debate on technology, see Tashjian, *Skyscraper Primitives*, p. 120.

15. William Carlos Williams, *Spring and All*, p. 88.

16. William Carlos Williams, "A Beginning on the Short Story (Notes)," p. 303.

17. William Carlos Williams, *I Wanted to Write a Poem*, p. 13.

18. Hemingway, *Death in the Afternoon*, p. 10. Also see Kenner, *A Homemade World*, p. 145.

19. Gertrude Stein, *The Autobiography of Alice B. Toklas*, p. 201.

20. Amy Lowell, "Is There a National Spirit in 'The New Poetry' of America?" p. 324.

21. William Carlos Williams, "Marianne Moore," p. 125. On Moore and the shift from realism to a poetry of real things, see Costello, *Marianne Moore*, pp. 204ff.

22. Simpson, *At the End of the Road*, p. 55. See Altieri, "The Objectivist Tradition," pp. 5–22; DuPlessis, "Objectivist Poetics and Political Vision," pp. 123–48; Kuberski, "Charles Olson and the American Thing," pp. 175–93.

23. Hartley, "Dissertation on Modern Painting," cited in Tashjian, *William Carlos Williams*, p. 50.

24. William Carlos Williams, "Yours, O Youth," p. 35.

25. William Carlos Williams, "Introduction," *Charles Sheeler—Paintings—Drawings—Photographs*, p. 143.

26. Zukovsky, "Sincerity and Objectification," p. 268. On Zukofsky, George Oppen, and the impact of photography on the 1930s Objectivists, see Kenner, "Oppen, Zukofsky, and the Poem as Lens," pp. 162–71.

27. William Carlos Williams, "The American Background," p. 32. Stieglitz's impact on Williams (including the photographer's works, exhibitions, and conversation) has been amply detailed by Dijkstra in *Cubism, Stieglitz, and the Early Poetry of William Carlos Williams*; Tashjian, *William Carlos Williams*, pp. 90–98; Thomas, *Literary Admirers of Alfred Stieglitz*.

28. William Carlos Williams, *The Embodiment of Knowledge*, p. 114; Williams, "Whitman's *Leaves of Grass* and Photography," p. 232. Williams's grandmother, Emily Wellcome, had been married to an itinerant photographer. See Mariani, *William Carlos Williams*, p. 7.

29. William Carlos Williams, *Spring and All*, p. 138.

30. See Riddel, *The Inverted Bell*, p. 226.

31. William Carlos Williams, *Collected Earlier Poems*, p. 353 (hereafter abbreviated as *CEP*). Other examples are "Della Primavera," *CEP*, p. 57; "Rapid Transit," *CEP*, p. 282; "Brilliant Sad Sun," *CEP*, p. 324.

32. See Sankey, *A Companion to William Carlos Williams's "Paterson,"* p. 17.

33. William Carlos Williams, *Spring and All*, pp. 110, 111.

34. William Carlos Williams, *Paterson*, p. 51 (hereafter cited as *P* in text). That the camera's objectivity could overpower the imagination is evident in another context, when Williams wrote Constance Rourke in 1938 that Sheeler himself may have gone too far—painting too much as the camera sees. "Someone should smash his camera and open his brain" (quoted in Weaver, *William Carlos Williams*, p. 62).

35. William Carlos Williams, "A Beginning on the Short Story (Notes)," p. 303.

36. See Altieri, "Objective Image and Act of Mind in Modern Poetry," pp. 101–14. Altieri says that "at their most triumphant moments, the modernists have glimpsed a vision in which the structures of consciousness and the diversity of experience seem dialectically related." As J. Hillis Miller put it, Williams gave up early on "those dramas of the interchange of subject and object, self and world, which have long been central in Western philosophy and literature. . . . He reaches at the age of twenty the place which Wallace Stevens attains only after decades of struggle to harmonize imagination and reality" (Miller, *Poets of Reality*, p. 287). In "The Credences of Summer," Stevens had written, "Let's see the very thing and nothing else. / Let's see it with the hottest fire of sight" (*The Collected Poems of Wallace Stevens*, p. 373). The process here is more heavily symbolist, however, and thus different from that of Williams, who thought of isolating the thing objectively in its own space. In Stevens the surface of the poem forms a translucent texture, rich in conceptual and linguistic complexity, whereas Williams strove for simplificaton and a certain opaqueness.

37. William Carlos Williams, *Spring and All*, pp. 123, 151.

38. William Carlos Williams, "January Morning," *CEP*, pp. 162–66.

39. William Carlos Williams, "This Florida: 1924," *CEP*, p. 329.

40. William Carlos Williams, "To a Solitary Disciple," *CEP*, p. 167.

41. This aspect of Williams has been richly treated by Dijkstra in *Cubism, Stieglitz, and the Early Poetry of William Carlos Williams*; Tashjian, *William Carlos Williams and the American Scene*; and Marling, *William Carlos Williams and the Painters, 1909–1923*.

42. Cf. E. E. Cummings: "the symbol of all art is the Prism. . . . The goal is unrealism. The method is destructive. To break up the white light of objective realism, into the secret glories which it contains." E. E. Cummings, unpublished notes, Houghton Library, Harvard University, quoted in E. E. Cummings, *Tulips and Chimneys*, p. x.

43. Hammett, *The Maltese Falcon*, p. 3.

44. William Carlos Williams, *Kora in Hell*, pp. 66–67.

45. Ibid., p. 78.

46. William Carlos Williams, "An Essay on *Leaves of Grass*," p. 331. Williams early on came to regard himself as a son of Whitman, building on what Whitman had started, developing further the accommodating free verse forms that were appropriate to a democracy. Yet Williams was not

blindly imitating Whitman: "The only way to be like Whitman is to write *unlike* him" (Williams, "America, Whitman, and the Art of Poetry," p. 31). For Williams's corrective view of Whitman, arguing that the poetic line needs a discipline Whitman did not himself exemplify, see "On Measure—Statement for Cid Corman," pp. 337–40. The significance of Whitman to Williams is treated extensively in Tapscott, *American Beauty*. On Williams's association of the new measure with modern science, see J. Hillis Miller, *Poets of Reality*, p. 343.

47. "Personally I have a distaste for miscellany," Stevens had written in response to Williams's recently published collection of poems, *Al Que Quiere*. "To fidget with points of view leads always to new beginnings and incessant new beginnings lead to sterility.... A single manner or mood thoroughly matured and exploited is that fresh thing" (Williams, "Prologue," *Kora in Hell*, pp. 16, 15).

48. William Carlos Williams, *The Descent of Winter*, p. 259. On broken forms and the "force of deconstruction," see introduction to *A Recognizable Image*, ed. Dijkstra, p. 41.

49. William Carlos Williams, *In the American Grain*, [p. v].

50. William Carlos Williams, "The Great American Novel," in *Imaginations*, p. 158 (hereafter abbreviated as *GAN* in text).

51. William Carlos Williams, *A Recognizable Image*, p. 65. See *CEP*, pp. 427–28.

52. Williams to Creeley, March 3, 1950, in *The Poetics of the New American Poetry*, ed. Allen and Tallman, p. 140.

53. William Carlos Williams, *Spring and All*, p. 133.

54. Quoted by Levin in "Revisiting Dos Passos's *U.S.A.*," p. 414.

55. Warshow, "The Legacy of the Thirties," p. 39.

56. Quoted in Dos Passos, *The Fourteenth Chronicle*, ed. Ludington, p. 463.

57. Dos Passos, "Against American Literature," p. 271.

58. Dos Passos, *Century's Ebb*, p. 352.

59. Lawrence, review of Dos Passos, *Manhattan Transfer*, pp. 363–64.

60. Dos Passos, "Contemporary Chronicles," cited in Diggins, "Visions of Chaos," p. 333.

61. Dos Passos, "Satire as a Way of Seeing," p. 21.

62. Dos Passos, introduction to Cendrars, *Panama, or the Adventures of My Seven Uncles*, pp. vii–viii.

63. Dos Passos, *The Fourteenth Chronicle*, ed. Ludington, p. 387.

64. Gingrich, "Editor's Note," p. 51.

65. William Carlos Williams, Author's introduction to *The Wedge*, p. 256. For a fuller discussion of Williams's notion of the poem as machine, as well as Dos Passos's use of the "gear and girder" conception of fictive structure, see Tichi, *Shifting Gears*.

66. See Lynn, introduction to *World in a Glass*, p. x. Lynn is thinking especially of Oscar Handlin's *The Americans* (1963).

67. Dos Passos, "Interview with D. Sanders," p. 163.

68. See Westerhoven, "Autobiographical Elements in the Camera Eye," pp. 340–64; Diggins, "Visions of Chaos and Visions of Order."

69. Dos Passos, *The Big Money, U.S.A.*, pp. 128–29.

70. Sartre, "John Dos Passos and *1919*," pp. 63, 65–66.

71. One of the best characterizations of Dos Passos's style in these narrative sections is Erich Auerbach's descripton of *Madame Bovary*: "The situation, then, is not presented simply as a picture, but we are first given Emma and then the situation through her.... Though the light which illuminates the picture proceeds from her, she is yet herself part of the picture, she is situated within it.... there is nothing of Flaubert's life in these words, but only Emma's; Flaubert does nothing but bestow the power of mature expression upon the material which she affords, in its complete subjectivity.... So she does not simply see, but is herself seen as one seeing, and is thus judged, simply through a plain description of her subjective life, out of her own feelings" (*Mimesis*, pp. 427–28).

72. Gado, ed., *First Person*, p. 42.

73. See Ludington, *John Dos Passos*, p. 226. Also see Carver, "The Newspaper and Other Sources of *Manhattan Transfer*." Cf. William Carlos Williams's use of newspapers in *Paterson*, in which the library's archives form a memory bank for the community. See Bollard, "The 'Newspaper Landscape' of William's *Paterson*." During the 1930s brief flashes of newspaper headlines became a convention in Hollywood movies as a way of adding to the texture of "reality" while also advancing the plot.

74. Dos Passos, *The 42nd Parallel, U.S.A.*, pp. 320–21.

75. Dos Passos, *Manhattan Transfer*, p. 3.

76. Dos Passos, *The 42nd Parallel, U.S.A.*, p. 98.

77. Dos Passos, *The Big Money, U.S.A.*, p. 413.

78. Ludington, *John Dos Passos*, p. 260.

79. Dos Passos, *The Big Money, U.S.A.*, p. 174. This phrase seems to have been with Dos Passos from early on. Cf. his notes for the novel: "The upside down image in the retina, / piece by piece immediately out of color..." (Ludington, *John Dos Passos*, p. 259).

80. Dos Passos, "Satire as a Way of Seeing," pp. 20–21.

81. Dos Passos, *1919, U.S.A.*, p. 12.

82. Dos Passos, *The Big Money, U.S.A.*, p. 461.

83. Dos Passos, "The Writer as Technician," p. 78.

84. Dos Passos, *The Big Money, U.S.A.*, p. 430.

85. Dos Passos, *The 42nd Parallel, U.S.A.*, p. 225.

86. Ibid., p. 241.

87. Dos Passos, *The Big Money, U.S.A.*, pp. 381, 378.

88. Dos Passos, "The Writer as Technician," p. 79.

89. Dos Passos, *The Big Money, U.S.A.*, p. 391.

90. Ibid., p. 413.

91. Ibid., pp. 414, 390.

92. For an account of the trip South, see Bergreen, *James Agee*, pp. 158–82.

93. Agee and Evans, *Let Us Now Praise Famous Men*, p. xv. Hereafter citations are incorporated in the text in parentheses. The text is identical in the 1941 and 1960 editions, except for the addition in 1960 of a foreword by Evans. The page numbers of the original edition and the 1960 edition are the same, except for the prefaces, which are paginated in roman numerals.

94. Agee, "Plans for Work." For discussions of *Let Us Now Praise Famous Men*, see Stott, *Documentary Expression and Thirties America*, pp. 261–314; and Puckett, *Five Photo-Textual Documentaries from the Great Depression*, pp. 111–51.

95. Agee: "In a novel, a house or person has his meaning, his existence, entirely through the writer. Here [on the tenant farm], a house or a person has only the most limited meaning through me: his true meaning is much huger. It is that he *exists*, in actual being, as you do and as I do, and as no character of the imagination can possibly exist. His great weight, mystery, and dignity are in this fact" (p. 12).

96. Continuing in this direction, the composer John Cage will pick up his own function in post–World War II America, working creatively with silence, becoming the composer as listener.

97. See Agee, *Letters of James Agee to Father Flye*, p. 53. Also, Barson, *A Way of Seeing*, pp. 33, 45ff.

98. At times Agee can move us too close to the object: "I should further describe the odor of corn: in sweat, or on the teeth, and breath, when it is eaten as much as they eat it, it is of a particular sweet stuffy fetor, to which the nearest parallel is the odor of the yellow excrement of a baby" (pp. 154–55). On such occasions, the Romantic temptation to confuse "reality" with life at the bottom, could run away with Agee, and even the experience of bedbugs could become a religious penance.

99. Dodson, "A Cropper Family," p. 85.

100. Agee, introduction to Levitt, *A Way of Seeing*, p. v.

101. Ibid., p. vi.

102. Agee, *The Collected Short Prose*, p. 151.

103. See Orvell, "Reproduction and 'The Real Thing,'" pp. 49–64.

104. Morris, "Photographs, Images, and Words," p. 466.

105. For a full catalogue of the FSA images, see Evans, *Walker Evans: Photographs for the Farm Security Administration, 1935–1938.*

106. Dos Passos, "The Writer as Technician," p. 79.

EPILOGUE

1. "Vanishing Backyards," pp. 77, 78, 81. On the transformation of junk and transient objects into valued durables, see Thompson, *Rubbish Theory*, and Culler, "Junk and Rubbish," pp. 2–12.

2. "Vanishing Backyards," p. 79.

3. Steiner confirms Walter Benjamin's contention that photography declares, willy nilly, that "the world is beautiful," and raises "every tin can into the realm of the All." But the European's cynicism constricts our understanding of the transformation process at issue here (Benjamin, "A Short History of Photography," p. 213).

4. Evans, "Walker Evans, Visiting Artist," p. 317.

5. Agee and Evans, *Let Us Now Praise Famous Men*, p. 166.

6. Ibid., p. 270. Wright Morris places Agee within what he considers a larger context of regional attitudes toward things: "It would appear that only Americans convert the new into trash, into junk, yet feel the presence of life in worn-out objects, made holy by use. It is common for the backward and rural folk to feel it. . . . In Agee, the burden of this intent is religious, and on occasion almost unbearably poignant" (Morris, *About Fiction* [New York: Harper and Row, 1975], p. 167).

7. William Carlos Williams, "Effie Deans," p. 129.

8. Ibid., p. 133.

9. Hartigan, "Joseph Cornell," p. 99. Cf. Ashton, *A Joseph Cornell Album*, p. 6. Cornell drew on a wide range of contemporary European artists— Dali, Magritte, de Chirico, Duchamp, Man Ray, Kurt Schwitters—and quickly became identified as a surrealist, but his art owed at least as much to Edgar Allan Poe, Emily Dickinson, and Mary Baker Eddy as to foreign sources. (He may have been the only Christian Scientist surrealist, yet these interests were in fact complementary—for both were ways of transcending the ordinary, escaping death.) See Ashton, *A Joseph Cornell Album*, pp. 55–57.

10. Lowell, "Hawthorne," p. 39.

11. Whitman, "As I Ebb'd with the Ocean of Life," pp. 254–55.

12. Stevens, "The Man on the Dump," pp. 201–3.

13. Barthelme, *Snow White*, p. 97. One of the great transformers of mass culture and junk was Andy Warhol. The Campbell's soup can was only the beginning. As Frederick Hughes, his friend and manager, put it on his death, "He was a massive shopper. . . . He considered shopping a part of his work, and every day he bought things that caught his eye on his rounds of flea markets and antique stores, anything from 19th-century sculpture and furniture to tiny little collectibles, like World's Fair items" (*New York Times*, February 26, 1987, C-21).

14. Oldenburg, statement for catalogue, "Environment, Situations, Spaces," pp. 11–12.

15. Oldenburg, "Items toward an introduction," p. 8.

16. Quoted in Johnson, *Claes Oldenburg*, pp. 17, 59.

17. If that sensibility is anticipated anywhere before 1940 it is in the work of the blackly humorous Nathanael West, who, in *A Cool Million* (1934), turns the proudest products of America into so much junk, a symptom of the overall shoddiness of American culture. West is humorous, he is satiric, but—unlike the postmodernist—he does not view the objects of his satire with any particular affection. Using as his spokesman an Indian chief whose tribal passions are intact but whose vocabulary has been adulterated by virtue of his Harvard education, West issues his indictment. To Chief Satinpenny, the paleface has filled the skies with smoke and the rivers with refuse. The land is now so flooded with "clever cigarette lighters," with "toilet paper, painted boxes to keep pins in, key rings, watch fobs, leatherette satchels," that "all the secret places of the earth are full. Now even the Grand Canyon will no longer hold razor blades." Little is left untouched in West's 1930s parody (which encompasses patriots and Indians, Horatio Alger and fascists), but underneath it is a sense of urgency, as if he too, in surveying civilization from the dump, found the scene more menacing than entertaining. West, *A Cool Million*, pp. 232–33.

18. Chase, *Mexico*, p. 47.

19. On Chase (together with a consideration of other critiques of American industrial civilization), see Susman, "Culture and Commitment," pp. 190–91.

20. Chase, *Mexico*, p. 9.

Abernethy, Peter I. "Frank Lloyd Wright and Walt Whitman: The Expatriates' Dream of Home." *American Studies* 18 (Fall 1977).

Abrahams, Edward. *The Lyrical Left: Randolph Bourne, Alfred Stieglitz, and the Origins of Cultural Radicalism in America.* Charlottesville: University Press of Virginia, 1986.

Adams, Henry. *The Education of Henry Adams.* 1918. Reprint. New York: Random House, 1931.

Adimari, Ralph, and Ralph Holloway, eds. *New York Dissected.* New York: Rufus Rockwell Wilson, 1936.

Adler, Felix. "The Influence of Manual Training on Character." *Proceedings of the National Conference of Charities and Corrections.* Boston, 1888.

Agee, James. *Letters of James Agee to Father Flye.* Boston: Houghton Mifflin, 1971.

———. "Plans for Work: October 1937." In *The Collected Short Prose,* edited by Robert Fitzgerald, 147–66. New York: Ballantine, 1970.

Agee, James, and Walker Evans. *Let Us Now Praise Famous Men.* 1941. Reprint. New York: Houghton Mifflin, 1980.

Agnew, Jean-Christophe. "The Consuming Vision of Henry James." In *The Culture of Consumption,* edited by Richard Wightman Fox and T. J. Jackson Lears, 65–100. New York: Pantheon, 1983.

Allen, Donald, and Warren Tallman, eds. *The Poetics of the New American Poetry.* New York: Grove Press, 1973.

Allen, Gay Wilson. *A Reader's Guide to Walt Whitman.* New York: Farrar, Straus and Giroux, Noonday Press, 1970.

———. *The Solitary Singer.* New York: New York University Press, 1967.

Allen, James Sloan. *The Romance of Commerce and Culture: Capitalism, Modernism, and the Chicago-Aspen Crusade for Cultural Reform.* Chicago: University of Chicago Press, 1983.

Allwood, John. *The Great Exhibitions.* London, 1977.

Altick, Richard. *The Shows of London.* Cambridge: Harvard University Press, Belknap Press, 1978.

Altieri, Charles. "Objective Image and Act of Mind in Modern Poetry." *PMLA* 91 (January 1976): 101–14.

———. "The Objectivist Tradition." *Chicago Review* 30 (Winter 1979): 5–22.

American Quarterly. Special issue on "Modernist Culture in America." 39 (Spring 1987).

Ames, Kenneth Leroy. "Grand Rapids Furniture at the Time of the Centennial." *Winterthur Portfolio* 10 (Spring 1975): 23–50.

_____. "Notes toward a Theory of Style: Three Episodes in the History of Nineteenth-Century American Furniture." Paper delivered at the American Studies Association Conference, Philadelphia, November 1983.

_____. "Renaissance Revival Furniture in America." Ph.D. dissertation, University of Pennsylvania, 1970.

_____. Review of Arthur J. Pulos, *American Design Ethic, Winterthur Portfolio*, 19 (Summer/Autumn 1984): 226–29.

_____. *Victorian Furniture.* Philadelphia: The Victorian Society, 1983.

Anderson, Charles. *Person, Place, and Thing in Henry James's Novels.* Durham, N.C.: Duke University Press, 1977.

Andre, Linda. "The Rhetoric of Power: Machine Art and Public Relations." *Afterimage* 11 (February 1984): 6–7.

Anscombe, Isabelle, and Charlotte Gere. *Arts and Crafts in Britain and America.* New York: Rizzoli, 1978.

Applebaum, Stanley. *The Chicago World's Fair of 1893: A Photographic Record.* New York: Dover, 1980.

Arms, George. "Howells's English Travel Books: Problems in Technique." *PMLA* 82 (March 1967): 104–16.

Arnheim, Rudolph. "On the Nature of Photography." In *The Camera Viewed,* edited by Peninah Petruck. Vol. 2. New York: E. P. Dutton, 1979.

Ashton, Dore. *A Joseph Cornell Album.* New York: Viking Press, 1974.

Atkinson, Brooks, ed. *Selected Writings of Ralph Waldo Emerson.* New York: Modern Library, 1940.

Auerbach, Erich. *Mimesis: The Representation of Reality in Western Literature.* Garden City, N.Y.: Doubleday, 1953.

Bach, Richard F. "Industrial Design: The Resurgence of Quality." In *Annual of American Design 1931,* edited by R. L. Leonard and C. A. Glassgold, 79–100. New York: Ives Washburn and the American Union of Decorative Artists and Craftsmen, 1930.

_____. *Museums and the Industrial World.* New York: The Metropolitan Museum of Art, 1926.

_____. "A Note on Producers of Industrial Art and Their Relation to the Public." *Arts and Decoration* 18 (January 1923).

_____. "What Is the Matter with Our Industrial Arts?" *Arts and Decoration* 18 (January 1923).

Banta, Martha. "Artists, Models, Real Things, and Recognisable Types." *Studies in the Literary Imagination* 16 (Fall 1983).

Barnouw, Erik. *The Magician and the Cinema.* Oxford: Oxford University Press, 1981.

Barson, A. T. *A Way of Seeing: A Critical Study of James Agee.* Amherst: University of Massachusetts Press, 1972.

Barth, Gunter. *City People: The Rise of Modern City Culture in Nineteenth-Century America.* New York: Oxford, 1980.

Barthelme, Donald. *Snow White.* New York: Bantam, 1968.

Bartlett, John. "Has the Brain a Photographic Function?" *American Journal of Photography* 18, no. 209 (May 1897): 195–200.

––––––. "On the Choice of a Subject Suitable for a Photographic Picture." *American Journal of Photography* 18, no. 210 (June 1897): 255–66.

Bassham, Ben L. *The Theatrical Photographs of Napoleon Sarony.* Kent, Ohio: Kent State University Press, 1978.

Batchelder, Ernest. "The Arts and Crafts Movement in America: Work or Play?" *The Craftsman* 16 (1909). Reprinted in *The Craftsman: An Anthology*, edited by Barry Sanders. Santa Barbara, Calif.: Peregrine Smith, 1978.

Baudrillard, Jean. "The Precession of Simulacra" (1983). In *Art after Modernism: Rethinking Representation*, edited by Brian Wallis. New York: The New Museum of Contemporary Art; and Boston: David R. Godine, 1984.

––––––. *Le Système des Objets.* Paris, Editions Gallimard, 1968.

Baym, Nina. *Woman's Fiction: A Guide to Novels by and about Women in America, 1820–1870.* Ithaca: Cornell University Press, 1978.

Beaver, Joseph. *Walt Whitman: Poet of Science.* New York: King's Crown Press, 1951.

Beecher, Catharine E. *A Treatise on Domestic Economy.* 1841. Reprint. New York: Schocken, 1977.

Beecher, Catharine E., and Harriet B. Stowe. *The American Woman's Home: or, Principles of Domestic Science.* 1869. Reprint. New York: Arno, 1971.

Beecher, Henry Ward. "Building a House." *Star Papers.* New York, 1855.

––––––. "A July 4 [1876] Oration." In *Democratic Vistas, 1860–1880*, edited by Alan Trachtenberg. New York: Braziller, 1970.

Bell, Daniel. "Modernism Mummified." *American Quarterly* 39 (Spring 1987).

Bell, Michael Davitt. "Frank Norris, Style, and the Problem of American Naturalism." *Studies in the Literary Imagination* 16 (Fall 1983).

Benedict, Burton. "The Anthropology of World's Fairs." In *The Anthropology of World's Fairs*, edited by Burton Benedict. Berkeley, Calif.: Scolar Press, 1983.

Benjamin, Walter. "The Author as Producer." In *Reflections: Essays, Aphorisms, Autobiographical Writings*, edited by Peter Demetz. New York: Harcourt Brace Jovanovich, 1978.

––––––. "Paris, Capital of the Nineteenth Century." In *Reflections: Essays, Aphorisms, Autobiographical Writings*, edited by Peter Demetz. New York: Harcourt Brace Jovanovich, 1978.

––––––. "A Short History of Photography." In *Classic Essays on Photography*, edited by Alan Trachtenberg. New Haven: Leete's Island Books, 1980.

––––––. "The Work of Art in the Age of Mechanical Reproduction." 1963. In *Illuminations*, edited by Hannah Arendt. New York: Schocken, 1969.

Bergmann, Hans. "Panoramas of New York, 1845–1860." *Prospects* 10 (1985): 119–37.

Bergon, Frank. *Stephen Crane's Artistry*. New York: Columbia University Press, 1975.

Bergreen, Laurence. *James Agee: A Life*. New York: Viking, 1984.

Berthoff, Warner. *The Ferment of Realism*. New York: Free Press, 1965.

Bigelow, Lyman G. *Artistic Photography and How to Attain It*. Philadelphia, 1876.

Bode, Carl. *The Anatomy of American Popular Culture*. Berkeley: University of California Press, 1959.

Bollard, Margaret Lloyd. "The 'Newspaper Landscape' of Williams's *Paterson*." *Contemporary Literature* 16 (Summer 1975): 317–27.

Boorstin, Daniel. *The Americans: The Democratic Experience*. New York: Random House, 1973.

———. *The Image: A Guide to Pseudo-Events in America*. 1962. Reprint. New York: Harper and Row, 1964.

Borcoman, James. "Notes on the Early Use of Combination Printing." In *One Hundred Years of Photographic History: Essays in Honor of Beaumont Newhall*, edited by Van Deren Coke. Albuquerque: University of New Mexico Press, 1975.

Boris, Eileen. *Art and Labor: Ruskin, Morris, and the Craftsman Ideal in America*. Philadelphia: Temple University Press, 1986.

Bowditch, H. P. "Are Composite Photographs Typical Pictures?" *McClure's Magazine* 3 (September 1894): 331–42.

Bowlby, Rachel. *Just Looking: Consumer Culture in Dreiser, Gissing, and Zola*. New York: Methuen, 1985.

Bradbury, Malcolm, and James McFarlane, eds. *Modernism, 1890–1930*. Harmondsworth, England: Penguin, 1976.

Bremner, Robert. *From the Depths: The Discovery of Poverty in the United States*. New York: New York University Press, 1956.

Brewster, David. *The Stereoscope: Its History, Theory, and Construction*. 1856. Reprint. Hastings-on-Hudson, N.Y.: Morgan and Morgan, 1971.

Brooks, Van Wyck. "America's Coming-of-Age." In *Three Essays on America*. 1934. Reprint. New York: E. P. Dutton, 1970.

Brown, Milton. *American Painting from the Armory Show to the Depression*. Princeton: Princeton University Press, 1955.

Bruce, Edward. *The Century: Its Fruits and Its Festival*. Philadelphia: Lippincott, 1877.

Buel, James William. *The Magic City: A Massive Portfolio of Original Photographic Views of the Great World's Fair*. Philadelphia: Historical Publishing Co., 1894.

Buell, Lawrence. "Transcendentalist Catalogue Rhetoric: Vision versus Form." *American Literature* 40 (November 1968): 325–39.

Bullock, Alan. "The Double Image." In *Modernism*, edited by Malcolm Bradbury and James McFarlane, 58–70. Harmondsworth, England: Penguin, 1976.

Bunnell, Peter, ed. *Edward Weston on Photography.* Salt Lake City: Gibbs Smith, 1983.

Burroughs, John. *Indoor Studies: Writings of John Burroughs* 8. Cambridge: Riverside Press, 1905.

Caffin, Charles. *Photography as a Fine Art.* 1901. Reprint. Hastings-on-Hudson, N.Y.: Morgan and Morgan, 1971.

Cahan, Abraham. *The Rise of David Levinsky.* 1917. Reprint. New York: Harper and Row, 1960.

Calinescu, Matei. *Faces of Modernity: Avant-Garde, Decadence, Kitsch.* Bloomington: Indiana University Press, 1977.

Carver, Craig. "The Newspaper and Other Sources of *Manhattan Transfer.*" *Studies in American Fiction* 3 (Autumn 1975): 167–79.

Cather, Willa. "The Novel Démeublé." In *Not Under Forty.* New York: Knopf, 1936.

Cathers, David M. *Furniture of the American Arts and Crafts Movement: Stickley and Roycroft Mission Oak.* New York: New American Library, 1981.

Cawelti, John. "America on Display." In *The Age of Industrialism in America: Essays in Social Structure and Cultural Values,* edited by Frederick Cople Jaher. New York: Free Press, 1968.

Chandler, Alfred D., Jr. *The Visible Hand: The Managerial Revolution in American Business.* Cambridge: Harvard University Press, 1977.

Chari, V. K. "The Structure of Whitman's Catalogue Poem." *Walt Whitman Review* 18 (1972): 3–17.

Chase, Stuart. *Mexico: A Study of Two Americas.* New York: Literary Guild, 1931.

———. *Your Money's Worth.* New York: Macmillan, 1927.

Chase, Stuart, and F. J. Schlink. *Men and Machines.* New York: Macmillan, 1929.

Cheney, Sheldon, and Martha Candler Cheney. *Art and the Machine: An Account of Industrial Design in 20th Century America.* New York: Whittlesey House, 1936.

Christman, Henry M. *Walt Whitman's New York.* New York: Macmillan, 1963.

Clark, Clifford Edward, Jr. *The American Family Home, 1800–1960.* Chapel Hill: University of North Carolina Press, 1986.

Clark, Judson Robert, ed. *The Arts and Crafts Movement in America, 1876–1916.* Princeton: Princeton University Press, 1972.

Coburn, Alvin Langdon. *Alvin Langdon Coburn: Photographer,* edited by Helmut and Alison Gernsheim. 1966. Reprint. New York: Dover, 1978.

———. "The Relation of Time to Art." *Camera Work* 36 (October 1911). Reprinted in *Camera Work: A Critical Anthology,* edited by Jonathan Green. Millerton, N.Y.: Aperture, 1973.

Cockerill, John A. "Some Phases of Contemporary Journalism." *Cosmopolitan* 13 (October 1892).

Coffman, Stanley K., Jr., " 'Crossing Brooklyn Ferry': A Note on the Catalogue Technique in Whitman's Poetry." *Modern Philology* 51 (May 1954): 225–32.

Cohen, Lizabeth. "Embellishing a Life of Labor: An Interpretation of the Material Culture of American Working-Class Homes, 1885–1915." In *Material Culture Studies in America*, edited by Thomas J. Schlereth. Nashville: American Association for State and Local History, 1982.

———. "Respectability at $50.00 Down, 20 Months to Pay! Furnishing a Working-class Victorian Home." In *Victorian Furniture*, edited by Kenneth L. Ames. Philadelphia: The Victorian Society, 1983.

Cohn, Jan. *The Palace or the Poorhouse: The American Home as a Cultural Symbol*. East Lansing: Michigan State University Press, 1979.

Coleman, A. D. "The Directorial Mode: Notes toward a Definition." *Artforum* (September 1976). Reprinted in *Photography in Print*, edited by Vicki Goldberg, 480–91. New York: Touchstone, 1981.

Colliers (September 28, 1907); (October 7, 1911); (March 22, 1913); (March 20, 1915); (April 4, 1931); (October 26, 1935).

Conn, Peter. *The Divided Mind: Ideology and Imagination in America, 1898–1917*. New York: Cambridge University Press, 1983.

Costello, Bonnie. *Marianne Moore: Imaginary Possessions*. Cambridge: Harvard University Press, 1981.

Crane, Stephen. "The Blue Hotel." In *The Red Badge of Courage and Selected Prose and Poetry*, edited by William M. Gibson. New York: Holt, Rinehart and Winston, 1968.

———. "Coney Island's Failing Days." *New York Press*, October 14, 1894. Reprinted in *Tales, Sketches, and Reports*. Vol. 8 of *The University of Virginia Edition of the Works of Stephen Crane*, edited by Fredson Bowers. Charlottesville: University Press of Virginia, 1973.

———. "An Experiment in Misery." In *Stephen Crane: Stories and Tales*, edited by Robert Wooster Stallman. New York: Vintage, 1955.

———. "Joys of Seaside Life." *New York Tribune*, July 17, 1892. Reprinted in *Tales, Sketches, and Reports*. Vol. 8 of *The University of Virginia Edition of the Works of Stephen Crane*, edited by Fredson Bowers. Charlottesville: University Press of Virginia, 1973.

———. *Maggie, A Girl of the Streets*. Edited by Thomas A. Gullason. New York: W. W. Norton, 1979.

———. *Maggie*. In *The Red Badge of Courage and Selected Prose and Poetry*, edited by William M. Gibson. New York: Holt, Rinehart and Winston, 1968.

———. "Manacled." In *Tales, Sketches, and Reports*. Vol. 8. of *The University of Virginia Edition of the Works of Stephen Crane*, edited by Fredson Bowers. Charlottesville: University Press of Virginia, 1973.

———. "The Open Boat." In *The Red Badge of Courage and Selected Prose and Poetry*, edited by William M. Gibson. New York: Holt, Rinehart and Winston, 1968.

———. *The Red Badge of Courage and Selected Prose and Poetry*, edited by William M. Gibson. New York: Holt, Rinehart and Winston, 1968.

Cranston, M. R. "Guild of Dames of the Household—One Practical Solution to the Servant Problem." *The Craftsman* 10 (June 1906): 335–39.

Crawford, William. *The Keepers of Light: A History and Working Guide to Early Photographic Processes*. Dobbs Ferry: Dobbs Ferry, 1979.

The Crayon 2 (no. 16).

Crihfield, A. R. "Relation of Backgrounds to Subjects." *Philadelphia Photographer* 8, no. 86 (February 1871).

Cronin, Morton. "Currier and Ives: A Content Analysis." *American Quarterly* 4 (1952): 317–30.

Crosby, Ernest. "Democracy." *The Craftsman* 10 (April 1906).

Cross, Charles. *A Picture of America: The Photostory of America—as It Is—and as It Might Be, Told by the News Camera*. New York: Simon and Schuster, 1932.

Culler, Jonathan. "Junk and Rubbish: A Semiotic Approach." *Diacritics* 15 (Fall 1985): 2–12.

Cummings, E. E. *Tulips and Chimneys*. 1922. Reprint. Introduction by Richard S. Kennedy. New York: Liveright, 1976.

Current-Garcia, Eugene, and Walton R. Patrick, eds. *Realism and Romanticism in Fiction: An Approach to the Novel*. Chicago: Scott, Foresman, 1962.

Curtis, Edward S. *The North American Indians*. 20 vols. 1907–30. Reprint. New York: Johnson, 1970. Vol. 1.

Curtis, James C., and Sheila Grannen. "Let Us Now Appraise Famous Photographs: Walker Evans and Documentary Photography." *Winterthur Portfolio* 15 (Spring 1980): 1–23.

Dana, John Cotton. *A Plan for a Useful Museum*. Woodstock, N.Y.: Elm Tree Press, 1920.

Danto, Arthur. "The Artworld." *Journal of Philosophy* 61 (October 15, 1964): 571–84.

Darrah, William. *The World of Stereographs*. Gettysburg: W. C. Darrah, 1987.

Darrow, Clarence S. "Realism in Literature and Art." *Arena* 9 (December 1893).

Dewey, John. *School and Society*. Revised ed. Chicago: University of Chicago Press, 1915.

De Zayas, Marius. "Modern Art—Theories and Representations." *Camera Work* 44 (October 1913).

————. *291* Nos. 5–6 (July–August 1915). Reprinted in *Camera Work: A Critical Anthology*, edited by Jonathan Green. Millerton, N.Y.: Aperture, 1973.

Diggins, John P. "Visions of Chaos and Visions of Order: Dos Passos as Historian." *American Literature* 46 (November 1974): 329–46.

Dijkstra, Bram. *Cubism, Stieglitz, and the Early Poetry of William Carlos Williams: The Hieroglyphics of a New Speech*. Princeton: Princeton University Press, 1969.

————, ed. *A Recognizable Image: William Carlos Williams on Art and Artists*. New York: New Directions, 1978.

Dines, Elaine, ed. *Paul Outerbridge: A Singular Aesthetic: Photographs and Drawings, 1921–1941*. Laguna Beach, Calif.: Laguna Beach Art Museum, 1981.

Dingus, Rick. *The Photographic Artifacts of Timothy O'Sullivan*. Albuquerque: University of New Mexico Press, 1982.

Doctorow, E. L. *World's Fair*. New York: Ballantine Books, 1985.

Dodson, L. S. "A Cropper Family." In *Living Conditions and Population Migration in Four Appalachian Counties*. Washington, D.C.: U.S. Department of Agriculture, 1937.

Dos Passos, John. "Against American Literature." *The New Republic* 8 (October 14, 1916).

———. *The Big Money, U.S.A.* Boston: Houghton Mifflin, 1946.

———. "The Camera Eye." *Esquire* (April 1936).

———. *Century's Ebb*. Boston: Gambit, 1975.

———. *The 42nd Parallel, U.S.A.* Boston: Houghton Mifflin, 1946.

———. *The Fourteenth Chronicle: Letters and Diaries of John Dos Passos*. Edited by Townsend Ludington. Boston: Gambit, 1973.

———. "Interview with D. Sanders." *Paris Review* 12 (Spring 1969).

———. Introduction to *Panama, or the Adventures of My Seven Uncles*, by Blaise Cendrars. New York: Harper and Brothers, 1931.

———. *Manhattan Transfer*. 1925. Reprint. Boston: Houghton Mifflin, 1953.

———. *1919, U.S.A.* Boston: Houghton Mifflin, 1953.

———. "Satire as a Way of Seeing." 1937. In *Occasions and Protests*. N.p.: Henry Regnery, 1964.

———. *U.S.A.* Boston: Houghton Mifflin, 1946.

———. "The Writer as Technician." In *The American Writers' Congress*, edited by Henry Hart. New York: International Publishers, 1935.

Doty, Robert. *Photo-Secession: Stieglitz and the Fine Art Movement in Photography*. 1960. Reprint. New York: Dover, 1978.

Douglas, Ann. *The Feminization of American Culture*. New York: Knopf, 1977.

Dow, Eddy. "Van Wyck Brooks and Lewis Mumford: A Confluence in the 'Twenties.'" In *Van Wyck Brooks: The Critic and Critics*, 238–51. Port Washington, N.Y.: Kennikat Press, 1979.

Downing, Andrew Jackson. *Country Houses*. Reprinted in *The Literature of Architecture*, edited by Don Gifford. New York: E. P. Dutton, 1966.

———. *Victorian Cottage Residences* (published as *Cottage Residences*, 1873). New York: Dover, 1981.

Dreiser, Theodore. *Fine Furniture*. 1930. Reprint. Brooklyn, N.Y.: Haskell House, 1975.

———. "A Remarkable Art." *Great Round World* (May 3, 1902).

———. *Sister Carrie*, edited by Donald Pizer. 1900. Reprint. New York: W. W. Norton, 1970.

———. *Twelve Men*. New York: Boni and Liveright, 1919.

Duffey, Joseph. "Mumford's Quest: The First Decade." *Salmagundi* 49 (Summer 1980).

Duncan, Hugh Dalziel. *Culture and Democracy.* Totowa, N.J.: Bedminster Press, 1965.

DuPlessis, Rachel Blau. "Objectivist Poetics and Political Vision: A Study of Oppen and Pound." In *George Oppen: Man and Poet,* edited by Burton Hatlen, 123–48. Orono, Maine: National Poetry Foundation, 1981.

Eagleson, Walter F. *Trick Photography.* Winterset, Ohio, 1902.

Earl, Polly Anne. "Craftsmen and Machines." In *Technological Innovation and Decorative Arts,* edited by Ian Quimby and Polly Anne Earl. Charlottesville: University Press of Virginia, 1974.

Earle, Edward W., ed. *Points of View: The Stereograph in America—a Cultural History.* Rochester: Visual Studies Workshop, 1979.

Eco, Umberto. *Travels in Hyperreality: Essays.* New York: Harcourt Brace Jovanovich, 1986.

Emerson, Ralph Waldo. "Nature." In *The Selected Writings of Ralph Waldo Emerson,* edited by Brooks Atkinson. New York: Modern Library, 1940.

———. "The Poet." In *The Selected Writings of Ralph Waldo Emerson,* edited by Brooks Atkinson. New York: Modern Library, 1940.

———. *The Selected Writings of Ralph Waldo Emerson.* Edited by Brooks Atkinson. New York: Modern Library, 1940.

Enyeart, James. *Bruguière, His Photographs and His Life.* New York: Knopf, 1977.

Epstein, Jean. "The New Conditions of Literary Phenomena." *Broom* 2 (April 1922): 6–7.

Erikson, Erik. *Childhood and Society.* 2d ed. New York: W. W. Norton, 1963.

Ettema, Michael J. "Technological Innovation and Design Economics in Furniture Manufacture." *Winterthur Portfolio* 16 (Summer/Autumn 1981).

Evans, Walker. "Handwritten Draft Memorandum Re Resettlement Administration Job, Spring 1935." In *Walker Evans at Work.* With an Introduction by Jerry L. Thompson. New York: Harper and Row, 1982.

———. "Photography." In *Quality: Its Image in the Arts,* edited by Louis Kronenberger. Reprinted in *Massachusetts Review* 19 (Winter 1978).

———. "The Reappearance of Photography." *Hound and Horn* 5 (October–November 1931).

———. Review of *Photo-Eye* by Franz Roh. 1929. In "The Reappearance of Photography." *Hound and Horn* 5 (October–November 1931).

———. "Unfinished Letter to Ernestine Evans, February 1934." In *Walker Evans at Work.* With an Introduction by Jerry L. Thompson. New York: Harper and Row, 1982.

———. *Walker Evans at Work.* With an Introduction by Jerry L. Thompson. New York: Harper and Row, 1982.

———. *Walker Evans: Photographs for the Farm Security Administration, 1935–1938.* Introduction by Jerrold Maddox. New York: Da Capo, 1973.

———. "Walker Evans, Visiting Artist: A Transcript of His Discussion with the Students of the University of Michigan." 1971. Reprinted in *Photog-*

raphy: Essays and Images, edited by Beaumont Newhall. New York: Museum of Modern Art, 1980.

Ewbank, Thomas. *The World a Workshop*. New York, 1855.

"Fargo Fakery." *Time* 28 (September 7, 1936).

Farrell, James T. *Judgment Day*. In *Studs Lonigan*. New York: Random House, 1938.

Fennimore, Donald L. "Fine Points of Furniture, American Empire: Late, Later, Latest." In *Victorian Furniture*, edited by Kenneth L. Ames. Philadelphia: The Victorian Society, 1983.

Ferebee, Ann. *A History of Design from the Victorian Era to the Present*. New York: Van Nostrand Reinhold, 1970.

Ferris, Hugh. "The Real Traditions of Architecture." In *Annual of American Design 1931*, edited by R. L. Leonard and C. A. Glassgold, 105–20. New York: Ives Washburn and the American Union of Decorative Artists and Craftsmen, 1930.

Fielding, Raymond. "Hale's Tours: Ultrarealism in the Pre-1910 Motion Picture." *Cinema Journal* 10 (Fall 1970): 34–47.

Fisher, Philip. "Acting, Reading, Fortune's Wheel: *Sister Carrie* and the Life History of Objects." In *American Realism: New Essays*, edited by Eric J. Sundquist. Baltimore: Johns Hopkins University Press, 1982.

Fitzgerald, F. Scott. *The Great Gatsby*. New York: Scribner's, 1925.

Flinn, John J., ed. *Official Guide to the World's Columbian Exposition in the City of Chicago*. Chicago: The Columbian Guide Company, 1893.

Frank, Waldo. *Our America*. New York: Boni and Liveright, 1919.

Frank, Waldo, Lewis Mumford, et al., eds. *America and Alfred Stieglitz: A Collective Portrait*. New York: The Literary Guild, 1934.

Frankenstein, Alfred. *After the Hunt: William Harnett and Other American Still Life Painters, 1870–1900*. Revised ed. Berkeley: University of California Press, 1969.

Frankl, Paul T. "The Home of Yesterday, Today and Tomorrow." In *Annual of American Design 1931*, edited by R. L. Leonard and C. A. Glassgold, 25–46. New York: Ives Washburn and the American Union of Decorative Artists and Craftsmen, 1930.

————. *New Dimensions*. New York: Payson and Clarke, 1928.

Frassanito, William. *Gettysburg: A Journey in Time*. New York: Scribner's, 1976.

French, Warren. *Frank Norris*. New York: Twayne, 1962.

Fuller, Henry Blake. "Dr. Gowdy and the Squash." *Under the Skylights*. New York: Appleton, 1902.

————. *With the Procession*. 1895. Reprint. Chicago: University of Chicago Press, 1965.

Furness, Clifton Joseph, ed. *Walt Whitman's Workshop: A Collection of Unpublished Manuscripts*. Cambridge: Harvard University Press, 1928.

Gado, Frank, ed. *First Person: Conversations on Writers and Writings*. New York: Union College Press, 1973.

Galton, Francis. *Inquiries into Human Faculty and Its Development.* 1883. Reprint. New York: E. P. Dutton, 1907.

Gardner, Alexander. *Gardner's Photographic Sketch Book of the Civil War.* 1866. Reprint. New York: Dover, 1959.

Garland, Hamlin. "An Ambitious French Novel and a Modest American Story." *The Arena* 8 (June 1893): xi–xii. Reprinted in *Maggie,* edited by Thomas A. Gullason. New York: W. W. Norton, 1979.

———. *Crumbling Idols: Twelve Essays on Art Dealing Chiefly with Literature, Painting and the Drama,* edited by Jane Johnson. Cambridge: Harvard University Press, 1960.

Garvin, James L. "Mail-Order House Plans and American Victorian Architecture." *Winterthur Portfolio* 16 (Winter 1981): 309–34.

Gebhard, David. "The Moderne in the U.S., 1920–1941." *Architectural Association Quarterly* 2 (July 1970).

Geddes, Norman Bel. *Horizons.* Boston: Little, Brown, 1932.

Geertz, Clifford. "Art as a Cultural System." *Modern Language Notes* 91 (December 1976).

———. "The Impact of the Concept of Culture on the Concept of Man." In *The Interpretation of Cultures,* 33–54. New York: Basic Books, 1973.

Gerdts, William. *Painters of the Humble Truth: Masterpieces of American Still Life, 1801–1939.* Columbia: University of Missouri Press, 1981.

Gernshein, Helmut. *Creative Photography: Aesthetic Trends, 1839–1960.* New York: Bonanza, 1962.

Gettings, Fred. *Ghosts in Photographs: The Extraordinary Story of Spirit Photography.* New York: Harmony, 1978.

Giedion, Siegfried. *Mechanization Takes Command: A Contribution to Anonymous History.* 1948. Reprint. New York: W. W. Norton, 1969.

Gilbert, James B. *Work without Salvation: America's Intellectuals and Industrial Alienation, 1880–1910.* Baltimore: Johns Hopkins University Press, 1977.

Ginger, Ray. *Age of Excess: The United States from 1877 to 1914.* New York: Macmillan, 1965.

[Gingrich, Arnold]. "Editor's Note." In "The Camera Eye." *Esquire* (April 1936).

Girouard, Marc. *Sweetness and Light.* New York: Oxford, 1979.

Glassgold, C. A. "Design in America." In *Annual of American Design 1931,* edited by R. L. Leonard and C. A. Glassgold, 174–75. New York: Ives Washburn and the American Union of Decorative Artists and Craftsmen, 1930.

Godkin, E. L. "Chromo-civilization." *The Nation,* September 17, 1874 and September 24, 1874.

———. "The Expenditure of Rich Men." *Scribner's Magazine* 20 (1896): 495–501.

Goldberg, Vicki, ed. *Photography in Print.* New York: Touchstone, 1981.

Graham, Don. *The Fiction of Frank Norris: The Aesthetic Context.* Columbia: University of Missouri Press, 1978.

Green, Harvey. "The Ironies of Style: Complexities and Contradictions in American Decorative Arts, 1850–1900." In *Victorian Furniture*, edited by Kenneth L. Ames. Philadelphia: The Victorian Society, 1983.
———. *The Light of the Home: An Intimate View of the Lives of Women in Victorian America.* New York: Pantheon, 1983.
Green, Jonathan. *American Photography: A Critical History 1945 to the Present.* New York: Abrams, 1984.
Greif, Martin. *Depression Modern: The Thirties Style in America.* New York: Universe Books, 1975.
Grimsted, David. "Melodrama as Echo of the Historically Voiceless." In *Anonymous Americans: Explorations in Nineteenth Century Social History,* edited by Tamara K. Hareven. Englewood Cliffs, N.J.: Prentice Hall, 1971.
Gutheim, Frederick. *In the Cause of Architecture.* New York: *Architectural Record,* McGraw-Hill, 1975.
Haas, Robert Bartlett. *Muybridge: Man in Motion.* Berkeley: University of California Press, 1976.
[Hale, Edward Everett]. Review of *Leaves of Grass* by Walt Whitman. *North American Review* (January 1856). Reprinted in *Walt Whitman: A Critical Anthology,* edited by Francis Murphy. Middlesex, England: Penguin, 1969.
Hales, Peter. *Silver Cities: The Photography of American Urbanization, 1839–1915.* Philadelphia: Temple University Press, 1984.
Halstead, Murat. *Camera Mosaics: A Portfolio of National Photography.* New York, 1894.
Halttunen, Karen. *Confidence Men and Painted Women: A Study of Middle-Class Culture in America, 1830–1870.* New Haven: Yale University Press, 1982.
Hammen, Scott. "Sheeler and Strand's 'Mannhatta': A Neglected Masterpiece." *Afterimage* 6 (January 1979): 6–7.
Hammett, Dashiell. *The Maltese Falcon.* 1929. Reprint. New York: Vintage, 1972.
Handlin, David. *The American: Home Architecture and Society, 1815–95.* Boston: Little, Brown, 1979.
Hanks, David. *The Decorative Designs of Frank Lloyd Wright.* New York: E. P. Dutton, 1979.
———. "Frank Lloyd Wright: 'The Art and Craft of the Machine.'" In *Victorian Furniture,* edited by Kenneth L. Ames. Philadelphia: The Victorian Society, 1983.
Harris, Neil. "The Drama of Consumer Desire." In *Yankee Enterprise: The Rise of American Manufactures,* edited by Otto Mayr and Robert C. Post. Washington, D.C.: Smithsonian Institution Press, 1981.
———. *Humbug: The Art of P. T. Barnum.* Boston: Little, Brown, 1973.
———. "Iconography and Intellectual History." In *New Directions in American Intellectual History,* edited by John Higham and Paul K. Conkin. Baltimore: Johns Hopkins University Press, 1979.
———. "Museums, Merchandising, and Popular Taste: The Struggle for

Influence." In *Material Culture and the Study of American Life*, edited by Ian M. G. Quimby, 140–74. New York: W. W. Norton, 1978.

Hartigan, Lynda Roscoe. "Joseph Cornell: A Biography." In *Joseph Cornell*, edited by Kynaston McShine. New York: Museum of Modern Art, 1980.

Hartley, Marsden. *Adventures in the Arts*. New York: Boni and Liveright, 1912.

Hartmann, Sadakichi. "On the Possibility of New Laws of Composition." *Camera Work* 30 (April 1910). Reprinted in *Camera Work: A Critical Anthology*, edited by Jonathan Green. Millerton, N.Y.: Aperture, 1973.

Hayden, Dolores. *Grand Domestic Revolution: A History of Feminist Designs for American Homes, Neighborhoods, and Cities*. Cambridge: MIT Press, 1982.

Heap, Jane. Editor's Introduction, "Machine-Age Exposition." *Little Review* (Spring Supplement, 1927).

Hemingway, Ernest. *Death in the Afternoon*. New York: Charles Scribner's Sons, 1932.

Hendricks, Gordon. *The Photographs of Thomas Eakins*. New York: Grossman, 1972.

Hendrickson, Robert. *The Grand Emporiums: The Illustrated History of America's Great Department Stores*. New York: Stein and Day, 1979.

Hennessey, William J. *Russel Wright, American Designer*. Cambridge: MIT Press, 1983.

Herrick, Robert. *The Common Lot*. 1904. Reprint. Upper Saddle River, N.Y.: Gregg Press, 1968.

Hillier, Bevis. *Victorian Studio Photographs*. Boston: David R. Godine, 1976.

Hine, Lewis. "Social Photography: How the Camera May Help in the Social Uplift." *National Conference of Charities and Correction Proceedings* (June 1909): 358–59.

Holloway, Emory, and Vernolian Schwarz, eds. *I Sit and Look Out: Editorials from the Brooklyn Daily Times, by Walt Whitman*. New York: Columbia University Press, 1932.

Holmes, Oliver Wendell. *Soundings from the Atlantic*. Boston, 1864.

———. "The Stereoscope and the Stereograph." *Atlantic* (June 1859). Reprinted in *Photography in Print*, edited by Vicki Goldberg. New York: Touchstone, 1981.

———. "Sun-Painting and Sun-Sculpture." *Atlantic* (July 1861).

Holton, Milne. *Cylinder of Vision: The Fiction and Journalistic Writing of Stephen Crane*. Baton Rouge: Louisiana State University Press, 1972.

Homer, William Innes. *Alfred Stieglitz and the American Avant-Garde*. Boston: New York Graphic Society, 1977.

Hopkins, Albert. *Magic, Stage Illusions and Scientific Diversions*. 1897. Reprint. New York: B. Blom, 1967.

Horowitz, Helen. *Culture and the City: Cultural Philanthropy in Chicago from the 1880s to 1917*. Lexington: University of Kentucky Press, 1976.

The Housekeeper's Quest. Pamphlet. New York, 1885.

Howe, Graham, and Jacqueline Markham. *Paul Outerbridge, Jr.: Photographs*. New York: Rizzoli, 1980.

Howells, William Dean. "A Case in Point." *Literature* (March 24, 1899). Reprinted in *Critical Essays on Frank Norris*, edited by Don Graham. Boston: G. K. Hall, 1980.

―――. "Editor's Study." *Harper's Monthly* 62 (May 1886).

―――. *A Hazard of New Fortunes*. 1890. Reprint. New York: E. P. Dutton, 1952.

―――. "James's Hawthorne." *Atlantic Monthly* (February 1880). Reprinted in *Criticism and Fiction and Other Essays*, edited by Clara Marbury Kirk and Rudolf Kirk. New York: New York University Press, 1959.

―――. *London Films*. New York: Harper and Brothers, 1905.

―――. "The Man of Letters as a Man of Business." *Scribner's Magazine* (October 1893). Reprinted in *Criticism and Fiction and Other Essays*, edited by Clara Marbury Kirk and Rudolf Kirk. New York: New York University Press, 1959.

―――. "Problems of Existence in Fiction." *Literature* (March 10, 1899). Reprinted in *Criticism and Fiction and Other Essays*, edited by Clara Marbury Kirk and Rudolf Kirk. New York: New York University Press, 1959.

―――. "A Sennight of the Centennial." *Atlantic Monthly* 38 (1876). Reprinted in *Democratic Vistas*, edited by Alan Trachtenberg. New York: George Braziller, 1970.

Hower, Ralph. *History of an Advertising Agency: N. W. Ayer and Son at Work, 1869–1949*. Cambridge: Harvard University Press, 1949.

―――. *History of Macy's of New York, 1858–1919*. Cambridge: Harvard University Press, 1943.

Hughes, H. Stuart. *Consciousness and Society*. New York: Knopf, 1966.

Hughes, Thomas Parke, ed. *Changing Attitudes toward American Technology*. New York: Harper and Row, 1975.

Hungerford, Edward. "Walt Whitman and His Chart of Bumps." *American Literature* 2 (May 1931): 350–84.

Iles, George. *Flame, Electricity, and the Camera: Man's Progress from the First Kindling of Fire to the Wireless Telegraph and the Photography of Color*. New York: Doubleday and McClure, 1900.

Irmas, Deborah. *Signs of the Times: Some Recurring Motifs in Twentieth-Century Photography*. San Francisco: San Francisco Museum of Modern Art, 1985.

Ivins, William M., Jr. *Prints and Visual Communication*. 1953. Reprint. Cambridge: MIT Press, 1969.

Jacknis, Ira. "Franz Boas and Photography." *Studies in Visual Communication* 10 (Winter 1984): 2–60.

James, Henry. *The Art of the Novel: Critical Prefaces*. Edited by R. P. Blackmur. New York: Charles Scribner's Sons, 1934.

―――. "Paste." In *The Complete Tales of Henry James*, edited by Leon Edel. Vol. 10. Philadelphia: J. B. Lippincott, 1964.

_____. *Portable Henry James*. Edited by Morton Dauwen Zabel. New York: Viking, 1951.

_____. *Portrait of a Lady*. 1881. Reprint. Boston: Houghton Mifflin, 1956.

_____. *Selected Short Stories*. Edited by Quentin Anderson. San Francisco: Rinehart, 1957.

_____. *The Spoils of Poynton*. 1897. Reprint. Harmondsworth, England: Penguin, 1963.

James, William. "The Hidden Self." *Scribner's Magazine* 7, no. 3 (March 1890): 361–73.

Jarves, James Jackson. *The Art Idea*. 1864. Reprint. Cambridge: Harvard University Press, 1960.

Jeffrey, Ian. "Photography and Nature." *Art Journal* 41 (Spring 1981).

Johnson, Alexander Bryan. *A Treatise on Language*. Edited by David Rynin. 1836. Reprint. New York: Dover, 1968.

Johnson, Benjamin P. "Great Exhibition of the Industry of All Nations, 1851." In *Readings in Technology and American Life*, edited by Carroll Pursell. New York: Oxford, 1969.

Johnson, Ellen H. *Claes Oldenburg*. Penguin New Art 4. Baltimore: Penguin, 1971.

Judson, Robert, ed. *The Arts and Crafts Movement in America 1876–1976*. Princeton: Princeton University Press, 1972.

Jussim, Estelle. *Slave to Beauty: The Eccentric Life and Controversial Career of F. Holland Day, Photographer, Publisher, Aesthete*. Boston: David R. Godine, 1981.

Jussim, Estelle, and Elizabeth Lindquist-Cock. *Landscape as Photograph*. New Haven: Yale University Press, 1985.

Kaplan, Justin. *Walt Whitman: A Life*. New York: Simon and Schuster, 1980.

Kaplan, Wendy, et al. *"The Art That Is Life": The Arts and Crafts Movement in America, 1875–1920*. Boston: Museum of Fine Arts, 1987.

Kasson, John F. *Amusing the Millions: Coney Island at the Turn of the Century*. New York: Hill and Wang, 1978.

_____. *Civilizing the Machine: Technology and Republican Values in America, 1776–1900*. New York: Viking, 1976.

Katz, Leslie. "Interview with Walker Evans." In *The Camera Viewed*, edited by Peninah R. Petruck, vol. 1. New York: E. P. Dutton, 1979.

Kenner, Hugh. *A Homemade World: The American Modernist Writers*. New York: Knopf, 1975.

_____. "Oppen, Zukofsky, and the Poem as Lens." In *Literature at the Barricades: The American Writer in the 1930s*, edited by Ralph F. Bogardus and Fred Hobson, 162–71. University: University of Alabama Press, 1982.

Kepes, Gyorgy, ed. *The Man-made Object*. New York: George Braziller, 1966.

Kern, Stephen. *The Culture of Time and Space, 1880–1918*. Cambridge: Harvard University Press, 1983.

Kimball, John C. "Machinery as a Gospel Worker." *Unitarian Christian Examiner* (November 1869).

King, Clarence. *Mountaineering in the Sierra Nevada*. Boston: James R. Osgood, 1872.

Kingdon, Frank. *John Cotton Dana: A Life*. Newark: The Public Library and Museum, 1940.

Kirkland, Joseph. "Realism versus Other Isms." *The Dial* 14 (February 16, 1893).

Kirstein, Lincoln. "Photographs of America: Walker Evans." *American Photographs*. 1938. Reprint. New York: East River Press, 1975.

Kouwenhoven, John. *The Arts in Modern American Civilization*. 1948. (Originally published as *Made in America*.) New York: W. W. Norton, 1967.

———. *The Columbia Historical Portrait of New York*. New York: Harper and Row, 1972.

Krauss, Rosalind. "Photography's Discursive Spaces: Landscape / View." *College Art Journal* 42 (Winter 1982): 311–19.

———. "Stieglitz / Equivalents." *October* 11 (Winter 1979): 129–40.

———. "Tracing Nadar." In *Reading into Photography*, edited by Thomas F. Barrow, 117–34. Albuquerque: University of New Mexico Press, 1982.

Kuberski, Philip. "Charles Olson and the American Thing: The Ideology of Revolution." *Criticism* 27 (Spring 1985): 175–93.

Kuenzli, Rudolf E., ed. *New York Dada*. New York: Willis Locker and Owens, 1986.

Kuhlmann, Susan. *Knave, Fool, and Genius: The Confidence Man as He Appears in Nineteenth-Century American Fiction*. Chapel Hill: University of North Carolina Press, 1973.

Kwiat, Joseph. "Dreiser and the Graphic Artist." *American Quarterly* 3 (Summer 1951): 127–41.

Kwolek-Folland, Angel. "The Elegant Dugout: Domesticity and Moveable Culture in the United States, 1870–1900." *American Studies* 25 (Fall 1984): 21–37.

Lambourne, Lionel. *Utopian Craftsmen: The Arts and Crafts Movement from the Cotswolds to Chicago*. Salt Lake City: Peregrine Smith, 1980.

Lavater, John Casper. *Essays in Physiognomy, Designed to Promote the Knowledge and the Love of Mankind*. Translated from the French by Henry Hunter. Vol. 1. London: John Murray, 1789.

Lawrence, D. H. Review of *Manhattan Transfer* by John Dos Passos. In *Calendar of Modern Letters* (April 1927). Reprinted in *Phoenix: The Posthumous Papers*, edited by Edward D. McDonald. 1936. Reprint. New York: Viking, 1968.

———. *Studies in Classic American Literature*. 1922. Reprint. Garden City, N.Y.: Doubleday, n.d.

———. "Things." In *The Complete Short Stories of D. H. Lawrence*. 1922. Reprint. 3 vols. New York: Viking, 1961.

Lears, T. J. Jackson. "From Salvation to Self-Realization: Advertising and the Therapeutic Roots of the Consumer Culture, 1880–1930." In *The Culture of Consumption*, edited by Richard Wightman Fox and T. J. Jackson Lears. New York: Pantheon, 1983.

_____. *No Place of Grace: Antimodernism and the Transformation of American Culture, 1880–1920*. New York: Pantheon, 1981.

_____. "Some Versions of Fantasy: Toward a Cultural History of American Advertising, 1880–1930." *Prospects* 9 (1984): 349–405.

Lee, Gerald Stanley. *Crowds: A Moving-Picture of Democracy*. Garden City, N.Y.: Doubleday, Page, 1913.

Léger, Fernand. "A New Realism—The Object: Its Plastic and Cinematic Value." *The Little Review* (Winter 1926). Reprinted in *Photography: Essays and Images*, edited by Beaumont Newhall. New York: Museum of Modern Art, 1980.

Leonard, Neil. "Alfred Stieglitz and Realism." *Art Quarterly* 29 (1966).

Levin, Harry. "Revisiting Dos Passos's *U.S.A.*" *Massachusetts Review* 20 (Autumn 1979).

Levitt, Helen. *A Way of Seeing*. Introduction by James Agee. New York: Horizon Press, 1981.

Life (May 24, 1937); (May 31, 1937); (October 6, 1941).

Lindsay, Vachel. *The Art of the Moving Picture*. New York: Macmillan, 1915.

Lippmann, Walter. *Public Opinion*. 1922. Reprint. New York: Free Press, 1965.

Loewy, Raymond. *Never Leave Well Enough Alone*. New York: Simon and Schuster, 1951.

Loftie, William John. *A Plea for Art in the House*. Philadelphia, 1877.

Lowe, Donald M. *History of Bourgeois Perception*. Chicago: University of Chicago Press, 1982.

Lowell, Amy. "Is There a National Spirit in 'The New Poetry' of America?" *The Craftsman* 30 (1916). Reprinted in *The Craftsman: An Anthology*, edited by Barry Sanders. Salt Lake City: Peregrine Smith, 1978.

Lowell, Robert. "Hawthorne." In *For the Union Dead*. New York: Farrar, Straus and Giroux, 1964.

Ludington, Townsend. *John Dos Passos: A Twentieth-Century Odyssey*. New York: E. P. Dutton, 1980.

Lyman, Christopher. *The Vanishing Race, and Other Illusions: Photographs of Indians by Edward S. Curtis*. New York: Pantheon, 1982.

Lynn, Kenneth. Introducton to *World in a Glass: A View of Our Century Selected from the Novels of John Dos Passos*. Boston: Houghton Mifflin, 1966.

_____. *William Dean Howells: An American Life*. New York: Harcourt Brace, 1970.

Lyons, Nathan, ed. *Photographers on Photography*. Englewood Cliffs, N.J.: Prentice Hall, 1966.

Maass, John. *The Glorious Enterprise: The Centennial Exhibition of 1876 and J. H. Schwartzmann, Architect-in-Chief.* Watkins Glen, N.Y.: American Life Foundation, 1973.

Mabie, Hamilton Wright. "The Interpretation of Idealism." *Books and Culture* (1896). Reprinted in *American Thought and Writing: The 1890s,* edited by Donald Pizer. Boston: Houghton Mifflin, 1972.

MacCannell, Dean. *The Tourist: A New Theory of the Leisure Class.* New York: Schocken, 1976.

McCausland, Elizabeth. "Documentary Photography." Lecture given on July 27, 1938. In "Elizabeth McCausland on Photography." *Afterimage* 12 (May 1985).

McClaugherty, Martha Crabill. "Household Art: Creating the Artistic Home, 1868–1893." *Winterthur Portfolio* 18 (Spring 1983): 1–26.

McDonald, Edward D., ed. *Phoenix: The Posthumous Papers of D. H. Lawrence.* 1936. Reprint. New York: Viking, 1968.

McElrath, Joseph R., Jr. "Frank Norris's *Vandover and the Brute*: Narrative Technique and the Socio-Critical Viewpoint." In *Critical Essays on Frank Norris,* edited by Don Graham. Boston: G. K. Hall, 1980.

Male, Roy. "Whitman's Mechanical Muse." In *Papers on Walt Whitman,* edited by Lester F. Zimmerman and Winston Weathers, 35–43. Tulsa, Okla: University of Tulsa Press, 1970.

Manville, Johns. "The Book of Roofs" (1923). In Collection of Architectural Trade Catalogues, Architecture Library, Columbia University.

Marcus, Leonard S. *The American Store Window.* New York: Whitney Library of Design, 1978.

Marcuse, Herbert. *The Aesthetic Dimension: Toward a Critique of Marxist Aesthetics.* Boston: Beacon Press, 1978.

———. *One Dimensional Man.* Boston: Beacon Press, 1964.

Marden, Orison Swett. *Little Visits with Great Americans.* New York: The Success Company, 1903.

Mariani, Paul. *William Carlos Williams: A New World Naked.* New York: McGraw-Hill, 1981.

Marling, William. *William Carlos Williams and the Painters, 1909–1923.* Athens, Ohio: Ohio University Press, 1982.

Marsh, John L. "Drama and Spectacle by the Yard: The Panorama in America." *Journal of Popular Culture* 10 (Winter 1976): 581–90.

Marx, Leo. *The Machine in the Garden: Technology and the Pastoral Ideal in America.* New York: Oxford University Press, 1964.

Marzio, Peter. *The Democratic Art: Pictures for a Nineteenth-Century America.* Boston: David R. Godine, 1979.

Mason, John B. "Walt Whitman's Catalogue." *American Literature* 45 (March 1973): 34–49.

May, Henry. *The End of American Innocence.* 1959. Reprint. Chicago: Quadrangle Books, 1964.

Mechling, Jay. "Mind, Messages, and Madness: Gregory Bateson Makes a Paradigm for American Culture Studies." *Prospects* 8 (1983): 11–30.

Meikle, Jeffrey L. *Twentieth Century Limited: Industrial Design in America.* Philadelphia: Temple University Press, 1979.

Merz, Charles. *The Great American Bandwagon.* New York: Literary Guild of America, 1928.

Michaels, Walter Benn. "The Gold Standard and the Logic of Naturalism." *Representations* 9 (Winter 1985): 123–29.

Michelis, P. A. "Aesthetic Distance and the Charm of Contemporary Art." In *Aesthetics and the Arts,* edited by Lee A. Jacobus. New York: McGraw-Hill, 1968.

Miller, Donald L. "Lewis Mumford, Master of Many Arts: The Forming Years." In *Contemporary Critiques of Technology, Technology Studies Resource Center: Working Papers Series,* 3:1–63. Bethlehem, Pa.: Lehigh University, 1985.

Miller, Henry. *Tropic of Capricorn.* 1939. Reprint. New York: Grove Press, 1961.

Miller, J. Hillis. *Poets of Reality: Six Twentieth-Century Writers.* New York: Atheneum, 1974.

Moers, Ellen. *Two Dreisers.* New York: Viking, 1969.

Moholy-Nagy, Laszlo. "A New Instrument of Vision." 1932. In *Moholy-Nagy,* edited by Richard Kostelanetz, 50–54. New York: Praeger, 1970.

Monroe, Harriet. "In the Galleries." *Chicago Examiner* (April 13, 1907). Reprinted in *Writings on Wright: Selected Comment on Frank Lloyd Wright,* edited by H. Allen Brooks. Cambridge: MIT Press, 1981.

Morgan, Hal, and Andreas Brown. *Prairie Fires and Paper Moons: The American Photographic Postcard, 1900–1920.* Boston: David R. Godine, 1981.

Morgan, Willard D., ed. *The Complete Photographer.* 10 vols. New York: National Educational Alliance, 1942–43.

Morris, Wright. "Photographs, Images, and Words." *American Scholar* 48 (Autumn 1979).

Morse, Florence. "About Furnishing." In *Household Art,* edited by Candace Wheeler. New York, 1893.

Morse, S. F. B. *The Life of Samuel F. B. Morse.* New York, 1875.

Morton, H. J. "Photography Indoors." *Philadelphia Photographer* 1, no. 7 (July 1864): 104–6.

Mottram, Ron. "Frank Norris and Photographic Representation." *Texas Studies in Literature and Language* 25, no. 4 (Winter 1983): 574–96.

Mumford, Lewis. "American Interiors." *New Republic* 41 (December 31, 1924): 139–40.

_____. *American Taste.* San Francisco: The Westgate Press, 1929. Reprinted in *The Culture of the Twenties,* edited by Loren Baritz. Indianapolis: Bobbs-Merrill, 1970.

_____. *The Brown Decades.* 1931. Reprint. New York: Dover, 1955.

_____. "A Camera and Alfred Stieglitz." *New Yorker* (December 22, 1934).

_____. "The City." In *Civilization in the United States*, edited by Harold Stearns. New York: Harcourt, Brace, 1922.

_____. "Culture and Machine Art." In *Annual of American Design 1931*, edited by R. L. Leonard and C. A. Glassgold, 9–10. New York: Ives Washburn and the American Union of Decorative Artists and Craftsmen, 1930.

_____. "Frank Lloyd Wright and the New Pioneers." *Architectural Record* 65 (April 1929). Reprinted in *Writings on Wright: Selected Comment on Frank Lloyd Wright*, edited by H. Allen Brooks. Cambridge: MIT Press, 1981.

_____. *The Golden Day*. New York: Boni and Liveright, 1926.

_____. "Machinery and Modern Style." *New Republic* 27 (August 3, 1921).

_____. "The Metropolitan Milieu." In *America and Alfred Stieglitz: A Collective Portrait*, edited by Waldo Frank et al. New York: The Literary Guild, 1934.

_____. *Sketches from Life*. Boston: Beacon Press, 1983.

_____. "Standardization, Reproduction and Choice." *Magazine of Art* 45 (February 1952).

_____. *Sticks and Stones*. 1924. Reprint. New York: Dover, 1955.

_____. *Technics and Civilization*. 1934. Reprint. New York: Harcourt Brace, 1963.

Murphy, Francis, ed. *Walt Whitman: A Critical Anthology*. Middlesex, England: Penguin, 1969.

Muybridge, Eadweard. *Animals in Motion*. London, 1899.

Naef, Weston J., and James N. Wood. *Era of Exploration: The Rise of Landscape Photography in the American West, 1860–1885*. Buffalo and New York: Albright-Knox Gallery and Metropolitan Museum of Art, 1975.

Nagel, James. *Stephen Crane and Literary Impressionism*. State College: Pennsylvania State University Press, 1980.

Nashville Banner. Review of Stephen Crane's *Maggie* (August 15, 1896). Reprinted in *Stephen Crane: The Critical Heritage*, edited by Richard M. Weatherford. London: Routledge and Kegan Paul, 1973.

Nelson, Raymond. *Van Wyck Brooks: A Writer's Life*. New York: E. P. Dutton, 1981.

Newhall, Beaumont. *The Daguerreotype in America*. New York Graphic Society, 1961.

_____. *Photography: Essays and Images*. New York: Museum of Modern Art, 1980.

New York Tribune. Review of Walt Whitman's *Leaves of Grass* (July 23, 1855). Reprinted in *New York Dissected*, edited by Ralph Adimari and Ralph Holloway. New York: Rufus Rockwell Wilson, 1936.

Norman, Dorothy. *Alfred Stieglitz: An American Seer*. New York: Random House, 1973.

_____. *Stieglitz Memorial Portfolio, 1864–1946*. New York: Twice a Year Press, 1947.

Norris, Frank. "Fiction Is Selection." *Wave* (September 11, 1897). Reprinted in *Literary Criticism of Frank Norris*, edited by Donald Pizer. Austin: University of Texas Press, 1964.

_____. "Frank Norris's Weekly Letter." *Chicago American* (August 3, 1901). Reprinted in *Literary Criticism of Frank Norris*, edited by Donald Pizer. Austin: University of Texas Press, 1964.

_____. "Novelists of the Future: The Training They Need." *Boston Evening Transcript* (November 27, 1901). Reprinted in *Literary Criticism of Frank Norris*, edited by Donald Pizer. Austin: University of Texas Press, 1964.

_____. "An Opening for Novelists: Great Opportunities for Fiction Writers in San Francisco." *Wave* (May 22, 1897). Reprinted in *Literary Criticism of Frank Norris*, edited by Donald Pizer. Austin: University of Texas Press, 1964.

_____. *The Pit.* 1903. Reprint. New York: Amsco, n.d.

_____. "A Plea for Romantic Fiction." In *Literary Criticism of Frank Norris*, edited by Donald Pizer. Austin: University of Texas Press, 1964.

_____. "Stephen Crane's Stories of Life in the Slums: *Maggie* and *George's Mother.*" *Wave* (July 4, 1896). Reprinted in *Literary Criticism of Frank Norris*, edited by Donald Pizer. Austin: University of Texas Press, 1964.

_____. *Vandover and the Brute.* New York: Doubleday, Page, 1914.

Novak, Barbara. *Nature and Culture: American Landscape and Painting, 1825–1875.* New York: Oxford, 1980.

Nye, David E. *Image Worlds: Corporate Identities at General Electric, 1890–1930.* Cambridge: MIT Press, 1985.

Nye, Russel Blaine. *Society and Culture in America 1830–1860.* New York: Harper and Row, 1974.

Official Guide Book of the New York World's Fair, 1939. New York: Exposition Publications, 1939.

O'Keeffe, Georgia. Introduction to *Georgia O'Keeffe, a Portrait.* Edited by Alfred Stieglitz. New York: Metropolitan Museum of Art, 1978.

Oldenburg, Claes. "Environment, Situation, Spaces." 1961. Expanded in *Store Days: Documents from the Store.* 1961. Reprinted in *Claes Oldenburg.* London: Arts Council of Great Britain, 1970.

_____. "Items toward an introduction." 1970. Reprinted in *Claes Oldenburg.* London: Arts Council of Great Britain, 1970.

Orvell, Miles. "Reproduction and 'The Real Thing': The Anxiety of Realism in the Age of Photography." In *The Technological Imagination: Theories and Fictions*, edited by Teresa De Lauretis et al., 49–64. Madison, Wis.: Coda Press, 1980; published for the Center for Twentieth-Century Studies, Milwaukee, 1980.

_____. Review of *Silver Cities: The Photography of American Urbanization, 1839–1915* by Peter Hales. In *Studies in Visual Communication* 10 (Fall 1984): 80–83.

Owens, Craig. "The Discourse of Others: Feminists and Postmodernism."

In *The Anti-Aesthetic: Essays on Postmodern Culture,* edited by Hal Foster. Port Townsend, Wash.: Bay Press, 1983.

Pach, Walter. *The Art Museum in America.* New York: Pantheon, 1984.

Panzer, Mary. *Philadelphia Naturalistic Photography, 1865–1906.* New Haven: Yale University Art Gallery, 1982.

Paul, Sherman. *Louis Sullivan: An Architect in American Thought.* Englewood Cliffs, N.J.: Prentice Hall, 1962.

Pearsall, A. A. "Instantaneous Portraiture." *Philadelphia Photographer* 8, no. 95 (November 1871): 385–86.

Pease, Donald. "Fear, Rage, and the Mistrials of Representation in *The Red Badge of Courage.*" In *American Realism: New Essays,* edited by Eric J. Sundquist, 155–75. Baltimore: Johns Hopkins University Press, 1982.

Peirce, Charles S. "How to Make Our Ideas Clear." 1878. In *Values in a Universe of Chance,* edited by Philip P. Wiener. Garden City, N.Y.: Doubleday Anchor, 1958.

Pilgrim, Dianne. "Decorative Art: The Domestic Environment." In *American Renaissance, 1876–1917* [catalogue]. Brooklyn, N.Y.: Brooklyn Institute of Arts and Sciences, 1979.

Pizer, Donald. "Evolutionary Ethical Dualism in Frank Norris's *Vandover and the Brute* and *McTeague.*" *PMLA* 76, no.5 (December 1961): 552–60.

———, ed. *Theodore Dreiser: A Selection of Uncollected Prose.* Detroit: Wayne State University Press, 1977.

Platt, Orville H. "Invention and Advancement." In *Popular Culture and Industrialism, 1865–1890,* edited by Henry Nash Smith. Garden City, N.Y.: Doubleday Anchor, 1967.

"The Poor Taste of the Rich." *House Beautiful* 17 (December 1904). Reprinted in *The Call of the Wild,* edited by Roderick Nash. New York: George Braziller, 1970.

Potter, David M. *People of Plenty.* Chicago: University of Chicago Press, 1954.

Praz, Mario. *An Illustrated History of Interior Decoration: From Pompeii to Art Nouveau.* New York: Thames and Hudson, 1982.

Presbrey, Frank. *The History and Development of Advertising.* New York: Doubleday, 1929.

Puckett, John Rogers. *Five Photo-Textual Documentaries from the Great Depression.* Ann Arbor, Mich.: UMI Research Press, 1984.

Pulos, Arthur. *American Design Ethic: A History of Industrial Design to 1940.* Cambridge: MIT Press, 1983.

Pultz, John, and Catherine B. Scallen. *Cubism and American Photography, 1910–1930.* Williamstown, Mass.: Clark Art Institute, 1981.

Pursell, Carroll W., Jr. *Readings in Technology and American Life.* New York: Oxford University Press, 1969.

Ray, Man. "The Age of Light." *Photographs, 1920–1934.* 1934. Reprint. New York: Dover, 1979.

_____. "Photography Is Not Art." In *Man Ray Photographs*. Introduction by Jean-Hubert Martin. New York: Thames and Hudson, 1982.

Reed, Michael D. "First Person Persona and the Catalogue in 'Song of Myself.'" *Walt Whitman Review* 23 (1977): 147–53.

Reisch, Marc S. "Poetry and Portraiture in Whitman's *Leaves of Grass*." *Walt Whitman Review* 27 (September 1981): 113–25.

Rice, Elmer. *The Adding Machine*. 1923. In *Three Plays by Elmer Rice*. New York: Hill and Wang, 1965.

_____. *A Voyage to Purilia*. New York: Cosmopolitan Book, 1930.

Richards, George D. "Pictorial Journalism." *The World Today* 9 (August 1905).

Riddel, Joseph. *The Inverted Bell, Modernism and the Counter-Poetics of William Carlos Williams*. Baton Rouge: Louisiana State University Press, 1974.

Riis, Jacob. *The Children of the Poor*. New York: Scribner's, 1892.

_____. *How the Other Half Lives*. 1890. Reprint. New York: Dover, 1971.

Rinhart, Floyd, and Marion Rinhart. *The American Daguerreotype*. Athens: University of Georgia Press, 1981.

Robinson, Henry P. *The Elements of a Pictorial Photograph*. 1896. Reprint. New York: Arno, 1973.

_____. *Pictorial Effect*. 1869. Reprint. Philadelphia, 1881.

Rodgers, Cleveland, and John Black, eds. *The Gathering of the Forces*. 2 vols. New York: G. P. Putnam's, 1920.

Roh, Franz. "Mechanism and Expression." In *Photo-Eye: 76 Photos of the Period*, edited by Franz Roh and Jan Tschichold. 1929. Reprint. New York: Arno, 1973.

Root, Marcus A. *The Camera and the Pencil*. Philadelphia: Lippincott, 1864. Reprint. Pawlett, Vt.: Helios, 1971.

Rosenberg, Nathan. *Technology and American Economic Growth*. White Plains, N.Y.: M. E. Sharpe, 1972.

Rosenfeld, Paul. "Stieglitz." *The Dial* 70 (April 1921). Reprinted in *Photography: Essays and Images*, edited by Beaumont Newhall. New York: Museum of Modern Art, 1980.

Ross, Denman W. "The Arts and Crafts: A Diagnosis." *The Craftsman* 7 (October 1904): 335–43.

Rothstein, Arthur. "Direction in the Picture Story." In *The Complete Photographer*, edited by Willard D. Morgan. 10 vols. New York: National Educational Alliance, 1942–43.

_____. "Setting the Record Straight." *Camera 35* 22 (April 1978): 50–51.

"A Rough Novel." *Boston Evening Transcript* (March 22, 1899). Reprinted in *Frank Norris: The Critical Reception*, edited by Joseph R. McElrath, Jr., and Katherine Knight. New York: Burt Franklin, 1981.

Rubin, Joseph Jay. *The Historic Whitman*. State College: Pennsylvania State University Press, 1973.

Rudisill, Richard. *Mirror Image: The Influence of the Daguerreotype on American Society*. Albuquerque: University of New Mexico Press, 1971.

Rugg, Harold. "The Artist and the Great Transition." In *America and Alfred Stieglitz: A Collective Portrait*, edited by Waldo Frank et al. New York: The Literary Guild, 1934.

"Russel Wright's 'American Way.'" *American Magazine of the Arts* (November 1940).

Rydell, Robert W. *All the World's a Fair: Visions of Empire at American International Expositions, 1876–1916*. Chicago: University of Chicago Press, 1984.

Saisselin, Remy G. *The Bourgeois and the Bibelot*. New Brunswick, N.J.: Rutgers University Press, 1984.

Salzman, Jack, ed. *Theodore Dreiser, the Critical Reception*. New York: David Lewis, 1972.

Sanders, Barry, ed. *The Craftsman: An Anthology*. Salt Lake City: Peregrine Smith, 1978.

Sandweiss, Martha A. *Master Works of American Photography: The Amon Carter Museum Collection*. Birmingham, Ala.: Oxmoor House, 1982.

Sankey, Benjamin. *A Companion to William Carlos Williams's "Paterson."* Berkeley: University of California Press, 1971.

Santayana, George. "The Genteel Tradition in American Philosophy." In *The Genteel Tradition*, edited by D. L. Wilson. Cambridge: Harvard University Press, 1967.

Sartre, Jean-Paul. "John Dos Passos and *1919*." In *Dos Passos: A Collection of Critical Essays*, edited by Andrew Hook, 63–66. Englewood Cliffs, N.J.: Prentice Hall, 1974.

Scherer, Joanna Cohan. Review of *The Vanishing Race and Other Illusions* by Christopher Lyman. In *Studies in Visual Communication* 11 (Summer 1985): 78–85.

Schiller, Dan. *Objectivity and the News: The Public and the Rise of Commercial Journalism*. Philadelphia: University of Pennsylvania Press, 1981.

Schlereth, Thomas J., ed. *Material Culture Studies in America*. Nashville: American Association for State and Local History, 1982.

Schwartz, Sanford. *The Matrix of Modernism: Pound, Eliot, and Early Twentieth-Century Thought*. Princeton: Princeton University Press, 1985.

Seale, William. *The Tasteful Interlude: American Interiors through the Camera's Eye, 1860–1917*. New York: Praeger, 1975.

Sears, Roebuck and Co. *Catalogue No. 117, The Great Price Maker*, edited by Joseph J. Schroeder. 1908. Reprint. Northfield, Ill.: DBI Books, 1971.

Sedgwick, Ellery, III. "The American Genteel Tradition in the Early Twentieth Century." *American Studies* 25 (Spring 1984): 49–76.

Segal, Howard P. *Technological Utopianism in American Culture*. Chicago: University of Chicago Press, 1985.

Sekula, Allan. "The Traffic in Photographs." *Art Journal* 41 (Spring 1981).

Shear, G. Willard. *Panorama of the Hudson.* New York, 1888.

Silliman, B., Jr., and C. R. Goodrich, eds. *The World of Science, Art, and Industry Illustrated from Examples in the New York Exhibition, 1853–54.* New York: G. P. Putnam, 1854.

Silverman, Jonathan. *For the World to See: The Life of Margaret Bourke-White.* New York: Viking Press, 1983.

Simpson, Louis. *At the End of the Road.* Middletown, Conn.: Wesleyan University Press, 1963.

Sinclair, Upton. *The Jungle.* 1905. New York: New American Library, 1980.

Singal, Daniel Joseph. "Towards a Definition of American Modernism." *American Quarterly* 39 (Spring 1987): 7–26.

Slater, Philip. *The Pursuit of Loneliness.* Boston: Beacon Press, 1970.

Smith, Henry Nash, ed. *Popular Culture and Industrialism, 1865–1890.* Garden City, N.Y.: Anchor Books, 1967.

Smith, Mary Ann. *Gustav Stickley: The Craftsman.* Syracuse, N.Y.: Syracuse University Press, 1983.

Smith, Thorne. "Advertising." In *Civilization in the United States,* edited by Harold Stearns. New York: Harcourt, Brace, 1922.

Snow, Robert E., and David Wright. "Coney Island: A Case Study in Popular Culture and Technological Change." *Journal of Popular Culture* (Spring 1976): 960–75.

Snyder, Joel. "Documentary without Ontology." *Studies in Visual Communication* 10 (Winter 1984): 87–88.

Snyder, Joel, and Doug Munson. *The Documentary Photograph as a Work of Art: American Photographs, 1860–1876.* Chicago: David and Alfred Smart Gallery, University of Chicago, 1976.

Sobieszek, Robert A. "Composite Imagery and the Origins of Photomontage; Part 1: The Naturalist Strain." *Artforum* 17, no. 1 (1978): 58–65.

————. "New Acquisitions: A Note on Early Photomontage Images." *Image: Journal of Photography in the George Eastman House* 15, no. 4 (1972): 19–24.

Sobieszek, Robert A., and Odette M. Appel. *The Spirit of Fact: The Daguerreotypes of Southworth and Hawes, 1843–1862.* Boston: David R. Godine, 1976.

Solomon, Eric. *Stephen Crane: From Parody to Realism.* Cambridge: Harvard University Press, 1967.

Solomon-Godeau, Abigail. "Back to Basics: The Return of Alfred Stieglitz." *Afterimage* 12 (Summer 1984): 21–25.

Sontag, Susan. *On Photography.* New York: Farrar, Straus and Giroux, 1977.

Spitzer, Leo. "American Advertising Explained as Popular Art." In *A Method of Interpreting Literature.* Northampton, Mass.: Smith College, 1949.

Spofford, Harriet. "Art Decoration as Applied to Furniture" (1877). In
    Late Victorian Decor: From Eastlake's Gothic to Cook's House Beautiful,
    edited by Hugh Guthrie. Watkins Glen, N.Y.: American Life, 1968.
Stallman, Robert Wooster, ed. *Stephen Crane: Stories and Tales*. New
    York: Vintage, 1952.
Stanley, Hiram M. "The Passion for Realism and What Is to Come of It."
    The Dial (April 16, 1893).
Stearns, Harold E. "The Intellectual Life." In *Civilization in the United
    States*, edited by Harold E. Stearns. New York: Harcourt, 1922.
Steichen, Edward. "Commercial Photography." In *Annual of American
    Design 1931*, edited by R. L. Leonard and C. A. Glassgold, 157–73. New
    York: Ives Washburn and the American Union of Decorative Artists
    and Craftsmen, 1930.
———. *A Life in Photography*. 1963. Reprint. New York: Bonanza, 1984.
Stein, Gertrude. *The Autobiography of Alice B. Toklas*. 1933. In *Selected
    Writings of Gertrude Stein*, edited by Carl Van Vechten. New York: Mod-
    ern Library, 1962.
———. "Composition as Explanation." 1926. In *Selected Writings of Ger-
    trude Stein*, edited by Carl Van Vechten. New York: Modern Library,
    1962.
———. "Pictures." In *Lectures in America*. 1935. Reprint. New York: Vin-
    tage, 1975.
Stein, Roger. *John Ruskin and Aesthetic Thought in America, 1840–1900*.
    Cambridge: Harvard University Press, 1967.
Stein, Sally A. "The Composite Photographic Image and the Composition
    of Consumer Ideology." *Art Journal* 41 (Spring 1981): 39–45.
Sternberger, Dolf. *Panorama of the 19th Century*. Translated by Joachim
    Neugroschel. 1955. American ed. New York: Mole Editions, 1977.
Stevens, Wallace. *The Collected Poems of Wallace Stevens*. New York:
    Knopf, 1967.
———. "The Credences of Summer." In *The Collected Poems of Wallace
    Stevens*. New York: Knopf, 1967.
———. "The Man on the Dump." In *The Collected Poems of Wallace Ste-
    vens*. New York: Knopf, 1967.
Stewart, Susan. *On Longing*. Baltimore: Johns Hopkins University Press,
    1984.
Stickley, Gustav. "Als Ik Kan: Art True and False." *The Craftsman* 8 (June
    1905).
———. *Craftsman Homes*. 1909. Reprint. New York: Dover, 1979.
———. "The Ethics of Home Furnishing." *The Craftsman* 29 (January
    1916).
———. "The Old Crafts and the Modern Factories." *The Craftsman* 20
    (May 1911).
———. "Ornament: Its Use and Abuse." *The Craftsman* 7 (July 1905). Re-
    printed in *The Forgotten Rebel: Gustav Stickley and His Craftsman Mis-*

sion Furniture, edited by John Crosby Freeman. Watkins Glen, N.Y.: Century House, 1966.

_____. "Thoughts Occasioned by an Anniversary." *The Craftsman* 12 (1907). Reprinted in *The Craftsman: An Anthology*, edited by Barry Sanders. Salt Lake City: Peregrine Smith, 1978.

_____. "The Use and Abuse of Machinery and Its Relation to the Arts and Crafts." *The Craftsman* 11 (November 1906). Reprinted in *The Forgotten Rebel: Gustav Stickley and His Craftsman Mission Furniture*, edited by John Crosby Freeman. Watkins Glen, N.Y.: Century House, 1966.

_____. "Waste: Our Heaviest National Liability." *The Craftsman* 20 (July 1911).

Stickley Craftsman Furniture Catalogs. Reprint. New York: Dover, 1979.

Stieglitz, Alfred. *Alfred Stieglitz, Photographs and Writings*. Edited by Sarah Greenough and Juan Hamilton. Washington, D.C.: National Gallery of Art, 1983.

Stilgoe, John R. "Molding the Industrial Zone Aesthetic: 1880–1929." *Journal of American Studies* 16 (April 1982): 6–24.

Stillinger, Elizabeth. *The Antiquers*. New York: Knopf, 1980.

Stoddard, John T. "Composite Photography." *Century Magazine* 33 (March 1887): 750–57.

Stott, William. *Documentary Expression and Thirties America*. New York: Oxford, 1973.

Stovall, Floyd. *The Foreground of "Leaves of Grass."* Charlottesville: University Press of Virginia, 1974.

Strand, Paul. "Alfred Stieglitz and a Machine." In *America and Alfred Stieglitz: A Collective Portrait*, edited by Waldo Frank et al. New York: The Literary Guild, 1934.

_____. "Photography and the New God." *Broom* 3 (1922). Reprinted in *Photographers on Photography*, edited by Nathan Lyons. Englewood Cliffs, N.J.: Prentice Hall, 1966.

_____. *Photo Notes* (March–April 1940).

_____. "Stieglitz: An Appraisal." *Popular Photography* (July 1947).

Struik, Dirk. *Yankee Science in the Making*. Boston: Little, Brown, 1948.

Stryker, Roy Emerson. "Documentary Photography." In *The Complete Photographer*, edited by Willard D. Morgan. 10 vols. New York: National Educational Alliance, 1942–43.

_____. "The FSA Collection of Photographs." 1973. In *Photography in Print*, edited by Vicki Goldberg. New York: Touchstone, 1981.

Stryker, Roy Emerson, and Nancy Wood, eds. *In This Proud Land*. New York: Galahad, 1973.

Studies in Visual Communication 11 (Summer 1985): 78–85.

Sullivan, Louis. *The Autobiography of an Idea*. 1924. Reprint. New York: Dover, 1956.

_____. "Characteristics and Tendencies of American Architecture."

Builders' Weekly Reporter (London) (1885). Reprinted in *Kindergarten Chats and Other Writings*. New York: George Wittenborn, 1947.

————. "Ornament in Architecture." *The Engineering Magazine* (August 1892). Reprinted in *Kindergarten Chats and Other Writings*. New York: George Wittenborn, 1947.

————. "What Is Architecture? A Study in the American People Today." *American Contractor* (January 1906). Reprinted in *Kindergarten Chats and Other Writings*. New York: George Wittenborn, 1947.

Sundquist, Eric J. "Country of the Blue." In *American Realism, New Essays*, edited by Eric J. Sundquist. Baltimore: Johns Hopkins University Press, 1982.

Susman, Warren. "Culture and Commitment." In *Culture as History: The Transformation of American Society in the Twentieth Century*. New York: Pantheon, 1984.

————. *Culture as History: The Transformation of American Society in the Twentieth Century*. New York: Pantheon, 1984.

Tapscott, Stephen. *American Beauty: William Carlos Williams and the Modernist Whitman*. New York: Columbia University Press, 1984.

Tashjian, Dickran. *Skyscraper Primitives: Dada and the American Avant-Garde, 1910–1925*. Middletown, Conn.: Wesleyan University Press, 1975.

————. *William Carlos Williams and the American Scene, 1920–1940*. New York: Whitney Museum of American Art, 1978.

Taylor, A. A. E. "Photographic View of the Inner Man." *Philadelphia Photographer* 3, no. 29 (May 1886): 138–39.

Taylor, Lisa, et al. *American Enterprise: Nineteenth Century Patent Models*. New York: Cooper-Hewitt Museum, 1984.

Teague, Walter. *Design This Day: The Technique of Order in the Machine Age*. New York: Harcourt, Brace, 1940.

Thomas, F. Richard. *Literary Admirers of Alfred Stieglitz*. Carbondale: Southern Illinois University Press, 1983.

Thompson, Maurice. "The Ethics of Literary Art." 1893. Reprinted in *American Thought and Writing: The 1890s*, edited by Donald Pizer. Boston: Houghton Mifflin, 1972.

Thompson, Michael. *Rubbish Theory: The Creation and Destruction of Value*. New York: Oxford, 1979.

Tibbetts, John. "The Real Thing: Arguments between Art and Science in the Work of P. H. Emerson and H. P. Robinson." *Journal of American Culture* 4 (Spring 1981): 149–72.

Tichi, Cecelia. *Shifting Gears: Technology, Literature, Culture in Modernist America*. Chapel Hill: University of North Carolina Press, 1987.

Tocqueville, Alexis de. *Democracy in America*. Translated by Henry Reeve. 1838. Reprint. 2 vols. New York: Vintage, 1945.

Tomsich, John. *A Genteel Endeavor: American Culture and Politics in the Gilded Age*. Stanford, Calif.: Stanford University Press, 1971.

Trachtenberg, Alan. "Albums of War: On Reading Civil War Photography."
Representations 9 (Winter 1985): 1–32.

———. "Brady's Portraits." *Yale Review* 73 (Winter 1984): 130–53.

———. "Experiments in Another Country: Stephen Crane's City
Sketches." In *American Realism*, edited by Eric Sundquist, 138–54. Baltimore: Johns Hopkins University Press, 1982.

———. *The Incorporation of America: Culture and Society in the Gilded
Age*. New York: Hill and Wang, 1982.

———. "Mumford in the Twenties: The Historian as Artist." *Salmagundi*
49 (Summer 1980): 28–42.

———. "Walker Evans's America: A Documentary Invention." In *Observations: Essays on Documentary Photography*, edited by David
Featherstone, 56–66. Carmel, Calif.: The Friends of Photography, 1984.

———, ed. *Democratic Vistas, 1860–1880*. New York: George Braziller,
1970.

Traubel, Horace. "Horace Traubel on Photography." *Camera Work* 46
(April 1914).

———. *With Walt Whitman in Camden*. 5 vols. New York: Mitchell Kennerley, 1914.

———. *With Walt Whitman in Camden, April 8–September 14, 1889*,
edited by Gertrude Traubel. Carbondale: Southern Illinois University
Press, 1964.

Triggs, Oscar L. *Chapters in the History of the Arts and Crafts Movement*.
Chicago: Bohemian Guild of the Industrial Art League, 1902.

———. "The New Industrialism." *The Craftsman* 3 (November 1902).

Trilling, Lionel. "William Dean Howells and the Roots of Modern Taste."
In *The Opposing Self*. New York: Viking, 1955.

Twain, Mark. *A Connecticut Yankee in King Arthur's Court*. 1889. Reprint.
New York: New American Library, 1963.

———. *Life on the Mississippi*. 1883. Reprint. New York: New American
Library, 1961.

Twombly, Robert. *Frank Lloyd Wright: His Life and His Architecture*. New
York: Wiley, 1979.

———. *Louis Sullivan: His Life and Work*. New York: Viking, 1986.

"Vanishing Backyards." *Fortune* 1 (May 1930).

Veblen, Thorstein. "Arts and Crafts." *Journal of Political Economy* 11
(December 1902).

Veeder, William. *The Lessons of the Master: Popular Fiction and Personal
Style in the Nineteenth Century*. Chicago: University of Chicago Press,
1979.

Vertrees, Alan. "The Picture Making of Henry Peach Robinson." In *Perspectives on Photography*, edited by David Oliphant and Thomas Zigal,
78–101. Austin: University of Texas Press, 1982.

Veysey, Lawrence. "Intellectual History and the New Social History." In
New Directions in American Intellectual History, edited by John

Higham and Paul K. Conkin. Baltimore: Johns Hopkins University Press, 1979.

"A Vital Expression in German Photographic Art: Illustrated by the Work of Rudolf Duhrkoop." *The Craftsman* 21, no. 1 (1911): 26–33.

Vogel, H. "Photography and Truth." *Philadelphia Photographer* 6 (August 1869).

Vos, George W. "Art and Machinery." *The Soil* 1, no. 1 (1916).

Walker, Timothy. "A Defence of Mechanical Philosophy." *North American Review* 33 (July 1832): 122–36.

Wanamaker, John. "On the Department Store." In *American Primer*, edited by Daniel Boorstin. New York: Mentor, 1968.

Warner, Charles Dudley. "Modern Fiction." *Atlantic Monthly* 51 (April 1883).

———. "What Is Your Culture to Me?" *Scribner's Monthly* 4 (1872). Reprinted in *Democratic Vistas: 1860–1880*, edited by Alan Trachtenberg. New York: George Braziller, 1970.

Warren, Samuel D., and Louis D. Brandeis. "The Right to Privacy." *Harvard Law Review* 4 (December 15, 1890): 193–220.

Warshow, Robert. "The Legacy of the Thirties." In *The Immediate Experience*. New York: Atheneum, 1974.

Weatherford, Richard M., ed. *Stephen Crane: The Critical Heritage*. London: Routledge and Kegan Paul, 1973.

Weaver, Mike. *William Carlos Williams: The American Background*. London: Cambridge University Press, 1971.

West, Nathanael. *A Cool Million*. 1934. Reprinted in *The Complete Works of Nathanael West*. New York: Farrar, Straus and Co., 1957.

———. *The Dream Life of Balso Snell*. 1931. Reprinted in *The Complete Works of Nathanael West*. New York: Farrar, Straus and Co., 1957.

Westerhoven, John. "Autobiographical Elements in the Camera Eye." *American Literature* 48 (November 1976): 340–64.

Weston, Edward. *Daybooks of Edward Weston*, edited by Nancy Newhall. 2 vols. Vol. 1, *Mexico*. Vol. 2, *California*. Millerton, N.Y.: Aperture, 1961.

———. "Letter Regarding Pictorialism and the Work of Alfred Stieglitz." In *Principles of Pictorial Photography*. 1923. Reprinted in *Edward Weston on Photography*, edited by Peter Bunnell. Salt Lake City: Gibbs Smith, 1983.

———. "Photographic Art." *Encyclopedia Britannica*. Reprinted in *The Camera Viewed: Writings on Twentieth-Century Photography*, vol. 1, edited by Peninah R. Petruck. New York: E. P. Dutton, 1979.

———. "Photography—Not Pictorial." In *Photographers on Photography*, edited by Nathan Lyons. Englewood Cliffs, N.J.: Prentice Hall, 1966.

———. "Seeing Photographically." In *The Complete Photographer*, vol. 9 (1943). Reprinted in *Photographers on Photography*, edited by Nathan Lyons. Englewood Cliffs, N.J.: Prentice Hall, 1966.

———. "Weston to Hagemeyer: New York Notes, 1922." *Center for Creative Photography* (November 1976). Reprinted in *Edward Weston on*

Photography, edited by Peter Bunnell. Salt Lake City: Gibbs Smith, 1983.

Wharton, Edith. *The Age of Innocence*. New York: Modern Library, 1920.

Wharton, Edith, and Ogden Codman, Jr. *The Decoration of Houses*. New York, 1897.

Wheelwright, Philip. *Metaphor and Reality*. Bloomington: Indiana University Press, 1962.

White, George Abbot. "Vernacular Photography: F.S.A. Images of Depression Leisure." *Studies in Visual Communication* 9 (Winter 1983).

Whitman, Walt. *An American Primer*. In *Walt Whitman: A Critical Anthology*, edited by Francis Murphy. Baltimore: Penguin, 1970.

———. "As I Ebb'd with the Ocean of Life." In *Leaves of Grass: A Norton Critical Edition*, edited by Sculley Bradley and Harold W. Blodgett. New York: W. W. Norton, 1973.

———. "A Backward Glance O'er Travel'd Roads." 1888. In *Leaves of Grass: A Norton Critical Edition*, edited by Sculley Bradley and Harold W. Blodgett. New York: W. W. Norton, 1973.

———. *The Complete Prose Works of Walt Whitman*. Edited by Richard Maurice Bucke. 9 vols. Camden Edition. New York: G. P. Putnam's Sons, 1902.

———. *Leaves of Grass*. 2d ed. Brooklyn, N.Y.: 1856.

———. *Leaves of Grass: A Norton Critical Edition*. Edited by Sculley Bradley and Harold W. Blodgett. New York: W. W. Norton, 1973.

———. *Leaves of Grass, and Selected Prose*, edited by John Kouwenhoven. New York: Modern Library, 1950.

———. "Notes on the Meaning and Intention of 'Leaves of Grass.'" In *The Complete Prose Works of Walt Whitman*, edited by Richard Maurice Bucke. 9 vols. Camden Edition. New York: G. P. Putnam's Sons, 1902.

———. *Prose Works 1892*. 2 vols. Edited by Floyd Stovall. New York: New York University Press, 1963.

———. *Specimen Days*. In *Prose Works 1892*. 2 vols. Edited by Floyd Stovall. New York: New York University Press, 1963.

———. "There Was a Child Went Forth." In *Leaves of Grass: A Norton Critical Edition*, edited by Sculley Bradley and Harold W. Blodgett. New York: W. W. Norton, 1973.

———. *The Uncollected Poetry and Prose of Walt Whitman*. Edited by Emory Holloway. 2 vols. Garden City, N.Y.: Doubleday, Page, 1921.

———. *Walt Whitman: Notebooks and Unpublished Prose Manuscripts*. Edited by Edward F. Grier. New York: New York University Press, 1984.

———. "Wicked Architecture." *Life Illustrated* (July 19, 1856). Reprinted in *New York Dissected*, edited by Ralph Adimari and Emory Holloway. New York: R. R. Wilson, 1936.

Wiebe, Robert H. *The Search for Order, 1877–1920*. New York: Hill and Wang, 1967.

Williams, Henry T., and Mrs. C. J. Jones. *Beautiful Homes, or Hints on House Furnishings* (1878).

Williams, William Carlos. "America, Whitman, and the Art of Poetry." *Poetry Journal* 8 (November 1917).

———. "The American Background." In *America and Alfred Stieglitz*, edited by Waldo Frank et al. New York: The Literary Guild, Doubleday, 1934.

———. Author's Introduction to *The Wedge*. 1944. Reprinted in *Selected Essays*. 1954. Reprint. New York: New Directions, 1969.

———. "A Beginning on the Short Story (Notes)." Reprinted in *Selected Essays*. 1954. Reprint. New York: New Directions, 1969.

———. *Collected Earlier Poems*. New York: New Directions, 1951.

———. *The Descent of Winter*. In *Imaginations*, edited by Webster Schott. New York: New Directions, 1979.

———. "Effie Deans." In *A Recognizable Image: William Carlos Williams on Art and Artists*, edited by Bram Dijkstra. New York: New Directions, 1978.

———. *The Embodiment of Knowledge*. Edited by Ron Loewinsohn. New York: New Directions, 1974.

———. "An Essay on *Leaves of Grass*." 1955. Reprinted in *Walt Whitman: A Critical Anthology*, edited by Francis Murphy. Baltimore: Penguin, 1969.

———. *The Great American Novel*. In *Imaginations*, edited by Webster Schott. New York: New Directions, 1979.

———. *In the American Grain*. 1925. Reprint. New York: New Directions, 1956.

———. Introduction to *Charles Sheeler—Paintings—Drawings—Photographs*. New York: Museum of Modern Art, 1939. Reprinted in *A Recognizable Image: William Carlos Williams on Art and Artists*, edited by Bram Dijkstra. New York: New Directions, 1978.

———. *I Wanted to Write a Poem*. Boston: Beacon Press. 1958.

———. "January Morning." In *Collected Earlier Poems*. New York: New Directions, 1951.

———. *Kora in Hell: Improvisations*. In *Imaginations*, edited by Webster Schott. New York: New Directions, 1979.

———. "Marianne Moore." Reprinted in *Selected Essays*. 1954. New York: New Directions, 1969.

———. "On Measure—Statement for Cid Corman." Reprinted in *Selected Essays*. 1954. Reprint. New York: New Directions, 1969.

———. *Paterson*. New York: New Directions, 1963.

———. *Spring and All*. In *Imaginations*, edited by Webster Schott. New York: New Directions, 1979.

———. "This Florida: 1924." In *Collected Earlier Poems*. New York: New Directions, 1951.

———. "To a Solitary Disciple." In *Collected Earlier Poems*. New York: New Directions, 1951.

———. "Whitman's *Leaves of Grass* and Photography." In *A Recognizable*

Image: William Carlos Williams on Art and Artists, edited by Bram Dijkstra. New York: New Directions, 1978.

———. "The Work of Gertrude Stein." Reprinted in *Selected Essays*. 1954. Reprint. New York: New Directions, 1969.

———. "Yours, O Youth." *Contact* 3 (1921). Reprinted in *Selected Essays*. Reprint. 1954. New York: New Directions, 1969.

Wilson, Christopher. "The Rhetoric of Consumption: Mass-Market Magazines and the Demise of the Gentle Reader, 1880–1920." In *The Culture of Consumption*, edited by Richard Wightman Fox and T. J. Jackson Lears, 39–64. New York: Pantheon, 1983.

Wilson, Edmund. "Mr. and Mrs. X." In *The American Earthquake*. Garden City, N.Y.: Doubleday, 1958.

Wilson, Richard Guy. "Architecture and the Reinterpretation of the Past in the American Renaissance." *Winterthur Portfolio* 18 (Spring 1983).

———. "*The Decoration of Houses* and Scientific Eclecticism." In *Victorian Furniture*, edited by Kenneth L. Ames, 193–204. Philadelphia: The Victorian Society, 1983.

Wilson, Richard Guy, Dianne H. Pilgrim, and Dickran Tashjian. *The Machine Age in America, 1918–1941*. New York: The Brooklyn Museum with Harry N. Abrams, 1986.

Wogan, Claudia C. "Crane's Use of Color in 'The Red Badge of Courage.'" *Modern Fiction Studies* 6 (Summer 1960).

Wood, Nancy. "Portrait of Stryker." In *In This Proud Land*, edited by Roy Emerson Stryker and Nancy Wood. New York: Galahad, 1973.

Woodbury, Walter E. *Photographic Amusements, Including a Number of Novel Effects Obtainable with the Camera*. New York, 1898.

"The Work of L. & J. G. Stickley (,) Fayetteville, New York." In *Stickley Furniture Catalogs*. Reprint. New York: Dover, 1979.

Wright, Frank Lloyd. "The Architect and the Machine." *Architectural Record* (May 1927). Reprinted in *In the Cause of Architecture*, edited by Frederick Gutheim. New York: *Architectural Record* and McGraw-Hill, 1975.

———. "The Art and Craft of the Machine." In *Frank Lloyd Wright: Writings and Buildings*, edited by Edgar Kaufmann and Ben Raeburn. Cleveland: World Publishing Company, Meridian Books, 1960.

———. *Autobiography*. Revised ed. New York: Duell, Sloan and Pearce, 1943.

———. *The Japanese Print: An Interpretation*. 1912. Reprint. New York: Horizon Press, 1967.

———. "Principles of Design." In *Annual of American Design 1931*, edited by R. L. Leonard and C. A. Glassgold, 101–4. New York: Ives Washburn and the American Union of Decorative Artists and Craftsmen, 1930.

———. "Standardization, the Soul of the Machine." *Architectural Record* (June 1927). Reprinted in *In the Cause of Architecture*, edited by Frederick Gutheim. New York: *Architectural Record*, McGraw-Hill, 1975.

Wright, Gwendolyn. *Building the Dream: A Social History of Housing in America*. Cambridge: MIT Press, 1983.

Wrobel, Arthur. "Whitman and the Phrenologists: The Divine Body and the Sensuous Soul." *PMLA* 89 (January 1974): 17–23.

Wyckoff, Walter A. *The Workers: An Experiment in Reality*. 2 vols. New York: Charles Scribner's Sons, 1901.

Zarobila, Charles. "Walt Whitman and the Panorama." *Walt Whitman Review* 25 (June 1979).

Ziff, Larzer. *The American 1890s: Life and Times of a Lost Generation*. New York: Viking, 1966.

Zimmerman, Lester F., and Winston Weathers, eds. *Papers on Walt Whitman*. Tulsa, Okla.: University of Tulsa Press, 1970.

Zukovsky, Louis. "Sincerity and Objectification." *Poetry* 37 (February 1931).

Zweig, Paul. *Walt Whitman: The Making of the Poet*. New York: Basic Books, 1984.

Adams, Henry, xix
Agee, James, 245–46, 272–86; and
  Fortune, 272, 273; and Evans,
  272, 278–83; structure of *Let Us
  Now Praise Famous Men*, 273–
  74; and documentary tradition,
  274; and Richards, 275; compared with Williams and Dos
  Passos, 275; prose style of, 275–
  77; and camera, 277–78; photography as prose model for, 278–
  82; Wright Morris on, 282–83;
  and commonplace collage, 290–
  92
Allen, Gay Wilson, 12
Altick, Richard, 34
Ames, Kenneth, 48
Arts and Crafts movement, 60, 158,
  176, 177, 186; style of, 159; relation to labor, 162
Ashbee, C. R., 162
Authenticity: as moral and aesthetic value, 154, 155, 186; in literature, 240. *See also* Culture: of
  authenticity
Avedon, Richard, 311 (n. 19)

Bach, Richard F., 181, 193; and
  function of museum, 325 (n. 76)
Barnum, P. T., 58; and *Gallery of
  American Female Beauty*, 17–18
Barthelme, Donald, 295–96
Bartlett, John, 85
Baudrillard, Jean, xxv, 50, 62
Bauhaus movement, 182, 186, 188
Baum, Frank L., 41
Beecher, Catharine E., 37, 50
Beecher, Henry Ward, 46–47
Belden, E. Porter, 21
Benedict, Burton, 55

Benjamin, Walter, xvii, 226, 290; on
  photography, 310 (n. 1)
Boorstin, Daniel, xxiv
Bourke-White, Margaret, 223, 226–
  27, 228, 234, 236; and Erskine
  Caldwell, *You Have Seen Their
  Faces*, 277–78
Brady, Mathew, 8, 9
Brooklyn Bridge, 170, 189, 197
Brooks, Van Wyck, xvi, 172, 200,
  232, 286, 299; on highbrow and
  lowbrow, 153; *America's Coming-
  of-Age*, 153–54; and "usable
  past," 168; and need for cultural
  synthesis, 189, 241; and split be-
  tween culture, 203–4; and ideal
  of national culture, 286
Browere, John H. I., 17
Bruce, Edward, 38–39
Buel, James William, 75
Burchfield, Charles, 288
Burroughs, John, 124

Caffin, Charles, 205
Cahan, Abraham, 52–53
Camera: as model for Whitman, 5–
  9; and Victorian culture, 73–102
  passim; as cultural symbol, 198–
  204, 227–28, 239; as literary
  model, 277–78
Camera Work, 204, 207
Catalogues (sales), 43–45; Sears,
  54–55
Cather, Willa, 243
Cawelti, John, 34
Cendrars, Blaise, 260
Centennial Exhibition (Philadel-
  phia, 1876), 38–39, 59, 147–48
Chaplin, Charlie, 147
Chase, Stuart, 298–99

Cheney, Martha Candler, 170, 191
Cheney, Sheldon, 170, 191
Chicago Exposition (1893). *See* World's Columbian Exposition of 1893 (Chicago)
Chromolithograph, cultural meaning of, 36–38
City: and consciousness, 5; and machine, 157
Class: conflict between labor and elite, 105; elite vs. lower, in Howells, 110
Coady, Robert, 236
Coburn, A. L., 203, 222
Coleman, A. D., 77–78
Colonial style, 167
Columbian Exposition. *See* World's Columbian Exposition of 1893 (Chicago)
Combination prints, 92
Composite portrait, 92–94
Confidence man, as type, 53, 58–59
Consumer culture, 41–72 passim, 141–47; manufacture of goods in, xvii, 157; growth of, xviii; and aesthetics of abundance, 42–46; and commercial aesthetic in furnishings, 48; and nostalgia for simpler life, 70–72. *See also* Catalogues; Chromolithograph, cultural meaning of; Department stores; Exhibition halls; Home, meaning of; Imitations; Victorian society; Warhol, Andy
Cornell, Joseph, 292–93
Craftsman movement: *Craftsman Farms*, 164; *The Craftsman*, 164, 165; Craftsman Building, 165–66; and objective photography, 329 (n. 24). *See also* Arts and Crafts movement; Stickley, Gustav
Crane, Hart, 203
Crane, Stephen, 104, 126–37; and

Alexander Gardner, 318 (n. 73). Works: *Maggie*, 126–27, 128–30; *Red Badge of Courage*, 127, 130–32; "The Blue Hotel," 132; "An Experiment in Misery," 133; "Manacled," 135; "The Open Boat," 135
Crosby, Ernest, 165
Cross, Charles, 227
Crystal Palace (London), 25, 59
Crystal Palace (New York), 25–27, 28
Cubism: and photography, 215; and modern poetry, 251
Culture: tension between imitation and authenticity, xv, xvi, 158, 299; artist's relationship to, xix–xx; levels of, xx; of authenticity, xx, xxi, 141, 155; of imitation, xx, 39, 141; of the factitious, xxiii; conflict between levels of, 117–19; nationalistic ideal of, 181; synthesis of levels, 286. *See also* Consumer culture; Replication
Cummings, E. E., 260
Curtis, Edward, 97–99

Daguerreotype, 7. *See also* Daguerreotype gallery
Daguerreotype gallery, 16–19
Dana, John Cotton, 180
Danto, Arthur, 301 (n. 12)
Darrow, Clarence, 106–7
Davis, Stuart, 249
Day, F. Holland, 86–88
Demuth, Charles, 251
Department stores, 41, 42–43
Depression, cultural effects of the, 226
De Zayas, Marius, 201, 203, 209
Doctorow, E. L., 193
Documentary photography, 94–99, 227, 230–31
Dodson, L. S., 276
Dos Passos, John, 150, 245–46,

257–72, 285, 286; and Whitman, 258–59; D. H. Lawrence on, 259; and *Leaves of Grass*, 259; on Cendrars, 260; and photography, 261; and Stieglitz, 267; epistemology in, 268; and Vertov, 268; and satire, 268, 269; compared with Williams, 269; and American language, 269–71; and Sacco-Vanzetti case, 271; and authenticity, 272. Works: *U.S.A.*, 259–72: as chronicle, 262–64; compared with *Paterson*, 263–64; narrative sections in, 264–65; Sartre on, 265; Biographies in, 265–66; Newsreels in, 266–67; Camera Eye in, 267–68; *Manhattan Transfer*, 267
Downing, Andrew Jackson, 46, 52
Dreiser, Theodore, 104; and Stieglitz, 125. Works: *Sister Carrie*, 42, 125; *Fine Furniture*, 53
Duchamp, Marcel, 274
Duncan, Hugh Dalziel, 62

Eakins, Thomas, 20, 104
Eco, Umberto, xxv
Eliot, George, 312 (n. 24)
Eliot, T. S., 148
Emerson, Ralph Waldo, 4, 24, 152, 242
Engineer, as cultural symbol, 166, 171–72
Engineering: design, 170; tradition of, 188. *See also* Functionalism
Epstein, Jean, 244
Erikson, Erik, 13
Europe, culture of: compared with America, xxv–xxvi; meaning of, for America, 59–65
Evans, Walker, 231–39, 272, 288, 290; compared with Stryker, 231–32; and authenticity, 233; and precisionist style, 234; and Strand, 238; Kirstein on, 239; on

Stieglitz, 239; *American Photographs*, 283, 290; photographs in *Let Us Now Praise Famous Men*, 283–85
Exhibition halls, 19

Facsimiles, xxiii
Farm Security Administration (FSA): photographic unit, 228–31, 232–33
Farrell, James T., 151
Federal Arts Project: *Index of American Design*, 196
Ferris, Hugh, 174
Fitzgerald, F. Scott, 71–72
Ford, Henry, 168
Form and function, 173, 174. *See also* Functionalism
Fortune, 287–88
Frank, Waldo, 152, 285
Frankl, Paul T., 185
Frassanito, William, 95
Frederic, Harold, 127
FSA. *See* Farm Security Administration
Fuller, Henry Blake: *With the Procession*, 69–70; "Dr. Gowdy and the Squash," 121–22
Functionalism, xvi, 173, 174, 184

Galton, Francis, 92–94
Gardner, Alexander, 95–96, 127
Garland, Hamlin, 106, 114, 128
Geddes, Norman Bel, 184–85, 191, 196
Geertz, Clifford, xx
Ginger, Ray, 42
Gingrich, Arnold, 261, 264
Godkin, E. L., 37–38, 62
Goldberg, Rube, 148
Grimsted, David, 19
Guy, F., 22

Haberle, John, 121
Hale, Edward Everett, 6

Hale's Tours, 35
Hammett, Dashiell, 252
Harnett, William, 121
Harris, Neil, xx
Hartley, Marsden, 203, 247
Hartmann, Sadakichi, 218
Haviland, Paul B., 201
Hawthorne, Nathaniel, 294
Heap, Jane, 166
Hemingway, Ernest, 246
Henri, Robert, 104
Herrick, Robert, 62
Highbrow and lowbrow, 153, 172,
  232. *See also* Culture
Hine, Lewis, 227, 312 (n. 24)
Holmes, Oliver Wendell, 75–77, 91
Home, meaning of, 46–49. *See also*
  Consumer culture
Homer, Winslow, 104
Horowitz, Helen, 62
Howells, William Dean, 105, 108–
  15, 147–48; and class conflict,
  110; and middle-class realism,
  119–20, 129; and photography,
  124, 125; and future of realism,
  136. Works: *A Hazard of New
  Fortunes*, 48–49, 109–13; *A Trav-
  eler from Altruria*, 109

Iles, George, 94
Illusion: in pictorial arts, 121–22
Imitation, culture of. *See* Culture:
  of imitation
Imitations: in home furnishings,
  52, 187. *See also* Consumer cul-
  ture
Industrial design, 180, 181
Industrial designer, 190–91
Insley, H. E., 21
Ivins, William, 76–77

Jackson, William Henry, 99, 311
  (n. 13)
James, Henry, 108, 152; and realism, 121, 122–23; and photography, 122–24; and "fact," 123; and

Coburn, 123–24, 317 (n. 59); and
  models, 316 (n. 56). Works: *Portrait of a Lady*, 65–67; *Spoils
  of Poynton*, 67–69; "The Real
  Thing," 122–23, 134; "Paste," 316
  (n. 57); *Turn of the Screw*, 317
  (n. 58)
Johnson, Alexander Bryan: theory
  of language, 332 (n. 9)
Junk: cultural significance of, 287;
  Morris on, 338 (n. 6)
Jussim, Estelle, 86

Keaton, Buster, 148
King, Clarence, 100
Kirkland, Joseph, 124
Kirstein, Lincoln, 233, 239
Krauss, Rosalind, 99
Krausz, Sigmund, 96

Lange, Dorothea, 228, 229, 230,
  234; *An American Exodus*, 282
Language: relationship between
  words and things, 172–73, 242–
  45, 332 (n. 9)
Lavater, John Caspar, 14, 15
Lawrence, D. H., xvi–xvii;
  "Things," 63–64
Leaves of Grass. See Whitman,
  Walt
Le Corbusier, 179
Lee, Gerald Stanley, 150, 157–58
Léger, Fernand, 215, 222
*Let Us Now Praise Famous Men.
  See* Agee, James
Lindsay, Vachel, 150, 244
Lippmann, Walter, 151
Loewy, Raymond, 185
Lowe, Donald, 46
Lowell, Amy, 247
Lowell, Robert, 294

Mabie, Hamilton Wright, 107–8
MacCannell, Dean, xxiv
Machine: and reproductions, xv,
  33; meaning of, xvi; and Victo-

rian aesthetic of replication, 49–
60 passim; and culture, 141; as
symbol, 142, 166; and labor, 147–
48, 163; social and psychological
effects of, 154; and design, 169
Manual training movement, 162–
63, 322 (n. 18)
Manufacturing, xvii, 157. *See also*
Consumer culture
Marcuse, Herbert, xix–xx, 148
Material culture, xxii
Mechanization, 24. *See also* Ma-
chine
Meikle, Jeffrey, 194
Melville, Herman, 55
Miller, Henry, 146–47
Modernism, literary, 242. *See also*
Culture: of authenticity
Monroe, Harriet, 179
Moore, Marianne, 243, 247
Morris, William, 160, 176
Morris, Wright, xxiv, 282–83
Mumford, Lewis, 153, 168–72; on
preindustrial culture, 70; on fail-
ures of urban culture, 149–50;
influence of, 158; and Brooks,
168; and "usable past," 168; and
ideal of organic community, 169;
and reproductions, 169; and
Sachlichkeit, 174–76, 247; on
right use of machine, 179, 180;
and machine design, 185–86;
and ideal of architect-craftsman,
190; changing views of, 196, 323
(n. 38); and Stieglitz, 202; on social function of photography,
219, 221–22. Works: *The Golden
Day*, 62; *Brown Decades*, 171;
Sticks and Stones, 171; *The City*
(film), 194
Muybridge, Eadweard, 94, 100–
101, 300 (n. 13), 316 (n. 56)

New York World's Fair (1939–40),
189–90, 193–95
Nietzsche, Friedrich, 69

Norris, Frank, 104, 114–19, 126,
129, 240; and the composite photograph, 313 (n. 44); and illusion
of realism, 316 (n. 53); on photographic realism, 317 (n. 63).
Works: *Vandover and the Brute*,
57–58, 116–19; *The Pit*, 63, 310
(n. 82); *McTeague*, 114–15, 116,
124
Norton, Charles Eliot, 62
Notman, William, 81
Nutting, Wallace, 167
Nye, David, 222

Objectivism (poetry), 247, 248
O'Keeffe, Georgia, 211–12
Oldenburg, Claes, 296–98
Omnibus form, 18–28
O'Sullivan, Timothy, 99, 100, 127
Outerbridge, Paul, 224–26

Panorama, 20–23
Parton, James, 37
Paul, Sherman, 172
Peirce, Charles Sanders, 92
Peto, John, 293
Photography, 73–102, 198–239; and
culture, xxi; portrait, 9–12, 78,
88–94; stereographic, 78; landscape, 78–79; panoramic, 79;
theatrical, 79–80; pictorial aesthetic, 86, 199; combination
prints, 92–94; documentary
mode, 94–99, 227, 230–31; and
problem of verisimilitude, 95–
99; Photo-Secession, 124, 202;
and advertising, 144, 223; and
cubism, 215; Farm Security Administration (FSA) photographic
unit, 228–31, 232–33; Caffin on,
311 (n. 20); as fusion of science
and art, 312 (n. 23)
Phrenology, 13–14
Physiognomy, 14–16
Pictorial aesthetic, 86, 199. *See also*
Photography

Platt, Orville H., 33
Popular culture: twentieth century, xv, 188–89; in literature, 141; and technology, 244
Portrait conventions. *See* Photography: portrait
Postmodernism, xxiv, 299; and junk, 295–98
Praz, Mario, 47–48

Realism: and types, xx; and facts, 107; and pictures, 162. *See also* Realism (literary); Realism (photographic); Types
Realism (literary), 103–37 passim; and reform, 106–7; "Higher," 107–8; and middle-class, 112–13; "photographic," 120; and melodrama, 129; and typicality, 129; and non-fiction journalism, 135; reaction against, 240–41, 245
Realism (photographic): "artificial," 77; types and typology in, 77, 81, 85, 312 (n. 28)
Real Thing, The (as phrase), xv, xvi, xvii; in advertising, 144–45
"Real Thing, The" (story by Henry James), 122–23
Replication: material, xv, xx, 33–34, 75; of experience, 35–36. *See also* Consumer culture; Culture: of imitation
Rice, Elmer, 150–51, 320 (n. 22)
Richards, I. A., 275
Richardson, H. H., 171, 174
Riis, Jacob, 96–97, 159, 126–27, 227. Works: *How the Other Half Lives*, 96, 97; *Children of the Poor*, 107
Robinson, Henry Peach, 81–85, 86
Roebling, John Augustus, 170, 174, 247
Roebling, Washington, 170
Root, Marcus A., 9, 84–85
Rosenfeld, Paul, 199–200
Rothstein, Arthur, 230–31

Rugg, Harold, 154–55
Ruskin, John, 108, 160, 176

Sachlichkeit, 174–76, 197, 247
Saisselin, Remy G., 5
Santayana, George, 152, 154
Sarony, Napoleon, 79–80
Science: changed conceptions of physical reality, xviii
Science and art: goal of fusion, 177, 203–4, 285; photography as synthesis of, 201, 214
Sheeler, Charles, 247
Simpson, Louis, 247
Sinclair, Upton, 146
Skyscraper, as modern form, 174
Snyder, Joel, 95
Social class. *See* Class
Sontag, Susan, xxiii, 6
Southworth, Albert, 85
Southworth and Hawes (photography studio), 91–92
Spitzer, Leo, 146
Spofford, Harriet, 160
Stearns, Harold, 212
Steerage, The (photograph), 207–11
Steichen, Edward, 223
Stein, Gertrude, 241, 243, 246; and language theories, 332 (n. 9)
Steinbeck, John, 266
Steiner, Ralph, 215, 217, 288, 289
Stevens, Wallace, 253; "Man on the Dump," 295
Stickley, Gustav, 158–66, 173, 189, 233; and *The Craftsman*, 159; and value of authenticity, 160–62; and Craftsman Farms, 162; Mumford on, 171; and functionalism, 185–86; and Craftsman ideal, 194
Stickley, L. & J. G., 164
Stieglitz, Alfred, 198–214, 228, 247; and instant photography, 101; and Dreiser, 125; and Emerson, 154–55; and Whitman, 154–55; and ideal of objectivity, 196–97,

219; as symbol, 199; Mumford on, 204, 212, 213, 233; Rosenfeld on, 204; Caffin on, 205; and urban subjects, 205, 206; as symbol of fusion of science and art, 205, 214, 328 (n. 17); *The Steerage*, 207–11; Strand on, 209–11, 214; and O'Keeffe, 211–12, 214; and the photographic series, 211–14; and Williams, 248; on the city, 327 (n. 4); on the machine, 327 (n. 4)

Stowe, Harriet Beecher, 37, 50

Strand, Paul, 209, 211, 215–19, 228; on Stieglitz, 214; and machine, 218

Streamlined design, 182–85. *See also* Functionalism

Stryker, Roy Emerson, 231, 232

Sullivan, Louis, 34, 158, 171–74, 185, 233, 247; on social function of architecture, 171; on engineers, 171–72; and discovery of form in function, 173; and real things, 173; influence on later designers, 174; and the skyscraper, 174. *See also* Functionalism; Streamlined design

Taylor, Frederick Winslow, 147, 164; and factory systems, 193

Teague, Walter, 184, 191

Technology: and middle-class culture, 33; and design, 170. *See also* Consumer culture: manufacture of goods in; Machine

Thayer, William, 34

Thompson, Maurice, 106

Trachtenberg, Alan, 237

Traubel, Horace, 200

Triggs, Oscar L. 162

Trompe l'oeil painting, 120–22

Twain, Mark, 105, 108; and authenticity of dialect, 316 (n. 51). Works: *Connecticut Yankee*, 38, 107; *Life on the Mississippi*, 53,

56; *Huckleberry Finn*, 56–57

Types: and metonymy, in photography, 88; aesthetic of, 101–2. *See also* Realism; Realism (literary); Realism (photographic)

U.S.A. See Dos Passos, John

"Usable past," 168. *See also* Brooks, Van Wyck; Mumford, Lewis

Vance, Robert H., 21

Veblen, Thorstein, 63, 163

Vernacular forms, xvi; and machine, 154. *See also* Authenticity; Machine

Verisimilitude (literary), reaction against, 245. *See also* Realism (literary)

Verisimilitude (photographic), 314 (n. 57). *See also* Realism (photographic)

Victorian society: and abundance, 42–46; nature and artifice in aesthetic of, 56. *See also* Consumer culture

Vogel, Hermann, 89–90

Vos, George W., 166

Wanamaker, John, 41

Warhol, Andy, 338 (n. 13)

Warner, Charles Dudley, 104–6, 116, 117, 124, 153, 299

Warshow, Robert, 258

West, Nathanael, 148–49; *A Cool Million*, 339 (n. 17)

Weston, Edward, 199, 219–21; and the close-up, 219–20; and authenticity, 220; Diego Rivera on, 220; on pictorialism, 220; and "super realism," 220

Wharton, Edith, 41, 173; and Ogden Codman, *The Decoration of Houses*, 60–61, 63

Wheelwright, Philip, xvi, xvii

Whitehead, Alfred North, 19

Whitman, Walt, xxi, 3–29, 101, 114,

115, 124, 130, 147, 150, 155, 159, 165, 200, 236, 258–59, 285, 296; as type of American artist, xxi; and free-verse catalogue, 3; and Brady, 8–9; *Leaves of Grass* frontispiece daguerreotype portrait of, 8–14; and phrenology, 13–14; and daguerreotype gallery, 16–19; and panorama, 20–23; and trade fairs, 25–28; as cultural symbol, 238; and modernism, 242, 328–29 (n. 20); and photography, 302 (n. 10); on Longfellow, 303 (n. 28). Works: *Leaves of Grass*, 3, 24; "Crossing Brooklyn Ferry," 7; "There Was a Child Went Forth," 7; "Faces," 14; "Pictures," 19; "Song of Myself," 20, 23; *Specimen Days*, 131; "As I Ebb'd with the Ocean of Life," 294

Williams, William Carlos, 241–57, 285, 286, 292; and Whitman, 250, 253; and cubism, 251. Works: *In the American Grain*, 148, 254; *Spring and All*, 246, 250; "Young Sycamore," 248; "The Red Wheelbarrow," 248–49; *Paterson*, 249–50, 254, 255–57; *Kora in Hell*, 250, 252–53, 254; "January Morning," 251; "To a Solitary Disciple," 251; *The Descent of Winter*, 254; *The Great American Novel*, 255; "To Elsie," 257

Williamsburg, Va., 167, 169

Wilson, Edmund, 146

Wilson, Edward, 81

Woodward, Calvin, 162

World's Columbian Exposition of 1893 (Chicago), 34–35, 59–61, 94, 190, 305–6 (n. 9)

World's Fair of 1939–40. *See* New York World's Fair (1939–40)

Wright, Frank Lloyd, 158, 171, 176–80, 262; and functionalism, 174; and right use of machine, 176–77, 324 (n. 62); and organic ideal, 177–78; and standardization, 177–78; and abstraction, 178–79; contrasted with streamlined design, 185; and Russel Wright, 188; and Whitman, 189; and middle-class market, 196

Wright, Russel, 158, 186–90, 194; and functional design, 186; and mass market, 186–88; and vernacular American tradition, 188–89

Zukovsky, Louis, 248

Zweig, Paul, 14